Programming F#

Programming F#

Chris Smith
foreword by Don Syme

O'REILLY®

Beijing · Cambridge · Farnham · Köln · Sebastopol · Taipei · Tokyo

Programming F#
by Chris Smith

Copyright © 2010 Chris Smith. All rights reserved.
Printed in the United States of America.

Published by O'Reilly Media, Inc., 1005 Gravenstein Highway North, Sebastopol, CA 95472.

O'Reilly books may be purchased for educational, business, or sales promotional use. Online editions are also available for most titles (*http://my.safaribooksonline.com*). For more information, contact our corporate/institutional sales department: (800) 998-9938 or *corporate@oreilly.com*.

Editor: Laurel Ruma
Production Editor: Loranah Dimant
Production Services: Newgen, Inc.

Indexer: Jay Marchand
Cover Designer: Karen Montgomery
Interior Designer: David Futato
Illustrator: Robert Romano

Printing History:
    October 2009:   First Edition.

RepKover.™   This book uses RepKover™, a durable and flexible lay-flat binding.

ISBN: 978-0-596-15364-9

[M]

1254505098

Table of Contents

Foreword

This book marks a transition point in the history of the F# language. From its origins as a research project at Microsoft Research, Cambridge, and its long heritage from languages such as OCaml and Haskell, F# has now emerged as a stable, efficient, and enjoyable productivity tool for compositional and succinct programming on the .NET platform. With the release of Visual Studio 2010, a whole new generation of programmers will have the language available to them as they build the future through the software they design, whether it be through beautiful code, groundbreaking software frameworks, high-performance websites, new software methodologies, better numerical algorithms, great testing, intelligent parallelization, better modelling, or any number of the other manifestations of "good programming" with F#. As the designer of F#, I am thrilled to see Chris Smith, a major contributor on the F# team, present F# in a way that is accessible to a wide audience.

F# combines the simplicity and elegance of typed functional programming with the strengths of the .NET platform. Although typed functional programming is relatively new to many programmers and thus requires some learning, it makes programming simpler in many ways. F# programs tend to be built from compositional, correct foundational elements, and type inference makes programs shorter and clearer. In this book, Chris first introduces the foundational paradigms of F#: functional programming, imperative programming, and object-oriented programming, and emphasizes how these can be used together. His focus is on simple, clear explanations of the foundational elements of the language, with an eye on the enjoyment that comes from programming in general, and programming with F# in particular.

When used at its best, F# makes things simple. For example, F# units of measure are covered in this book and are a landmark feature in the history of programming languages, taming much of the complexity of working with floating-point numbers in common application areas. Furthermore, the huge, generation-defining shift toward asynchronous and parallel processing forms part of the background to the development of F#. In this book, Chris tackles the foundations F# and .NET provide to help you work in this world. Likewise, F# has great strengths in language-oriented programming, a topic dear to Chris's heart, and again well covered here.

Above all, F# is a practical language, and Chris has ensured that the reader is well equipped with the information needed to use the current generation of F# tools well, with a notable emphasis on F# scripting. Chris's book describes F# "1.0" as it appears in Visual Studio 2010, the first officially supported release of the language. The F# team and I are very grateful to Chris for his contributions to the development of the language and its tools. I hope you enjoy your programming with F# as much as Chris and I have enjoyed working as part of the F# team.

—Don Syme
Principal Researcher and F# Designer, Microsoft Research

Preface

There is a new language in Visual Studio called F#. It will help you write more expressive, easier-to-maintain code while enabling you to take advantage of the breadth of the .NET platform. Learning F# will not only make you more productive, it will also make you a better programmer. Once you have mastered concepts such as functional programming introduced in F#, you can apply them to programs written in other languages, as well as have a new perspective on programming.

Introducing F#

So what actually is F#? In a nutshell, F# is a *multiparadigm* programming language built on .NET, meaning that it supports several different *styles* of programming natively. I'll spare you the history of the language and instead just go over the big bullets:

- F# supports functional programming, which is a style of programming that emphasizes *what* a program should do, not explicitly *how* the program should work.

- F# supports object-oriented programming. In F#, you can abstract code into classes and objects, enabling you to simplify your code.

- F# supports imperative programming. In F# you can modify the contents of memory, read and write files, send data over the network, and so on.

- F# is statically typed. Being statically typed means that type information is known at compile time, leading to type-safe code. F# won't allow you to put a square peg into a round hole.

- F# is a .NET language. It runs on the Common Language Infrastructure (CLI) and so it gets things like garbage collection (memory management) and powerful class libraries for free. F# also supports all .NET concepts natively, such as delegates, enumerations, structures, P/Invoke, and so on.

Even without all the jargon, it is clear that F# is a broad and powerful language. But don't worry, we'll cover it all step by step.

Who This Book Is For

This book isn't intended to be an introductory text on programming and assumes familiarity with basic concepts like looping, functions, and recursion. However, no previous experience with functional programming or .NET is required.

If you come from a C# or VB.NET background, you should feel right at home. While F# approaches programming from a different viewpoint, you can apply all of your existing .NET know-how to programming in F#.

If you come from an OCaml or Haskell background, the syntax of F# should look very familiar. F# has most of the features of those languages, and adds many more to integrate well with .NET.

What You Need to Get Going

F# is included as part of Visual Studio 2010. This includes the F# compiler and project system, and contains all the features like syntax highlighting and IntelliSense that you would expect. A full version of Visual Studio 2010 is not required to use F#, however. F# will work on top of the Visual Studio 2008 shell, which is a free, slimmed-down version of Visual Studio. You can download the Visual Studio 2008 shell (Integrated Mode) at:

> *http://www.microsoft.com/downloads/details.aspx?FamilyID=40646580-97FA*
> *-4698-B65F-620D4B4B1ED7*

Once you have the Visual Studio 2008 shell, you can install the latest F# Community Technology Preview, from the Microsoft F# Developer Center (*http://fsharp.net*).

On non-Microsoft platforms, you can still write and deploy F# applications using the open source (*http://open-source.org*) Mono platform (*http://www.mono-project.com/*).

How the Book Is Organized

This book is divided into two parts. Part I focuses on multiparadigm programming in F#. Early chapters will be devoted to programming in a specific F# paradigm, while later ones will help flesh out your understanding of language capabilities. By the end of Part I, you will be fluent in the F# language and its idioms.

Part II will introduce a few lingering concepts but primarily focus on applying F# in specialized areas. By the end of Part II, you will know how to utilize F# as a scripting language for parallel programming, and for creating domain-specific languages.

Part I, Multiparadigm Programming

Chapter 1, *Introduction to F#*, presents the F# language and the Visual Studio 2010 integrated development environment (IDE). Even if you are familiar with Visual Studio, I recommend you read this chapter, as F# has some unique characteristics when it comes to building and running projects.

Chapter 2, *Fundamentals*, introduces the core types and concepts that will be the foundation for all other chapters.

Chapter 3, *Functional Programming*, introduces functional programming and how to write F# code using this style.

Chapter 4, *Imperative Programming*, describes how to mutate values and change program state in an imperative manner.

Chapter 5, *Object-Oriented Programming*, covers object-oriented programming from creating simple types to inheritance and polymorphism.

Chapter 6, *.NET Programming*, goes over some style-independent concepts exposed by the .NET Framework and CLI.

Chapter 7, *Applied Functional Programming*, covers more advanced topics in functional programming such as tail recursion and functional design patterns.

Chapter 8, *Applied Object-Oriented Programming*, describes how to develop and take advantage of a rich type system. Special attention will be paid to how to leverage the functional aspects of F# to make object-oriented code better.

Part II, Programming F#

Chapter 9, *Scripting*, examines F# as a scripting language and how to make the most of F# script files.

Chapter 10, *Computation Expressions*, introduces an advanced F# language feature that will enable you to eliminate redundant code and add new capabilities to the core F# language.

Chapter 11, *Asynchronous and Parallel Programming*, takes a look at how to use F# to take advantage of multiple cores on a processor and the facilities in the F# and .NET libraries for parallel programming.

Chapter 12, *Reflection*, provides a look at the .NET reflection library and how to use it to create declarative programs.

Chapter 13, *Quotations*, introduces F# quotation expressions and how they can be used to do metaprogramming, as well as execute F# code on other computational platforms.

Appendixes

This book also features a couple of appendixes to flesh out any extra concepts you might be interested in.

Appendix A does a quick sweep through the existing technologies available on the .NET platform and how to use them from F#.

Appendix B covers how to write F# to interoperate with existing libraries as well as unmanaged code using P/Invoke and COM-interop.

Conventions Used in This Book

The following font conventions are used in this book:

Italic
> Used for new concepts as they are defined.

`Constant width`
> Used for code examples and F# keywords.

`Constant width bold`
> Used for emphasis within program code.

Pay special attention to note styles within this text.

Notes like this are used to add more detail for the curious reader.

Warnings are indicated in this style to help you avoid common mistakes.

How to Contact Us

Please address comments and questions concerning this book to the publisher:

> O'Reilly Media, Inc.
> 1005 Gravenstein Highway North
> Sebastopol, CA 95472
> 800-998-9938 (in the U.S. or Canada)
> 707-829-0515 (international/local)
> 707-829-0104 (fax)

Although we've tested and verified the information in this book, you may find that some aspects of the F# language have changed since this writing (or perhaps even a bug in an example!). We have a web page for the book, where we list examples and any plans for future editions. You can access this page at:

> *http://oreilly.com/catalog/9780596153649*

You can also send messages electronically. To be put on the mailing list or request a catalog, send email to:

> *info@oreilly.com*

To comment on the book, send email to:

> *bookquestions@oreilly.com*

For information about this book and others, as well as additional technical articles and discussion on F#, see the O'Reilly website:

> *http://www.oreilly.com*

or the O'Reilly .NET DevCenter:

> *http://www.oreillynet.com/dotnet*

or the Microsoft Developer Network portal for F#:

> *http://www.msdn.com/fsharp*

Using Code Examples

This book is here to help you get your job done. In general, you may use the code in this book in your programs and documentation. You do not need to contact us for permission unless you're reproducing a significant portion of the code. For example, writing a program that uses several chunks of code from this book does not require permission. Selling or distributing a CD-ROM of examples from O'Reilly books does require permission. Answering a question by citing this book and quoting example code does not require permission. Incorporating a significant amount of example code from this book into your product's documentation does require permission.

We appreciate, but do not require, attribution. An attribution usually includes the title, author, publisher, and ISBN. For example: "*Programming F#*, by Chris Smith. Copyright 2010 Chris Smith, 978-0-596-15364-9."

If you feel your use of code examples falls outside fair use or the permission given above, feel free to contact us at *permissions@oreilly.com*.

Safari® Books Online

Safari Safari Books Online is an on-demand digital library that lets you easily
Books Online search over 7,500 technology and creative reference books and videos to
find the answers you need quickly.

With a subscription, you can read any page and watch any video from our library online.
Read books on your cell phone and mobile devices. Access new titles before they are
available for print, and get exclusive access to manuscripts in development and post
feedback for the authors. Copy and paste code samples, organize your favorites, download chapters, bookmark key sections, create notes, print out pages, and benefit from
tons of other time-saving features.

O'Reilly Media has uploaded this book to the Safari Books Online service. To have full
digital access to this book and others on similar topics from O'Reilly and other pub-
lishers, sign up for free at *http://my.safaribooksonline.com*.

Acknowledgments

I get all the credit for writing this book, but the real effort for putting together the F#
language comes from F# teams at Microsoft in Redmond and Microsoft Research in
Cambridge, England. I've had immense pleasure working with a ridiculously talented
group of people and without their effort F# would just be a TODO sticky note on Don
Syme's monitor.

Here are the people at Microsoft who made F# happen:

Anar Alimov	Joe Pamer
Andrew Kennedy	Jomo Fisher
Baofa Feng	Kyle Ross
Brian McNamara	Laurant Le Blun
Daniel Quirk	Luke Hoban
Dmitry Lomov	Matteo Taveggia
Dominic Cooney	Ralf Herbrich
Don Syme	Santosh Zachariah
Gordon Hogenson	Sean Wang
Greg Neverov	Timothy Ng
James Margetson	Tomas Petricek

Also, from the amazing editors at O'Reilly to the outstanding people in the F# com-
munity, this book could not have been possible without the help of many others: John
Osborn, Laurel Ruma, Brian MacDonald, Matt Ellis, André van Meulebrouck, Stephen
Toub, Jared Parsons, Dustin "honorary member" Campbell, Michael de la Maza, Alex
Peake, Ryan Cavanaugh, Brian Peek, Matthew Podwysocki, Richard Minerich, Kate
Moore, and finally Stuart Bowers—you're easily a level-9 F# ninja by now.

PART I

Multiparadigm Programming

CHAPTER 1

Introduction to F#

F# is a powerful language that spans multiple paradigms of development. This chapter provides a brief introduction to the heart of F#—the F# compiler, tools, and its place in Visual Studio 2010.

In this chapter, you will create a couple of simple F# applications and then I'll point out key Visual Studio features for F# development. I won't cover much of Visual Studio here, so I encourage you to explore the IDE on your own to learn more, or refer to the documentation online at *http://msdn.microsoft.com/en-us/vstudio/default.aspx*.

If you are already familiar with Visual Studio, you should still skim through this chapter. Creating and debugging F# projects works just like C# or VB.NET; however, F# has a unique characteristic when it comes to multiple-file projects. In addition, F# has a feature called *F# Interactive* that will dramatically increase your productivity. Not to be missed!

Getting to Know F#

As with all programming books, it is customary to write a Hello, World application, and I don't want to deviate from tradition. Open up Notepad or your favorite text editor and create a new file named *HelloWorld.fs* with the following text:

```
// HelloWorld.fs

printfn "Hello, World"
```

Success! You've just written your first F# application. To compile this application, use the F# compiler, `fsc.exe`, located in the *Program Files\Microsoft F#\v4.0* folder. (Or, if you are using the Mono, wherever you chose to install F#.) The following snippet shows calling the F# compiler on the command line to build and run your application:

```
C:\Program Files\Microsoft F#\v4.0>fsc HelloWorld.fs
Microsoft F# Compiler, (c) Microsoft Corporation, All Rights Reserved
F# Version 1.9.8.0, compiling for .NET Framework Version v4.0.21017

C:\Program Files\Microsoft F#\v4.0>HelloWorld.exe
Hello, World!
```

Visual Studio 2010

Tools are the lifeblood of any programming language, and F# is no different. While you can be successful writing F# code in your favorite text editor and invoking the compiler exclusively from the command line, you'll likely be more productive using tools. Like C# and VB.NET, F# is a first-class citizen in Visual Studio. F# in Visual Studio has all the features you would expect, such as debugger support, IntelliSense, project templates, and so on.

To create your first F# project, open up the Visual Studio IDE and select File→New Project from the menu bar to open the New Project dialog, as shown in Figure 1-1. Select Visual F# in the left pane, select F# Application in the right pane, and click OK.

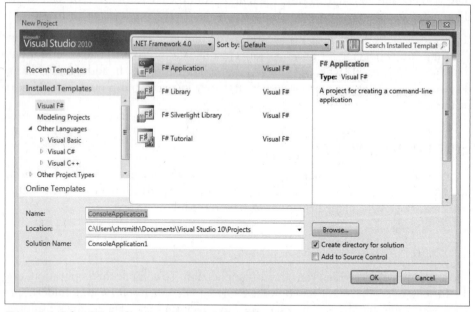

Figure 1-1. Select F# Application to start your first F# project

After you click OK in the New Project dialog, you'll see an empty code editor, a blank canvas ready for you to create your F# masterpiece.

To start with, let's revisit our Hello, World application. Type the following code into the F# editor:

```
printfn "Hello, World"
```

Now press Control + F5 to run your application. When your application starts, a console window will appear and display the entirely unsurprising result shown in Figure 1-2.

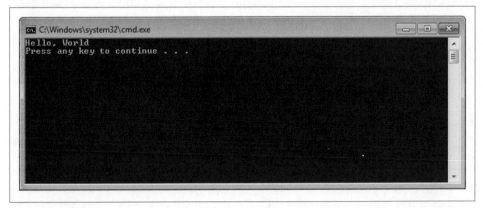

Figure 1-2. Hello, World in F#

Your Second F# Program

It may be startling to see a program work without an explicit `Main` method. You will see why this is admissible in the next chapter, but for now let's create a more meaningful Hello, World–type program to get a feel for basic F# syntax.

The code in Example 1-1 will create a program that accepts two command-line parameters and prints them to the console. In addition, it displays the current time.

Example 1-1. Mega Hello World

```
(*
Mega Hello World:
Take two command line parameters and then print
them along with the current time to the console.
*)

open System

[<EntryPoint>]
let main (args : string[]) =

    if args.Length <> 2 then
        failwith "Error: Expected arguments <greeting> and <thing>"
```

```
let greeting, thing = args.[0], args.[1]
let timeOfDay = DateTime.Now.ToString("hh:mm tt")

printfn "%s, %s at %s" greeting thing timeOfDay

// Program exit code
0
```

Now that you have actual F# code, hopefully you are curious about what is going on. Let's look at this program line by line to see how it works.

Values

Example 1-1 introduces three values named greeting, thing, and timeOfDay:

```
let greeting, thing = args.[0], args.[1]
let timeOfDay = DateTime.Now.ToString("hh:mm tt")
```

The key thing here is that the let keyword binds a *name* to a *value*. It is worth pointing out that unlike most other programming languages, in F# values are *immutable* by default, meaning they cannot be changed once initialized. We will cover why values are immutable in Chapter 3, but for now it is sufficient to say it has to do with functional programming.

F# is also case-sensitive, so any two values with names that only differ by case are considered different:

```
let number = 1
let Number = 2
let NUMBER = 3
```

A value's name can be any combination of letters, numbers, an underscore _, or an apostrophe '. However, the name must begin with a letter or an underscore.

> You can enclose the value's name with a pair of tickmarks, in which case the name can contain any character except for tabs and newlines. This allows you to refer to values and functions exposed from other .NET languages that may conflict with F# keywords:
>
> ```
> let ``this.Isn't %A% good value Name$!@#`` = 5
> ```

Whitespace Matters

Other languages, like C#, use semicolons and curly braces to indicate when statements and blocks of code are complete. However, programmers typically indent their code to make it more readable anyway, so these extra symbols often just add syntactic clutter to the code.

In F#, whitespace—spaces and newlines—is significant. The F# compiler allows you to use whitespace to delimit code blocks. For example, anything indented more than

---

the `if` keyword is considered to be in the body of the `if` statement. Because tab characters can indicate an unknown number of space characters, they are prohibited in F# code.

 You can configure the Visual Studio editor to automatically convert tab characters into spaces by changing the relevant setting under Tools→Options→Text Editor→F#.

Reviewing Example 1-1, notice that the body of the `main` method was indented by four spaces, and the body of the `if` statement was indented by another four spaces:

```
let main (args : string[]) =

    if args.Length <> 2 then
        failwith "Error: Expected arguments <greeting> and <thing>"

    let greeting, thing = args.[0], args.[1]
    let timeOfDay = DateTime.Now.ToString("hh:mm tt")

    printfn "%s, %s at %s" greeting thing timeOfDay

    // Program exit code
    0
```

If the body of the `if` statement, the `failwith`, was dedented four spaces and therefore lined up with the `if` keyword, the F# compiler would yield a warning. This is because the compiler wouldn't be able to determine if the `failwith` was meant for the body of the `if` statement:

```
[<EntryPoint>]
let main (args : string[]) =

    if args.Length <> 2 then
    failwith "Error: Expected arguments <greeting> and <thing>"

Warning FS0058: possible incorrect indentation: this token is offside of
context started at position (25:5). Try indenting this token further or
using standard formatting conventions
```

The general rule is that anything belonging to a method or statement must be indented further than the keyword that began the method or statement. So in Example 1-1, everything in the `main` method was indented past the first `let` and everything in the `if` statement was indented past the `if` keyword. As you see and write more F# code, you will quickly find that omitting semicolons and curly braces makes the code easier to write and also much easier to read.

.NET Interop

Example 1-1 also demonstrated how F# can interoperate with existing .NET libraries:

```
open System

// ...

let timeOfDay = DateTime.Now.ToString("hh:mm tt")
```

The .NET Framework contains a broad array of libraries for everything from graphics to databases to web services. F# can take advantage of any .NET library natively by calling directly into it. In Example 1-1, the `DateTime.Now` property was used in the `System` namespace in the `mscorlib.dll` assembly. Conversely, any code written in F# can be consumed by other .NET languages.

For more information on .NET libraries, you can skip ahead to Appendix A for a quick tour of what's available.

Comments

Like any language, F# allows you to comment your code. To declare a single-line comment, use two slashes, `//`; everything after them until the end of the line will be ignored by the compiler:

```
// Program exit code
```

For larger comments that span multiple lines, you can use multiline comments, which indicate to the compiler to ignore everything between the (* and *) characters:

```
(*
Mega Hello World:
Take two command line parameters and then print
them along with the current time to the console.
*)
```

For F# applications written in Visual Studio, there is a third type of comment: an *XML documentation comment*. If a comment starting with three slashes, `///`, is placed above an identifier, Visual Studio will display the comment's text when you hover over it.

Figure 1-3 shows applying an XML documentation comment and its associated tooltip.

F# Interactive

So far you have written some F# code and executed it, and the rest of the book will have many more examples. While you *could* leave a wake of new projects while working through this book and trying out the samples, Visual Studio comes with a tool called F# Interactive or FSI. Using the FSI window, you will not only find it much easier to work through the examples in this book, but it will also help you write applications.

```
/// Compute the greatest common divisor of
/// two numbers.
let rec gcd x y =
    if y = 0 then x
    else gcd y (x % y)


let x = gcd 1024 12
```

val gcd : int -> int -> int

Compute the greatest common divisor of
two numbers.

Full name: ProgrammingFS.Ch1.gcd

Figure 1-3. XML documentation comments

F# Interactive is a tool known as a *REPL*, which stands for read-evaluate-print loop.
It accepts F# code, compiles and executes it, then prints the results. This allows you
to quickly and easily experiment with F# code without needing to create new projects
or build a full application to see the result of a five-line snippet.

In C# and VB.NET, you must compile and then run your application in order to see
its results, which makes it cumbersome to try out and experiment with small code
fragments. Even if you use the Visual Studio Immediate Window while debugging, you
are limited to just evaluating expressions and cannot actually write code, such as defining new functions and classes.

In Visual Studio, most profiles launch the F# Interactive window by using the Control
+Alt+F keyboard combination. Once the FSI window is available, it accepts F# code
until you terminate the input with ;; and a newline. The code entered will be compiled
and executed just as shown in Figure 1-4.

After each code snippet is sent to FSI, for every name introduced, you will see val *<name>*.
If an expression was left unnamed, by default, it will be called it. After the name of the
identifier will be a colon and the *type* of the code evaluated, followed by its value. For
example, in Figure 1-4, the value x was introduced, of type int, with value 42.

 If you are running F# without Visual Studio, you can find a console
version of F# Interactive named fsi.exe in the same directory you found
fsc.exe.

Try running these other snippets in FSI. Note that every code snippet is terminated
with ;;:

```
> 2 + 2;;
val it : int = 4
> // Introduce two values
let x = 1
```

```
let y = 2.3

val x : int
val y : float

> float x + y;;
val it : float = 3.3
> let cube x = x * x * x;;

val cube : int -> int

> cube 4;;
val it : int = 64
```

FSI dramatically simplifies testing and debugging your applications because you can send F# code from your current project to the FSI window by highlighting the code in Visual Studio and pressing Alt+Enter.

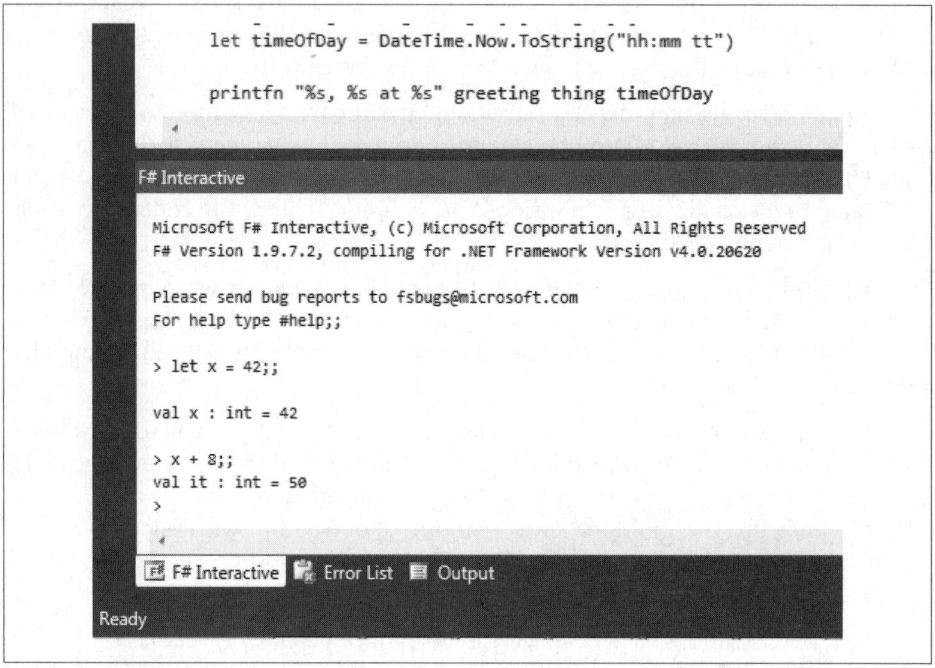

```
let timeOfDay = DateTime.Now.ToString("hh:mm tt")

printfn "%s, %s at %s" greeting thing timeOfDay
```

F# Interactive

```
Microsoft F# Interactive, (c) Microsoft Corporation, All Rights Reserved
F# Version 1.9.7.2, compiling for .NET Framework Version v4.0.20620

Please send bug reports to fsbugs@microsoft.com
For help type #help;;

> let x = 42;;

val x : int = 42

> x + 8;;
val it : int = 50
>
```

F# Interactive   Error List   Output

Ready

Figure 1-4. The F# Interactive window

After selecting all the code in Example 1-1 within the code editor and pressing Alt+Enter, you will see the following in the FSI window:

```
>

val main : string array -> int
```

This allows you to write code in the Visual Studio editor—which offers syntax highlighting and IntelliSense—but test your code using the FSI window. You can test the `main` method you sent to FSI simply by calling it:

```
> main [| "Hello"; "World" |];;
Hello, World at 10:52 AM
val it : int = 0
```

The majority of the samples in this book are taken directly from FSI sessions. I encourage you to use FSI as well to follow along and experiment with the F# language's syntax.

Managing F# Source Files

When you are starting out in F# programming, most of the programs you write will live only in FSI or perhaps in a single code file. Your F# projects, however, will quickly grow and be broken up across multiple files and eventually multiple projects.

The F# language has some unique characteristics when it comes to managing projects with multiple source files. In F#, the order in which code files are compiled is significant.

You can only call into functions and classes defined earlier in the code file or in a separate code file compiled before the file where the function or class is used. If you rearrange the order of the source files, your program may no longer build!

The reason for this significance in compilation order is *type inference*, a topic covered in the next chapter.

F# source files are compiled in the order they are displayed in Visual Studio's Solution Explorer, from top to bottom. Whenever you add a new code file, it is added to the bottom of the list, but if you want to rearrange the source files, you can right-click a code file and select Move Up or Move Down, as shown in Figure 1-5. The keyboard shortcut for reordering project files is Alt+Up and Alt+Down.

Now that you are armed with the logistical know-how for compiling F# applications, the rest of this book will focus exclusively on the syntax and semantics of the F# programming language.

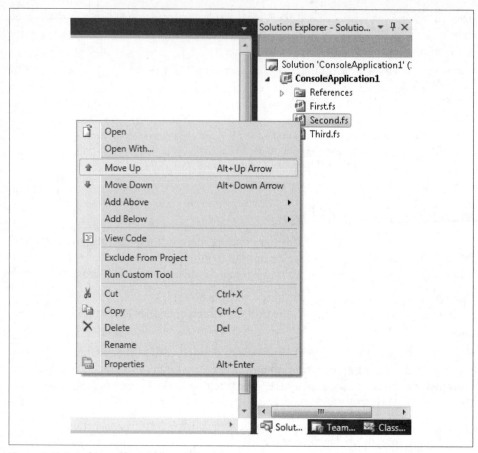

Figure 1-5. Reordering files within an F# project

CHAPTER 2

Fundamentals

In Chapter 1, you wrote your first F# program. I broke it down to give you a feel for what you were doing, but much of the code is still a mystery. In this chapter, I'll provide the necessary foundation for you to understand that code fully, but more importantly, I'll present several more examples that you can use to grasp the basics of F# before you move on to the more complex features.

The first section of this chapter covers primitive types, like `int` and `string`, which are the building blocks for all F# programs. I'll then cover functions so that you can manipulate data.

The third section details foundational types such as `list`, `option`, and `unit`. Mastering how to use these types will enable you to expand into the object-oriented and functional styles of F# code covered in later chapters.

By the end of this chapter, you will be able to write simple F# programs for processing data. In future chapters, you will learn how to add power and expressiveness to your code, but for now let's master the basics.

Primitive Types

A *type* is a concept or abstraction and is primarily about enforcing safety. Types represent a proof of sorts if a conversion will work. Some types are straightforward—representing an integer—while others are far more abstract—like a function. F# is statically typed, meaning that type checking is done at compile time. For example, if a function accepts an integer as a parameter, you will get a compiler error if you try to pass in a string.

Like C# and VB.NET, F# supports the full cast and crew of *primitive .NET types* (which are the same for most programming languages). They are built into the F# language and separate from *user-defined types*, which you define yourself.

To create a value, simply use a *let binding*.

You can do much more with `let` bindings, but we'll save that for Chapter 3. For now, just know that you can use a `let` binding (via the `let` keyword) to introduce a new identifier. For example, the following code defines a new value x in an FSI session:

```
> let x = 1;;

val x : int = 1
```

Numeric Primitives

Numeric primitives come in two varieties: integers and floating-point numbers. Integer types vary by size, so that some types take up less memory and can represent a smaller range of numbers. Integers can also be signed or unsigned based on whether or not they can represent negative numbers.

Floating-point types vary in size, too; in exchange for taking up more memory, they provide more precision on the numbers they hold.

To define new numeric values, use a `let` binding followed by an integer or floating-point literal with an optional suffix. The suffix determines the type of integer or floating-point number. For a full list of available primitive numeric types and their suffixes, see Table 2-1.

```
> let answerToEverything = 42UL;;

val everything : uint64 = 42UL

> let pi = 3.1415926M;;

val pi : decimal = 3.1415926M

> let avogadro = 6.022e-23;;

val avogadro : float = 6.022e-23
```

Table 2-1. Numerical primitives in F#

Type	Suffix	.NET type	Range
byte	uy	System.Byte	0 to 255
sbyte	y	System.SByte	−128 to 127
int16	s	System.Int16	−32,768 to 32,767
uint16	us	System.UInt16	0 to 65,535
int, int32		System.Int32	$−2^{31}$ to $2^{31}−1$
uint, uint32	u	System.UInt32	0 to $2^{32}−1$
int64	L	System.Int64	$−2^{63}$ to $2^{63}−1$
uint64	UL	System.UInt64	0 to $2^{64}−1$

Type	Suffix	.NET type	Range
float		System.Double	A double-precision floating point based on the IEEE64 standard. Represents values with approximately 15 significant digits.
float32	f	System.Float	A single-precision floating point based on the IEEE32 standard. Represents values with approximately 7 significant digits.
decimal	M	System.Decimal	A fixed-precision floating-point type with precisely 28 digits of precision.

F# will also allow you to specify values in hexadecimal (base 16), octal (base 8), or binary (base 2) using a prefix 0x, 0o, or 0b:

```
> let hex = 0xFCAF;;

val hex : int = 64687

> let oct = 0o7771L;;

val oct : int64 = 4089L

> let bin = 0b00101010y;;

val bin : sbyte = 42y

> (hex, oct, bin);;
val it : int * int64 * sbyte = (64687, 4089, 42)
```

If you are familiar with the IEEE32 and IEEE64 standards, you can also specify floating-point numbers using hex, octal, or binary. F# will convert the binary value to the floating-point number it represents. When using a different base to represent floating-point numbers, use the LF suffix for float types and lf for float32 types:

```
> 0x401E000000000000LF;;
val it : float = 7.5

> 0x000000001f;;
val it : float32 = 0.0f
```

Arithmetic

You can use standard arithmetic operators on numeric primitives. Table 2-2 lists all supported operators. Like all CLR-based languages, integer division rounds down to the next lowest number discarding the remainder.

Table 2-2. Arithmetic operators

Operator	Description	Example	Result
+	Addition	1 + 2	3
–	Subtraction	1 - 2	-1
*	Multiplication	2 * 3	6

Operator	Description	Example	Result
/	Division	8L / 3L	2L
**	Power[a]	2.0 ** 8.0	256.0
%	Modulus	7 % 3	1

[a] Power, the ** operator, only works for float and float32 types. To raise the power of an integer value, you must either convert it to a floating-point number first or use the pown function.

By default, arithmetic operators do not check for overflow, so if you exceed the range allowed by an integer value by addition, it will overflow to be negative. (Similarly, subtraction will result in a positive number if the number is too small to be stored in the integer type.)

```
> 32767s + 1s;;
val it : int16 = -32768s

> -32768s + -1s;;
val it : int16 = 32767s
```

If integer overflow is a cause for concern, you should consider using a larger type or using checked arithmetic, discussed in Chapter 7.

F# features all the standard math functions you would expect; see a full listing in Table 2-3.

Table 2-3. Common math functions

Routine	Description	Example	Result
abs	Absolute value of a number	abs -1.0	1.0
ceil	Round up to the nearest integer	ceil 9.1	10
exp	Raise a value to a power of e	exp 1.0	2.718
floor	Round down to the nearest integer	floor 9.9	9.0
sign	Sign of the value	sign -5	-1
log	Natural logarithm	log 2.71828	1.0
log10	Logarithm in base 10	log10 1000.0	3.0
sqrt	Square root	sqrt 4.0	2.0
cos	Cosine	cos 0.0	1.0
sin	Sine	sin 0.0	0.0
tan	Tangent	tan 1.0	1.557
pown	Compute the power of an integer	pown 2L 10	1024L

Conversion Routines

One of the tenets of the F# language is that there are no implicit conversions. This means that the compiler will not automatically convert primitive data types for you behind the scenes, for example, converting an int16 to an int64. This eliminates subtle bugs by removing surprise conversions. Instead, to convert primitive values, you must use an explicit conversion function listed in Table 2-4. All of the standard conversion functions accept all other primitive types—including strings and chars.

Table 2-4. Numeric primitive conversion routines

Routine	Description	Example	Result
sbyte	Converts data to an sybte	sbyte -5	-5y
byte	Converts data to a byte	byte "42"	42uy
int16	Converts data to an int16	int16 'a'	97s
uint16	Converts data to a uint16	uint16 5	5us
int32, int	Converts data to an int	int 2.5	2
uint32, uint	Converts data to a uint	uint32 0xFF	255
int64	Converts data to an int64	int64 -8	-8L
uint64	Converts data to a uint64	uint64 "0xFF"	255UL
float	Converts data to a float	float 3.1415M	3.1415
float32	Converts data to a float32	float32 8y	8.0f
decimal	Converts data to a decimal	decimal 1.23	1.23M

While these conversion routines accept strings, they parse strings using the underlying System.Convert family of methods, meaning that for invalid inputs they throw System.FormatException exceptions.

BigInt

If you are dealing with data larger than 2^{64}, F# has the BigInt type for representing arbitrarily large integers. While the BigInt type is simply an alias for the System.Numerics.BigInteger type, it is worth noting that neither C# nor VB.NET has syntax to support arbitrarily large integers.

BigInt uses the I suffix for literals. Example 2-1 defines data storage sizes as BigInts.

Example 2-1. The BigInt type for representing large integers

```
> open System.Numerics

// Data storage units
let megabyte = 1024I    * 1024I
let gigabyte = megabyte * 1024I
```

```
let terabyte  = gigabyte * 1024I
let petabyte  = terabyte * 1024I
let exabyte   = petabyte * 1024I
let zettabyte = exabyte  * 1024I;;

val megabyte : BigInteger = 1048576
val gigabyte : BigInteger = 1073741824
val terabyte : BigInteger = 1099511627776
val petabyte : BigInteger = 1125899906842624
val exabyte  : BigInteger = 1152921504606846976
val zettabyte : BigInteger = 1180591620717411303424
```

 Although `BigInt` is heavily optimized for performance, it is much slower than using the primitive integer data types.

Bitwise Operations

Primitive integer types support bitwise operators for manipulating values at a binary level. Bitwise operators are typically used when reading and writing binary data from files. See Table 2-5.

Table 2-5. Bitwise operators

Operator	Description	Example	Result
&&&	Bitwise 'And'	0b1111 &&& 0b0011	0b0011
|||	Bitwise 'Or'	0xFF00 ||| 0x00FF	0xFFFF
^^^	Bitwise 'Exclusive Or'	0b0011 ^^^ 0b0101	0b0110
<<<	Left Shift	0b0001 <<< 3	0b1000
>>>	Right Shift	0b1000 >>> 3	0b0001

Characters

The .NET platform is based on Unicode, so characters are represented using 2-byte UTF-16 characters. To define a character value, you can put any Unicode character in single quotes. Characters can also be specified using a Unicode hexadecimal character code.

The following code defines a list of vowel characters and prints the result of defining a character using a hexadecimal value:

```
> let vowels = ['a'; 'e'; 'i'; 'o'; 'u'];;

val vowels : char list = ['a'; 'e'; 'i'; 'o'; 'u']

> printfn "Hex u0061 = '%c'" '\u0061';;
Hex u0061 = 'a'
val it : unit = ()
```

To represent special control characters, you need to use an escape sequence, listed in Table 2-6. An escape sequence is a backslash followed by a special character.

Table 2-6. Character escape sequences

Character	Meaning
\'	Single quote
\"	Double quote
\\	Backslash
\b	Backspace
\n	Newline
\r	Carriage return
\t	Horizontal tab

If you want to get the numeric representation of a .NET character's Unicode value, you can pass it to any of the conversion routines listed earlier in Table 2-3. Alternatively, you can get the byte value of a character literal by adding a B suffix:

```
> // Convert value of 'C' to an integer
int 'C';;
val it : int = 67
> // Convert value of 'C' to a byte
'C'B;;
val it : byte = 67uy
```

Strings

String literals are defined by enclosing a series of characters in double quotes, which can span multiple lines. To access a character from within a string, use the indexer syntax, .[ ], and pass in a zero-based character index:

```
> let password = "abracadabra";;

val password : string = "abracadabra"

> let multiline = "This string
takes up
multiple lines";;

val multiline : string = "This string
takes up
multiple lines";;

> multiline.[0];;
val it : char = 'T'
> multiline.[1];;
val it : char = 'h'
> multiline.[2];;
val it : char = 'i'
```

```
> multiline.[3];;
val it : char = 's'
```

If you want to specify a long string, you can break it up across multiple lines using a single backslash, \. If the last character on a line in a string literal is a backslash, the string will continue on the next line after removing all leading whitespace characters:

```
let longString = "abc-\
                      def-\
              ghi";;

> longString;;
val it : string = "abc-def-ghi"
```

You can use the escape sequence characters such as \t or \\ within a string if you want, but this makes defining file paths and registry keys problematic. You can define a verbatim string using the @ symbol, which takes the verbatim text between the quotation marks and does not encode any escape sequence characters:

```
> let normalString = "Normal.\n.\n.\t.\t.String";;

val normalString : string = "Normal.
.
.        .      .String

> let verbatimString = @"Verbatim.\n.\n.\t.\t.String";;

val verbatimString : string = "Verbatim.\n.\n.\t.\t.String"
```

Similar to adding the B suffix to a character to return its byte representation, adding B to the end of a string will return the string's characters in the form of a byte array. (Arrays will be covered in Chapter 4.)

```
> let hello = "Hello"B;;

val hello : byte array = [|72uy; 101uy; 108uy; 108uy; 111uy|]
```

Boolean Values

For dealing with values that can only be true or false, F# has the bool type (System.Boolean), as well as standard Boolean operators listed in Table 2-7.

Table 2-7. Boolean operators

Operator	Description	Example	Result
&&	Boolean 'And'	true && false	false
||	Boolean 'Or'	true || false	true
not	Boolean 'Not'	not false	true

Example 2-2 builds truth tables for Boolean functions and prints them. It defines a function called printTruthTable that takes a function named f as a parameter. That function is called for each cell in the truth table and its result is printed. Later the operators && and || are passed to the printTruthTable function.

Example 2-2. Printing truth tables

```
> // Print the truth table for the given function
let printTruthTable f =
    printfn "        |true  | false |"
    printfn "        +-------+-------+"
    printfn " true  | %5b | %5b |" (f true  true) (f true  false)
    printfn " false | %5b | %5b |" (f false true) (f false false)
    printfn "        +-------+-------+"
    printfn ""
    ();;

val printTruthTable : (bool -> bool -> bool) -> unit

> printTruthTable (&&);;
        |true  | false |
        +-------+-------+
 true  | true  | false |
 false | false | false |
        +-------+-------+

val it : unit = ()
> printTruthTable (||);;
        |true  | false |
        +-------+-------+
 true  | true  | true  |
 false | true  | false |
        +-------+-------+

val it : unit = ()
```

 F# uses short-circuit evaluation when evaluating Boolean expressions, meaning that if the result can be determined after evaluating the first of the two expressions, the second value won't be evaluated. For example:

```
true || f()
```

will evaluate to true, without executing function f. Likewise:

```
false && g()
```

will evaluate to false, without executing function g.

Comparison and Equality

You can compare numeric values using standard greater than, less than, and equality operators listed Table 2-8. All comparison and equality operators evaluate to a Boolean value; the compare function returns –1, 0, or 1, depending on whether the first parameter is less than, equal to, or greater than the second.

Table 2-8. Comparison operators

Operator	Description	Example	Result
<	Less than	1 < 2	true
<=	Less than or equal	4.0 <= 4.0	true
>	Greater than	1.4e3 > 1.0e2	true
>=	Greater than or equal	0I >= 2I	false
=	Equal to	"abc" = "abc"	true
<>	Not equal to	'a' <> 'b'	true
compare	Compare two values	compare 31 31	0

> Equality in .NET is a complex topic. There is *value equality* and *refer-ential equality*. For value types, comparison means that the values are identical, such as 1 = 1. For reference types, however, equality is deter-mined by overriding the `System.Object` method `Equals`. For more infor-mation, refer to the section "Object Equality" on page 119.

Functions

Now that we have all of F#'s primitive types under our control, let's define functions in order to manipulate them.

You define functions the same way you define values, except everything after the name of the function serves as the function's parameters. The following defines a function called `square` that takes an integer, `x`, and returns its square:

```
> let square x = x * x;;

val square : int -> int

> square 4;;
val it : int = 16
```

Unlike C#, F# has no `return` keyword. So when you define a function, the last ex-pression to be evaluated in the function is what the function returns.

Let's try another function to add `1` to the function's input:

```
> let addOne x = x + 1;;

val addOne : int -> int
```

The output from FSI shows the function has type `int -> int`, which is read as "a function taking an integer and returning an integer." The signature gets a bit more complicated when you add multiple parameters:

```
> let add x y = x + y

val add : int -> int -> int
```

Technically speaking, the type `int -> int -> int` is read as "a function taking an integer, which returns a function which takes an integer and returns an integer." Don't worry about this "functions returning functions" jazz just yet. The only thing you need to know for now is that to call a function, simply provide its parameters separated by spaces:

```
> add 1 2;;

Val it : 3
```

Type Inference

Because F# is statically typed, calling the `add` method you just created with a floating-point value will result in a compiler error:

```
> add 1.0 2.0;;

  add 1.0 2.0;;
  ----^^^^

stdin(3,5): error FS0001: This expression has type
        float
but is here used with type
        int.
```

You might be wondering, then, why does the compiler think that this function takes only integers? The + operator also works on floats, too!

The reason is because of *type inference*. Unlike C#, the F# compiler doesn't require you to explicitly state the types of all the parameters to a function. The compiler figures it out based on usage.

 Be careful not to confuse type inference with *dynamic typing*. Although F# allows you to omit types when writing code, that doesn't mean that type checking is not enforced at compile time.

Because the + operator works for many different types such as `byte`, `int`, and `decimal`, the compiler simply defaults to `int` if there is no additional information.

The following FSI session declares a function that will multiply two values. Just as when + was used, the function is inferred to work on integers because no usage information is provided:

```
> // No additional information to infer usage
let mult x y = x * x;;

val mult : int -> int -> int
```

Now if we have FSI snippet that not only defines the `mult` function but also calls it passing in floats, then the function's signature will be inferred to be of type `float -> float -> float`:

```
> // Type inference in action
let mult x y = x * y
let result = mult 4.0 5.5;;

val mult : float -> float -> float
val result : float
```

However, you can provide a *type annotation*, or hint, to the F# compiler about what the types are. To add a type annotation, simply replace a function parameter with the following form:

ident -> (*ident* : *type*)

where *type* is the type you wish to force the parameter to be. To constrain the first parameter of our add function to be a `float`, simply redefine the function as:

```
> let add (x : float) y = x + y;;

val add : float -> float -> float
```

Notice that because you added the type annotation for value `x`, the type of the function changed to `float -> float -> float`. This is because the only overload for `+` that takes a `float` as its first parameter is `float -> float -> float`, so the F# compiler now infers the type of `y` to be `float` as well.

Type inference dramatically reduces code clutter by having the compiler figure out what types to use. However, the occasional type annotation is required and can sometimes improve code readability.

Generic Functions

You can write functions that work for any type of a parameter, for example, an identity function that simply returns its input:

```
> let ident x = x;;

val ident : 'a -> 'a

> ident "a string";;
val it : string = "a string"
> ident 1234L;;
val it : int64 = 1234L
```

Because the type inference system could not determine a fixed type for value `x` in the `ident` function, it was generic. If a parameter is *generic*, it means that the parameter can be of any type, such as an integer, string, or float.

The type of a generic parameter can have the name of any valid identifier prefixed with an apostrophe, but typically letters of the alphabet starting with 'a'. The following code redefines the ident function using a type annotation that forces x to be generic:

```
> let ident2 (x : 'a) = x;;

val ident2 : 'a -> 'a
```

Writing generic code is important for maximizing code reuse. We will continue to dive into type inference and generic functions as the book progresses, so don't sweat the details just yet. Just note that whenever you see an 'a, it can be an int, float, string, user-defined type, etc.

Scope

Each value declared in F# has a specific scope, which is the range of locations where the value can be used. (More formally, this is called a *declaration space*.) By default values have module scope, meaning that they can be used anywhere after their declaration. However, values defined within a function are scoped only to that function. So a function can use any value defined previously on the "outside" of the function, but the "outside" cannot refer to values defined inside of a function.

In the following example, a value named moduleValue is defined with module scope and used inside of a function, while another value named functionValue is defined within a function and raises an error when used outside of its scope:

```
> // Scope
let moduleValue = 10
let functionA x =
    x + moduleValue;;

val moduleValue : int = 10
val functionA : int -> int

> // Error case
let functionB x =
    let functionValue = 20
    x + functionValue

// 'functionValue' not in scope
functionValue;;

    functionValue;;
    ^^^^^^^^^^^^^
error FS0039: The value or constructor 'functionValue' is not defined.
```

The scoping of values may not seem that important a detail, but it is important in F# because it allows nested functions. In F#, you can declare new function values within the body of a function. Nested functions have access to any value declared in a higher scope, such as the parent function or module, as well as any new values declared within the nested function.

The following code shows nested functions in action. Notice how function g is able to use its parent function f 's parameter fParam:

```
> // Nested functions
let moduleValue = 1

let f fParam =
    let g gParam = fParam + gParam + moduleValue

    let a = g 1
    let b = g 2
    a + b;;

val moduleValue : int = 1
val f : int -> int
```

It may seem as though defining functions within functions can only lead to confusion, but the ability to limit the scope of functions is very useful. It helps prevent pollution of the surrounding module by allowing you to keep small, specific functions local to just where they are needed. This will become more apparent once we start programming in the functional style in Chapter 3.

Once you do start using nested functions, it might become tedious to keep all the values in scope straight. What if you want to declare a value named x, but that value is already used in a higher scope? In F#, having two values with the same name doesn't lead to a compiler error; rather it simply leads to *shadowing*. When this happens, both values exist in memory, except there is no way to access the previously declared value. Instead, the last one declared "wins."

The following code defines a function which takes a parameter x, and then defines several new values each named x as well:

```
> // Convert bytes to gigabytes
let bytesToGB x =
    let x = x / 1024I //  B to KB
    let x = x / 1024I // KB to MB
    let x = x / 1024I // MB to GB
    x;;

val bytesToGB : System.Numerics.BigInteger -> System.Numerics.BigInteger

> let hardDriveSize = bytesToGB 268435456000I;;
val hardDriveSize : System.Numerics.BigInt = 250I
```

After each `let` binding in the previous example, the value named x is shadowed and replaced with a new one. It may look as if the value of x is changing, but actually it is just creating a new value of x and giving it the same name. The following shows an example of how the code gets compiled:

```
let bytesToGB x =
    let x_2 = x   / 1024I //  B to KB
    let x_3 = x_2 / 1024I // KB to MB
```

```
let x_4 = x_3 / 1024I // MB to GB
x_4
```

This technique of intentionally shadowing values is useful for giving the illusion of updating values without relying on mutation. If you want to actually update the value of x, you would need to resort to mutability, which is covered in Chapter 4.

Control Flow

Within a function, you can branch control flow using the `if` keyword. The condition expression must be of type `bool` and if it evaluates to `true`, the given code is executed, which in the following snippet prints a message to the console:

```
> // If statements
let printGreeting shouldGreet greeting =
    if shouldGreet then
        printfn "%s" greeting;;

val printGreeting : bool -> string -> unit

> printGreeting true "Hello!";;
Hello!
val it : unit = ()
> printGreeting false "Hello again!";;
val it : unit = ()
```

More complex code branching can be done using `if` *expressions*.

`if` expressions work just as you would expect: if the condition expression evaluates to `true` then the first block of code executes, otherwise, the second block of code executes. However, something that makes F# very different from other languages is that `if` expressions return a value.

In the following example, the value `result` is bound to the result of the `if` expression. So if `x % 2 = 0`, `result`'s value will be `"Yes it is"`; otherwise, its value will be `"No it is not"`:

```
> // If expressions
let isEven x =
    let result =
        if x % 2 = 0 then
            "Yes it is"
        else
            "No it is not"
    result;;

val isEven : int -> string

> isEven 5;;
val it : string = "No it is not"
```

You can nest `if` expressions to model more complicated branching, but this quickly becomes difficult to maintain:

```
let isWeekend day =
    if day = "Sunday" then
        true
    else
        if day = "Saturday" then
            true
        else
            false
```

F# has some syntactic sugar to help you combat deeply nested if expressions with the elif keyword. With it, you can chain together multiple if expressions without the need for nesting:

```
let isWeekday day =
    if    day = "Monday"    then true
    elif day = "Tuesday"    then true
    elif day = "Wednesday"  then true
    elif day = "Thursday"   then true
    elif day = "Friday"     then true
    else false
```

Because the result of the if expression is a value, every clause of an if expression must return the same type:

```
> // ERROR: Different types for if expression clauses
let x =
    if 1 > 2 then
        42
    else
        "a string";;

      else              "a string";;
    ------------------^^^^^^^^^^^^

stdin(118,19): error FS0001: This expression has type
        string
but is here used with type
        int.
stopped due to error
```

But what if you only have a single if and no corresponding else? Then, the clause must return unit. unit is a special type in F# that means essentially "no value." (C# developers can think of unit as a manifestation of void.) We'll cover it in more detail shortly.

The if statements in the following example work because printfn returns unit:

```
> // If statement bodies returning unit
let describeNumber x =
    if x % 2 = 0 then
        printfn "x is a multiple of 2"
    if x % 3 = 0 then
        printfn "x is a multiple of 3"
    if x % 5 = 0 then
        printfn "x is a multiple of 5"
    ();;
```

```
val describeNumber : int -> unit

> describeNumber 18;;
x is a multiple of 2
x is a multiple of 3
val it : unit = ()
```

Core Types

Earlier we covered the primitive types available on the .NET platform, but those alone are insufficient for creating meaningful programs. The F# library includes several core types that will allow you to organize, manipulate, and process data. Table 2-9 lists a set of foundational types you will use throughout your F# applications.

Table 2-9. Common types in F#

Signature	Name	Description	Example
unit	Unit	A unit value	()
int, float	Concrete type	A concrete type	42, 3.14
'a, 'b	Generic type	A generic (free) type	
'a -> 'b	Function type	A function returning a value	fun x -> x + 1
'a * 'b	Tuple type	An ordered collection of values	(1, 2), ("eggs", "ham")
'a list	List type	A list of values	[1; 2; 3], [1 .. 3]
'a option	Option type	An optional value	Some(3), None

Unit

The unit type is a value signifying nothing of consequence. unit can be thought of as a concrete representation of **void** and is represented in code via ():

```
> let x = ();;

val x : unit

> ();;
val it : unit = ()
```

if expressions without a matching else must return unit because if they did return a value, what would happen if else was hit? Also, in F#, every function must return a value, so if the function doesn't conceptually return anything—like printf—then it should return a unit value.

The ignore function can swallow a function's return value if you want to return unit. It is typically used when calling a function for its side effect and you want to ignore its return value:

```
> let square x = x * x;;
```

```
val square : int -> int

> ignore (square 4);;
val it : unit = ()
```

Tuple

A tuple (pronounced "two-pull") is an ordered collection of data, and an easy way to group common pieces of data together. For example, tuples can be used to track the intermediate results of a computation.

 F# tuples use the underlying System.Tuple<_> type, though, in practice, you will never use the Tuple<_> class directly.

To create an instance of a tuple, separate a group of values with commas, and optionally place them within parentheses. A tuple type is described by a list of the tuple's elements' types, separated by asterisks. In the following example, dinner is an instance of a tuple, while string * string is the tuple's type:

```
> let dinner = ("green eggs", "ham");;

val dinner : string * string = ("green eggs", "ham")
```

Tuples can contain any number of values of any type. In fact, you can even have a tuple that contains other tuples!

The following code snippet defines two tuples. The first, named zeros, contains a tuple of various manifestations of zero. The second, nested, defines a nested tuple. The tuple has three elements, the second and third of which are themselves tuples:

```
> let zeros = (0, 0L, 0I, 0.0);;

val zeros : int * int64 * bigint * float = (0, 0L, 0I, 0.0)

> let nested = (1, (2.0, 3M), (4L, "5", '6'));;

val nested : int * (float * decimal) * (int64 * string * char) = ...
```

To extract values from two-element tuples, you can use the fst and snd functions. fst returns the first element of the tuple and snd returns the second:

```
> let nameTuple = ("John", "Smith");;

val nameTuple : string * string = ("John", "Smith")

> fst nameTuple;;
val it : string = "John"
> snd nameTuple;;
val it : string = "Smith"
```

Alternately, you can extract values from tuples by simply using a `let` binding. If you have `let` followed by multiple identifiers separated by commas, those names capture the tuple's values.

The following example creates a tuple value named `snacks`. Later the tuple's values are extracted into new identifiers named x, y, and z:

```
> let snacks = ("Soda", "Cookies", "Candy");;

val snacks : string * string * string = ("Soda", "Cookies", "Candy")

> let x, y, z = snacks;;

val z : string = "Soda"
val y : string = "Cookies"
val x : string = "Candy"

> y, z;;
val it : string * string = ("Cookies", "Candy")
```

You will get a compile error if you try to extract too many or too few values from a tuple:

```
> let x, y = snacks;;

  let x, y = snacks;;
  -----------^^^^^^

stdin(8,12): error FS0001: Type mismatch. Expecting a
        string * string
but given a
        string * string * string.
The tuples have differing lengths of 2 and 3.
```

It is possible to pass tuples as parameters to functions, like any value. Functions taking a single tuple as a parameter have a very different meaning when it comes to the functional style of programming; see "Partial function application" on page 51.

In the following example, the function `tupledAdd` takes two parameters, x and y, in tupled form. Notice the difference in type signature between the `add` and the `tupledAdd` functions:

```
> let add x y = x + y;;

val add : int -> int -> int

> let tupledAdd(x, y) = x + y;;

val tupledAdd : int * int -> int

> add 3 7;;
val it : int = 10

> tupledAdd(3, 7);;
val it : int = 10
```

Lists

Whereas tuples group values into a single entity, lists allow you link data together to form a chain. Doing so allows you to process list elements in bulk using aggregate operators, discussed shortly.

The simplest way to define a list is as a semicolon-delimited list of values enclosed in brackets, though later you will learn to declare lists using the more powerful list comprehension syntax. The empty list, which contains no items, is represented by []:

```
> // Declaring lists
let vowels = ['a'; 'e'; 'i'; 'o'; 'u']
let emptyList = [];;

val vowels : char list = ['a'; 'e'; 'i'; 'o'; 'u']
val emptyList : 'a list = []
```

In our example, the empty list had type `'a list` because it could be of any type and the type inference system was unable to pin down a specific type.

Unlike list types in other languages, F# lists are quite restrictive in how you access and manipulate them. In fact, for a list there are only two operations you can perform. (To see how this limitation can be used to your advantage, refer to Chapter 7.)

The first primitive list operation is *cons*, represented by the :: or cons operator. This joins an element to the front or *head* of a list. The following example attaches the value 'y' to the head of the vowels list:

```
> // Using the cons operator
let sometimes = 'y' :: vowels;;

val sometimes : char list = ['y'; 'a'; 'e'; 'i'; 'o'; 'u']
```

The second primitive list operation, known as append, uses the @ operator. Append joins two lists together. The following example joins the list odds and the list evens together, resulting in a new list:

```
> // Using the append operator
let odds = [1; 3; 5; 7; 9]
let evens = [2; 4; 6; 8; 10]

val odds : int list = [1; 3; 5; 7; 9]
val evens : int list = [2; 4; 6; 8; 10]

> odds @ evens;;
val it : int list = [1; 3; 5; 7; 9; 2; 4; 6; 8; 10]
```

List ranges

Declaring list elements as a semicolon-delimited list quickly becomes tedious, especially for large lists. To declare a list of ordered numeric values, use the list range syntax.

The first expression specifies the lower bound of the range and the second specifies the upper bound. The result then is a list of values from the lower bound to the upper bound, each separated by one:

```
> let x = [1 .. 10];;

val x : int list = [1; 2; 3; 4; 5; 6; 7; 8; 9; 10]
```

If an optional step value is provided, then the result is a list of values in the range between two numbers separated by the stepping value. Note that the stepping value can be negative:

```
> // List ranges
let tens = [0 .. 10 .. 50]
let countDown = [5L .. -1L .. 0L];;

val tens : int list = [0; 10; 20; 30; 40; 50]
val countDown : int list = [5L; 4L; 3L; 2L; 1L; 0L]
```

List comprehensions

The most expressive method for creating lists is to use *list comprehensions*, which is a rich syntax that allows you to generate lists inline with F# code. At the simplest level, a list comprehension is some code surrounded by rectangular brackets [ ]. The body of the list comprehension will be executed until it terminates, and the list will be made up of elements returned via the `yield` keyword. (Note that the list is fully generated in memory; lists elements are not lazily evaluated, like F#'s `seq<_>` type, discussed in the next chapter.)

```
> // Simple list comprehensions
let numbersNear x =
    [
        yield x - 1
        yield x
        yield x + 1
    ];;

val numbersNear : int -> int list

> numbersNear 3;;
val it : int list = [2; 3; 4]
```

Most any F# code can exist inside of list comprehensions, including things like function declarations and `for` loops. The following code snippet shows a list comprehension that defines a function **negate** and returns the numbers 1 through 10, negating the even ones:

```
> // More complex list comprehensions
let x =
    [ let negate x = -x
      for i in 1 .. 10 do
          if i % 2 = 0 then
              yield negate i
```

```
                else
                    yield i ];;

        val x : int list = [1; -2; 3; -4; 5; -6; 7; -8; 9; -10]
```

When using for loops within list comprehensions, you can simplify the code by using -> instead of do yield. The following two code snippets are identical:

```
// Generate the first ten multiples of a number
let multiplesOf  x = [ for i in 1 .. 10 do yield x * i ]

// Simplified list comprehension
let multiplesOf2 x = [ for i in 1 .. 10 -> x * i ]
```

Using list comprehension syntax will enable you to quickly and concisely generate lists of data, which can then be processed in your code. Example 2-3 shows how you can use list comprehensions to generate all prime numbers smaller than a given integer.

The example works by looping through all numbers between 1 and the given max value. Then, it uses a list comprehension to generate all the factors of that number. It checks if the generated list of factors has only two elements, then it yields the value because it is prime. There certainly are more efficient ways to compute primes, but this demonstrates just how expressive list comprehensions can be.

Example 2-3. Using list comprehensions to compute primes

```
> // List comprehension for prime numbers
let primesUnder max =
    [
        for n in 1 .. max do
            let factorsOfN =
                [
                    for i in 1 .. n do
                        if n % i = 0 then
                            yield i
                ]

            // n is prime if its only factors are 1 and n
            if List.length factorsOfN = 2 then
                yield n
    ];;

val primesUnder : int -> int list

> primesUnder 50;;
val it : int list = [2; 3; 5; 7; 11; 13; 17; 19; 23; 29; 31; 37; 41; 43; 47]
```

List module functions

The F# Library's List module contains many methods to help you process lists. These built-in methods listed in Table 2-10 will be the primary way you will use lists in F#.

Table 2-10. Common List module functions

Function and type	Description
`List.length` `'a list -> int`	Returns the length of a list.
`List.head` `'a list -> 'a`	Returns the first element in a list.
`List.tail` `'a list -> 'a list`	Returns the given list without the first element.
`List.exists` `('a -> bool) -> 'a list -> bool`	Returns whether or not an element in the list satisfies the search function.
`List.rev` `'a list -> 'a list`	Reverses the elements in a list.
`List.tryfind` `('a -> bool) -> 'a list -> 'a option`	Returns `Some(x)` where x is the first element for which the given function returns `true`. Otherwise returns None. (Some and None will be covered shortly.)
`List.zip` `'a list -> 'b list -> ('a * 'b) list`	Given two lists with the same length, returns a joined list of tuples.
`List.filter` `('a -> bool) -> 'a list -> 'a list`	Returns a list with only the elements for which the given function returned `true`.
`List.partition` `('a -> bool) -> 'a list -> ('a list * 'a list)`	Given a predicate function and a list returns two new lists, the first where the function returned `true`, the second where the function returned `false`.

Initially, it may not be clear how to use some of the `List` module functions, but you'll soon be able to identify what a function does by simply looking at its type signature.

The following example demonstrates the `List.partition` function, partitioning a list of numbers from 1 to 15 into two new lists: one comprised of multiples of five and the other list made up of everything else. The tricky part to note is that `List.partition` returns a tuple, and in the example values `multOf5` and `nonMultOf5` are elements of that tuple being bound at the same time:

```
> // Using List.partition
let isMultipleOf5 x = (x % 5 = 0)

let multOf5, nonMultOf5 =
    List.partition isMultipleOf5 [1 .. 15];;

val isMultipleOf5 : int -> bool
val nonMultOf5 : int list = [1; 2; 3; 4; 6; 7; 8; 9; 11; 12; 13; 14]
val multOf5 : int list = [5; 10; 15]
```

What is `List` anyway? All of these functions are defined in the `List` module in the `Microsoft.FSharp.Collections` namespace. Because the `Microsoft.FSharp.Collections` module is imported by default to access any of these methods, you need to qualify the `List` module name and call the function.

Aggregate Operators

Although lists offer a way to chain together pieces of data, there really isn't anything special about them. The true power of lists lies in *aggregate operators*, which are a set of powerful functions that are useful for any collection of values. You'll see this set of methods again in the discussion of sequences (Chapter 3) and arrays (Chapter 4).

List.map

`List.map` is a projection operation that creates a new list based on a provided function. Each element in the new list is the result of evaluating the function. It has type:

```
('a -> 'b) -> 'a list -> 'b list
```

You can visually represent mapping a function *f* to list [x; y; z] as shown in Figure 2-1.

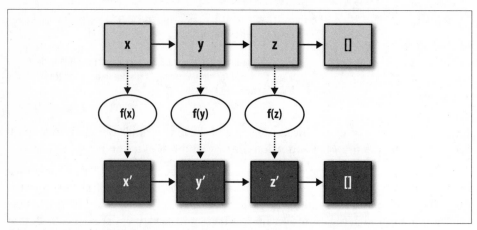

Figure 2-1. Visualizing List.map

Example 2-4 shows the result of mapping a square function to a list of integers.

Example 2-4. Using List.map to square numbers in a list

```
> let squares x = x * x;;

val squares : int -> int

> List.map squares [1 .. 10];;
val it : int list = [1; 4; 9; 16; 25; 36; 49; 64; 81; 100]
```

It may not seem like it right now, but `List.map` is one of the most useful functions in the F# language. It provides an elegant way for you to transform data and when used repeatedly can simplify the structure of the code you write.

List.fold

Folds represent the most powerful type of aggregate operator and not surprisingly the most complicated. When you have a list of values and you want to distill it down to a single piece of data, you use a fold.

There are two main types of folds you can use on lists. Let's start with `List.reduce`, which has type:

```
('a -> 'a -> 'a) -> 'a list -> 'a
```

`List.reduce` iterates through each element of a list, building up an *accumulator value*, which is the summary of the processing done on the list so far. Once every list item has been processed, the final accumulator value is returned. The accumulator's initial value in `List.reduce` is the first element of the list.

Example 2-5 demonstrates how to use `List.reduce` to comma-separate a list of strings. The function `insertCommas` takes the accumulator and a value and simply returns a new string that joins the accumulator and the value separated by a comma. When passed to `List.reduce`, the initial value of the accumulator is the first item in the list, so the net result after processing every item in the list is a single string containing all of the list's values separated by commas.

Example 2-5. Comma-separating a list of strings using List.reduce

```
> let insertCommas (acc : string) item = acc + ", " + item;;

val insertCommas : string -> string -> string

> List.reduce insertCommas ["Jack"; "Jill"; "Jim"; "Joe"; "Jane"];;
val it : string = "Jack, Jill, Jim, Joe, Jane"
```

The following table shows how the accumulator was built up after processing each list element:

Accumulator	List element
"Jack" (the first list element)	"Jill" (the second list element)
"Jack, Jill"	"Jim"
"Jack, Jill, Jim"	"Joe"
"Jack, Jill, Jim, Joe"	"Jane"

While the `reduce` fold is helpful, it forces the type of the accumulator to have the same type as the list. But what if you wanted something more powerful? For example, reducing a list of items in a shopping cart to a cash value.

If you want to use a custom accumulator type, you can use `List.fold`. The `fold` function takes three parameters. First, a function that when provided an accumulator and list element returns a new accumulator. Second, an initial accumulator value. The final parameter is the list to fold over. The return value of the function is the final state of the accumulator. Officially the type is:

```
('acc -> 'b -> 'acc) -> 'acc -> 'b list -> 'acc
```

To provide a simple example, consider folding a list of integers into their sum:

```
> let addAccToListItem acc i = acc + i;;

val addAccToListItem : int -> int -> int

> List.fold addAccToListItem 0 [1; 2; 3];;
val it : int = 6
```

But again, the accumulator for `fold` does not need to be the same as the list's elements. Example 2-6 folds the characters of a **string** into a tuple counting the occurrences of each vowel. (The number of a's, e's, i's, etc.)

When the folding function is applied to each letter in the list, if the letter is a vowel, we return an updated accumulator value, otherwise, we just return the existing accumulator.

Example 2-6. Counting vowels using List.fold

```
> // Count the number of vowels in a string
let countVowels (str : string) =
    let charList = List.ofSeq str

    let accFunc (As, Es, Is, Os, Us) letter =
        if   letter = 'a' then (As + 1, Es, Is, Os, Us)
        elif letter = 'e' then (As, Es + 1, Is, Os, Us)
        elif letter = 'i' then (As, Es, Is + 1, Os, Us)
        elif letter = 'o' then (As, Es, Is, Os + 1, Us)
        elif letter = 'u' then (As, Es, Is, Os, Us + 1)
        else                   (As, Es, Is, Os, Us)

    List.fold accFunc (0, 0, 0, 0, 0) charList;;

val countVowels : string -> int * int * int * int * int

> countVowels "The quick brown fox jumps over the lazy dog";;
val it : int * int * int * int * int = (1, 3, 1, 4, 2)
```

Folding right-to-left

`List.reduce` and `List.fold` process the list in a left-to-right order. There are alternative functions `List.reduceBack` and `List.foldBack` for processing lists in right-to-left order. Depending on what you are trying to do, processing a list in reverse order can have a substantial impact on performance. (For a more in-depth look at the performance implications of list processing, refer to Chapter 7.)

List.iter

The final aggregate operator, `List.iter`, iterates through each element of the list and calls a function that you pass as a parameter. It has type:

```
('a -> unit) -> 'a list -> unit
```

Because `List.iter` returns `unit`, it is predominately used for evaluating the side effect of the given method. The term *side effect* simply means that executing the function has some side effect other than its return value; for example, `printfn` has the side effect of printing to the console in addition to returning `unit`.

Example 2-7 uses `List.iter` to iterate through each number in a list and print it to the console.

Example 2-7. Using List.iter to print numbers in a list

```
> // Using List.iter
let printNumber x = printfn "Printing %d" x
List.iter printNumber [1 .. 5];;

val printNumber : int -> unit

Printing 1
Printing 2
Printing 3
Printing 4
Printing 5
```

Option

If you want to represent a value that may or may not exist, the best way to do so is to use the `option` type. The `option` type has only two possible values: `Some('a)` and `None`.

Consider the problem of parsing a `string` as an `int`. If the string is properly formatted, the function should return the integer value; but what if the string is improperly formatted? This is a prime situation where you would use an `option` type.

Example 2-8 defines a function `isInteger`, which tries to parse an integer using the `Int32.TryParse` function. If the parsing is successful, the function will return `Some(result)`; otherwise, it will return `None`. This enables consumers of the function to know that for some inputs the result may not be defined, hence returning `None`.

Example 2-8. The option type storing if a string parses as an integer

```
> // Using option to return a value (or not)
open System

let isInteger str =
    let successful, result = Int32.TryParse(str)
    if successful
    then Some(result)
    else None;;
```

```
val isInteger : string -> int option

> isInteger "This is not an int";;
val it : int option = None
> isInteger "400";;
val it : int option = Some 400
```

 A common idiom in C# is to use null to mean the absence of a value. However, null is also used to indicate an uninitialized value. This duality can lead to confusion and bugs. If you use the option type, there is no question what the value represents.

option can be thought of as similar to the System.Nullable type.

To retrieve the value of an option, you can use Option.get. (If Option.get is called on None, an exception will be thrown.) The following snippet defines a function containsNegativeNumbers which returns Some(_) for all negative numbers in a list. Then, the list's negative numbers are retrieved using Option.get:

```
> // Using Option.get
Let isLessThanZero x = (x < 0)

let containsNegativeNumbers intList =
    let filteredList = List.filter isLessThanZero intList
    if List.length filteredList > 0
    then Some(filteredList)
    else None;;

val containsNegativeNumbers : int list -> int list option

> let negativeNumbers = containsNegativeNumbers [6; 20; -8; 45; -5];;

val negativeNumbers : int list option = Some [-8; -5]

> Option.get negativeNumbers;;
val it : int list = [-8; -5]
```

The Option module contains other helpful functions listed in Table 2-11.

Table 2-11. Common Option module methods

Function and type	Description
Option.isSome	Returns true if the option is Some, otherwise, false
'a option -> bool	
Option.isNone	Returns false if the option is Some, otherwise, true
'a option -> bool	

Printfn

Writing data to the console is the simplest way to perform I/O and is done using the printf family of functions. printf comes in three main flavors: printf, printfn, and sprintf.

printf takes the input and writes it to the screen, whereas printfn writes it to the screen and adds a line continuation:

```
> // printf and printfn
printf "Hello, "
printfn "World";;

Hello, World
```

> The existing .NET System.Console class can be used for writing text to the screen, but printf is better suited for the functional style because its arguments are strongly typed and therefore contribute to type inference. System.Console should still be used for input, however.

Printing text to the console isn't especially exciting, but printf adds a lot of power in that it has formatting and checking built-in. By providing a *format specifier*, listed in Table 2-12, you can drop in data as well. This greatly simplifies printing data:

```
> // Format specifiers
let mountain = "K2"
let height   = 8611
let units    = 'm';;

val mountain : string = "K2"
val height : int = 8611
val units : char = 'm'

> printfn "%s is %d%c high" mountain height units;;
K2 is 28251m high
val it : unit = ()
```

Best of all, when using F#'s type inference system, the compiler will give you an error if the data doesn't match the given format specifier:

```
> printfn "An integer = %d" 1.23;;

  printfn "An integer = %d" 1.23;;
  --------------------------^^^^

stdin(2,27): error FS0001: The type 'float' is not compatible with any of the
types byte,int16,int32,int64,sbyte,uint16,uint32,uint64,nativeint,unativeint,
arising from the use of a printf-style format string.
stopped due to error
```

In addition, because the F# compiler knows what type to expect given a list of format specifiers, the type inference system can pin down the types of those values. For example, in the following snippet, the types of the function's parameters are inferred based on usage:

```
> // Type inference from printf
let inferParams x y z =
    printfn "x = %f, y = %s, z = %b" x y z;;

val inferParams : float -> string -> bool -> unit
```

Table 2-12. Printf format specifiers

Hole	Description	Example	Result
%d, %i	Print any integer	printf "%d" 5	5
%x, %o	Print any integer in Hex or Octal format	printfn "%x" 255	ff
%s	Print any string	printf "%s" "ABC"	ABC
%f	Print any floating-point number	printf "%f" 1.1M	1.100000
%c	Print any character	printf "%c" '\097'	a
%b	Print any Boolean	printf "%b" false	false
%O	Print any object	printfn "%O" (1,2)	(1, 2)
%A	Print anything	printf "%A" (1, [])	(1, [])

The %O format specifier boxes the object and calls the Object.ToString virtual method. The %A printf format specifier works the same way, except that it checks for any special printing instructions from a [<StructuredFormatDisplay>] attribute before calling Object.ToString.

sprintf is used when you want the result of the printing as a string:

```
> let location = "World";;

val location : string

> sprintf "Hello, %s" location;;
val it : string = "Hello, World"
```

Anatomy of an F# Program

By now, you might want to learn how to take the F# code we have been writing in the FSI window and convert it into actual F# programs. But in reality, every code snippet you have seen so far has been a full program!

Most other languages, like C#, require an explicit program entry point, often called a *main* method. Yet our F# programs so far haven't declared any special markup indicating where the program should begin. In F#, for single-file applications, the contents of the code file are executed from top to bottom in order (without the need for declaring a specific main method).

For multifile projects, however, code needs to be divided into organization units called *modules* or *namespaces*.

Modules

All the code we have written so far has been in a module. By default, F# puts all your code into an *anonymous module* with the same name as the code file with the first letter capitalized. So, if you have a value named value1, and your code is in *file1.fs*, you can refer to it by using the fully qualified path: File1.value1.

Creating modules

You can explicitly name your code's module by using the module keyword at the top of a code file. After that point, every value, function, or type defined will belong to that module:

```
module Alpha

// To refer to this value outside the module
// use: Alpha.x
let x = 1
```

Nested modules

Files can contain nested modules as well. To declare a nested module, use the module keyword followed by the name of your module and an equals sign =. Nested modules must be indented to be disambiguated from the "top-level" module:

```
module Utilities

module ConversionUtils =

    // Utilities.ConversionUtils.intToString
    let intToString (x : int) = x.ToString()

    module ConvertBase =
        // Utilities.ConversionUtils.ConvertBase.convertToHex
        let convertToHex x = sprintf "%x" x

        // Utilities.ConversionUtils.ConvertBase.convertToOct
        let convertToOct x = sprintf "%o" x

module DataTypes =

    // Utilities.DataTypes.Point
    type Point = Point of float * float * float
```

Namespaces

The alternative to modules is namespaces. Namespaces are a unit of organizing code just like modules with the only difference being that namespaces cannot contain values, only type declarations. Also, namespaces cannot be nested in the same way that modules can. Instead, you can simply add multiple namespaces to the same file.

Example 2-9 defines several types inside of two namespaces.

Example 2-9. Namespaces

```
namespace PlayingCards

// PlayingCard.Suit
type Suit =
    | Spade
    | Club
    | Diamond
    | Heart

// PlayingCards.PlayingCard
type PlayingCard =
    | Ace   of Suit
    | King  of Suit
    | Queen of Suit
    | Jack  of Suit
    | ValueCard of int * Suit

namespace PlayingCards.Poker

// PlayingCards.Poker.PokerPlayer
type PokerPlayer = { Name : string; Money : int; Position : int  }
```

It may seem strange to have both namespaces and modules in F#. Modules are optimized for rapid prototyping and quickly exploring a solution, as you have seen so far. Namespaces, on the other hand, are geared toward larger-scale projects with an object-oriented solution.

Program Startup

In F#, the program starts executing at the top of the last code file, which needs to be a module. Consider this simple F# program consisting of a single code file:

```
// Program.fs
let numbers = [1 .. 10]
let square x = x * x

let squaredNumbers = List.map square numbers

printfn "SquaredNumbers = %A" squaredNumbers

open System

printfn "(press any key to continue)"
Console.ReadKey(true)
```

Now open that project in Visual Studio, and then add a new, empty F# code file. When you press F5 to run your program, nothing will happen. This is because the newest file added to the project—which is blank—was added "last" and thus is what ran when the program started up.

 Having code execute seemingly randomly should probably be setting off alarm bells in your head. Modules are not recommended for large-scale projects, but we will go over using modules for real-world applications in Chapter 7.

For more formal program-startup semantics, you can use the [<EntryPoint>] attribute to define a main method. To qualify, your main method must:

- Be the last function defined in the last compiled file in your project. This ensures there is no confusion as to where the F# program starts.
- Take a single parameter of type **string array**, which are the arguments to your program. (Arrays will be covered in Chapter 4.)
- Return an integer, which is your program's exit code.

To make the main method explicit, you could rewrite the previous application as:

```
// Program.fs
open System

[<EntryPoint>]
let main (args : string[]) =
    let numbers = [1 .. 10]
    let square x = x * x

    let squaredNumbers = List.map square numbers

    printfn "SquaredNumbers = %A" squaredNumbers

    printfn "(press any key to continue)"
    Console.ReadKey(True) |> ignore

    // Return 0
    0
```

Now you have all the tools you need to write simple F# programs. In the next chapter, you will learn to program using the functional style, enabling you to write more powerful F# applications and advance on your journey to becoming a level-9 F# ninja master.

CHAPTER 3

Functional Programming

With the basics out of the way, you can begin to examine F# from the approach of a particular style. This chapter is devoted to F#'s main paradigm: functional programming. In a nutshell, functional programming is about being more declarative in your code. In imperative programming (covered in Chapter 4), you spend your time listing out the specific steps to perform a task. In functional programming, you specify *what* is to be done, but not *how*. Even though functional programming is no silver bullet, the result is that programs are much clearer, and some problems like concurrency and parallel programming are solved much more easily.

Functional programming isn't going to replace imperative or object-oriented programming on its own; rather, it just provides a different approach to use so that in certain applications you can be much more productive.

For a language to be considered "functional," it typically needs to support a few key features:

- Immutable data
- Ability to compose functions
- Functions can be treated as data
- Lazy evaluation
- Pattern matching

We will go into each of these raw, functional concepts and what they offer throughout the chapter. By the end you will be able to write purely functional code, and leverage the elegance and simplicity of declarative programming. A deeper look at functional concepts, such as tail recursion and closures, will come in Chapter 7.

Programming with Functions

The heart of functional programming is thinking about code in terms of mathematical functions. Consider two functions f and g:

```
f(x) = x^2 + x
g(x) = x + 1
```

It follows that:

```
f(2) = (2)^2 + (2)
g(2) = (2) + 1
```

And if you compose the two functions, or put them together, you get:

```
f g (2) = f(g(2))
        = (g(2))^2 + (g(2))
        = (2+1)^2 + (2+1)
        = 12
```

You don't have to be a mathematician to program in F#, but some of the ideas of mathematics translate to functional programming. For example, in the previous snippets there was no explicit return type specified. Does f(x) take an integer or a float? This mathematical notation isn't concerned with data types or return values. The equivalent F# code is:

```
let f x = x ** 2.0 + x
let g x = x + 1.0
```

The fact the F# code resembles the mathematical notation isn't a coincidence. Functional programming in essence is thinking about computations in an abstract way— again, what is to be computed but not how it gets computed.

You can even think of entire programs as functions with their inputs being mouse and keyboard strokes and the output being the process exit code. When you begin to view programming in this way, some of the complexity associated with normal programming models goes away.

First, if you think about your program as a series of functions, then you don't need to spend all your time in the details explaining step by step how to complete a task. Functions simply take their input and produce an output. Second, algorithms are expressed in terms of functions and not classes or objects, so it is easier to translate those concepts into functional programming.

You will see examples of how functional programming can simplify complex code throughout the chapter, but first you need to start thinking in terms of functions. To do so, you need to abandon some of the mindset built up from existing imperative languages. In the next sections, I will introduce the notion of immutability, functions as values, and function composition to demonstrate how to use functional programming.

Immutability

You may have noticed that I have suspiciously not used the word *variable* before, and instead referred to everything as a *value*. The reason for this is that in functional programming, the names of things you declare are *immutable* by default, meaning they cannot be changed.

If a function somehow changes the state of the program—such as writing to a file or mutating a global variable in memory—that is known as a *side effect*. For example, calling the `printfn` function returns `unit` but has the side effect of printing text to the screen. Similarly, if a function updates the value of something in memory, that too is a side effect—something extra the function does in addition to returning a value.

Side effects aren't all that bad, but unintended side effects are the root of many bugs. Even the most well-intentioned programmers can make mistakes if they aren't aware of the side effects of a function. Immutable values help you write safer code because you can't screw up what you can't change.

If you are used to an imperative programming language, then not being able to have variables may seem like a burden. But immutability offers some significant benefits. Consider Example 3-1; both functions simply sum the squares of a list of numbers, with one using the imperative style of mutating data and the other the functional style. The imperative style makes use of a *mutable* variable, meaning that the value of `total` changes during the execution of `imperativeSum`.

Example 3-1. Summing a list of squares using imperative and functional styles

```
let square x = x * x

let imperativeSum numbers =
    let mutable total = 0
    for i in numbers do
        let x = square i
        total <- total + x
    total

let functionalSum numbers =
    numbers
    |> Seq.map square
    |> Seq.sum
```

Both snippets of code return the same value for the same input, so what is the benefit of the functional style? The first thing you might notice is readability. With the imperative style, you have to read through the code to understand what is going on. The functional style, however, is more declarative; the code maps directly to what you want to have happen. (That is, squaring each element in the list, and then summing them.) Also, if you wanted to run the imperative version in parallel, you would have to rewrite the code entirely. Because you were so detailed in how you specified the program to be run, if you want it in parallel, you have to detail the steps for doing it in parallel. The functional version, however, wasn't prescriptive on how to do things, so you can easily swap out a parallel implementation for map and sum. You will see just how easy F# makes parallel programming in Chapter 11.

 Functional programming languages are referred to as *pure* if they do not allow side effects. F#, in this regard, is considered impure as it will allow you to change the values of variables when programming in the imperative style.

Function Values

In most other programming languages, functions and data are regarded as two very different things. However, in a functional programming language, functions are treated just like any other piece of data. For example, functions can be passed as parameters to other functions. In addition, functions can create and return new functions! Functions that take or return other functions as their inputs or outputs are known as *higher-order functions*, and are key for idiomatic functional programming.

This capability enables you to abstract and reuse algorithms in your code. You saw an example of this in the previous chapter with List.iter, List.map, and List.fold.

Example 3-2 defines a function, negate, which negates a single integer. When that function is passed as a parameter to List.map, the function is then applied to a whole list, negating every list element.

Example 3-2. Example of higher-order functions

```
> let negate x = -x;;

val negate : int -> int

> List.map negate [1 .. 10];;
val it : int list = [-1; -2; -3; -4; -5; -6; -7; -8; -9; -10]
```

Using function values is very convenient, but the result is that you end up writing many simple functions that don't have a lot of value on their own. For example, our negate function in Example 3-2 will probably never be used anywhere else in the program except when negating a list.

Rather than naming all the little functions you pass as parameters, you can use an *anonymous function*, also known as a *lambda expression*, to create a function inline.

To create a lambda expression, simply use the fun keyword followed by the function's parameters and an arrow, ->.

The following snippet creates a lambda expression and passes the value 5 as a parameter. When the function is executed, the parameter x is incremented by 3 and the result is 8:

```
> (fun x -> x + 3) 5;;
val it : int = 8
```

We can rewrite our negate list example using a lambda that takes a single parameter i:

```
> List.map (fun i -> -i) [1 .. 10];;
val it : int list = [-1; -2; -3; -4; -5; -6; -7; -8; -9; -10]
```

 Be careful to keep lambdas simple. As they grow larger, they become more difficult to debug. This is especially true if you find yourself copying and pasting lambdas around in your code.

Partial function application

Another aspect of functional programming is partial function application, also known as *currying*. Let's start by writing a simple function that appends text to a file using the existing .NET libraries:

```
> // Append text to a file
open System.IO

let appendFile (fileName : string) (text : string) =
    use file = new StreamWriter(fileName, true)
    file.WriteLine(text)
    file.Close();;

val appendFile : string -> string -> unit

> appendFile @"D:\Log.txt" "Processing Event X...";;
val it : unit = ()
```

The appendFile function seems simple enough, but what if you wanted to repeatedly write to the same log file? You would have to keep around the path to your log file and always pass it in as the first parameter. It would be nice, however, to create a new version of appendFile where the first parameter is fixed to our verbatim string, @"D:\Log.txt".

Partial function application is the ability to specify some parameters of a function, and produce a new function where those parameters are fixed. You can "curry" the first parameter of appendFile and produce a new function that takes only one parameter, the message to be logged:

```
> // Curry appendFile so that the first parameter is fixed
let curriedAppendFile = appendFile @"D:\Log.txt";;

val curriedAppendFile : (string -> unit)

> // Appends text to to 'D:\Log.txt'
curriedAppendFile "Processing Event Y...";;

val it : unit = ()
```

Currying is why function types have arrows between arguments. The `appendFile` function had type:

```
string -> string -> unit
```

so after the first `string` parameter was passed in, the result was a function that took a `string` and returned `unit`, or `string -> unit`.

 While curried functions can make code simpler, they can also make code harder to debug. Be careful not to abuse currying to make your programs any more complex than they need to be.

All you need to do to curry a function is specify a subset of its required parameters, and the result will be a function that only requires the parameters not yet specified. For this reason, you can only curry a function's arguments from left to right.

Currying and partial function application may not look particularly powerful, but they can dramatically improve the elegance of your code. Consider the `printf` function that takes a format string as a parameter followed by the values to fill in that format string. If you just supply the first parameter of `"%d"`, the result is a partially applied function that accepts an integer and prints it to the screen.

The following example shows how you can pass a partially applied version of `printf` to avoid the need for a lambda expression:

```
> // Non curried
List.iter (fun i -> printfn "%d" i) [1 .. 3];;
1
2
3
val it : unit = ()
> // Using printfn curried
List.iter (printfn "%d") [1 .. 3];;
1
2
3
val it : unit = ()
```

You will see how to take full advantage of partial function application when you get to function composition and the pipe-forward operator.

Functions returning functions

With functional programming treating functions like data, it is possible for functions to return other functions as values. This can cause some interesting results when you consider values in scope.

Example 3-3 defines a function `generatePowerOfFunc`, which returns a function that raises a given number to a power. Two functions are created, `powerOfTwo` and `powerOf Three`, which raise two or three to a given power.

Example 3-3. Functions returning functions

```
> // Functions returning functions
let generatePowerOfFunc base = (fun exponent -> base ** exponent);;

val generatePowerOfFunc : float -> float -> float

> let powerOfTwo = generatePowerOfFunc 2.0;;

val powerOfTwo : (float -> float)

> powerOfTwo 8.0;;
val it : float = 256.0
> let powerOfThree = generatePowerOfFunc 3.0;;

val powerOfThree : (float -> float)

> powerOfThree 2.0;;
val it : float = 9.0
```

If you look closer at our generatePowerOfFunc function, notice that its parameter base is used in the two lambdas it returned. But when you call values powerOfTwo and powerOfThree later, where does base come from if it isn't a parameter to the function? When generatePowerOfFunc was initially called with the value 2.0 as a parameter, where was that 2.0 stored?

There is a bit of magic going on here known as a *closure*. Don't concern yourself with this for now, or how it works. Just know that if a value is in scope, it can be used and perhaps returned by a function. In Chapter 7, I will cover closures in depth and show you the sorts of things you can do by abusing this magic performed by the F# compiler.

Recursive Functions

A function that calls itself is known to be *recursive*, and when programming in the functional style, these can be very useful, as you will see shortly.

To define a recursive function, you simply need to add the rec keyword. The following snippet defines a function for calculating the factorial of a number. (That is, the product of all positive integers up to and including the number. For example, the factorial of 4 is 4 * 3 * 2 * 1.)

```
> // Define a recursive function
let rec factorial x =
    if x <= 1 then
        1
    else
        x * factorial (x - 1);;

val factorial : int -> int

> factorial 5;;
val it : int = 120
```

The rec keyword may stand out as an artifact because other languages don't require you to explicitly call out recursive functions. The actual purpose of the rec keyword is to inform the type inference system to allow the function to be used as part of the type inference process. rec allows you to call the function before the type inference system has determined the function's type.

Using recursion combined with higher-order functions, you can easily simulate the sort of looping constructs found in imperative languages without the need for mutating values. The following example creates functional versions of common for and while loops. Notice that in the example of the *for* loop, an updated counter is simply passed as a parameter to the recursive call:

```
> // Functional for loop
let rec forLoop body times =
    if times <= 0 then
        ()
    else
        body()
        forLoop body (times - 1)

// Functional while loop
let rec whileLoop predicate body =
    if predicate() then
        body()
        whileLoop predicate body
    else
        ();;

val forLoop : (unit -> unit) -> int -> unit
val whileLoop : (unit -> bool) -> (unit -> unit) -> unit

> forLoop (fun () -> printfn "Looping...") 3;;
Looping...
Looping...
Looping...
val it : unit = ()
> // A typical work week...
open System

whileLoop
    (fun () -> DateTime.Now.DayOfWeek <> DayOfWeek.Saturday)
    (fun () -> printfn "I wish it were the weekend...");;
I wish it were the weekend...
I wish it were the weekend...
I wish it were the weekend...
    * * * This goes on for several days * * *
val it : unit = ()
```

Mutual recursion

Two functions that call each other are known as *mutually recursive*, and present a unique challenge to the F# type inference system. In order to determine the type of the first function, you need to know the type of the second function and vice versa.

In Example 3-4, the mutually recursive functions fail to compile because when processing the isOdd function, the isEven function has not been declared yet.

Example 3-4. Mutually recursive functions

```
> // Error: Can't define isOdd without isEven, and vice versa
let isOdd  x = if x = 1 then true else not (isEven (x - 1))
let isEven x = if x = 0 then true else not (isOdd (x - 1));;

  let isOdd x = if x = 0 then true else not (isEven (x - 1))
  ---------------------------------------------^^^^^^^

stdin(4,44): error FS0039: The value or constructor 'isEven' is not defined.
stopped due to error
```

In order to define mutually recursive functions, you must join them together with the and keyword, which tells the F# compiler to perform type inference for both functions at the same time:

```
> // Define mutually recursive functions
let rec isOdd  n = (n = 1) || isEven (n - 1)
and     isEven n = (n = 0) || isOdd (n - 1);;

val isOdd : int -> bool
val isEven : int -> bool

> isOdd 13;;
val it : bool = true
```

Symbolic Operators

Think how difficult programming would be if you couldn't write 1 + 2 and instead had to write add 1 2 every time. Fortunately, F# not only has built-in symbolic operators for things like addition and subtraction, but it also allows you to define your own symbolic operators, enabling you to write code in a cleaner, more elegant way.

 Don't think of symbolic functions as a form of operator overloading, but rather as functions whose names are made out of symbols.

A symbolic operator can be made up of any sequence of !%&*+-./<=>?@^|~ symbols (including : provided it is not the first character). The following code defines a new function ! that computes the factorial of a number:

```
> // Factorial
let rec (!) x =
    if x <= 1 then 1
    else x * !(x - 1);;

val ( ! ) : int -> int

> !5;;
val it : int = 120
```

By default, symbolic functions use *infix* notation when they have more than one parameter. This means that the first parameter comes before the symbol, which is how you most commonly apply symbolic functions. The following example defines a function ===, which compares a string with a regular expression:

```
> // Define (===) to compare strings based on regular expressions
open System.Text.RegularExpressions;;

let (===) str (regex : string) =
    Regex.Match(str, regex).Success;;

val ( === ) : string -> string -> bool

> "The quick brown fox" === "The (.*) fox";;
val it : bool = true
```

To have symbolic operators that come before their parameters, also known as *prefix notation*, you must prefix the function with a tilde ~, exclamation point !, or question mark ?. In the following code, the function ~+++ is prefixed with a tilde, and thus to call it, you write ~+++ 1 2 3 rather than 1 ~+++ 2 3. This enables you to use symbolic operators that more naturally fit the style of the function being defined:

```
> let (~+++) x y z = x + y + z;;

val ( ~+++ ) : int -> int -> int -> int

> ~+++ 1 2 3;;
val it : int = 6
```

In addition to allowing you to name functions that map more closely to mathematics, symbolic operators can also be passed around to higher-order functions if you simply put parentheses around the symbol. For example, if you want to sum or multiply the elements of a list, you can simply write:

```
> // Sum a list using the (+) symbolic function
List.fold (+) 0 [1 .. 10];;
val it : int = 55
> // Multiply all elements using the (*) symbolic function
List.fold (*) 1 [1 .. 10];;
val it : int = 3628800
```

```
> let minus = (-);;

val minus : (int -> int -> int)

> List.fold minus 10 [3; 3; 3];;
val it : int = 1
```

Function Composition

Once you get a strong grasp on functions, you can begin to look at combining them to form larger, more powerful functions. This is known as *function composition* and is another tenet of functional programming.

Before we go over how to combine functions, let's look at the problem it solves. Here is an example of what not to do: put everything into one massive function. Consider this code for getting the size of a given folder on disk (I've added type annotations to help clarify return values):

```
open System
open System.IO

let sizeOfFolder folder =

    // Get all files under the path
    let filesInFolder : string [] =
        Directory.GetFiles(
            folder, "*.*",
            SearchOption.AllDirectories)

    // Map those files to their corresponding FileInfo object
    let fileInfos : FileInfo [] =
        Array.map
            (fun file -> new FileInfo(file))
            filesInFolder

    // Map those fileInfo objects to the file's size
    let fileSizes : int64 [] =
        Array.map
            (fun (info : FileInfo) -> info.Length)
            fileInfos

    // Total the file sizes
    let totalSize = Array.sum fileSizes

    // Return the total size of the files
    totalSize
```

There are three main problems with this code:

- The type inference system cannot determine the correct types automatically, so we must provide a type annotation to the parameters in each lambda expression.

This is because type inference processes code from left to right, top to bottom, so it sees the lambda passed to `Array.map` before it sees the type of the array elements passed. (Therefore, the type of the lambda's parameter is unknown.)

- The result of each computation is just fed as a parameter into the next step of the computation, so the function is littered with unnecessary `let` statements.

- It's kind of ugly. It takes more time to decipher what is going on than it should.

Function composition is about taking code like this and breaking it down into smaller functions, then composing those into a final result.

The previous example kept feeding the computation of one function into the next. Mathematically, if we want the result of `f(x)` passed into `g(x)`, we write: `g(f(x))`. We could have avoided all those `let` bindings by nesting all the intermediate results, but that is extremely unreadable, as you can see here:

```
let uglySizeOfFolder folder =
    Array.sum
        (Array.map
            (fun (info : FileInfo) -> info.Length)
            (Array.map
                (fun file -> new FileInfo(file))
                (Directory.GetFiles(
                    folder, "*.*",
                    SearchOption.AllDirectories))))
```

Pipe-forward operator

Fortunately, F# solves this problem of passing an intermediate result on to the next function concisely with the pipe-forward operator, `|>`. It is defined as:

```
let (|>) x f = f x
```

The pipe-forward operator allows you to rearrange the parameters of a function so that you present the last parameter of the function first. Whereas the last parameter to `List.iter` is the list to iterate through, by using the pipe-forward operator, you can now "pipe" the list into `List.iter` so you specify which list to iterate through first:

```
> [1 .. 3] |> List.iter (printfn "%d");;
1
2
3
val it : unit = ()
```

 Technically speaking, the pipe-forward operator and its sister function, the pipe-backward operator, are not actually composing functions. Rather, they just deal in function application.

The benefit of the pipe-forward operator is that you can continually reapply it to chain functions together. So, the result of one function is then piped into the next. We can then rewrite our `sizeOfFolder` function as the following. Note that `Directory.Get Files` takes its parameters as a tuple and therefore cannot be curried:

```
let sizeOfFolderPiped folder =

    let getFiles folder =
        Directory.GetFiles(folder, "*.*", SearchOption.AllDirectories)

    let totalSize =
        folder
        |> getFiles
        |> Array.map (fun file -> new FileInfo(file))
        |> Array.map (fun info -> info.Length)
        |> Array.sum

    totalSize
```

The simplicity achieved by using the pipe-forward operator is an example of how useful function currying is. The pipe-forward operator takes a value and a function that only takes one parameter; however, the functions that we used, such as `Array.map`, clearly take two (a function to map and the array itself). The reason this works is that we curried one argument, resulting in a function that takes only one parameter and therefore can easily be used with the pipe-forward operator.

 While the pipe-forward operator can greatly simplify code by removing unnecessary declarations for immediate results, this makes debugging piped sequences more difficult because you cannot inspect the value of any intermediate results.

An added benefit of the pipe-forward operator is that it can help the type inference process. You cannot access any properties or methods of a value if the compiler doesn't know what its type is. Therefore, you must use a type annotation to specifically pin down types:

```
> // ERROR: Compiler doesn't know s has a Length property
List.iter
    (fun s -> printfn "s has length %d" s.Length)
    ["Pipe"; "Forward"];;

    (fun s -> printfn "s has length %d" s.Length)
-----------------------------------------^^^^^^^^^

stdin(89,41): error FS0072: Lookup on object of indeterminate type based on
information prior to this program point. A type annotation may be needed prior
to this program point to constrain the type of the object. This may allow the
lookup to be resolved
stopped due to error
```

Because the pipe-forward operator allows the compiler to "see" the last parameter of a function earlier, the type inference system can determine the correct types of a function sooner, eliminating the need for type annotations.

In the following snippet, because the pipe-forward operator is used, the parameter of the lambda passed to `List.iter` is known to be of type **string**, and therefore does not need a type annotation:

```
> ["Pipe"; "Forward"] |> List.iter (fun s -> printfn "s has length %d" s.Length);;
s has length 4
s has length 7
val it : unit = ()
```

Forward composition operator

The forward composition operator, >>, joins two functions together, with the function on the left being called first:

```
let (>>) f g x = g(f x)
```

When using the pipe-forward operator in functions, you need a placeholder variable to "kick off" the pipelining. In our last example, the function took a **folder** parameter that we directly passed into the first piped function:

```
let sizeOfFolderPiped2 folder =

    let getFiles folder =
        Directory.GetFiles(folder, "*.*", SearchOption.AllDirectories)

    folder
    |> getFiles
    |> Array.map (fun file -> new FileInfo(file))
    |> Array.map (fun info -> info.Length)
    |> Array.sum
```

Using the function composition operator, however, no parameter is needed. We simply compose all of those functions together, resulting in a new function that takes a parameter and computes the result:

```
> // Function Composition

open System.IO

let sizeOfFolderComposed (*No Parameters!*) =

    let getFiles folder =
        Directory.GetFiles(folder, "*.*", SearchOption.AllDirectories)

    // The result of this expression is a function that takes
    // one parameter, which will be passed to getFiles and piped
    // through the following functions.
    getFiles
    >> Array.map (fun file -> new FileInfo(file))
    >> Array.map (fun info -> info.Length)
    >> Array.sum;;

val sizeOfFolderComposed : (string -> int64)
```

```
> sizeOfFolderComposed
    (Environment.GetFolderPath(Environment.SpecialFolder.MyPictures));;
val it : int64 = 904680821L
```

A simpler example of composing simple functions would be:

```
> // Basic Function Composition
let square x = x * x
let toString (x : int) = x.ToString()
let strLen (x : string) = x.Length
let lenOfSquare = square >> toString >> strLen;;

val square : int -> int
val toString : int -> string
val strLen : string -> int
val lenOfSquare : (int -> int)

> square 128;;
val it : int = 16384
> lenOfSquare 128;;
val it : int = 5
```

Pipe-backward operator

At first glance, the pipe-backward operator, <|, accepts a function on the left and applies
it to a value on the right. This seems unnecessary because all it does is separate a function and its last parameter, which you can do without the need of some special operator:

```
let (<|) f x = f x
```

Here's an example of the pipe-backward operator in action:

```
> List.iter (printfn "%d") [1 .. 3];;
1
2
3
val it : unit = ()

> List.iter (printfn "%d") <| [1 .. 3];;
1
2
3
val it : unit = ()
```

You might be surprised, but the pipe-backward operator actually does serve an important purpose: it allows you to change precedence. I've avoided mentioning operator
precedence so far, but it is the order in which functions are applied. Function arguments
are evaluated left to right, meaning if you want to call a function and pass the result to
another function, you have two choices, add parentheses around the expression or use
the pipe-backward operator:

```
> printfn "The result of sprintf is %s" (sprintf "(%d, %d)" 1 2);;
The result of sprintf is (1, 2)
```

```
val it : unit = ()

> printfn "The result of sprintf is %s" <| sprintf "(%d, %d)" 1 2;;
The result of sprintf is (1, 2)
val it : unit = ()
```

The pipe-backward operator isn't as common as the pipe-forward or function composition operators, but it serves a solid role in cleaning up F# code.

Backward composition operator

Just like the pipe-backward operator, the composable equivalent is the backward composition operator, <<. The backward composition operator takes two functions and applies the right function first and then the left. It is useful when you want to express ideas in reverse order. It is defined as:

```
let (<<) f g x = f(g x)
```

The following code shows how to take the square of the negation of a number. Using the backward composition operator allows the program text to read exactly in the way the function operates, in other words, have the program code read more like it actually operates:

```
> // Backward Composition
let square x = x * x
let negate x = -x;;

val square : int -> int
val negate : int -> int

> // Using (>>) negates the square
(square >> negate) 10;;
val it : int = -100
> (* But what we really want is the square of the negation
so we need to use (<<) *)
(square << negate) 10;;
val it : int = 100
```

Another example of the backward composition operator would be using it to filter out empty lists in a list of lists. Again, the backward composition operator is used to change the way the code reads to the programmer:

```
> // Filtering lists
[ [1]; []; [4;5;6]; [3;4]; []; []; []; [9] ]
|> List.filter(not << List.isEmpty);;

val it : int list list = <1]; [4; 5; 6]; [3; 4]; [9>
```

Pattern Matching

All programs need to sift and sort through data; to do this in functional programming, you use pattern matching. Pattern matching is similar to a *switch* statement from C#

---

or C++, but it is much more powerful. A pattern match is a series of rules that will execute if the pattern matches the input. The pattern-match expression then returns the result of the rule that was matched; therefore, all rules in a pattern match must return the same type.

To do pattern matching, you use the `match` and `with` keywords with a series of pattern rules, each followed by an arrow, `->`. The following snippet shows using a pattern matching against the expression `isOdd x` to mimic the behavior of an `if` expression. The first rule matches the `true` value, and if that rule matches, it will print `"x is odd"` to the console:

```
> // Simple pattern matching
let isOdd x = (x % 2 = 1)

let describeNumber x =
    match isOdd x with
    | true  -> printfn "x is odd"
    | false -> printfn "x is even";;

val isOdd : int -> bool
val describeNumber : int -> unit

> describeNumber 4;;
x is even
val it : unit = ()
```

The simplest sort of pattern matching is against constant values. Example 3-5 constructs a truth table for the Boolean function `And` by matching both values of a tuple simultaneously.

Example 3-5. Constructing a truth table using pattern matching

```
> // Truth table for AND via pattern matching
let testAnd x y =
    match x, y with
    | true,  true  -> true
    | true,  false -> false
    | false, true  -> false
    | false, false -> false;;

val testAnd : bool -> bool -> bool

> testAnd true true;;
val it : bool = true
```

Note that type inference works on pattern matches. In Example 3-5, because the first rule matches x with the Boolean value `true` and y with another Boolean value, both x and y are inferred to be Boolean values.

The underscore, _, is a wildcard that matches anything. So you can simplify the previous example by using a wildcard to capture any input but `true true`:

```
let testAnd x y =
    match x, y with
    | true,  true -> true
    | _, _         -> false
```

Pattern-matching rules are checked in the order they are declared. So if you had wild-card matches first, subsequent rules would never be checked.

Match Failure

You might have been wondering, what would happen if we left out one of the possible truth table matches in the original version of testAnd? For example:

```
let testAnd x y =
    match x, y with
    | true,  true -> true
    | true,  false -> false
    // | false, true -> false - Oops! false, true case omitted!
    | false, false -> false
```

If no match is found during a pattern matching, an exception of type Microsoft.FSharp.Core.MatchFailureException is raised. You can avoid this by making sure that all possible cases are covered. Fortunately, the F# compiler will issue a warning when it can determine that pattern-match rules are incomplete:

```
> // Incomplete pattern matching. OOPS! Not every letter matched.
let letterIndex l =
    match l with
    | 'a' -> 1
    | 'b' -> 2;;

    match l with
    ----------^

stdin(48,11): warning FS0025: Incomplete pattern matches on this expression.
For example, the value '' '' may indicate a case not covered by the pattern(s).

val letterIndex : char -> int

> letterIndex 'k';;
Microsoft.FSharp.Core.MatchFailureException: The match cases were incomplete
   at FSI_0040.letterIndex(Char l)
   at <StartupCode$FSI_0041>.$FSI_0041.main@()
stopped due to error
```

Named Patterns

So far we have just matched constant values, but you can also use named patterns to actually extract data and bind it to a new value. Consider the following example. It matches against a specific string, but for anything else it captures a new value, x:

```
> // Named patterns
let greet name =
    match name with
    | "Robert"  -> printfn "Hello, Bob"
    | "William" -> printfn "Hello, Bill"
    | x -> printfn "Hello, %s" x;;

val greet : string -> unit

> greet "Earl";;
Hello, Earl
val it : unit = ()
```

The last match rule doesn't match a constant value; instead, it binds the value being matched to a new value you can then use in the match rule's body. Value captures, like wildcards, match anything, so make sure to put more specific rules first.

Matching Literals

Naming patterns is great, but it also prevents you from using an existing value as part of a pattern match. In the previous example, hardcoding the names as part of the pattern match would make the code more difficult to maintain and potentially lead to bugs.

If you want to match against a well-known value, but don't want to copy and paste the literal value into every match rule, you could make the mistake of using a named pattern. This, however, does not work as you intend and just outscopes the existing value.

In the following example, the first pattern-match rule doesn't compare the value name against the value bill, rather it just introduces a new value named bill. This is why the second pattern-match rule yields a warning, because the previous rule already catches all pattern-match input:

```
> // ERROR: Unintentional value captures
let bill = "Bill Gates"
let greet name =
    match name with
    | bill -> "Hello Bill!"
    | x    -> sprintf "Hello, %s" x;;

      | x     -> sprintf "Hello, %s" x;;
  ------^^

stdin(56,7): warning FS0026: This rule will never be matched.

val bill : string = "Bill Gates"
val greet : string -> string
```

In order to match against an existing value, you must add the [<Literal>] attribute, which allows any literal value (a constant) to be used inside of a pattern match. Note that values marked with [<Literal>] must begin with a capital letter.

Attributes are a way to annotate .NET code. For more information about attributes and .NET metadata, refer to Chapter 12.

```
> // Define a literal value
[<Literal>]
let Bill = "Bill Gates";;

val Bill : string = "Bill Gates"

> // Match against literal values
let greet name =
    match name with
    | Bill -> "Hello Bill!"
    | x    -> sprintf "Hello, %s" x;;

val greet : string -> string

> greet "Bill G.";;
val it : string = "Hello, Bill G."
> greet "Bill Gates";;
val it : string = "Hello Bill!"
```

Only integers, characters, Booleans, strings, and floating-point numbers can be marked as literals. If you want to match against more complex types, like a dictionary or map, you must use a when guard.

when Guards

While pattern matching is a powerful concept, sometimes you need custom logic to determine whether a rule should match. This is what when guards are for. If a pattern is matched, the optional when guard will execute and the rule will fire if and only if the when expression evaluates to true.

The following example implements a simple game where you guess a random number. when guards are used to check if the guess is higher, lower, or equal to the secret number:

```
> // High / Low game
open System

let highLowGame () =

    let rng = new Random()
    let secretNumber = rng.Next() % 100

    let rec highLowGameStep () =

        printfn "Guess the secret number:"
        let guessStr = Console.ReadLine()
        let guess = Int32.Parse(guessStr)
```

```
    match guess with
    | _ when guess > secretNumber
        -> printfn "The secret number is lower."
           highLowGameStep()

    | _ when guess = secretNumber
        -> printfn "You've guessed correctly!"
           ()

    | _ when guess < secretNumber
        -> printfn "The secret number is higher."
           highLowGameStep()

    // Begin the game
    highLowGameStep();;

val highLowGame : unit -> unit

> highLowGame();;
Guess the secret number: 50
The secret number is lower.
Guess the secret number: 25
The secret number is higher.
Guess the secret number: 37
You've guessed correctly!
val it : unit = ()
```

Grouping Patterns

As your pattern matches contain more and more rules, you might want to combine patterns. There are two ways to combine patterns. The first is to use Or, represented by a vertical pipe |, which combines patterns together so the rule will fire if any of the grouped patterns match. The second is to use And, represented by an ampersand &, which combines patterns together so that the rule will fire only if all of the grouped patterns match:

```
let vowelTest c =
    match c with
    | 'a' | 'e' | 'i' | 'o' | 'u'
        -> true
    | _ -> false

let describeNumbers x y =
    match x, y with
    | 1, _
    | _, 1
        -> "One of the numbers is one."
    | (2, _) & (_, 2)
        -> "Both of the numbers are two"
    | _ -> "Other."
```

The And pattern has little use in normal pattern matching; however, it is invaluable when using active patterns (Chapter 7).

Matching the Structure of Data

Pattern matching can also match against the structure of data.

Tuples

You have already seen how to match against tuples. If the tuple's elements are separated by commas in the pattern match, each element will be matched individually. However, if a tuple input is used in a named pattern, the bound value will have a tuple type.

In the following example, the first rule binds value `tuple`, which captures both values x and y. Other rules match against tuple elements individually:

```
let testXor x y =
    match x, y with
    | tuple when fst tuple = snd tuple
        -> true
    | true,  true  -> false
    | false, false -> false
```

Lists

Example 3-6 demonstrates how you can pattern match against the structure of lists. The function `listLength` matches against lists of fixed size, otherwise it recursively calls itself with the tail of the list.

Example 3-6. Determining the length of a list

```
let rec listLength l =
    match l with
    | []          -> 0
    | [_]         -> 1
    | [_; _]      -> 2
    | [_; _; _]   -> 3
    | hd :: tail -> 1 + listLength tail
```

The first four pattern-match rules match against lists of specific lengths, using wildcards to indicate that list elements are not important. The last line of the pattern match, however, uses the cons operator `::` to match the first element of the list, hd, to the rest of the list; tail. tail could be any list, from an empty list `[]` on up to a list with a million elements. (Though owing to the previous rules in the function, we can infer that `tail` is at least three elements long.)

Options

Pattern matching also provides a more functional way to use `option` types:

```
let describeOption o =
    match o with
    | Some(42) -> "The answer was 42, but what was the question?"
    | Some(x)  -> sprintf "The answer was %d" x
    | None     -> "No answer found."
```

Outside of Match Expressions

Pattern matching is an extremely powerful concept, but its best aspect is that it doesn't have to be used exclusively in a 'match with' expression. Pattern matching occurs throughout the F# language.

let bindings

let bindings are actually pattern-match rules. So if you write:

```
let x = f()
...
```

you can think of it as if you had written:

```
match f() with
| x -> ...
```

This is how we use let bindings to extract values from tuples:

```
// This...
let x, y = (100, 200)

// ... is the same as this...
match (100, 200) with
| x, y -> ...
```

Anonymous functions

Parameters to anonymous functions are pattern matches in disguise, too!

```
// Given a tuple of option values, return their sum
let addOptionValues = fun (Some(x), Some(y)) -> x + y
```

Wildcard patterns

Imagine you wanted to write a function but didn't care about one of the parameters, or perhaps wanted to ignore values from a tuple. In that case, you could use a wildcard pattern:

```
> List.iter (fun _ -> printfn "Step...") [1 .. 3];;
Step...
Step...
Step...
val it : unit = ()

> let _, second, _ = (1, 2, 3);;

val second : int = 2
```

Alternate Lambda Syntax

The final use for pattern matching is a simplified lambda syntax. When writing F# code, you will find that it's common to pass the parameter directly into a pattern-match expression, such as:

```
let rec listLength theList =
    match theList with
    | []         -> 0
    | [_]        -> 1
    | [_; _]     -> 2
    | [_; _; _]  -> 3
    | hd :: tail -> 1 + listLength tail
```

A simpler way to write this would be to use the function keyword, which acts much like the fun keyword for creating lambdas, except that function lambdas accept only one parameter that must be placed within a pattern match. The following example rewrites the listLength function using the function keyword:

```
> // The 'function' keyword
let rec funListLength =
    function
    | []         -> 0
    | [_]        -> 1
    | [_; _]     -> 2
    | [_; _; _]  -> 3
    | hd :: tail -> 1 + funListLength tail;;

val funListLength : 'a list -> int

> funListLength [1 .. 5];;
val it : int = 5
```

Discriminated Unions

A foundational type in functional programming is the *discriminated union*, which is a type that can only be one of a set of possible values. Each possible value of a discriminated union is referred to as a *union case*. With the invariant that discriminated unions can only be one of a set of values, the compiler can do additional checks to make sure your code is correct, in particular, making sure that pattern matches against discriminated union types are exhaustive.

To define a discriminated union, use the type keyword, followed by the type's name, and then each union case separated by a pipe, |. In a standard deck of cards, a card's suit can be represented with the following discriminated union:

```
> // Discriminated union for a card's suit
type Suit =
    | Heart
    | Diamond
    | Spade
    | Club;;
```

```
type Suit =
  | Heart
  | Diamond
  | Spade
  | Club

> let suits = [ Heart; Diamond; Spade; Club ];;

val suits : Suit list = [Heart; Diamond; Spade; Club]
```

You can also optionally associate data with each union case. To continue the playing-card example, each card can be associated with a suit, and value cards with an integer and suit pair. (The `int * Suit` syntax may look familiar—it is the type signature of a tuple.)

```
// Discriminated union for playing cards
type PlayingCard =
    | Ace    of Suit
    | King   of Suit
    | Queen of Suit
    | Jack   of Suit
    | ValueCard of int * Suit

// Use a list comprehension to generate a deck of cards
let deckOfCards =
    [
        for suit in [ Spade; Club; Heart; Diamond ] do
            yield Ace(suit)
            yield King(suit)
            yield Queen(suit)
            yield Jack(suit)
            for value in 2 .. 10 do
                yield ValueCard(value, suit)
    ]
```

It is also possible to declare discriminated unions on the same line, with the first pipe | optional.

```
type Number = Odd | Even
```

Discriminated unions can also be recursive. If you need to define a set of mutually recursive discriminated unions, then just like functions, they need to be linked together with the and keyword.

The following defines a simple format for describing a programming language:

```
// Program statements
type Statement =
    | Print    of string
    | Sequence of Statement * Statement
    | IfStmt   of Expression * Statement * Statement
```

```
// Program expressions
and Expression =
    | Integer     of int
    | LessThan    of Expression * Expression
    | GreaterThan of Expression * Expression

(*
    if (3 > 1)
        print "3 is greater than 1"
    else
        print "3 is not"
        print "greater than 1"
*)
let program =
    IfStmt(
        GreaterThan(
            Integer(3),
            Integer(1)),
        Print("3 is greater than 1"),
        Sequence(
            Print("3 is not"),
            Print("greater than 1")
        )
    )
```

Using Discriminated Unions for Tree Structures

Discriminated unions are ideal for representing tree structures. Example 3-7 defines a
binary tree and a function for traversing it in only 11 lines of code. This expressiveness
of discriminated unions makes them ideal in any situation where you are working with
a tree-like data structure.

Example 3-7. Binary tree using discriminated unions

```
type BinaryTree =
    | Node of int * BinaryTree * BinaryTree
    | Empty

let rec printInOrder tree =
    match tree with
    | Node (data, left, right)
        -> printInOrder left
           printfn "Node %d" data
           printInOrder right
    | Empty
        -> ()

(*
        2
       / \
      1   4
         / \
        3   5
*)
```

```
let binTree =
    Node(2,
        Node(1, Empty, Empty),
        Node(4,
            Node(3, Empty, Empty),
            Node(5, Empty, Empty)
        )
    )
```

When evaluated within an FSI session, the previous example prints the following:

```
> printInOrder binTree;;
Node 1
Node 2
Node 3
Node 4
Node 5
val it : unit = ()
```

Pattern Matching

You can pattern match against discriminated unions by using just the case labels as patterns. If the union label has data associated with it, you can pattern match against a constant, use a wildcard, or capture the value just like a normal pattern match.

The following example demonstrates the power of pattern matching and discriminated unions by describing two hole cards in a game of poker:

```
// Describe a pair of cards in a game of poker
let describeHoleCards cards =
    match cards with
    | []
    | [_]
        -> failwith "Too few cards."
    | cards when List.length cards > 2
        -> failwith "Too many cards."

    | [ Ace(_);  Ace(_)  ] -> "Pocket Rockets"
    | [ King(_); King(_) ] -> "Cowboys"

    | [ ValueCard(2, _); ValueCard(2, _)]
        -> "Ducks"

    | [ Queen(_); Queen(_) ]
    | [ Jack(_);  Jack(_)  ]
        -> "Pair of face cards"

    | [ ValueCard(x, _); ValueCard(y, _) ] when x = y
        -> "A Pair"

    | [ first; second ]
        -> sprintf "Two cards: %A and %A" first second
```

You can also have recursive discriminated unions in pattern matches. Notice in the following example, the third rule uses a nested pattern to match only `Manager` values that have exactly two `Worker` employees:

```
type Employee =
    | Manager of string * Employee list
    | Worker  of string

let rec printOrganization worker =
    match worker with
    | Worker(name) -> printfn "Employee %s" name

    // Manager with a worker list with one element
    | Manager(managerName, [ Worker(employeeName) ])
        -> printfn "Manager %s with Worker %s" managerName employeeName

    // Manager with a worker list of two elements
    | Manager(managerName, [ Worker(employee1); Worker(employee2) ])
        -> printfn
                "Manager %s with two workers %s and %s"
                managerName employee1 employee2

    // Manager with a list of workers
    | Manager(managerName, workers)
        -> printfn "Manager %s with workers..." managerName
            workers |> List.iter printOrganization
```

The previous example would result in the following FSI session:

```
> let company = Manager("Tom", [ Worker("Pam"); Worker("Stuart") ] );;

val company : Employee = Manager ("Tom",[Worker "Pam"; Worker "Stuart"])

> printOrganization company;;
Manager Tom with two workers Pam and Stuart
val it : unit = ()
```

Because the compiler knows every possible data tag associated with a discriminated union at compile time, any incomplete pattern match will issue a warning. For example, if the `Ace` union case were left out of the pattern match, F# compiler would know:

```
> // OOPS! Forgot about the Ace union case...
let getCardValue card =
    match card with
    | King(_) | Queen(_) | Jack(_) -> 10
    | ValueCard(x, _)              -> x;;

    match card with
    ----------^^^^

stdin(53,11): warning FS0025: Incomplete pattern matches on this expression.
For example, the value 'Ace (_)' may indicate a case not covered by the pattern(s).

val getCardValue : PlayingCard -> int
```

Be careful when using a wildcard to match against a discriminated union. If the union is ever extended later, you will get a warning for each instance where the pattern match is not exhaustive. However, no warning will be issued if you use a wildcard because it will consume all additional cases. Being warned where your code could cause a match failure at runtime goes a long way toward preventing defects.

Methods and Properties

You can add more power to discriminated unions by adding methods and properties, which are functions you can call off an instance of a discriminated union. (For more information on adding methods and properties, refer to Chapter 5.)

```
type PlayingCard =
    | Ace    of Suit
    | King   of Suit
    | Queen of Suit
    | Jack   of Suit
    | ValueCard of int * Suit

    member this.Value =
        match this with
        | Ace(_) -> 11
        | King(_) | Queen (_)| Jack(_)  -> 10
        | ValueCard(x, _) when x <= 10 && x >= 2
                        -> x
        | ValueCard(_) -> failwith "Card has an invalid value!"

let highCard = Ace(Spade)
let highCardValue = highCard.Value
```

Records

Discriminated unions are great for defining a hierarchy of data, but when you are trying to get values out of a discriminated union they have the same problem as tuples, namely, that there is no meaning associated with each value—rather, data is lumped together in some fixed ordering. For example, consider a single-case discriminated union for describing a person. Are its two string fields referring to the first and then last name, or the last and then first name? This can lead to confusion and bugs down the road.

```
type Person =
    | Person of string * string * int

let steve = Person("Steve", "Holt", 17)
let gob = Person("Bluth", "George Oscar", 36)
```

When you want to group your data into a structured format without needing hefty syntax, you can use the F# *record* type. Records give you a way to organize values into a type, as well as name those values through *fields*.

To define a record, you simply define a series of name/type pairs enclosed in curly braces. To create an instance of a record, simply provide a value for each record field and type inference will figure out the rest. See Example 3-8.

Example 3-8. Constructing and using records

```
> // Define a record type
type PersonRec = { First : string; Last : string; Age : int};;

type PersonRec =
  {First: string;
   Last: string;
   Age: int;}

> // Construct a record
let steve = { First = "Steve"; Last = "Holt"; Age = 17 };;

val steve : PersonRec = {First = "Steve";
                         Last = "Holt";
                         Age = 17;}

> // Use '.field' to access record fields
printfn "%s is %d years old" steve.First steve.Age;;
Steve is 17 years old
val it : unit = ()
```

 To the seasoned .NET developer, it may look as if records are just a simplified version of standard .NET classes. You can easily create properties and methods in F#, so why use a record? Records offer several distinct advantages over traditional object-oriented data structures:

- Type inference can infer a record's type. No need for superfluous type annotations.

- Record fields are immutable by default, whereas class types offer no safety guarantee.

- Records cannot be inherited, giving a future guarantee of safety.

- Records can be used as part of standard pattern matching; classes cannot without resorting to active patterns or when guards.

- Records (and discriminated unions) get structural comparison and equality semantics for free. Equality and comparison in .NET will be covered in Chapter 6.

Cloning Records

Records can easily be cloned using the with keyword:

```
type Car =
    {
        Make  : string
        Model : string
        Year  : int
```

```
        }
    let thisYear's = { Make = "FSharp"; Model = "Luxury Sedan"; Year = 2010 }
    let nextYear's = { thisYear's with Year = 2011 }
```

This is equivalent to writing:

```
    let nextYear's =
        {
            Make  = thisYear's.Make
            Model = thisYear's.Model
            Year  = 2011
        }
```

Pattern Matching

You can pattern match on records, providing value capture and literal matching. Note that not every record field needs to be a part of the pattern match.

In the following example, a list of Car is filtered to just those where the Model field is equal to "Coup":

```
    let allCoups =
        allNewCars
        |> List.filter
            (function
                | { Model = "Coup" } -> true
                | _                  -> false)
```

Type Inference

One distinct advantage of records is how they work with F#'s type inference system. Whereas .NET class types must be annotated in order to be used, record types can be inferred by the fields you access.

In Example 3-9, no type annotation is provided for values pt1 and pt2. Because fields X and Y were accessed and the compiler knows of a record type with an X and Y field, the type of pt1 and pt2 was inferred to be of type Point.

Example 3-9. Type inference for records

```
> type Point = { X : float; Y : float };;

type Point =
  {X: float;
   Y: float;}

> // Distance between two points
let distance pt1 pt2 =
    let square x = x * x
    sqrt <| square (pt1.X - pt2.X) + square (pt1.Y - pt2.Y);;

val distance : Point -> Point -> float
```

```
> distance {X = 0.0; Y = 0.0} {X = 10.0; Y = 10.0};;
val it : float = 14.14213562
```

When using two records that have identical field names, the type inference system will either issue an error or infer types that were different from what you intended. To combat this, you can either provide type annotations or fully qualify the record fields:

```
type Point   = { X: float; Y: float;}
type Vector3 = { X : float; Y : float; Z : float }

// Provide a type annotation to not infer pt1 and pt2 to be Vector3
// (since Vector3 was defined last with fields X and Y)
let distance (pt1 : Point) (pt2 : Point) =
    let square x = x * x
    sqrt <| square (pt1.X - pt2.X) + square (pt1.Y - pt2.Y)

// Disambiguate a Point from the Vector type by
// fully qualifying record fields.
let origin  = { Point.X = 0.0; Point.Y = 0.0 }
```

This provides all the necessary information for the type inference system to figure out what you mean.

Methods and Properties

Just like discriminated unions, you can add methods and properties to records as well:

```
> // Add a property to a record type Vector =
type Vector =
    { X : float; Y : float; Z : float }
    member this.Length =
        sqrt <| this.X ** 2.0 + this.Y ** 2.0 + this.Z ** 2.0;;

type Vector =
  {X: float;
   Y: float;
   Z: float;}
  with
    member Length : float
  end

> let v = { X = 10.0; Y = 20.0; Z = 30.0 };;

val v : Vector = {X = 10.0;
                  Y = 20.0;
                  Z = 30.0;}

> v.Length;;
val it : float = 37.41657387
```

Lazy Evaluation

The code we have written so far has been evaluated *eagerly*, meaning as soon as we sent it to FSI, it was executed. The same is true if you compiled and ran your F# program. However, there are situations when you only want to evaluate code on demand, for example, when you want to perform computationally expensive operations only if necessary. This is known as *lazy evaluation*.

Using lazy evaluation can lead to a dramatic reduction in memory footprint because you are only creating values in memory as you need them.

F# supports lazy evaluation in two ways—through the `Lazy` type and sequences (the `seq<'a>` type).

Lazy Types

A `Lazy` type is a thunk or placeholder for some computation. Once created, you can pass around the lazy value as though it has been evaluated. But it will only be evaluated once, and only when forced.

Example 3-10 creates two values, x and y, both of which have the side effect of printing to the console. Because they are initialized lazily, they are not evaluated when declared. Only when the value of y is desired is y's evaluation forced, which in turn forces the evaluation of x.

To construct a lazy value, you can use the `lazy` keyword or `Lazy<_>.Create`.

Example 3-10. Using lazy evaluation

```
> // Define two lazy values
let x = Lazy<int>.Create(fun () -> printfn "Evaluating x..."; 10)
let y = lazy (printfn "Evaluating y..."; x.Value + x.Value);;

val x : Lazy<int> = <unevaluated>
val y : Lazy<int> = <unevaluated>

> // Directly requesting y's value will force its evaluation
y.Value;;
Evaluating y...
Evaluating x...
val it : int = 20

> // Accessing y's value again will use a cached value (no side effects)
y.Value;;
val it : int = 20
```

Sequences

The most common use of lazy evaluation is through the sequence or **seq** type in F#, which represents an ordered sequence of items, much like a List. The following snippet defines a sequence of five elements and iterates through them using the **Seq.iter** function. (Just like the List module, there is a whole slew of available functions to use on sequences.)

```
> let seqOfNumbers = seq { 1 .. 5 };;

val seqOfNumbers : seq<int>

> seqOfNumbers |> Seq.iter (printfn "%d");;
1
2
3
4
5
val it : unit = ()
```

 The difference between a seq and a list is that only one element of a sequence exists in memory at any given time. seq is just an alias for the .NET interface System.Collections.Generic.IEnumerable<'a>.

So why have this limitation? Why have two types when you can just use a list? Because having all list contents in memory means you are resource-constrained. You can define an infinite sequence quite easily, but an infinite list would run out of memory. Also, with lists, you must know the value of each element ahead of time, whereas sequences can unfold dynamically (in so-called pull fashion).

Example 3-11 defines a sequence of all possible 32-bit integers represented as strings. It then tries to create an equivalent list, but fails due to memory.

Example 3-11. A sequence of all integers

```
> // Sequence of all integers
let allIntsSeq = seq { for i = 0 to System.Int32.MaxValue -> i };;

val allIntsSeq : seq<int>

> allIntsSeq;;
val it : seq<int> = seq [0; 1; 2; 3; ...]
> // List of all integers - ERROR: Can't fit in memory!
let allIntsList = [ for i = 0 to System.Int32.MaxValue -> i ];;
System.OutOfMemoryException: Exception of type 'System.OutOf MemoryException' was thrown.
```

Sequence Expressions

We can use the same list comprehension syntax to define sequences (technically referred to as *sequence expressions*). You begin a sequence by writing **seq** followed by curly braces:

```
> let alphabet = seq { for c in 'A' .. 'Z' -> c };;

val alphabet : seq<char>

> Seq.take 4 alphabet;;
val it : seq<char> = seq ['A'; 'B'; 'C'; 'D']
```

Sequences are evaluated lazily, so every time an element is yielded, the code executing inside the sequence is still running. Let's try the previous example again, but this time adding a side effect every time an element is returned. Instead of returning a letter of the alphabet, it will print that letter to the console as well:

```
> // Sequence with a side effect
let noisyAlphabet =
    seq {
        for c in 'A' .. 'Z' do
            printfn "Yielding %c..." c
            yield c
    };;

val noisyAlphabet : seq<char>

> let fifthLetter = Seq.nth 4 noisyAlphabet;;
Yielding A...
Yielding B...
Yielding C...
Yielding D...
Yielding E...

val fifthLetter : char = 'E'
```

An interesting aspect of sequence expressions is that they can be recursive. By using the **yield!** (pronounced *yield bang*) keyword, you can return a subsequence, the result of which is merged into the main sequence in order.

Example 3-12 shows how to leverage **yield!** within a sequence expression. The function **allFilesUnder** returns a **seq<string>**, which recursively gets all files under a given folder. **Directory.GetFiles** returns an array of strings containing all the files in the **basePath** folder. Because **array** is compatible with **seq**, the **yield!** returns all of those files.

Example 3-12. Sequence for listing all files under a folder

```
let rec allFilesUnder basePath =
    seq {
        // Yield all files in the base folder
        yield! Directory.GetFiles(basePath)
```

```
        // Yield all files in its sub folders
        for subdir in Directory.GetDirectories(basePath) do
            yield! allFilesUnder subdir
}
```

Seq Module Functions

The Seq module contains many helpful functions for using sequence types.

Seq.take

Returns the first *n* items from a sequence:

```
> // Sequence of random numbers
open System
let randomSequence =
    seq {
        let rng = new Random()
        while true do
            yield rng.Next()
    };;

val randomSequence : seq<int>

> randomSequence |> Seq.take 3;;
val it : seq<int> = seq [2101281294; 1297716638; 1114462900]
```

Seq.unfold

Generates a sequence using a given function. It has type ('a -> ('b * 'a) option) -> 'a -> seq<'b>.

The supplied function provides an input value, and its result is an option type with a tuple of the next value in the sequence combined with the input to the next iteration of Seq.unfold. The function returns None to indicate the end of the sequence. Example 3-13 generates all Fibonacci numbers under 100. (The nth Fibonacci number is the sum of the two previous items in the sequence; for example, 1, 1, 2, 3, 5, 8, and so on.) The example also uses the Seq.tolist function, which converts a sequence to a list.

Example 3-13. Using Seq.unfold

```
> // Generate the next element of the Fibonacci sequence give the previous
// two elements. To be used with Seq.unfold.
let nextFibUnder100 (a, b) =
    if a + b > 100 then
        None
    else
        let nextValue = a + b
        Some(nextValue, (nextValue, a));;

val nextFibUnder100 : int * int -> (int * (int * int)) option
```

```
> let fibsUnder100 = Seq.unfold nextFibUnder100 (0, 1);;

val fibsUnder100 : seq<int>

> Seq.tolist fibsUnder100;;
val it : int list = [1; 1; 2; 3; 5; 8; 13; 21; 34; 55; 89]
```

Other useful Seq module functions can be found in Table 3-1.

Table 3-1. Common Seq module functions

Function and type	Description
Seq.length seq<'a> -> int	Returns the length of the sequence.
Seq.exists ('a -> bool) -> seq<'a> -> bool	Returns whether or not an element in the sequence satisfies the search function.
Seq.tryFind ('a -> bool) -> seq<'a> -> 'a option	Returns Some(x) for the first element x, in which the given function returns true. Otherwise, returns None.
Seq.filter ('a -> bool) -> seq<'a> -> seq<'a>	Filters out all sequence elements for which the provided function does not evaluate to true.
Seq.concat (seq< #seq<'a> > -> seq<'a>	Flattens a series of sequences so that all of their elements are returned in a single seq.

Aggregate Operators

The Seq module also contains the same aggregate operators available in the List module.

Seq.iter

Iterates through each item in the sequence:

```
> // Print odd numbers under 10
let oddsUnderN n = seq { for i in 1 .. 2 .. n -> i }
Seq.iter (printfn "%d") (oddsUnderN 10);;
1
3
5
7
9

val oddsUnderN : int -> seq<int>
```

Seq.map

Produces a new sequence by mapping a function onto an existing sequence:

```
> // Sequence of words (Arrays are compatible with sequences)
let words = "The quick brown fox jumped over the lazy dog".Split( [| ' ' |]);;

val words : string [] =
  [|"The"; "quick"; "brown"; "fox"; "jumped"; "over"; "the"; "lazy"; "dog"|]

> // Map strings to string, length tuples
words |> Seq.map (fun word -> word, word.Length);;
val it : seq<string * int> =
  seq [("The", 3); ("quick", 5); ("brown", 5); ("fox", 3); ...]
```

Seq.fold

Reduces the sequence to a single value. Because there is only one way to iterate through sequences, there is no equivalent to `List.foldBack`:

```
> Seq.fold (+) 0 <| seq { 1 .. 100 };;
val it : int = 5050
```

You now know the main aspects for writing functional code. Although, it is perfectly OK if the advantages of function composition and lazy evaluation aren't immediately obvious. The majority of the examples in this book are written in the functional style and over time, you will begin to see how they approach problem solving from a different perspective.

CHAPTER 4

Imperative Programming

Until now most programs we have written have been *pure*, meaning that they never changed state. Whenever a function does something other than just return a value, it is known as a *side effect*. While pure functions have some interesting features like composability, the fact of the matter is that programs aren't interesting unless they do something: save data to disk, print values to the screen, issue network traffic, and so on. These side effects are where things actually get done.

This chapter will cover how to change program state and alter control flow, which is known as *imperative programming*. This style of programming is considered to be more error-prone than functional programming because it opens up the opportunity for getting things wrong. The more detailed the instructions you give the computer to branch, or write certain values into certain memory locations, the more likely the programmer will make a mistake. When you programmed in the functional style, all of your data was immutable, so you couldn't assign a wrong value by accident. However, if used judiciously, imperative programming can be a great boon for F# development.

Some potential benefits for imperative programming are:

- Improved performance
- Ease of maintenance through code clarity
- Interoperability with existing code

Imperative programming is a style in which the program performs tasks by altering data in memory. This typically leads to patterns where programs are written as a series of statements or commands. Example 4-1 shows a hypothetical program for using a killer robot to take over the earth. The functions don't return values, but do impact some part of the system, such as updating an internal data structure.

Example 4-1. Taking over the earth with imperative programming

```
let robot = new GiantKillerRobot()

robot.Initialize()

robot.EyeLaserIntensity <- Intensity.Kill
robot.Target <- [| Animals; Humans; Superheroes |]

// Sequence for taking over the Earth
let earth = Planets.Earth
while robot.Active && earth.ContainsLife do
    if robot.CurrentTarget.IsAlive then
        robot.FireEyeLaserAt(robot.CurrentTarget)
    else
        robot.AquireNextTarget()
```

Although the code snippet makes taking over the earth look fairly easy, you don't see all the hard work going on behind the scenes. The `Initialize` function may require powering up a nuclear reactor; and if `Initialize` is called twice in a row, the reactor might explode. If `Initialize` were written in a purely functional style, its output would depend only on the function's input. Instead, what happens during the function call to `Initialize` depends on the current state of memory.

While this chapter won't teach you how to program planet-conquering robots, it will detail how to write F# programs that can change the environment they run in. You will learn how to declare *variables*, whose values you can change during the course of your program. You'll learn how to use mutable collection types, which offer an easier-to-use alternative to F#'s `list` type. Finally, you will learn about control flow and exceptions, allowing you to alter the order in which code executes.

Understanding Memory in .NET

Before you can start making changes to memory, you first need to understand how memory works in .NET. Values in .NET applications are stored in one of two locations: on the *stack* or in the *heap*. (Experienced programmers may already be familiar with these concepts.) The stack is a fixed amount of memory for each process where *local variables* are stored. Local variables are temporary values used only for the duration of the function, like a loop counter. The stack is relatively limited in space, while the heap (also called RAM) may contain several gigabytes of data. .NET uses both the stack and the heap to take advantage of the cheap memory allocations on the stack when possible, and store data on the heap when more memory is required.

The area in memory where a value is stored affects how you can use it.

Value Types Versus Reference Types

Values stored on the stack are known as *value types*, and values stored on the heap are known as *reference types*.

Value types have a fixed size of bytes on the stack. `int` and `float` are both examples of value types, because their size is constant. Reference types, on the other hand, only store a *pointer* on the stack, which is the address of some blob of memory on the heap. So while the pointer has a fixed size—typically four or eight bytes—the blob of memory it points to can be much larger. `list` and `string` are both examples of reference types.

This is visualized in Figure 4-1. The integer 5 exists on the stack, and has no counterpart on the heap. A string, however, exists on the stack as a memory address, pointing to some sequence of characters on the heap.

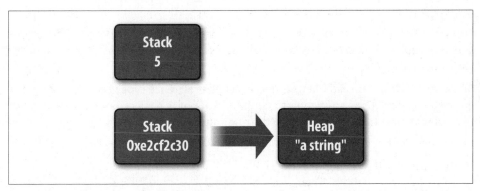

Figure 4-1. Stack types versus reference types

Default Values

So far, each value we have declared in F# has been initialized as soon as it has been created, because in the functional style of programming values cannot be changed once declared. In imperative programming, however, there is no need to fully initialize values because you can update them later. This means there is a notion of a *default value* for both value and reference types, that is, the value something has before it has been initialized.

To get the default value of a type, use the type function `Unchecked.defaultof<'a>`. This will return the default value for the type specified.

A *type function* is a special type of function that takes no arguments other than a generic type parameter. There are several helpful type functions that we will explore in forthcoming chapters:

Unchecked.defaultof<'a>
> Gets the default value for 'a

typeof<'a>
> Returns the System.Type object describing 'a

sizeof<'a>
> Returns the underlying stack size of 'a

For value types, their default value is simply a zero-bit pattern. Because the size of a value type is known once it is created, its size in bytes is allocated on the stack, with each byte being given the value 0b00000000.

The default value for reference types is a little more complicated. Before reference types are initialized they first point to a special address called null. This is used to indicate an uninitialized reference type.

In F#, you can use the null keyword to check if a reference type is equal to null. The following code defines a function to check if its input is null or not, and then calls it with an initialized and an uninitialized string value:

```
> let isNull = function null -> true | _ -> false;;

val isNull : obj -> bool

> isNull "a string";;
val it : bool = false
> isNull (null : string);;
val it : bool = true
```

However, reference types defined in F# do not have null as a proper value, meaning that they cannot be assigned to be null:

```
> type Thing = Plant | Animal | Mineral;;

type Thing =
  | Plant
  | Animal
  | Mineral

> // ERROR: Thing cannot be null
let testThing thing =
    match thing with
    | Plant   -> "Plant"
    | Animal  -> "Animal"
    | Mineral -> "Mineral"
    | null    -> "(null)";;

    | null -> "(null)";;
```

```
_____^^^^^
   stdin(9,7): error FS0043: The type 'Thing' does not have 'null' as a proper value.
```

This seems like a strange restriction, but it eliminates the need for excessive null checking. (If you call a method on an uninitialized reference type, your program will throw a NullReferenceException, so defensively checking all function parameters for null is typical.) If you do need to represent an uninitialized state in F#, consider using the Option type instead of a reference type with value null, where the value None represents an uninitialized state and Some('a) represents an initialized state.

 You can attribute some F# types to accept null as a proper value to ease interoperation with other .NET languages; see Appendix B for more information.

Reference Type Aliasing

It is possible that two reference types point to the same memory address on the heap. This is known as *aliasing*. When this happens, modifying one value will silently modify the other because they both point to the same memory address. This situation can lead to bugs if you aren't careful.

Example 4-2 creates one instance of an array (which we'll cover shortly), but it has two values that point to the same instance. Modifying value x also modifies y and vice versa.

Example 4-2. Aliasing reference types

```
> // Value x points to an array, while y points
// to the same value that x does
let x = [| 0 |]
let y = x;;

val x : int array = [|0|]
val y : int array = [|0|]

> // If you modify the value of x...
x.[0] <- 3;;
val it : unit = ()
> // ... x will change...
x;;
val it : int array = [|3|]
> // ... but so will y...
y;;
val it : int array = [|3|]
```

Changing Values

Now that you understand the basics of where and how data is stored in .NET, you can look at how to change that data. *Mutable values* are those that you can change, and can be declared using the `mutable` keyword. To change the contents of a mutable value, use the left arrow operator, `<-`:

```
> let mutable message = "World";;

val mutable message : string = "World"

> printfn "Hello, %s" message;;
Hello, World
val it : unit = ()

> message <- "Universe";;
val it : unit = ()
> printfn "Hello, %s" message;;
Hello, Universe
val it : unit = ()
```

There are several limitations on mutable values, all stemming from security-related CLR restrictions. This prevents you from writing some code using mutable values. Example 4-3 tries to define an inner-function `incrementX`, which captures a mutable value `x` in its closure (meaning it can access `x`, even though it wasn't passed in as a parameter). This leads to an error from the F# compiler because mutable values can only be used in the same function they are defined in.

Example 4-3. Errors using mutable values in closures

```
> // ERROR: Cannot use mutable values except in the function they are defined
let invalidUseOfMutable() =
    let mutable x = 0

    let incrementX() = x <- x + 1
    incrementX()

    x;;

    let incrementX() = x <- x + 1
    ---------------------^^^^^^^^^^

stdin(16,24): error FS0407: The mutable variable 'x' is used in an invalid way.
Mutable variables may not be captured by closures. Consider eliminating this use
 of mutation or using a heap-allocated mutable reference cell via 'ref' and '!'.
```

The full list of restrictions related to mutable values is as follows:

- Mutable values cannot be returned from functions (a copy is made instead).
- Mutable values cannot be captured in inner-functions (closures).

If you ever run into one of these issues, the simple workaround is to store the mutable data on the heap using a `ref` cell.

Reference Cells

The `ref` type, sometimes referred to as a `ref` *cell*, allows you to store mutable data on the heap, enabling you to bypass limitations with mutable values that are stored on the stack. To retrieve the value of a `ref` cell, use the ! symbolic operator and to set the value use the := operator.

`ref` is not only the name of a type, but also the name of a function that produces `ref` values, which has the signature:

```
val ref: 'a -> 'a ref
```

The `ref` function takes a value and returns a copy of it wrapped in a `ref` cell. Example 4-4 shows passing a list of planets to the `ref` function and then later altering the contents of the returned `ref` cell.

Example 4-4. Using ref cells to mutate data

```
let planets =
    ref [
        "Mercury";  "Venus";    "Earth";
        "Mars";     "Jupiter";  "Saturn";
        "Uranus";   "Neptune";  "Pluto"
    ]

// Oops! Sorry Pluto...

// Filter all planets not equal to "Pluto"
// Get the value of the planets ref cell using (!),
// then assign the new value using (:=)
planets := !planets |> List.filter (fun p -> p <> "Pluto")
```

 C# programmers should take care when using `ref` types and Boolean values. !x is simply the value of x, not the Boolean not function applied to x:

```
> let x = ref true;;

val x : bool ref

> !x;;

val it : bool = true
```

The F# library has two functions, `decr` and `incr`, to simplify incrementing and decrementing `int ref` types:

```
> let x = ref 0;;

val x : int ref = {contents = 0;}

> incr x;;
val it : unit = ()
> x;;
```

```
val it : int ref = {contents = 1;}
> decr x;;
val it : unit = ()
> x;;
val it : int ref = {contents = 0;}
```

Mutable Records

Mutability can be applied to more than just single values; record fields can be marked as mutable as well. This allows you to use records with the imperative style. To make a record field mutable, simply prefix the field name with the `mutable` keyword.

The following example creates a record with a mutable field `Miles`, which can be modified as if it were a mutable variable. Now you can update record fields without being forced to clone the entire record:

```
> // Mutable record types
open System

type MutableCar = { Make : string; Model : string; mutable Miles : int }

let driveForASeason car =
    let rng = new Random()
    car.Miles <- car.Miles + rng.Next() % 10000;;

type MutableCar =
  {Make: string;
   Model: string;
   mutable Miles: int;}
val driveForASeason : MutableCar -> unit

> // Mutate record fields
let kitt = { Make = "Pontiac"; Model = "Trans Am"; Miles = 0 }

driveForASeason kitt
driveForASeason kitt
driveForASeason kitt
driveForASeason kitt;;

val kitt : MutableCar = {Make = "Pontiac";
                         Model = "Trans Am";
                         Miles = 4660;}
```

Arrays

Until now, when you've needed to join multiple pieces of data together, you've used lists. Lists are extremely efficient at adding and removing elements from the beginning of a list, but they aren't ideal for every situation. For example, random access of list elements is very slow. In addition, if you needed to change the last element of a list, you would need to clone the entire list. (The performance characteristics of lists will be covered more in-depth in Chapter 7.)

When you know ahead of time how many items you will need in your collection and would like to be able to update any given item, arrays are the ideal type to use.

Arrays in .NET are a contiguous block of memory containing zero or more elements, each of which can be modified individually (unlike lists, which are immutable).

Arrays can be constructed using *array comprehensions*, which are identical to list comprehensions (discussed in Chapter 2), or manually via a list of values separated by semicolons and enclosed between [| |]:

```
> // Using the array comprehension syntax
let perfectSquares = [| for i in 1 .. 7 -> i * i |];;

val perfectSquares : int array

> perfectSquares;;
val it : int array = [|1; 4; 9; 16; 25; 36; 49|]

> // Manually declared
let perfectSquares2 = [| 1; 4; 9; 16; 25; 36; 49; 64; 81 |];;

val perfectSquares2 : int array
```

Indexing an Array

To retrieve an element from the array, you can use an indexer, .[], which is a zero-based index into the array:

```
> // Indexing an array
printfn
    "The first three perfect squares are %d, %d, and %d"
    perfectSquares.[0]
    perfectSquares.[1]
    perfectSquares.[2];;
The first three perfect squares are 1, 4, and 9
val it : unit = ()
```

Example 4-5 uses array indexers to change individual characters of a character array to implement a primitive form of encryption known as ROT13. ROT13 works by simply taking each letter and rotating it 13 places forward in the alphabet. This is achieved in the example by converting each letter to an integer, adding 13, and then converting it back to a character.

Example 4-5. ROT13 encryption in F#

```
open System

// Encrypt a letter using ROT13
let rot13Encrypt (letter : char) =

    // Move the letter forward 13 places in the alphabet (looping around)
    // Otherwise ignore.
    if Char.IsLetter(letter) then
```

```
        let newLetter =
            (int letter)
            |> (fun letterIdx -> letterIdx - (int 'A'))
            |> (fun letterIdx -> (letterIdx + 13) % 26)
            |> (fun letterIdx -> letterIdx + (int 'A'))
            |> char
        newLetter
    else
        letter

// Loop through each array element, encrypting each letter
let encryptText (text  : char[]) =

    for idx = 0 to text.Length - 1 do
        let letter = text.[idx]
        text.[idx] <- rot13Encrypt letter

let text =
    Array.ofSeq "THE QUICK BROWN FOX JUMPED OVER THE LAZY DOG"

printfn "Origional = %s" <| new String(text)
encryptText(text)
printfn "Encrypted = %s" <| new String(text)

// A unique trait of ROT13 is that to decrypt, simply encrypt again
encryptText(text)
printfn "Decrypted = %s" <| new String(text)
```

The output of our simple program is:

```
Origional = THE QUICK FOX JUMPED OVER THE LAZY DOG
Encrypted = GUR DHVPX SBK WHZCRQ BIRE GUR YNML QBT
Decrypted = THE QUICK FOX JUMPED OVER THE LAZY DOG
```

Unlike C# and VB.NET, indexers in F# require using the dot notation.
You can think of an indexer, then, as just another method or property:

```
// Incorrect
x[0]
// Correct
x.[0]
```

Attempting to access an element in the array with an index either less than zero
or greater than or equal to the number of elements in the array will raise an Index
OutOfRangeException exception. (Exceptions will be covered later in this chapter.) Fortunately, arrays have a Length property, which will return the number of items in the
array. Because array indexes are zero-based, you need to subtract 1 from Length to get
the index of the last element in the array:

```
> let alphabet = [| 'a' .. 'z' |];;

val alphabet : char array
```

```
> // First letter
alphabet.[0];;

val it : char = 'a'
> // Last leter
alphabet.[alphabet.Length - 1];;

val it : char = 'z'
> // Some non-existant letter
alphabet.[10000];;

System.IndexOutOfRangeException: Index was outside the bounds of the array.
   at <StartupCode$FSI_0012>.$FSI_0012._main()
stopped due to error
```

Array Slices

When you're analyzing data stored in arrays, it is sometimes convenient to just work
with a subset of the data. In F#, there is a special syntax for taking a *slice* of an array,
where you specify optional lower and upper bounds for the subset of data. The syntax
for taking a slice is:

   array.[*lowerBound..upperBound*]

If no lower bound is specified, 0 is used. If no upper bound is specified, the length of
the array -1 is used. If neither a lower nor upper bound is specified, you can us an * to
copy the entire array.

Example 4-6 shows the various ways for taking a slice of an array, but we will break it
down line by line shortly.

Example 4-6. Using array slices

```
open System
let daysOfWeek = Enum.GetNames( typeof<DayOfWeek> )

// Standard array slice, elements 2 through 4
daysOfWeek.[2..4]

// Just specify lower bound, elements 4 to the end
daysOfWeek.[4..]

// Just specify an upper bound, elements 0 to 2
daysOfWeek.[..2]

// Specify no bounds, get all elements (copies the array)
daysOfWeek.[*]
```

The first way we sliced an array was specifying both an upper and lower bound; this returned all array elements within that range:

```
> // Standard array slice, elements 2 through 4
daysOfWeek.[2..4];;
val it : string [] = [|"Tuesday"; "Wednesday"; "Thursday"|]
```

Next we specified just a lower or just an upper bound. This returns each element from the lower bound to the end of the array, or from the beginning of the array to the upper bound:

```
> // Just specify lower bound, elements 4 to the end
daysOfWeek.[4..];;
val it : string [] = [|"Thursday"; "Friday"; "Saturday"|]

> // Just specify an upper bound, elements 0 to 2
daysOfWeek.[..2];;
val it : string [] = [|"Sunday"; "Monday"; "Tuesday"|]
```

And finally we just copied the entire array using *. Note that for every slice operation a new array is returned, so there will never be problems with aliasing:

```
> // Specify no bounds, get all elements (copies the array)
daysOfWeek.[*];;
```

Creating Arrays

Array comprehensions and manually specifying each element aren't the only ways to construct arrays. You can also use the `Array.init` function; `Array.init` takes a function used to generate each array element based on its index. To create an uninitialized array, use the `Array.zeroCreate` function. With that function, each element is initialized to its default value: zero or `null`.

Example 4-7 shows how to use `Array.init` and `Array.zeroCreate` to construct arrays.

Example 4-7. Initializing arrays using Array.init

```
> // Initialize an array of sin-wave elements
let divisions = 4.0
let twoPi = 2.0 * Math.PI;;

val divisions : float = 4.0
val twoPi : float = 6.283185307

> Array.init (int divisions) (fun i -> float i * twoPi / divisions);;
val it : float array = [|0.0; 1.570796327; 3.141592654; 4.71238898|]
> // Construct empty arrays
let emptyIntArray    : int array    = Array.zeroCreate 3
let emptyStringArray : string array = Array.zeroCreate 3;;

val emptyIntArray : int array = [|0; 0; 0|]
val emptyStringArray : string array = [|null; null; null|]
```

The CLR limits arrays to take up no more than 2GB of memory, even on 64-bit machines. If you need to allocate an array to store a massive amount of data, use a custom data structure instead.

Pattern Matching

Pattern matching against arrays is just as easy as using lists. And just like pattern matching against lists, when matching against arrays, you can capture element values, as well as match against the structure of the array. Example 4-8 shows matching an array value against null or an array with 0, 1, or 2 elements.

Example 4-8. Pattern matching against arrays

```
> // Describe an array
let describeArray arr =
    match arr with
    | null       -> "The array is null"
    | [| |]      -> "The array is empty"
    | [| x |]    -> sprintf "The array has one element, %A" x
    | [| x; y |] -> sprintf "The array has two elements, %A and %A" x y
    | a -> sprintf "The array had %d elements, %A" a.Length a;;

val describeArray : 'a array -> string

> describeArray [| 1 .. 4 |];;
val it : string = "The array had 4 elements, [|1; 2; 3; 4|]"
> describeArray [| ("tuple", 1, 2, 3) |];;
val it : string = "The array has one element, ("tuple", 1, 2, 3)"
```

Array Equality

Arrays in F# are compared using structural equality. Two arrays are considered equal if they have the same rank, length, and elements. (Rank is the dimensionality of the array, something we will cover in the next section.)

```
> [| 1 .. 5 |] = [| 1; 2; 3; 4; 5 |];;
val it : bool = true
> [| 1 .. 3 |] = [| |];;
val it : bool = false
```

 This is different from the behavior of equality on arrays in C#. In F#, the = operator contains special logic for comparing arrays so the default referential equality is not used. For more information on object equality in .NET, refer to Chapter 5.

Array Module Functions

Just like the `List` and `Seq` modules, there is an `Array` module detailed in Table 4-1 that contains nearly identical functions for manipulating arrays.

Table 4-1. Common methods in the Array module

Function	Description
`Array.length` `'a[] -> int`	Returns the length of an array. Arrays already have a `Length` property as well, but this function is useful for function composition.
`Array.init` `int -> (int -> 'a) -> 'a[]`	Creates a new array with the given number of elements; each element is initialized by the result of the provided function.
`Array.zeroCreate` `int -> 'a[]`	Creates an array with the given length where each entry is the type's default value.
`Array.exists` `('a -> bool) -> 'a[] -> bool`	Tests if any element in the array satisfies the given function.

partition

`Array.partition` divides the given array into two new arrays. The first array contains only elements where the provided function returns `true`; the second array contains elements where the provided function returns `false`:

```
> // Simple Boolean function
let isGreaterThanTen x =
    if x > 10
    then true
    else false;;

val isGreaterThanTen : int -> bool

> // Partitioning arrays
[| 5; 5; 6; 20; 1; 3; 7; 11 |]
|> Array.partition isGreaterThanTen;;
val it : int array * int array = ([|20; 11|], [|5; 5; 6; 1; 3; 7|])
```

tryFind and tryFindIndex

`Array.tryFind` returns `Some` of the first element for which the given function returns `true`. Otherwise, it returns `None`. `Array.tryFindIndex` works just like `Array.tryFind`, except rather than returning the element, it returns its index in the array:

```
> // Simple Boolean function
let rec isPowerOfTwo x =
    if x = 2 then
        true
    elif x % 2 = 1  (* is odd *) then
        false
    else isPowerOfTwo (x / 2);;
```

```
val isPowerOfTwo : int -> bool

> [| 1; 7; 13; 64; 32 |]
|> Array.tryFind isPowerOfTwo;;
val it : int option = Some 64
> [| 1; 7; 13; 64; 32 |]
|> Array.tryFindIndex isPowerOfTwo;;
val it : int option = Some 3
```

 Array.tryFind and Array.tryFindIndex illustrate why the Option type is so powerful. In C#, functions similar to tryFindIndex will return -1 to indicate failure (opposed to None). However, if you are trying to implement tryFind, -1 could indicate either a failure to find an array element or finding an element with value -1.

Aggregate operators

The Array module also contains the aggregate operators of the List module, namely: fold, foldBack, map, and iter. In addition, there are also index-aware versions of these methods. Example 4-9 demonstrates the iteri function, which behaves just like iter except that in addition to the array element, the element's index is provided as well.

Example 4-9. Using the iteri array aggregate function

```
> let vowels = [| 'a'; 'e'; 'i'; 'o'; 'u' |];;

val vowels : char array = [|'a'; 'e'; 'i'; 'o'; 'u'|]

> Array.iteri (fun idx chr -> printfn "vowel.[%d] = %c" idx chr) vowels
vowel.[0] = a
vowel.[1] = e
vowel.[2] = i
vowel.[3] = o
vowel.[4] = u
val it : unit = ()
```

Multidimensional Arrays

Arrays are helpful for storing data in a linear fashion, but what if you need to represent data as a two-, three-, or higher-dimensional grid? You can create *multidimensional arrays*, which enable you to treat data as a block indexed by several values.

Multidimensional arrays come in two flavors: rectangular and jagged; the difference is illustrated in Figure 4-2. Rectangular arrays are in a solid block, while jagged arrays are essentially arrays of arrays.

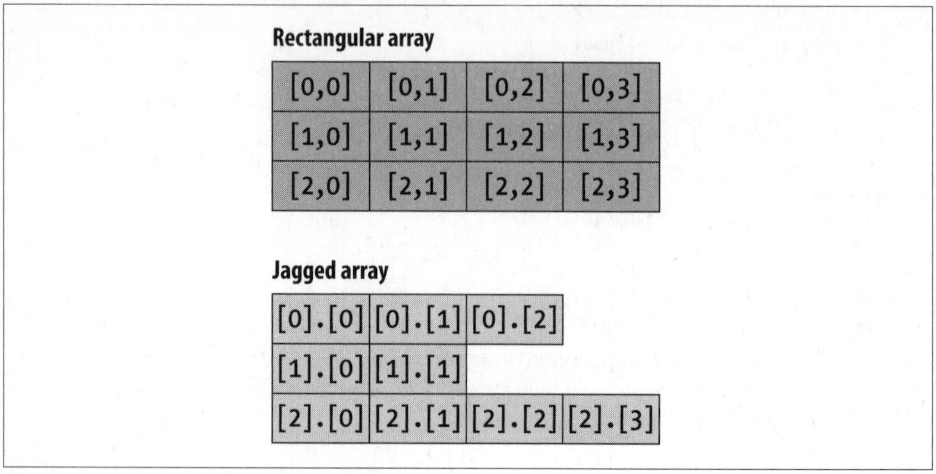

Rectangular array

[0,0]	[0,1]	[0,2]	[0,3]
[1,0]	[1,1]	[1,2]	[1,3]
[2,0]	[2,1]	[2,2]	[2,3]

Jagged array

[0].[0]	[0].[1]	[0].[2]	
[1].[0]	[1].[1]		
[2].[0]	[2].[1]	[2].[2]	[2].[3]

Figure 4-2. Rectangular and jagged arrays

Which type of multidimensional array to use depends on the situation. Using jagged arrays allows you to save memory if each row doesn't need to be the same length; however, rectangular arrays are more efficient for random access because the elements are stored in a contiguous block of memory. (And therefore can benefit from your processor's cache.)

Rectangular arrays

Rectangular arrays are rectangular blocks of *n* by *m* elements in memory. Rectangular arrays are indicated by rectangular brackets with a comma separating them for each new dimension. Also, just like single-dimensional arrays, there are the `Array2D` and `Array3D` modules for creating and initializing rectangular arrays:

```
> // Creating a 3x3 array
let identityMatrix : float[,] = Array2D.zeroCreate 3 3
identityMatrix.[0,0] <- 1.0
identityMatrix.[1,1] <- 1.0
identityMatrix.[2,2] <- 1.0;;


val identityMatrix : float [,] = <1.0; 0.0; 0.0]
                                 [0.0; 1.0; 0.0]
                                 [0.0; 0.0; 1.0>
```

2D rectangular arrays can also take slices, using the same syntax but providing a slice for each dimension:

```
> // All rows for columns with index 1 through 2
identityMatrix.[*, 1..2];;
val it : float [,] = <0.0; 0.0]
                     [1.0; 0.0]
                     [0.0; 1.0>
```

Jagged arrays

Jagged arrays are simply single-dimensional arrays of single-dimensional arrays. Each row in the main array is a different array, each needing to be initialized separately:

```
> // Create a jagged array
let jaggedArray : int[][]  = Array.zeroCreate 3
jaggedArray.[0] <- Array.init 1 (fun x -> x)
jaggedArray.[1] <- Array.init 2 (fun x -> x)
jaggedArray.[2] <- Array.init 3 (fun x -> x);;


val jaggedArray : int [] [] = [|[|0|]; [|0; 1|]; [|0; 1; 2|]|]
```

Mutable Collection Types

Often you will need to store data, but you won't know how many items you will have ahead of time. For example, you might be loading records from a database. If you use an array, you run the risk of wasting memory by allocating too many elements, or even worse, not enough.

Mutable collection types allow you to dynamically add and remove elements over time. While mutable collection types can be problematic when doing parallel and asynchronous programming, they are very simple to work with.

List<'T>

The List type in the System.Collections.Generic namespace—not to be confused with the F# list type—is a wrapper on top of an array that allows you to dynamically adjust the size of the array when adding and removing elements. Because List is built on top of standard arrays, retrieving and adding values is typically very fast. But once the internal array is filled up a new, larger one will need to be created and the List's contents copied over.

Example 4-10 shows basic usage of a List. Again, we're denying poor Pluto the title of planet.

Example 4-10. Using the List type

```
> // Create a List< > of planets
open System.Collections.Generic
let planets = new List<string>();;

val planets : Collections.Generic.List<string>

> // Add individual planets
planets.Add("Mercury")
planets.Add("Venus")
planets.Add("Earth")
planets.Add("Mars");;
> planets.Count;;
```

```
val it : int = 4
> // Add a collection of values at once
planets.AddRange( [| "Jupiter"; "Saturn"; "Uranus"; "Neptune"; "Pluto" |] );;
val it : unit = ()
> planets.Count;;
val it : int = 9
> // Sorry bro
planets.Remove("Pluto");;
val it : bool = true
> planets.Count;;
val it : int = 8
```

Table 4-2 shows common methods on the `List` type.

Table 4-2. Methods and properties on the List<'T> type

Function and type	Description
Add: 'a -> unit	Adds an element to the end of the list.
Clear: unit -> unit	Removes all elements from the list.
Contains: 'a -> bool	Returns whether or not the item can be found in the list.
Count: int	Property for the number of items in the list.
IndexOf: 'a -> int	Returns a zero-based index of the given item in the list. If it is not present, returns –1.
Insert: int * 'a -> unit	Inserts the given item at the specified index into the list.
Remove: 'a -> bool	Removes the given item if present from the list.
RemoveAt: int -> unit	Removes the item at the specified index.

Dictionary<'K,'V>

The `Dictionary` type in the `System.Collections.Generic` namespace that contains key-value pairs. Typically, you would use a dictionary when you want to store data and require a friendly way to look it up, rather than an index, such as using a name to look up someone's phone number.

Example 4-11 shows using a dictionary to map element symbols to a custom `Atom` type. It uses a language feature called *units of measure* to annotate the weight of each atom in atomic mass units. We will cover the units of measure feature in Chapter 7.

Example 4-11. Using a dictionary

```
// Atomic Mass Units
[<Measure>]
type amu

type Atom = { Name : string; Weight : float<amu> }

open System.Collections.Generic
let periodicTable = new Dictionary<string, Atom>()

periodicTable.Add( "H", { Name = "Hydrogen";  Weight = 1.0079<amu> })
periodicTable.Add("He", { Name = "Helium";    Weight = 4.0026<amu> })
periodicTable.Add("Li", { Name = "Lithium";   Weight = 6.9410<amu> })
periodicTable.Add("Be", { Name = "Beryllium"; Weight = 9.0122<amu> })
periodicTable.Add( "B", { Name = "Boron ";    Weight = 10.811<amu> })
// ...

// Lookup an element
let printElement name =

    if periodicTable.ContainsKey(name) then
        let atom = periodicTable.[name]
        printfn
            "Atom with symbol with '%s' has weight %A."
            atom.Name atom.Weight
    else
        printfn "Error. No atom with name '%s' found." name

// Alternate syntax to get a value. Return a tuple of 'success * result'
let printElement2 name =

    let (found, atom) = periodicTable.TryGetValue(name)
    if found then
        printfn
            "Atom with symbol with '%s' has weight %A."
            atom.Name atom.Weight
    else
        printfn "Error. No atom with name '%s' found." Name
```

Table 4-3 shows common methods on the `Dictionary<'k,'v>` type.

Table 4-3. Methods and properties on the Dictionary<'k,'v> type

Function and type	Description
`Add:` `'k * 'v -> unit`	Adds a new key-value pair to the dictionary.
`Clear:` `unit -> unit`	Removes all items from the dictionary.
`ContainsKey:` `'k -> bool`	Checks if the given key is present in the dictionary.

Function and type	Description
ContainsValue: 'v -> bool	Checks if the given value is present in the dictionary.
Count: int	Returns the number of items in the dictionary.
Remove: 'k -> unit	Removes a key-value pair from the dictionary with the given key.

HashSet<'T>

A HashSet, also defined in the System.Collections.Generic namespace, is an efficient collection for storing an unordered set of items. Let's say you were writing an application to crawl web pages. You would need to keep track of which pages you have visited before so you didn't get stuck in an infinite loop; however, if you stored the page URLs you had already visited in a List, it would be very slow to loop through each element to check whether a page had been visited before. A HashSet stores a collection of unique values based on their *hash code*, so checking if an element exists in the set can be done rather quickly.

Hash codes will be better explained in the next chapter; for now you can just think of them as a way to uniquely identify an object. They are the reason why looking up elements in a HashSet and a Dictionary is fast.

Example 4-12 shows using a HashSet to check whether a movie has won the Oscar for Best Picture.

Example 4-12. Using the HashSet type

```
Open System.Collections.Generic

let bestPicture = new HashSet<string>()
bestPicture.Add("No Country for Old Men")
bestPicture.Add("The Departed")
bestPicture.Add("Crash")
bestPicture.Add("Million Dollar Baby")
// ...

// Check if it was a best picture
if bestPicture.Contains("Manos: The Hands of Fate") then
    printfn "Sweet..."
    // ...
```

Table 4-4 shows common methods on the HashSet<'T> type.

Table 4-4. Methods and properties on the HashSet<'T> type

Function and type	Description
Add: 'a -> unit	Adds a new item to the HashSet.
Clear: unit -> unit	Removes all items from the HashSet.
Count: int	Returns the number of items in the HashSet.
IntersectWith: seq<'a> -> unit	Modifies the HashSet to contain only elements that intersect with the given sequence.
IsSubsetOf: seq<'a > -> bool	Returns whether the HashSet is a subset of the sequence; that is, every element in the HashSet is found in the sequence.
IsSupersetOf: seq<'a > -> bool	Returns whether the HashSet is a superset of the sequence; that is, every element in the sequence is contained in the HashSet.
Remove: 'a -> unit	Removes the given item from the HashSet.
UnionWith: seq<'a> -> unit	Modifies the HashSet to contain at least every element in the given sequence.

Looping Constructs

F# has the traditional sorts of looping constructs seen in imperative languages. These allow you to repeat the same function or piece of code a set number of times or until a condition is met.

While Loops

while expressions loop until a Boolean predicate evaluates to false. (For this reason, while loops cannot be used in a purely functional style, otherwise, the loop would never terminate because you could never update the predicate.)

Note that the while loop predicate must evaluate to bool and the body of the loop must evaluate to unit. The following code shows how to use a while loop to count up from zero:

```
> // While loop
let mutable i = 0
while i < 5 do
    i <- i + 1
    printfn "i = %d" i;;
i = 1
i = 2
i = 3
i = 4
i = 5

val mutable i : int = 5
```

The predicate for the `while` loop is checked before the loop starts, so if the initial value of the predicate is `false`, the loop will never execute.

For Loops

When you need to iterate a fixed number of times, you can use a `for` expression, of which there are two flavors in F#: simple and enumerable.

Simple for loops

Simple `for` loops introduce a new integer value and count up to a fixed value. The loop won't iterate if the counter is greater than the maximum value:

```
> // For loop
for i = 1 to 5 do
    printfn "%d" i;;
1
2
3
4
5
val it : unit = ()
```

To count down, use the `downto` keyword. The loop won't iterate if the counter is less than the minimum value:

```
> // Counting down
for i = 5 downto 1 do
    printfn "%d" i;;
5
4
3
2
1
val it : unit = ()
```

Numerical `for` loops are only supported with integers as the counter, so if you need to loop more than `System.Int32.MaxValue` times, you will need to use enumerable `for` loops.

Enumerable for loop

The more common type of `for` loop is one that iterates through a sequence of values. Enumerable `for` loops work with any `seq` type, such as `array` or `list`:

```
> // Enumerable loop
for i in [1 .. 5] do
    printfn "%d" i;;
1
2
3
4
5
val it : unit = ()
```

What makes enumerable `for` loops more powerful than a `foreach` loop in C# is that enumerable `for` loops can take advantage of pattern matching. The element that follows the `for` keyword is actually a pattern-match rule, so if it is a new identifier like `i`, it simply captures the pattern-match value. But more complex pattern-match rules can be used instead.

In Example 4-13, a discriminated union is introduced with two union cases, `Cat` and `Dog`. The `for` loop iterates through a list but executes only when the element in the list is an instance of the `Dog` union case.

Example 4-13. for loops with pattern matching

```
> // Pet type
type Pet =
    | Cat of string * int // Name, Lives
    | Dog of string       // Name
;;

type Pet =
   | Cat of string * int
   | Dog of string

> let famousPets = [ Dog("Lassie"); Cat("Felix", 9); Dog("Rin Tin Tin") ];;

val famousPets : Pet list = [Dog "Lassie"; Cat ("Felix",9); Dog "Rin Tin Tin"]

> // Print famous dogs
for Dog(name) in famousPets do
    printfn "%s was a famous dog." name;;
Lassie was a famous dog.
Rin Tin Tin was a famous dog.
val it : unit = ()
```

There are no `break` or `continue` keywords in F#. If you want to exit prematurely in the middle of a `for` loop, you will need to create a mutable value and convert the `for` loop to a `while` loop.

Exceptions

Every programmer knows things don't always happen as planned. I've been careful in examples so far to avoid showing you code where things fail. But dealing with the unexpected is a crucial aspect of any program, and fortunately the .NET platform supports a powerful mechanism for handling the unexpected.

An *exception* is a failure in a .NET program that causes an abnormal branch in control flow. If an exception occurs, the function immediately exits, as well as its calling function, and so on until the exception is *caught* by an *exception handler*. If the exception is never caught, the program terminates.

The simplest way to report an error in an F# program is to use the `failwith` function. This function takes a string as a parameter, and when called, throws an instance of `System.Exception`. An alternate version calls `failwithf` that takes a format string similar to `printf` and `sprintf`:

```
> // Using failwithf
let divide x y =
    if y = 0 then failwithf "Cannot divide %d by zero!" x
    x / y;;

val divide : int -> int -> int

> divide 10 0;;
System.Exception: Cannot divide 10 by zero!
   at FSI_0003.divide(Int32 x, Int32 y)
   at <StartupCode$FSI_0004>.$FSI_0004._main()
stopped due to error
```

In the previous example FSI indicated an exception was thrown, displaying the two most important properties on an exception type: the exception message and stack trace. Each exception has a `Message` property, which is a programmer-friendly description of the problem. The `Stacktrace` property is a string printout of all the functions waiting on a return value before the exception occurred, and is invaluable for tracking down the origin of an exception. Because the stack *unwinds* immediately after an exception is thrown, the exception could be caught far away from where the exception originated.

While a descriptive message helps programmers debug the exception, it is a best practice in .NET to use a specific exception type. To throw a more specific exception, you use the `raise` function. This takes a custom exception type (any type derived from `System.Exception`) and throws the exception just like `failwith`:

```
> // Raising a DivideByZeroException
let divide2 x y =
    if y = 0 then raise <| new System.DivideByZeroException()
    x / y;;

val divide2 : int -> int -> int

> divide2 10 0;;
```

```
System.DivideByZeroException: Attempted to divide by zero.
   at FSI_0005.divide2(Int32 x, Int32 y)
   at <StartupCode$FSI_0007>.$FSI_0007._main()
stopped due to error
```

 It is tempting to throw exceptions whenever your program reaches an unexpected state; however, throwing exceptions incurs a significant performance hit. Whenever possible, situations that would throw an exception should be obviated.

Handling Exceptions

To handle an exception you catch it using a **try-catch** expression. Any exceptions raised while executing code within a **try-catch** expression will be handled by a **with** block, which is a pattern match against the exception type.

Because the exception handler to execute is determined by pattern matching, you can combine exception handlers using Or or use a wildcard to catch any exception. If an exception is thrown within a **try-catch** expression and an appropriate exception handler cannot be found, the exception will continue bubbling up until caught or the program terminates.

try-catch expressions return a value, just like a pattern match or **if** expression. So naturally the last expression in the **try** block must have the same type as each rule in the **with** pattern match.

Example 4-14 shows some code that runs through a minefield of potential problems. Each possible exception will be caught with an appropriate exception handler. In the example, the **:?** dynamic type test operator is used to match against the exception type; this operator will be covered in more detail in the next chapter.

Example 4-14. try-catch expressions

```
open System.IO

[<EntryPoint>]
let main (args : string[]) =

    let exitCode =
        try
            let filePath = args.[0]

            printfn "Trying to gather information about file:"
            printfn "%s" filePath

            // Does the drive exist?
            let matchingDrive =
                Directory.GetLogicalDrives()
                |> Array.tryFind (fun drivePath -> drivePath.[0] = filePath.[0])

            if matchingDrive = None then
                raise <| new DriveNotFoundException(filePath)
```

```
        // Does the folder exist?
        let directory = Path.GetPathRoot(filePath)
        if not <| Directory.Exists(directory) then
            raise <| new DirectoryNotFoundException(filePath)

        // Does the file exist?
        if not <| File.Exists(filePath) then
            raise <| new FileNotFoundException(filePath)

        let fileInfo = new FileInfo(filePath)
        printfn "Created  = %s" <| fileInfo.CreationTime.ToString()
        printfn "Access   = %s" <| fileInfo.LastAccessTime.ToString()
        printfn "Size     = %d" fileInfo.Length

        0

    with
    // Combine patterns using Or
    | :? DriveNotFoundException
    | :? DirectoryNotFoundException
        ->  printfn "Unhandled Drive or Directory not found exception"
            1
    | :? FileNotFoundException as ex
        ->  printfn "Unhandled FileNotFoundException: %s" ex.Message
            3
    | :? IOException as ex
        ->  printfn "Unhandled IOException: %s" ex.Message
            4
    // Use a wild card match (result will be of type System.Exception)
    | _ as ex
        ->  printfn "Unhandled Exception: %s" ex.Message
            5

// Return the exit code
printfn "Exiting with code %d" exitCode
exitCode
```

Because not catching an exception might prevent unmanaged resources from being freed, such as file handles not being closed or flushing buffers, there is a second way to catch process exceptions: **try-finally** expressions. In a **try-finally** expression, the code in the **finally** block is executed whether or not an exception is thrown, giving you an opportunity to do required cleanup work.

Example 4-15 demonstrates a **try-finally** expression in action.

Example 4-15. try-finally expressions

```
> // Try-finally expressions
let tryFinallyTest() =
    try
        printfn "Before exception..."
        failwith "ERROR!"
        printfn "After exception raised..."
    finally
```

```
        printfn "Finally block executing..."

let test() =
    try
        tryFinallyTest()
    with
    | ex -> printfn "Exception caught with message: %s" ex.Message;;

val tryFinallyTest : unit -> unit
val test : unit -> unit

> test();;
Before exception...
Finally block executing...
Exception caught with message: ERROR!
val it : unit = ()
```

> Unlike in C#, there is no `try-catch-finally` expression. If you need to
> clean up any resources within an exception handler, you must do it for
> each exception handler or simply after the `try-catch` block.

Reraising Exceptions

Sometimes, despite your best efforts to take corrective action, you just can't fix the
problem. In those situations, you can *reraise* the exception, which will allow the original
exception to continue bubbling up from within an exception handler.

Example 4-16 demonstrates reraising an exception by using the `reraise` function.

Example 4-16. Reraise exceptions

```
open Checked

let reraiseExceptionTest() =
    try
        let x = 0x0fffffff
        let y = 0x0fffffff

        x * y
    with
    | :? System.OverflowException as ex
        -> printfn "An overflow exception occured..."
           reraise()
```

Defining Exceptions

Throwing specialized exceptions is key for consumers of your code to only catch the
exceptions they know how to handle. Other exceptions will then continue to bubble
up until an appropriate exception handler is found.

You can define your own custom exceptions by creating types that inherit from System.Exception, which you will see in Chapter 5. However, in F#, there is an easier way to define exceptions using a lightweight exception syntax. Declaring exceptions in this way allows you to define them with the same syntax as discriminated unions.

Example 4-17 shows creating several new exception types, some of which are associated with data. The advantage of these lightweight exceptions is that when they are caught, it is easier to extract the relevant data from them because you can use the same syntax for pattern matching against discriminated unions. Also, there is no need for a dynamic type test operator :?, which we saw in previous examples.

Example 4-17. Lightweight F# exception syntax

```
open System
open System.Collections.Generic

exception NoMagicWand
exception NoFullMoon of int * int
exception BadMojo of string

let castHex (ingredients : HashSet<string>) =
    try

        let currentWand = Environment.MagicWand

        if currentWand = null then
            raise NoMagicWand

        if not <| ingredients.Contains("Toad Wart") then
            raise <| BadMojo("Need Toad Wart to cast the hex!")

        if not <| isFullMoon(DateTime.Today) then
            raise <| NoFullMoon(DateTime.Today.Month, DateTime.Today.Day)

        // Begin the incantation...
        let mana =
            ingredients
            |> Seq.map (fun i -> i.GetHashCode())
            |> Seq.fold (+) 0

        sprintf "%x" mana

    with
    | NoMagicWand
        -> "Error: A magic wand is required to hex!"
    | NoFullMoon(month, day)
        -> "Error: Hexes can only be cast during a full moon."
    | BadMojo(msg)
        -> sprintf "Error: Hex failed due to bad mojo [%s]" msg
```

In Chapter 3, we looked at the functional style of programming, which provides some interesting ways to write code, but doesn't quite stand on its own. The purely functional style doesn't integrate well with the existing .NET framework class libraries and sometimes requires complicated solutions for simple problems.

In this chapter, you learned how to update values, which enables you to write new types of programs. Now you can use efficient collections to store program results, loop as necessary, and should any problems occur, throw exceptions.

Now you can make a choice as to how to approach problems, and you can begin to see the value of multiparadigm computing. Some problems can be solved by simply building up a mutable data structure, while others can be built up through combining simple functions to transform immutable data. You have options with F#.

In the next chapter, we will look at object-oriented programming. This third paradigm of F# doesn't necessarily add much more computational power, but it does provide a way for programmers to organize and abstract code. In much the same way that pure functions can be composed, so can objects.

CHAPTER 5

Object-Oriented Programming

In this chapter, we will cover the most widely used programming paradigm today: object-oriented programming. Mastering object-oriented programming (OOP) is crucial for taking advantage of the existing frameworks and libraries available on .NET, as well as writing F# code that can be integrated into those libraries.

Programming with Objects

Software systems are some of the most complex things created by man. Consider your typical .NET program: thousands if not millions of lines of source code, transformed into some intermediate language by compilers, then compiled again to machine code via a JITer, which then executes on a processor. Knowing the details about how each step works is just too much to handle.

Rather than sweating all the details of a program, object-oriented programming is about breaking problems into conceptual objects, and manipulating those. By modeling the world in terms of abstract objects, you can simplify the complexities of the underlying code.

For example, imagine you have a web log file. You can write several functions to parse and analyze the data. But conceptually it is a log file, which has properties such as file size and number of records, and actions such as delete, copy, find, backup, etc. By adding one more layer of abstraction, you can forget about all the complications of the layer below.

The Benefits of OOP

There are several benefits to object-oriented programming:

Encourages code reuse
> By encapsulating your code into objects, you can reuse the code, which ultimately saves time and enhances productivity.

Tames complexity

> Rather than dealing with myriad individual functions and global variables, OOP allows you to deal with one item at a time. So any mutable state is scoped to just the object.

Specialization through inheritance

> Using polymorphism, you can write code that deals with a base type of object, and still accepts any specialized instances of that type. This is another form of code reuse and will be discussed later in this chapter.

When OOP Breaks Down

While OOP may work well for modeling some concepts, it isn't a silver bullet. To quote Bernard Baruch:

> If all you have is a hammer, everything looks like a nail.

OOP has a tough time encoding algorithms and abstract concepts. In order to represent these concepts, *design patterns* have cropped up to help describe abstractions in terms of objects and their relationships.

While design patterns are helpful, they are simply compensation for OOP's inability to simply express certain concepts. In addition, they are a burden to the programmer, forcing you to write boilerplate code in order to define the contract and relationships between objects.

F# not only offers object-oriented constructs, but also a new set of functional primitives—like discriminated unions and function values. These augment existing object-oriented facilities and remove the need for most boilerplate code found when implementing design patterns. In fact, some design patterns aren't necessary when using a functional language. For example, the *Command Pattern* (from *Design Patterns*, by Gamma et al., Addison-Wesley) describes an object that can be passed around and executed. You can achieve the same result by using higher-order functions, which are baked into the F# language.

Understanding System.Object

.NET offers a rich type system that can check the identity of objects and guarantee type safety at runtime. By keeping track of the type of an object, the .NET runtime can ensure that square pegs aren't put into round holes.

To achieve this notion of object identity, everything from integers to strings to discriminated unions are instances of `System.Object`, abbreviated in F# by `obj`. An instance of `System.Object` isn't useful on its own because it doesn't have any customizations. However, it is important to know the methods available on `System.Object` because they are available on every object you encounter in .NET.

Common Methods

Each instance of `System.Object` comes with several methods that can be overwritten or customized. For custom F# types (discriminated unions and records), some of these methods are overwritten by the F# compiler.

ToString

`ToString` produces a human-readable string representation of the object. In F# this is the value the `printf` format specifier `%A` or `%O` displays to the console. No formal guidelines exist for what this should return, though the result from `ToString` should be adequate to differentiate the object from others, as well as an aid in debugging. The default value is the full name of the class itself.

The following example defines a type `PunctionMark` and provides an implementation of its `ToString` method. Without overriding `ToString`, the default message would look something like `FSI_0002+PunctuationMark`:

```
> // Overriding ToString
type PunctuationMark =
    | Period
    | Comma
    | QuestionMark
    | ExclamationPoint
    override this.ToString() =
        match this with
        | Period -> "Period (.)"
        | Comma  -> "Comma (,)"
        | QuestionMark      -> "QuestionMark (?)"
        | ExclamationPoint  -> "ExclamationPoint (!)";;

type PunctuationMark =
  | Period
  | Comma
  | QuestionMark
  | ExclamationPoint
  with
    override ToString : unit -> string
  end

> let x = Comma;;

val x : PunctuationMark = Comma

> x.ToString();;
val it : string = "Comma (,)"
```

GetHashCode

`GetHashCode` returns a hash value for the object. Overriding this function is crucial for the type to be used in collections such as `Dictionary`, `HashSet`, and `Set`. A hash code is a pseudo-unique identifier that describes a particular instance of the type. This makes it much more efficient to compare whether two objects are identical.

```
> "alpha".GetHashCode();;
val it : int = -1898387216
> "bravo".GetHashCode();;
val it : int = 1946920786
> "bravo".GetHashCode();;
val it : int = 1946920786
```

The default implementation is good enough for most applications, but if you ever override Equals, you should override GetHashCode.

When overriding GetHashCode, you must ensure the following invariants in order for the type to work correctly in collections:

- If two objects are equal, then their hash code must be identical. The converse is not true; two different objects may have the same hash code. However, you should take care to avoid these hash collisions whenever possible.

- An object's hash code must remain consistent if no changes have occurred to the object. If its internal state has been changed, then the hash code may change accordingly.

Equals

The equals function compares if two objects are equal. Equality in .NET is a complex topic (see "Object Equality" on page 119):

```
> "alpha".Equals(4);;
val it : bool = false
> "alpha".Equals("alpha");;
val it : bool = true
```

If you override Equals, you must also override GetHashCode because if two objects are considered equal, their hash codes must match.

GetType

Finally, the GetType method returns an instance of System.Type, which is the type of the actual object. This is important for understanding what something is at runtime, and you will see much more of this when we cover reflection in Chapter 12.

```
> let stringType = "A String".GetType();;

val stringType : System.Type

> stringType.AssemblyQualifiedName;;
val it : string
```

```
= "System.String, mscorlib, Version=4.0.0.0, Culture=neutral, Public
KeyToken=b77a5c561934e089"
```

Object Equality

Equality among .NET types is a difficult subject and revolves around the fundamental type or identity of the object. As mentioned in Chapter 4, there are value types and reference types, and each has a different default mechanism for equality.

By default, value types are compared using a bit pattern, so for two objects that exist on the stack, each byte is compared to determine if they are identical. This is sufficient for primitive types:

```
> // Value type equality
let x = 42
let y = 42;;

val x : int = 42
val y : int = 42

> x = y;;
val it : bool = true
```

Reference types, on the other hand, need more complex semantics. In Example 5-1, values x and y are both instances of class ClassType constructed with the same value. However, despite having the same conceptual meaning they are not considered equal.

Example 5-1. Referential equality

```
> // Referential Equality
type ClassType(x : int) =
    member this.Value = x

let x = new ClassType(42)
let y = new ClassType(42);;

type ClassType =
  class
    new : x:int -> ClassType
    member Value : int
  end
val x : ClassType
val y : ClassType

> x = y;;
val it : bool = false
> x = x;;
val it : bool = true
```

The default meaning of equality for reference types is *referential equality*, which means that the two references point to the same object. In the previous example, x = x evaluated to true because x and x refer to the same memory address. However x = y evaluated to `false` because x and y refer to different memory addresses. This is not sufficient for many applications.

By overriding `Object.Equals` for a type, you can customize the meaning of equality. The following example defines `ClassType2`, which has a more meaningful notion of equality:

```
> // Overriding Equals
type ClassType2(x : int) =
    member this.Value = x
    override this.Equals(o : obj) =
        match o with
        | :? ClassType2 as other -> (other.Value = this.Value)
        | _ -> false
    override this.GetHashCode() = x

let x = new ClassType2(31)
let y = new ClassType2(31)
let z = new ClassType2(10000);;

type ClassType2 =
  class
    new : x:int -> ClassType2
    override Equals : o:obj -> bool
    override GetHashCode : unit -> int
    member Value : int
  end
val x : ClassType2
val y : ClassType2
val z : ClassType2

> x = y;;
val it : bool = true
> x = z;;
val it : bool = false
```

Generated Equality

Tuples, discriminated unions, and records behave exactly as you would expect; that is, two instances with the same set of values are considered equal, just like value types.

Tuples are considered equal if both tuples have the same number of elements, and each element is equal:

```
> let x = (1, 'a', "str");;

val x : int * char * string = (1, 'a', "str")

> x = x;;
val it : bool = true
> x = (1, 'a', "different str");;
val it : bool = false
> // Nested tuples
(x, x) = (x, (1, 'a', "str"));;
val it : bool = true
```

Records are considered equal if all of their fields have the same value:

```
> // Record equality
type RecType = { Field1 : string; Field2 : float }

let x = { Field1 = "abc"; Field2 = 3.5 }
let y = { Field1 = "abc"; Field2 = 3.5 }
let z = { Field1 = "XXX"; Field2 = 0.0 };;

type RecType =
  {Field1: string;
   Field2: float;}
val x : RecType = {Field1 = "abc";
                    Field2 = 3.5;}
val y : RecType = {Field1 = "abc";
                    Field2 = 3.5;}
val z : RecType = {Field1 = "XXX";
                    Field2 = 0.0;}

> x = y;;
val it : bool = true
> x = z;;
val it : bool = false
```

Discriminated unions are considered equal if both values are of the same data tag, and the tuples of data associated with the tags are equal:

```
> // Discriminated Union Equality
type DUType =
    | A of int * char
    | B

let x = A(1, 'k')
let y = A(1, 'k')
let z = B;;

type DUType =
    | A of int * char
    | B
val x : DUType = A (1,'k')
val y : DUType = A (1,'k')
val z : DUType = B

> x = y;;
val it : bool = true
> x = z;;
val it : bool = false
```

In reality tuples, discriminated unions, and records are all reference types. So by default, they should use reference equality, meaning that all the comparisons in the previous examples would evaluate to false. The reason this works is because the F# compiler overrides Equals and GetHashCode for you (providing what is known as *structural equality* semantics).

You can change the default behavior of generated equality should the need arise, either by overriding `Equals` and `GetHashCode` yourself, or by adding the `ReferenceEquality` attribute.

Example 5-2 shows creating a discriminated union type that uses referential equality.

Example 5-2. Customizing generated equality

```
> // Referential Equality on Functional Types
[<ReferenceEquality>]
type RefDUType =
    | A of int * char
    | B;;

type RefDUType =
    | A of int * char
    | B

> // Declare two conceputally equal values
let x = A(4, 'A')
let y = A(4, 'A');;

val x : RefDUType = A (4,'A')
val y : RefDUType = A (4,'A')

> x = y;;
val it : bool = false
> x = x;;
val it : bool = true
```

Understanding Classes

Now that you understand the basics about what an object is, you can begin creating custom types of your own. Classes on the simplest level are functions glued to data. Data associated with a class are known as *fields*. Functions associated with a class are known as *properties* or *members*. (Properties are simply parameter-less methods.)

I'll cover each aspect of fields, methods, and properties in time. But creating a new class isn't going to be useful unless you can initialize it with some initial state. Classes have special methods called *constructors*, whose job is to initialize the class's fields.

A class's constructor is called when it is created by a call to `new`, and it may not be invoked again once the class has been instantiated.

F# features two separate syntaxes for defining class constructors: explicit constructors and implicit constructors. One is in line with F#'s simple yet terse syntax, while the other allows for more explicit control over how the class is generated.

Explicit Construction

The explicit class construction syntax is the least pleasant way to construct a class, but it provides the greatest degree of control. When you define a class using this syntax, you must explicitly name each class field and initialize each field with a constructor.

Class fields are prefixed with the **val** keyword and are accessed by using the *self identifier*, discussed later. Example 5-3 defines a new class called `Point`, which has two fields, m_x and m_y. The class has two constructors, one that takes two parameters and another that takes none.

Example 5-3. Explicit class construction syntax

```
type Point =
    val m_x : float
    val m_y : float

    // Constructor 1 - Takes two parameters
    new (x, y) = { m_x = x; m_y = y }

    // Constructor 2 - Takes no parameters
    new () = { m_x = 0.0; m_y = 0.0 }

    member this.Length =
        let sqr x = x * x
        sqrt <| sqr this.m_x + sqr this.m_y

let p1 = new Point(1.0, 1.0)
let p2 = new Point()
```

 In C#, a default constructor is provided if you don't define any custom constructors. This is not the case in F#. In F# you can define a class without a constructor, but then there would be no way to instantiate that class!

You can have arbitrary code execute before or after the class's fields are initialized to perform a limited set of setup actions. To perform an action before the class's fields are set, simply write code after the equals sign; to perform actions after the fields are initialized, use the **then** keyword followed by an expression, which must evaluate to **unit**.

Example 5-4 adds an explicit constructor to our `Point` type that takes a string, called `text`, as a parameter. Then, several new values are introduced as the string is parsed. Next, the class's fields m_x and m_y are initialized. Finally, after the fields are initialized, a message is printed to the console.

Example 5-4. Arbitrary execution before explicit constructor

```
open System

type Point2 =
    val m_x : float
```

```
    val m_y : float

    // Parse a string, e.g. "1.0, 2.0"
    new (text : string) as this =
        // Do any required pre processing
        if text = null then
            raise <| new ArgumentException("text")

        let parts = text.Split([| ',' |])
        let (successX, x) = Double.TryParse(parts.[0])
        let (successY, y) = Double.TryParse(parts.[1])

        if not successX || not successY then
            raise <| new ArgumentException("text")
        // Initialize class fields
        { m_x = x; m_y = y }
        then
            // Do any post processing
            printfn
                "Initialized to [%f, %f]"
                this.m_x
                this.m_y
```

Implicit Class Construction

While explicit class construction follows typical object-oriented programming styles, it seems rather unnatural in functional programming. Implicit class construction is a simpler way to define classes, and it fits more naturally with the F# language.

With an implicit constructor there are no explicit fields (**val**-bindings); instead, you can use **let**-bindings inside of the type's definition. When the class is compiled, the **let**-bindings will be compiled as class fields or simply optimized away. So although the implicit class construction syntax doesn't allow you to explicitly specify class fields, it does clean up the code for creating classes.

To create a type with an implicit constructor, simply add parentheses and arguments after the type name. The arguments will serve as parameters to the type's *primary constructor*. Any **let**-bindings or **do**-bindings in the body of the class will execute during its construction. Additional constructors defined must end up calling the primary constructor, to ensure all **let**-bindings are initialized.

Example 5-5 shows creating a class using the implicit class construction syntax. The example performs the same task of parsing a 2D point from a string, except it adds an additional constructor that takes two floating-point values. This will serve as the class's primary constructor.

Example 5-5. Implicit class construction

```
type Point3(x : float, y : float) =

    let length =
        let sqr x = x * x
```

```
            sqrt <| sqr x + sqr y
    do printfn "Initialized to [%f, %f]" x y

    member this.X = x
    member this.Y = y
    member this.Length = length

    // Define custom constructors, these must
    // call the 'main' constructor
    new() = new Point(0.0, 0.0)

    // Define a second constructor.
    new(text : string) =
        if text = null then
            raise <| new ArgumentException("text")

        let parts = text.Split([| ',' |])
        let (successX, x) = Double.TryParse(parts.[0])
        let (successY, y) = Double.TryParse(parts.[1])
        if not successX || not successY then
            raise <| new ArgumentException("text")
        // Calls the primary constructor
        new Point(x, y)
```

The primary constructor's parameters, as well as any let-bindings, are accessible anywhere within the class and do not need to be prefixed with the self-identifier. In the
previous example, the values x and y—parameters of the primary constructor—were
available as well as the length value defined in a let-binding.

> Having two syntaxes for creating classes seems redundant. The prefer-
> red way to create classes is to use the implicit class construction format,
> and rely only on the explicit class construction syntax when you need
> to have explicit control over the class's fields.

Generic Classes

In Chapter 2, we covered generic functions, or functions that accepted input of any
type. This concept also extends to classes, enabling you to define a type that can be a
collection of other types. For example, the F# list and seq types are generic because
you can have lists and sequences of any type, such as a list of strings or a seq of floats.

To add a generic type parameter to a class, use angle brackets after the class name.
From then on, refer to the type parameter name if you need to refer to the generic type.
For example:

```
    type GenericClass<'a, 'b>() = ...
```

Just like generic functions, generic type parameters are prefixed with an apostrophe,
'. It is the convention in F# to name generic type parameters 'a, 'b, 'c, and so on.

Example 5-6 defines a generic class `Arrayify` whose primary constructor takes a generic parameter, x, and contains properties that return arrays filled with x of various sizes.

Example 5-6. Defining generic classes

```
> // Define a generic class
type Arrayify<'a>(x : 'a) =
    member this.EmptyArray : 'a[] = [| |]
    member this.ArraySize1 : 'a[] = [| x |]
    member this.ArraySize2 : 'a[] = [| x; x |]
    member this.ArraySize3 : 'a[] = [| x; x; x |];;

type Arrayify<'a> =
  class
    new : x:'a -> Arrayify<'a>
    member ArraySize1 : 'a []
    member ArraySize2 : 'a []
    member ArraySize3 : 'a []
    member EmptyArray : 'a []
  end

> let arrayifyTuple = new Arrayify<int * int>( (10, 27) );;

val arrayifyTuple : Arrayify<int * int>

> arrayfiyTuple.ArraySize3;;
val it : (int * int) [] = [|(10, 27); (10, 27); (10, 27)|]
```

It is worth noting that the generic type may be omitted by using a wildcard < _ > and having the parameter's type be inferred by the F# compiler. In the following snippet, based on the value of x passed to `Arrayify`'s constructor, the generic type parameter is inferred to be of type **string**:

```
> let inferred = new Arrayify<_>( "a string" );;

val inferred : Arrayify<string>
```

Records and discriminated unions can be declared generic as well. The following snippet defines a generic discriminate union type:

```
> // Generic discriminated union
type GenDU<'a> =
    | Tag1 of 'a
    | Tag2 of string * 'a list;;

type GenDU<'a> =
  | Tag1 of 'a
  | Tag2 of string * 'a list

> Tag2("Primary Colors", [ 'R'; 'G'; 'B' ]);;
val it : GenDU<char> = Tag2 ("Primary Colors",['R'; 'G'; 'B'])
```

The following snippet defines a generic record type:

```
> type GenRec<'a, 'b> = { Field1 : 'a; Field2 : 'b };;

type GenRec<'a,'b> =
  {Field1: 'a;
   Field2: 'b;}

> let x = { Field1 = "Blue"; Field2 = 'C' };;

val x : GenRec<string,char> = {Field1 = "Blue";
                               Field2 = 'C';}
```

The Self-Identifier

In the previous examples, you may have noticed a curious **'this'** before each method
name. It was the name of the self-identifier, which allows you to refer to the instance
of the class inside of any of its methods. It doesn't have to be called this; in fact it can
be called any valid identifier.

Example 5-7 shows defining a class with oddly named self-identifiers. Note that the
identifier used to name the self-identifier is scoped only to the method or property.

Example 5-7. Naming the this-pointer

```
open System

type Circle =
    val m_radius : float

    new(r) = { m_radius = r }
    member foo.Radius = foo.m_radius
    member bar.Area = Math.PI * bar.Radius * bar.Radius
```

Obviously, the name of the self identifier should be consistent for every
member of a class.

The examples in this book typically name it this, to closer match the
C# equivalent, though in idiomatic F# code, you'll rarely need to refer
to the self-identifier, so it is common to give it a short name such as x,
or even __.

Methods and Properties

Classes are given meaning by their methods and properties. Methods are actions—
verbs—that describe what the type can do or have done to it. Properties, on the other
hand, are attributes—adjectives—that help describe the type.

Properties

Properties come in three different flavors: read-only, write-only, and read-write. A property *getter* is defined with the get keyword and returns the property value, whereas a property *setter*, defined with the set keyword, updates the property value.

The syntax for defining a read-only property is simply a method with no arguments. For more explicit control, you can provide with get and with set methods.

Example 5-8 shows creating a simple read-only property as well as a more complex property with both a getter and a setter. To invoke the setter, use the left arrow operator, <-, as if setting a mutable value.

Example 5-8. Defining class properties

```
> // Define a WaterBottle type with two properties
[<Measure>]
type ml

type WaterBottle() =
    let mutable m_amount = 0.0<ml>

    // Read-only property
    member this.Empty = (m_amount = 0.0<ml>)

    // Read-write property
    member this.Amount with get ()      = m_amount
                       and  set newAmt = m_amount <- newAmt;;


[<Measure>]
type ml
type WaterBottle =
  class
    new : unit -> WaterBottle
    member Amount : float<ml>
    member Empty : bool
    member Amount : float<ml> with set
  end

> let bottle = new WaterBottle();;

val bottle : WaterBottle

> bottle.Empty;;
val it : bool = true
> bottle.Amount <- 1000.0<ml>;;
val it : unit = ()
> bottle.Empty;;
val it : bool = false
```

Setting Properties in the Constructor

Properties simply provide an easy way to access data for a type, but it is worth noting that you can set properties as additional arguments to a class's constructor. This simplifies the code required to construct an object and set it up the way you want.

Example 5-9 shows two identical ways to construct a new `Form` object, in the `System.Windows.Forms` namespace. The first constructs the object and sets properties individually, and the second sets the properties as part of the class's constructor. This is just syntactic sugar for setting the properties individually after the constructor has executed.

Example 5-9. Setting properties after the class's constructor

```
open System.Windows.Forms

// Attempt one - The hard way
let f1 = new Form()
f1.Text     <- "Window Title"
f1.TopMost <- true
f1.Width    <- 640
f1.Height   <- 480
f1.ShowDialog()

// Attempt two - The easy way
let f2 = new Form(Text     = "Window Title",
                  TopMost = true,
                  Width   = 640,
                  Height  = 480)
f2.ShowDialog()
```

Methods

To add methods to a class, specify a self identifier followed by the function name. Just like function values, any pattern rules after the function's name are its parameters. And, just like functions, to define a method that takes no parameters, simply have it take `unit` as a parameter:

```
    type Television =

        val mutable m_channel : int
        val mutable m_turnedOn : bool

        new() = { m_channel = 3; m_turnedOn = true }

        member this.TurnOn () =
            printfn "Turning on..."
            this.m_turnedOn <- true

        member this.TurnOff () =
            printfn "Turning off..."
            this.m_turnedOn <- false
```

```
    member this.ChangeChannel (newChannel : int) =
        if this.m_turnedOn = false then
            failwith "Cannot change channel, the TV is not on."

        printfn "Changing channel to %d..." newChannel
        this.m_channel <- newChannel

    member this.CurrentChannel = this.m_channel
```

Class methods can be curried, or partially applied, just like function values. However, this is not recommended because other .NET languages do not support function currying. The best practice is to have all parameters wrapped in a single tuple. When referenced from other languages, your F# code won't look like it takes a single parameter of type Tuple, but rather a parameter for each element of the tuple, as you would expect:

```
> // Curryable class methods
type Adder() =
    // Curried method arguments
    member this.AddTwoParams x y = x + y
    // Normal arguments
    member this.AddTwoTupledParams (x, y) = x + y;;

type Adder =
  class
    new : unit -> Adder
    member AddTwoParams : x:int -> y:int -> int
    member AddTwoTupledParams : x:int * y:int -> int
  end

> let adder = new Adder();;

val adder : Adder

> let add10 = adder.AddTwoParams 10;;

val add10 : (int -> int)

> adder.AddTwoTupledParams(1, 2);;
val it : int = 3
```

A notable difference between class methods and function values is that class methods can be recursive without needing to use the rec keyword.

.NET design guidelines state that methods and properties should be named in Pascal Case, meaning every word is capitalized, including the first word. So DoStuff is a recommending naming instead of doStuff or do_stuff.

Static Methods, Properties, and Fields

We've now see methods and properties, which are functions associated with a particular instance of a type. But what if you want a method that is associated with the type itself and not a particular instance? For example, the Environment class in the System namespace has properties to describe the current computer, like the machine name. The current machine name isn't conceptually associated with a particular instance of System.Environment, so it seems strange to require an instance of the type in order to access the MachineName property.

To declare a method or property that can be accessed without an instance of the type, you need to mark it as *static*. This means that the method or property cannot access anything referenced from the self-identifier, such as class fields, but it can be called without having an instance of the type.

To define a static method, simply use the static keyword before a method declaration without declaring a self identifier. Example 5-10 shows creating a static method for class SomeClass. To call a static method, you must fully qualify the type and the method name, otherwise, it will lead to a compiler error.

Example 5-10. Static methods

```
> // Declaring a static method
type SomeClass() =
    static member StaticMember() = 5;;

type SomeClass =
  class
    new : unit -> SomeClass
    static member StaticMember : unit -> int
  end

> SomeClass.StaticMember();;
val it : int = 5
> let x = new SomeClass();;

val x : SomeClass

> x.StaticMember();;

  x.StaticMember();;
  ^^^^^^^^^^^^^^^^

stdin(39,1): error FS0809: StaticMember is not an instance method
```

Static methods are usually associated with utility classes and are not typical in F# code. When you find the need to write many static methods relating to a type, consider organizing them into a module.

Static fields

Class fields can also be marked as **static**, meaning there is a piece of data associated with a type that is accessible through any instance. (Rather than having a custom copy of the value for each instance of the class.)

Static fields typically serve as global constants. However, mutable static fields can be useful as well. Example 5-11 defines a class RareType such that whenever its primary constructor executes, the static field is decremented by one. Once the static field m_num Left is zero, an exception is raised preventing the class from being instantiated again. Without one shared value between each instance of RareType, this wouldn't be possible.

Example 5-11. Creating and using static fields

```
// Static fields
type RareType() =

    // There is only one instance of m_numLeft for all instances of RareType
    static let mutable m_numLeft = 2

    do
        if m_numLeft <= 0 then
            failwith "No more left!"
        m_numLeft <- m_numLeft - 1
        printfn "Initialized a rare type, only %d left!" m_numLeft

    static member NumLeft = m_numLeft
```

The following FSI session shows the type winding down:

```
> let a = new RareType();;

val a : RareType

Initialized a rare type, only 1 left!
> let b = new RareType();;

val b : RareType

Initialized a rare type, only 0 left!
> let c = new RareType();;

val c : RareType

System.Exception: No more left!
   at FSI_0012.RareType..ctor() in C:\Users\chrsmith\Desktop\Ch05.fsx:line 18
   at <StartupCode$FSI_0015>.$FSI_0015._main()
stopped due to error
> RareType.NumLeft;;
val it : int = 0
```

Method Overloading

Often you'll create a very useful method that you want to customize with different sets of parameters. This saves you the hassle of needing to convert your data into the exact types the method needs. Creating a method with the same name but that accepts a different number or different types of arguments is known as *method overloading*.

For example, the `System.Console.Writeline` method has 19 different overloads! This might seem like a lot, but if you want to print an integer, you can use the overload that takes an `int`:s

```
System.Console.WriteLine(42)
```

Otherwise, you would need to convert the `int` parameter to a `string` first, which would quickly become annoying:

```
System.Console.WriteLine((42).ToString())
```

In Example 5-12, the method `CountBits` is overridden to accept arguments of any primitive integer types.

Example 5-12. Method overloading in F#

```
type BitCounter =

    static member CountBits (x : int16) =
        let mutable x' = x
        let mutable numBits = 0
        for i = 0 to 15 do
            numBits <- numBits + int (x' &&& 1s)
            x' <- x' >>> 1
        numBits

    static member CountBits (x : int) =
        let mutable x' = x
        let mutable numBits = 0
        for i = 0 to 31 do
            numBits <- numBits + int (x' &&& 1)
            x' <- x' >>> 1
        numBits

    static member CountBits (x : int64) =
        let mutable x' = x
        let mutable numBits = 0
        for i = 0 to 63 do
            numBits <- numBits + int (x' &&& 1L)
            x' <- x' >>> 1
        numBits
```

Accessibility Modifiers

You can now create classes to encapsulate the complex inner workings of your abstractions. However, if consumers of your classes can access every method, property, or field, they could inadvertently modify some internal state and introduce bugs.

Limiting member visibility is important so that when you share your type across assembly boundaries consumers can only use the methods and properties you specify.

In F#, you can control the visibility of a type or method by providing an *accessibility modifier*. In Example 5-13, the type Ruby is marked internal, and its primary constructor is private, while its other constructors are all public. Attempting to call or access a private value, method, property, or constructor will lead to a compiler error.

Example 5-13. Accessibility modifiers

```
type internal Ruby private(shininess, carats) =

    let mutable m_size = carats
    let mutable m_shininess = shininess

    // Polishing increases shiness but decreases size
    member this.Polish() =
        this.Size    <- this.Size - 0.1
        m_shininess <- m_shininess + 0.1

    // Public getter, private setter
    member public  this.Size with get ()       = m_size
    member private this.Size with set newSize = m_size <- newSize

    member this.Shininess = m_shininess

    public new() =
        let rng = new Random()
        let s = float (rng.Next() % 100) * 0.01
        let c = float (rng.Next() % 16) + 0.1
        new Ruby(s, c)

    public new(carats) =
        let rng = new Random()
        let s = float (rng.Next() % 100) * 0.01
        new Ruby(s, carats)
```

The specifics for all three types of accessibility modifiers in F# are described in Table 5-1. The default accessibility for types, values, and functions in F# is public. The default accessibility for class fields (val and let bindings) is private.

Table 5-1. Accessibility modifiers

Accessibility modifier	Visibility
public	public visibility means that the method or property is visible from anywhere. This is the default for all types, values, and functions in F#.
private	private visibility limits the value to only be available in that class. Outside callers cannot access the value, nor can derived classes. This is the default for class fields.
internal	internal visibility is the same as public; however, this extends only to the current assembly. internal types will not be accessible from another assembly—as if they had originally been declared private.

Unlike in C#, there is *no protected visibility*. However, F# will honor protected visibility on types inherited from languages that support protected inheritance.

Accessibility modifiers on module values

Accessibility modifiers can be applied to more than just classes; they work on values defined in modules as well.

Example 5-14 defines a Logger module, which has a private mutable value m_filesToWriteTo. This value is only visible from within the module, so it can safely expose methods AddLogFile and LogMessage without needing to whether m_filesToWriteTo is null. (Since if m_filesToWriteTo were public, a caller could accidentally replace its value.)

Example 5-14. Accessibility modifiers in modules

```
open System.IO
open System.Collections.Generic

module Logger =

    let mutable private m_filesToWriteTo = new List<string>()

    let AddLogFile(filePath) = m_filesToWriteTo.Add(filePath)

    let LogMessage(message : string) =
        for logFile in m_filesToWriteTo do
            use file = new StreamWriter(logFile, true)
            file.WriteLine(message)
            file.Close()
```

F# signature files

Accessibility modifiers are key to limiting scope and encapsulation, but providing the correct accessibility modifiers to every type method and value adds a lot of clutter to your code. The best way to control accessibility across an entire file is to use an *F#*

signature file. A signature file, suffixed with the *.fsi* extension, allows you to specify a signature for an entire code file. Anything in the code file, but not in the signature, is assumed to have `private` accessibility. This provides a simple way to bulk annotate your code.

Example 5-15 shows a code file and the corresponding signature file. The signature file defines a class with a constructor and two methods. In the corresponding implementation file there are additional methods and properties, and even though those methods and properties aren't explicitly marked `private` they will be compiled as such. Also, because the signature file specifies the type is `internal` it will be compiled with that accessibility. If no accessibility is specified in the *.fsi* file, the member will have `public` accessibility.

An error will be raised if the implementation file has a lower visibility than the signature file.

 While *.fsi* signature files are not provided for any of the samples in this book, they are an important part of large-scale F# code bases.

Example 5-15. Example .fsi and .fs files

```
// File.fsi
namespace MyProject.Utilities

type internal MyClass =
    new : unit -> MyClass
    member public Property1 : int
    member private Method1 : int * int -> int

// File.fs
namespace MyProject.Utilities

type internal MyClass() =
    member this.Property1 = 10
    member this.Property2 with set (x : int) = ()
    member this.Method1 (x, y) = x + y
    member this.Method2 () = true
```

Inheritance

So far I have covered classes, but not *polymorphism*, which is the magic that makes object-oriented programming so powerful. Consider the following two classes, a delicious `BLTSandwich` and the standard `TurkeyAndSwissSandwich`:

```
type BLTSandwich() =
    member this.Ingredients = ["Bacon"; "Lettuce"; "Tomato"]
    member this.Calories = 450
    override this.ToString() = "BLT"
```

```
type TurkeySwissSandwich() =
    member this.Ingredients = ["Turkey"; "Swiss"]
    member this.Calories = 330
    override this.ToString() = "Turkey and Swiss"
```

Even though both classes are nearly identical, they are different entities. So in order to write a function that accepts both an instance of BLTSandwich and an instance of TurkeySwissSandwich, you will need to resort to method overloading. Also, we would have to add a new overload method whenever we added a new sandwich type.

```
member this.EatLunch(sandwich : BLTSandwich) = (*...*)

member this.EatLunch(sandwich : TurkeySwissSandwich) = (*...*)

// This will need to be added later...
member this.EatLunch(sandwich : ClubSandwich) = (*...*)
```

The right way to think about this is that both of these tasty snacks are specializations of the same base type: Sandwich; and can customize the general properties and methods of a Sandwich. Each specialization of Sandwich will have a different calorie count and list of ingredients.

Moreover, you can continue to create a *class hierarchy* to specialize even further: Perhaps create a BLTWithPickelsSandwich type. This is exactly how inheritance and polymorphism work.

Inheritance is the ability to create a new class that inherits the methods and properties of a *base class*, as well as the ability to add new methods and properties and/or customize existing ones. So in this example, BLTSandwich is a specialization, or *derived class*, of Sandwich, with its own custom implementations of the Calories and Ingredients properties.

Polymorphism is the ability to treat any derived class like an instance of its base class. (Since you know that the derived class has all of the same methods and properties of its base.)

The syntax for inheriting from a class is to add the line **inherit** *type* under the type declaration. The syntax is slightly different between explicit and implicit class construction.

When using the implicit class construction syntax, simply add the base class constructor you want to call immediately after the inherit declaration in the primary constructor. Make sure to provide any applicable parameters to the base class's constructor:

```
// Base class
type BaseClass =
    val m_field1 : int

    new(x) = { m_field1 = x }
    member this.Field1 = this.m_field1
```

```
// Derived class using implicit class construction
type ImplicitDerived(field1, field2) =
    inherit BaseClass(field1)

    let m_field2 : int = field2

    member this.Field2 = m_field2
```

When using explicit class construction, you call the desired base class constructor by putting **inherit** *type* in the field initialization of the class:

```
// Derived class using explicit class construction
type ExplicitDerived =
    inherit BaseClass

    val m_field2 : int

    new(field1, field2) =
        {
            inherit BaseClass(field1)
            m_field2 = field2
        }

    member this.Field2 = this.m_field2
```

Method Overriding

The key to customization in derived classes is a technique called *method overriding*, which allows you to redefine what a method does.

To communicate that a method or property can be overridden in F#, mark it as abstract. In Example 5-16, type Sandwich has two abstract properties, Ingredients and Calories. To provide a default implementation for these methods, you use the default keyword before the member declaration.

To override or customize the implementation of a base class's method in a derived class, use the override keyword before the member declaration. (Just as you have seen for overriding System.Object's ToString method.) From then on, when that method is called, the derived class's version will be used instead of the base class's.

Example 5-16. Method overriding in F#

```
type Sandwich() =
    abstract Ingredients : string list
    default this.Ingredients = []

    abstract Calories : int
    default this.Calories = 0

type BLTSandwich() =
    inherit Sandwich()
```

```
    override this.Ingredients = ["Bacon"; "Lettuce"; "Tomato"]
    override this.Calories   = 330

type TurkeySwissSandwich() =
    inherit Sandwich()

    override this.Ingredients = ["Turkey"; "Swiss"]
    override this.Calories = 330
```

To access the base class explicitly, you use the **base** keyword. Example 5-17 defines a new class **BLTWithPickleSandwich**, which accesses its base class to print its new ingredients and increase its calories.

Example 5-17. Accessing the base class

```
> // BLT with pickles
type BLTWithPickleSandwich() =
    inherit BLTSandwich()

    override this.Ingredients = "Pickles" :: base.Ingredients
    override this.Calories    = 50 + base.Calories;;

type BLTWithPickleSandwich =
  class
    inherit BLTSandwich
    new : unit -> BLTWithPickleSandwich
    override Calories : int
    override Ingredients : string list
  end

> let lunch = new BLTWithPickleSandwich();;

val lunch : BLTWithPickleSandwich

> lunch.Ingredients;;
val it : string list = ["Pickles"; "Bacon"; "Lettuce"; "Tomato"]
```

Categories of Classes

With the ability to create a class hierarchy, you have the choice of what to do with the classes higher in the tree and the ones at the very bottom.

Nodes at the top may represent *abstract classes*, which are so general that they might not actually exist. In a previous example, we defined a Sandwich class, for which we provided a default implementation for its abstract members. But not every abstract member has a meaningful default implementation.

To continue with our sandwich example, type Sandwich might inherit from Food, which inherits from System.Object. Class Food cannot provide any meaningful defaults for its methods, and thus would need to be declared abstract.

At the bottom of the class hierarchy are things so specific that they cannot further be specialized. Although BLTNoPicklesLightMayo could be the foundation for

BLTNoPicklesLightMayoOrganicLettuce, there isn't a need to customize the behavior of System.String.

In .NET, you can annotate these topmost and bottommost classes a special way to help define how your classes get used.

Abstract classes

Abstract classes are typically the root objects in hierarchies and are not whole on their own. In fact, you cannot instantiate a class marked as abstract; otherwise, you could potentially call a method that hasn't been defined.

To create an abstract class, simply apply the [<AbstractClass>] attribute to the class declaration. Otherwise, you will get an error for not providing a default implementation for abstract remembers.

```
> // ERROR: Define a class without providing an implementation to its members
type Foo() =
    member this.Alpha() = true
    abstract member Bravo : unit -> bool;;

  type Foo() =
  -----^^^

stdin(2,6): error FS0365: No implementation was given for 'abstract member
 Foo.Bravo : unit -> bool'
> // Properly define an abstract class
[<AbstractClass>]
type Bar() =
    member this.Alpha() = true
    abstract member Bravo : unit -> bool;;

type Bar =
  class
    new : unit -> Bar
    abstract member Bravo : unit -> bool
    member Alpha : unit -> bool
  end
```

Sealed classes

If abstract classes are those that you must inherit from, *sealed classes* are those that you cannot inherit from. To seal a class, simply add the [<Sealed>] attribute:

```
> // Define a sealed class
[<Sealed>]
type Foo() =
    member this.Alpha() = true;;

type Foo =
  class
    new : unit -> Foo
    member Alpha : unit -> bool
  end
```

```
> // ERROR: Inherit from a sealed class
type Bar() =
    inherit Foo()
    member this.Barvo() = false;;

      inherit Foo()
  ----^^^^^^^^^^^^
```

stdin(19,5): error FS0945: Cannot inherit a sealed type

Sealing a class enables certain compiler optimizations, because the compiler knows that virtual methods cannot be overwritten. It also prevents a certain kind of security bug where a malicious user creates a derived class for an object used for authentication and can spoof credentials.

Casting

A key advantage of polymorphism is that you can take an instance of a derived class and treat it like its base class. So in our previous examples, every class in the Sandwich hierarchy had a Calories property and an Ingredients property. To take an instance of a type and convert it to another type in the class hierarchy, you can use a *cast* operator.

Casting is a way to convert types between one another. There are two types of casts—*static* and *dynamic*—which are based on the direction you cast (up or down) an inheritance chain.

Static upcast

A static upcast is where an instance of a derived class is cast as one of its base classes, or cast to something higher up the inheritance tree. It is done using the static cast operator :>. The result is an instance of the targeted class.

Example 5-18 creates a class hierarchy where Pomeranian is a type of Dog, which is a type of Animal. By using a static upcast, we can convert an instance of Pomeranian into an instance of Dog or Animal. Anything can be upcast to obj.

Example 5-18. Static upcasts

```
> // Define a class hierarchy
[<AbstractClass>]
type Animal() =
    abstract member Legs : int

[<AbstractClass>]
type Dog() =
    inherit Animal()
    abstract member Description : string
    override this.Legs = 4
```

```
type Pomeranian() =
    inherit Dog()
    override this.Description = "Furry";;

... snip ...


> let steve = new Pomeranian()

val steve : Pomeranian

> // Casting Steve as various types
let steveAsDog    = steve :> Dog
let steveAsAnimal = steve :> Animal
let steveAsObject = steve :> obj;;

val steveAsDog : Dog
val steveAsAnimal : Animal
val steveAsObject : obj
```

Dynamic cast

A dynamic cast is when you cast a base type as a derived type, or cast something down the inheritance tree. (Therefore, this type of cast cannot be checked statically by the compiler.) This allows you to cast any peg—circular or not—into a round hole, which could lead to failures at runtime.

The most common use of a dynamic cast is when you have an instance of System.Object and you know that it is actually something else. To perform a dynamic cast, use the dynamic cast operator :?>. Building off our previous example, we can cast our steveAsObj value, which is of type obj, to a Dog by employing a dynamic cast:

```
> let steveAsObj = steve :> obj;;

val steveAsObj : obj

> let steveAsDog = steveAsObj :?> Dog;;

val steveAsDog : Dog

> steveAsDog.Description;;
val it : string = "Furry"
```

If a type is converted to something it is not, the error will be caught at runtime and result in a System.InvalidCastException exception:

```
> let _ = steveAsObj :?> string;;
System.InvalidCastException: Unable to cast object of type 'Pomeranian' to type
'System.String'.
   at <StartupCode$FSI_0022>.$FSI_0022._main()
stopped due to error
```

Pattern matching against types

When you use dynamic casts, if the cast fails, an exception is raised, so you cannot test the type of an object without the unnecessary overhead of exception handling. Fortunately, you can use a dynamic type test as part of a pattern match to simplify type checking using the :? operator.

Example 5-19 shows a function whatIs, which takes an object and matches it against several known types. If the type is not known, it calls the GetType method, from System.Object, and prints the name to the console.

It is worth noting that the **as ident** trailing the dynamic type test in the pattern match binds a new value with type equal to the type tested. So in the example, value **s** has type **string** and not **obj**.

Example 5-19. Type tests in a pattern match

```
> // Pattern matching against types
let whatIs (x : obj) =
    match x with
    | :? string    as s -> printfn "x is a string \"%s\"" s
    | :? int       as i -> printfn "x is an int %d" i
    | :? list<int> as l -> printfn "x is an int list '%A'" l
    | _ -> printfn "x is a '%s'" <| x.GetType().Name;;

val whatIs : obj -> unit

> whatIs [1 .. 5];;
x is an int list '[1; 2; 3; 4; 5]'
val it : unit = ()
> whatIs "Rosebud";;
x is a string "Rosebud"
val it : unit = ()
> whatIs (new System.IO.FileInfo(@"C:\config.sys"));;
x is a 'FileInfo'
val it : unit = ()
```

While there is plenty more to learn about OOP, and especially object-oriented design, you now can create classes and use inheritance to organize and reuse your code. This enables you to write code in F# to utilize its strengths—data exploration, quantitative computing, and so on—and package the code to integrate with object-oriented languages like C#.

CHAPTER 6

.NET Programming

The .NET platform is a general-purpose programming platform that can do more than just object-oriented or functional programming. This chapter will cover some additional concepts available when using .NET that will offer advantages when you put them to use in your F# code.

In this chapter, you will learn how to use interfaces to build better abstractions, enums, and structs, which can help performance, and how to use F#'s object expressions for boosting programmer productivity.

The .NET Platform

Let's begin our look at .NET-specific concepts by examining the runtime on which .NET applications execute. This will help you understand how to take full advantage of the platform by seeing the features F# gets for free.

The CLI

The foundation of the .NET platform is the CLI, or Common Language Infrastructure. This is a specification for a runtime system that actually runs your F# code. The F# compiler produces a binary file called an *assembly*, which is composed of a high-level assembly language called *MSIL* or Microsoft Intermediate Language.

An implementation of the CLI compiles this MSIL to machine code at runtime to execute the code faster than if it were just interpreted. The compilation happens "just-in-time" as the code is needed, or JIT.

Code that is compiled to MSIL and executed through the JITter is referred to as *managed code*, as opposed to *unmanaged code*, which is simply raw machine code (typically from programs written in C or C++).

There are several benefits of running through the CLI/managed code and not compiling your F# directly down to the machine level:

Interoperability among languages
> It would be much more difficult to share code among C#, VB.NET, and F# projects if it weren't for a common language (MSIL).

Ability to work cross-platform
> Since the CLI specification can be implemented anywhere, it is possible to run .NET code on other platforms, such as on the Web with Microsoft Silverlight, on the X-Box with XNA and the .NET Compact Framework, or even on Linux through the Mono project.

Machine independence
> The JIT layer takes care of compiling down to machine code, so you don't have to worry about compiling your source code to target a specific architecture like x86 or x64.

In addition, the .NET platform offers garbage collection. This frees the programmer from the error-prone process of tracking the allocation and freeing of memory, and (mostly) eliminates an entire class of bugs.

Most of the benefits you don't even need to think about, as things "just work." But the one aspect of .NET programming you should be cognizant about is how the garbage collector works.

Garbage Collection

The garbage collector is an aspect of the .NET runtime that will automatically free any memory that is no longer referenced. As soon as a value is no longer accessible, typically because the execution has left the function scope, the memory the object occupied is marked for deletion and will be freed later by the garbage collector. For example, if a function declares a value named x, as soon as that function exits, there is no longer a way to refer to x and therefore the garbage collector can safely reclaim its memory.

As the programmer, you usually don't need to worry about whether or not a section of memory should be freed or not; the garbage collector will take care of that for you.

However, it is still possible to have a memory leak in managed code. If you unintentionally keep a reference to something that you don't need, then the garbage collector won't free it because you could potentially access that memory later.

Having the garbage collector to manage all memory works fine for managed resources, which are the ones created and referenced by the CLI. But things get more complicated when you're dealing with unmanaged resources, which include pretty much anything existing outside of the CLI environment, such as file handles, operating system handles, shared memory, etc. Those resources must be explicitly managed and freed by the developer.

If for whatever reason you need to manually deal with allocating and freeing resources, the recommended pattern to use is the IDisposable interface. (Interfaces will be covered later in this chapter.) The IDisposable interface just contains one method, Dispose, which frees the resources. You customize the implementation of Dispose to take care of any cleanup you need, such as closing a file:

```
type IDisposable =
    interface
        abstract member Dispose : unit -> unit
    end
```

But remembering to call Dispose is problematic; in fact, it is just as error-prone as manually managing memory in the first place. Fortunately, F# has some syntactic sugar to help you.

If you use the use keyword, the F# code will dispose of the item as soon as it is done being used, that is, as it leaves scope. Syntactically, the use keyword behaves exactly like the let keyword.

The following example defines a new class called MultiFileLogger that implements IDisposable and prints some text to the console window when Dispose is called. Because the value logger is bound with use, as soon as the value leaves scope—such as when the function exits—Dispose will automatically be called:

```
> // Implementing IDisposable
open System
open System.IO
open System.Collections.Generic

type MultiFileLogger() =
    do printfn "Constructing..."
    let m_logs = new List<StreamWriter>()

    member this.AttachLogFile file =
        let newLogFile = new StreamWriter(file, true)
        m_logs.Add(newLogFile)

    member this.LogMessage (msg : string) =
        m_logs |> Seq.iter (fun writer -> writer.WriteLine(msg))

    interface IDisposable with
        member this.Dispose() =
            printfn "Cleaning up..."
            m_logs |> Seq.iter (fun writer -> writer.Close())
            m_logs.Clear();;

type MultiFileLogger =
  class
    interface IDisposable
    new : unit -> MultiFileLogger
    member AttachLogFile : file:string -> unit
    member LogMessage : msg:string -> unit
  end
```

```
> // Write some code using a MultiFileLogger
let task1() =
    use logger = new MultiFileLogger()
    // ...
    printfn "Exiting the function task1.."
    ();;

val task1 : unit -> unit

> task1();;
Constructing...
Exiting the function task1..
Cleaning up...
val it : unit = ()
```

Interfaces

So far in object-oriented programming, we have modeled a couple of different relationships. *Is a* relationships can be modeled through inheritance, and *has a* relationships are modeled through aggregation (fields and properties). For example, a BMW *is a* car (inherits from type `Car`) and *has a* motor (contains a field named `m_motor` of type `Engine`).

There is, however, a third type of relationship, the *can do* relationship, which means that type X can do the operations described by type Y. For example, people, cars, and wine all age. While there may be no clear relationship between people, cars, and wine, they are all capable of aging.

In .NET programming, the *can do* relationship is modeled via an *interface*, which is a contract that a type can implement to establish that it can perform a certain set of actions.

An interface is just a collection of methods and properties. A type can declare that it implements the interface if it provides an implementation for each method or property. Once this contract has been implemented, then the type *can do* whatever the interface describes.

In Example 6-1, several types implement the `IConsumable` interface. To implement an interface, use the `interface` keyword followed by the implementation of each interface method or property to fulfill the contract. If a class implements the `IConsumable` interface, it means that the class has a `Tastiness` property and an `Eat` method.

Example 6-1. Interfaces in F#

```
type Tastiness =
    | Delicious
    | SoSo
    | TrySomethingElse
```

```
type IConsumable =
    abstract Eat : unit -> unit
    abstract Tastiness : Tastiness

// Protip: Eat one of these a day
type Apple() =
    interface IConsumable with
        member this.Eat() = printfn "Tastey!"
        member this.Tastiness = Delicious

// Not that tastey, but if you are really hungry will do a bind
type CardboardBox() =
    interface IConsumable with
        member this.Eat() =  printfn "Yuck!"
        member this.Tastiness = TrySomethingElse
```

In C# it is possible to partially implement an interface, and allow derived classes to provide the rest of the contract. This is not possible in F#. If a type is declared to implement an interface, it must implement each method and property explicitly.

Using Interfaces

Unlike other .NET languages, in F#, the methods and properties of implemented interfaces are not in scope by default, so in order to call interface methods, you must cast the type to the corresponding interface. Once you have an instance of the interface, that object can do exactly what the interface specifies, no more and no less.

Needing to cast F# objects to interfaces before calling interface members is a common source of confusion when interoperating with existing .NET code. This requirement, however, makes it clear whether you are relying on the interface's functionality or the type's.

```
> let apple = new Apple();;

val apple : Apple

> apple.Tastiness;;

  apple.Tastiness;;
  ------^^^^^^^^^

stdin(81,7): error FS0039: The field, constructor or member 'Tastiness' is not defined.
> let iconsumable = apple :> IConsumable;;

val iconsumable : IConsumable

> iconsumable.Tastiness;;
val it : Tastiness = Delicious
```

Defining Interfaces

To create an interface, you simply define a new class type with only abstract methods. The type inference system will infer the type to be an interface. Alternatively, you can use the interface keyword, followed by abstract members and properties, followed by the end keyword.

In .NET code it is a convention to prefix interfaces with the letter I. This is a relic of Hungarian notation, which was a programming convention to prefix variables with the type of data something contained or the purpose of that value. For example, an integer that contained a column index would be named colX or nX, rather than the ambiguous x.

Because .NET code relies less on tracking machine-level primitives and more on abstractions, the .NET style guidelines dictate that you should not use it, with interface definitions being an exception.

```
> // Define a type inferred to be an interface
type IDoStuff =
    abstract DoThings : unit -> unit;;

// Define an interface explicitly
type IDoStuffToo =
    interface
        abstract member DoThings : unit -> unit
    end;;

type IDoStuff =
    interface
        abstract member DoThings : unit -> unit
    end

type IDoStuffToo =
    interface
        abstract member DoThings : unit -> unit
    end
```

Interfaces can inherit from one another, with the derived interface extending the contract of the first. However, consumers must implement the entire inheritance chain, implementing each interface fully.

This is another departure from the way C# handles interfaces. It may seem strange to explicitly implement the base interface if you implement the derived interface, but this provides an extra degree of explicitness in the F# language. The less the compiler does behind the scenes for you, the fewer surprises you will find in your programs.

Example 6-2 defines two interfaces, IDoStuff and IDoMoreStuff, which inherit from IDoStuff. When creating a class that implements the derived interface but not its base, an error is raised.

Example 6-2. Implementing a derived interface

```
> // Inherited interfaces
type IDoStuff =
    abstract DoStuff : unit -> unit

type IDoMoreStuff =
    inherit IDoStuff

    abstract DoMoreStuff : unit -> unit;;

 ... snip ...

> // ERROR: Doesn't implement full interface inheritance heirarchy
type Foo() =
    interface IDoMoreStuff with
        override this.DoMoreStuff() = printfn "Stuff getting done...";;

    interface IDoMoreStuff with
  ----^

stdin(116,5): error FS0366: No implementation was given for 'abstract member
IDoStuff.DoStuff : unit -> unit'. Note that all interface members must be
implemented and listed under an appropriate 'interface' declaration,
e.g. 'interface ... with member ...'
> // Works
type Bar() =
    interface IDoStuff with
        override this.DoStuff() = printfn "Stuff getting done..."

    interface IDoMoreStuff with
        override this.DoMoreStuff() = printfn "More stuff getting done...";;

type Bar =
  class
    interface IDoMoreStuff
    interface IDoStuff
    new : unit -> Bar
  end
```

Object Expressions

Interfaces are useful in .NET, but sometimes you just want an implementation of an interface without going through the hassle of defining a custom type. For example, in order to sort the elements in a List<_>, you must provide a type that implements the IComparer<'a> interface. As you require more ways to sort that List<_>, you will quickly find your code littered with types that serve no purpose other than to house the single method that defines how to compare two objects.

In F#, you can use an *object expression*, which will create an anonymous class and return an instance of it for you. (The term "anonymous class" just means the compiler will generate the class for you and that you have no way to know its name.) This simplifies the process of creating one-time-use types, much in the same way using a lambda expression simplifies creating one-time-use functions.

The syntax for creating object expressions is a pair of curly braces { } beginning with the new keyword followed by the name of an interface, declared just as you would normally use them. An object expression's result is an instance of the anonymous class.

Object Expressions for Interfaces

Example 6-3 shows both using an object expression and an implementation of the IComparer<'a> interface, which is used to sort items in a collection. Each object expression defines a different way to sort a list of names. Without the use of object expressions, this would take two separate type definitions, each implementing IComparer<'a>. But, from the use of object expressions, no new explicit types were required.

Example 6-3. Sorting a list using IComparer<'a>

```
open System.Collections.Generic

type Person =
    { First : string; Last : string }
    override this.ToString() = sprintf "%s, %s" this.Last this.First

let people =
    new List<_>(
        [|
            { First = "Jomo";  Last = "Fisher" }
            { First = "Brian"; Last = "McNamara" }
            { First = "Joe";   Last = "Pamer" }
        |] )

let printPeople () =
    Seq.iter (fun person -> printfn "\t %s" (person.ToString())) people

// Now sort by last name

printfn "Initial ordering:"
printPeople()

// Sort people by first name
people.Sort(
    {
        new IComparer<Person> with
            member this.Compare(l, r) =
                if   l.First > r.First then  1
                elif l.First = r.First then  0
                else                        -1
    } )
```

```
printfn "After sorting by first name:"
printPeople()

// Sort people by last name
people.Sort(
    {
        new IComparer<Person> with
            member this.Compare(l, r) =
                if   l.Last > r.Last then  1
                elif l.Last = r.Last then  0
                else                      -1
    } )

printfn "After sorting by last name:"
printPeople()
```

The output in FSI is as follows:

```
Initial ordering:
        Fisher, Jomo
        McNamara, Brian
        Pamer, Joe
After sorting by first name:
        McNamara, Brian
        Pamer, Joe
        Fisher, Jomo
After sorting by last name:
        Fisher, Jomo
        McNamara, Brian
        Pamer, Joe
```

Object Expressions for Derived Classes

In addition to implementing interfaces, you can also use object expressions to create derived classes. However, types declared in object expressions cannot add any new methods or properties; they can only override abstract members of the base type.

Example 6-4 uses an object expression to create a new instance of the abstract class Sandwich, without explicitly declaring a type.

Example 6-4. Object expressions for creating derived classes

```
> // Abstract class
[<AbstractClass>]
type Sandwich() =
    abstract Ingredients : string list
    abstract Calories : int

// Object expression for a derived class
let lunch =
```

```
{
    new Sandwich() with
        member this.Ingredients = ["Peanutbutter"; "Jelly"]
        member this.Calories = 400
    };;
type Sandwich =
  class
    abstract member Calories : int
    abstract member Ingredients : string list
    new : unit -> Sandwich
  end
val lunch : Sandwich

> lunch.Ingredients;;
val it : string list = ["Peanutbutter"; "Jelly"]
```

Object expressions are especially useful when writing unit tests. In unit tests, you typically want to create a *mock object*, or a class that simulates behavior that is otherwise slow or complicated to isolate, such as mocking out the database connection so your tests don't hit a real database. Using object expressions, you can easily create anonymous types that can serve as mock objects without the need for defining a plethora of custom types.

Extension Methods

There are times when you are working with a type and may not be able to make changes, either because you don't have the source code or because you are programming against an older version. This poses a problem when you want to extend that type in some way.

Extension methods provide a simple extension mechanism without needing to modify a type hierarchy or modify existing types. Extension methods are special types of methods you can use to augment existing types and use as if they were originally members of the type. This prevents you from having to rebuild base libraries or resort to using inheritance in order to add a few methods. Once extension methods have been added, you can use types as though they had the additional methods and properties, even if they weren't originally written for the type.

To declare an extension method, write `type` *ident* `with` followed by the extension methods, where *ident* is the fully qualified class name.

Note that because extension methods are not actually part of the class, they cannot access private or internal data. They are simply methods that can be called as though they were members of a class.

In Example 6-5, `System.Int32` is extended to provide the `ToHexString` method.

Example 6-5. Using an extension method

```
> (1094).ToHexString();;

  (1094).ToHexString();;
  -------^^^^^^^^^^^

stdin(131,8): error FS0039: The field, constructor or member 'ToHexString' is not defined.

> // Extend the Int32 AKA int type
type System.Int32 with
    member this.ToHexString() = sprintf "0x%x" this;;

  type Int32 with
    member ToHexString : unit -> string

> (1094).ToHexString();;
val it : string = "0x446"
```

Type extensions must be defined within modules and are only available once the given module has been opened. In other words, people need to opt-in to using extension methods by opening the defining module.

 Extension methods created in F# are not proper extension methods, in that they cannot be consumed from C# and VB.NET as extension methods. Rather, extension methods defined in F# code only extend types in other F# assemblies.

Extending Modules

Modules in F# can be extended by simply creating a new module with the same name. As long as the new module's namespace is opened, all new module functions, types, and value will be accessible.

The following snippet creates a new namespace called FSCollectionExtensions. Once this namespace is opened, its two modules will be available, adding new functions to the List and Seq modules:

```
namespace FSCollectionExtensions

open System.Collections.Generic

module List =

    /// Skips the first n elements of the list
    let rec skip n list =
        match n, list with
        | _, []      -> []
        | 0, list    -> list
        | n, hd :: tl -> skip (n - 1) tl

module Seq =
```

```
/// Reverse the elements in the sequence
let rec rev (s : seq<'a>) =
    let stack = new Stack<'a>()
    s |> Seq.iter stack.Push
    seq {
        while stack.Count > 0 do
            yield stack.Pop()
    }
```

Enumerations

We have covered discriminated unions, which are helpful for defining types of things within a set. However, each discriminated union case is a distinctly different class and is too heavyweight a construct in some situations. Many times you simply want to define a group of related constant integral values, and in those situations, you can use *enumerations*.

An enumeration is a primitive integral type, such as `int` or `sbyte`, which also contains a series of named constant values. An enumeration is just a wrapper over that integral type, however, so an instance of an enumerated type can have a value not defined within that enumeration.

Creating Enumerations

To create an enumeration, you use the same syntax as for creating discriminated unions, but each data tag must be given a constant value of the same type. Example 6-6 shows creating an enumeration type for chess pieces. Each enumeration field value must be unique. In the example, the field values correspond to the chess pieces' material value.

Example 6-6. Declaring an enumeration

```
type ChessPiece =
    | Empty  = 0
    | Pawn   = 1
    | Knight = 3
    | Bishop = 4
    | Rook   = 5
    | Queen  = 8
    | King   = 1000000
```

To use an enumeration value, simply use the fully qualified field name. Example 6-7 initializes an 8×8 array to represent locations on a chessboard.

With our `ChessPiece` enum as is, it would be impossible to differentiate between a black piece and a white piece. However, because each `ChessPiece` value is simply an integer, we can get sneaky and treat black pieces as their `ChessPiece` values, and white pieces as the negative. So `-1 * ChessPiece.Bishop` would represent a white bishop. I will cover the mechanics of converting enumeration values between their underlying primitives in the next section.

Example 6-7. Initializing a chessboard enum array

```
/// Create a 2D array of the ChessPiece enumeration
let createChessBoard() =
    let board = Array2D.init 8 8 (fun _ _ -> ChessPiece.Empty)

    // Place pawns
    for i = 0 to 7 do
        board.[1,i] <- ChessPiece.Pawn
        board.[6,i] <- enum<ChessPiece> (-1 * int ChessPiece.Pawn)

    // Place black pieces in order
    [| ChessPiece.Rook; ChessPiece.Knight; ChessPiece.Bishop; ChessPiece.Queen;
       ChessPiece.King; ChessPiece.Bishop; ChessPiece.Knight; ChessPiece.Rook |]
    |> Array.iteri(fun idx piece -> board.[0,idx] <- piece)

    // Place white pieces in order
    [| ChessPiece.Rook;  ChessPiece.Knight; ChessPiece.Bishop; ChessPiece.King;
       ChessPiece.Queen; ChessPiece.Bishop; ChessPiece.Knight; ChessPiece.Rook |]
    |> Array.iteri(fun idx piece ->
                        board.[7,idx] <- enum<ChessPiece> (-1 * int piece))

    // Return the board
    Board
```

Enumerations can be used in pattern matching, but unlike discriminated unions, each enumeration field again must be fully qualified through its type name:

```
let isPawn piece =
    match piece with
    | ChessPiece.Pawn
        -> true
    | _ -> false
```

Conversion

To construct an enumeration value, simply use the enum<_> function. The function converts its argument to the enum type of its generic type parameter.

The following snippet converts the value 42 to an instance of ChessPiece:

```
let invalidPiece = enum<ChessPiece>(42)
```

To get values from an enumeration, simply use the typical primitive value conversion functions, such as int:

```
let materialValueOfQueen = int ChessPiece.Queen
```

When to Use an Enum Versus a Discriminated Union

Enumerations and discriminated unions have two significant differences. First, enumerations don't offer a safety guarantee. Whereas a discriminated union can only be one of a known set of possible values, an enumeration is syntactic sugar over a primitive type. So if you are given an enumeration value, there is no implicit guarantee that the value is something meaningful.

For example, if the value –711 were converted to a `ChessPiece` enum, it would make no sense and likely introduce bugs when encountered. When you obtain an enum value from an external source, be sure to check it with the `Enum.IsDefined` method:

```
> System.Enum.IsDefined(typeof<ChessPiece>, int ChessPiece.Bishop);;
val it : bool = true
> System.Enum.IsDefined(typeof<ChessPiece>, -711);;
val it : bool = false
```

Second, enumerations only hold one piece of data—their value. Discriminated union data tags can each hold a unique tuple of data.

However, enumerations represent a common .NET idiom and offer significant performance benefits over discriminated unions. Whereas enums are simply a few bytes on the stack, discriminated unions are reference types and require separate memory allocations. So populating an array with a large number of enums will be much faster than populating that array with discriminated unions.

A useful benefit to enums is bit flags. Consider Example 6-8. By giving the enum fields powers of two as values, you can treat an instance of the enumeration as a set of bit flags. You can then use bitwise OR, `|||`, to combine the values, which you can then mask against to check if the given bit is set. Using this technique, you can store 32 binary flags within an `int`-based enum, or 64 in an `int64`-based enum.

Example 6-8. Combining enumeration values for flags

```
open System

// Enumeration of flag values
type FlagsEnum =
    | OptionA = 0b0001
    | OptionB = 0b0010
    | OptionC = 0b0100
    | OptionD = 0b1000

let isFlagSet (enum : FlagsEnum) (flag : FlagsEnum) =
    let flagName = Enum.GetName(typeof<FlagsEnum>, flag)
    if enum &&& flag = flag  then
        printfn "Flag [%s] is set." flagName
    else
        printfn "Flag [%s] is not set." flagName
```

The following FSI session is from Example 6-8:

```
> // Check if given flags are set
let customFlags = FlagsEnum.OptionA ||| FlagsEnum.OptionC

isFlagSet customFlags FlagsEnum.OptionA
isFlagSet customFlags FlagsEnum.OptionB
isFlagSet customFlags FlagsEnum.OptionC
isFlagSet customFlags FlagsEnum.OptionD
;;
Flag [OptionA] is set.
Flag [OptionB] is not set.
Flag [OptionC] is set.
Flag [OptionD] is not set.

val customFlags : FlagsEnum = 5
```

Structs

We have covered classes before and gone through the complexities of overriding
Equals to create equality semantics that make sense. However, there is a better way for
simple types. Rather than trying to simulate value type semantics through overriding
Equals, why not just create a new value type? *Structs* are similar to classes, the main
difference being that they are a value type, and therefore may be put on the stack. Struct
instances take up much less memory than a class and, if stack allocated, will not need
to be garbage collected.

Creating Structs

To create a struct, define a type as you normally would, but add the [<Struct>] attribute. Or, you could use the struct and end keywords before and after the struct's body:

```
[<Struct>]
type StructPoint(x : int, y : int) =
    member this.X = x
    member this.Y = y

type StructRect(top : int, bottom : int, left : int, right : int) =
    struct
        member this.Top    = top
        member this.Bottom = bottom
        member this.Left   = left
        member this.Right  = right

        override this.ToString() =
            sprintf "[%d, %d, %d, %d]" top bottom left right
    end
```

Structs have many of the features of classes but may be stored on the stack rather than
the heap. Therefore, equality (by default) is determined by simply comparing the values
on the stack rather than references:

```
> // Define two different struct values
let x = new StructPoint(6, 20)
let y = new StructPoint(6, 20);;

val x : StructPoint = FSI_0011+StructPoint
val y : StructPoint = FSI_0011+StructPoint

> x = y;;
val it : bool = true
```

One difference between structs and classes, however, is how they are constructed. Classes have only the constructors you provide, whereas structs automatically get a *default constructor*, which assigns the default value to each struct field. (Which you might recall is zero for value types and null for reference types.)

```
> // Struct for describing a book
[<Struct>]
type BookStruct(title : string, pages : int) =
    member this.Title = title
    member this.Pages = pages

    override this.ToString() =
        sprintf "Title: %A, Pages: %d" this.Title this.Pages;;

type BookStruct =
  struct
    new : title:string * pages:int -> BookStruct
    override ToString : unit -> string
    member Pages : int
    member Title : string
  end

> // Create an instance of the struct using the constructor
let book1 = new BookStruct("Philosopher's Stone", 309);;

val book1 : BookStruct = Title: "Philosopher's Stone", Pages: 309

> // Create an instance using the default constructor
let namelessBook = new BookStruct();;

val namelessBook : BookStruct = Title: <null>, Pages: 0
```

To create a struct in which you can modify its fields, you must explicitly declare each mutable field in a val binding. In addition, in order to mutate a struct's fields the instance of that struct must be declared mutable.

The following snippet defines a struct MPoint with two mutable fields. It then creates a mutable instance of that struct, pt, and updates the struct's fields:

```
> // Define a struct with mutable fields
[<Struct>]
type MPoint =
    val mutable X : int

    val mutable Y : int
```

```
      override this.ToString() =
          sprintf "{%d, %d}" this.X this.Y;;

type MPoint =
  struct
    val mutable X: int
    val mutable Y: int
    override ToString : unit -> string
  end

> let mutable pt = new MPoint();;

val mutable pt : MPoint = {0, 0}

> // Update the fields
pt.X <- 10
pt.Y <- 7;;
> pt;;
val it : MPoint = {10, 7}
> let nonMutableStruct = new MPoint();;

val nonMutableStruct : MPoint = {0, 0}

> // ERROR: Update a non-mutable struct's field
nonMutableStruct.X <- 10;;

  nonMutableStruct.X <- 10;;
  ^^^^^^^^^^^^^^^^^^^

stdin(54,1): error FS0256: A value must be mutable in order to mutate the contents
of a value type, e.g. 'let mutable x = ...'
```

Restrictions

Structs have several restrictions in place in order to enforce their characteristics:

- Structs cannot be inherited; they are implicitly marked with [<Sealed>].
- Structs cannot override the default constructor (because the default constructor always exists and zeros out all memory).
- Structs cannot use let bindings as with the implicit constructor syntax from class types.

When to Use a Struct Versus a Record

Because F# offers both structs and records as lightweight containers for data, it can be confusing to know when to use which.

The main benefit of using structs over records is the same as the benefit of using structs over classes, namely that they offer different performance characteristics. When you're dealing with a large number of small objects, allocating the space on the stack to create new structs is much faster than allocating many small objects on the heap. Similarly, with structs, there is no additional garbage collection step because the stack is cleared as soon as the function exits.

For the most part, however, the performance gain for struct allocation is negligible. In fact, if used thoughtlessly, structs can have a detrimental impact on performance as a result of excessive copying when passing them as parameters. Also, the .NET garbage collector and memory manager are designed for high-performance applications. When you think you have a performance problem, use the Visual Studio code profiler to identify what the bottleneck is first before prematurely converting all of your classes and records to structs.

CHAPTER 7

Applied Functional Programming

Most of the programming we have done so far has been in the functional style. While this has enabled us to write succinct, powerful programs, we haven't quite used the functional style to its full potential. Functional programming means more than just treating functions as values. Embracing the functional programming paradigm and letting it help shape your thought process will enable you to write programs that would otherwise be prohibitively difficult in an imperative style.

In this chapter, we will build on what you learned about functional programming back in Chapter 3, and I'll introduce new language features that will help you be more productive in the functional style. For example, using active patterns will allow you to increase the power of your pattern matching and eliminate the need for when guards; and by creating auto-opened modules, you can extend common F# modules.

In addition, we will look at some of the more mind-bending aspects of functional programming. You will learn how to use advanced forms of recursion to avoid stack overflows in your code and write more efficient programs using lists. And we will take a look at some common design patterns for functional code.

Our journey into exploring applied functional programming begins with looking at how you can harness the power of F#'s type checking and type inference systems to eliminate bugs in your code.

Units of Measure

There are several universal truths in this world: gravity is 9.8 meters per second squared; water will boil at over 100 degrees Celsius; and any programmer, no matter how talented or careful, will have bugs related to units of measure.

If you are ever writing code that deals with real-world units, you will invariably get it wrong. For example, you might pass in seconds when the function takes minutes, or mistake acceleration for velocity. The result of these sorts of bugs in software has ranged from minor annoyances to loss of life.

The problem is that if you represent a value with just a floating-point number, you have no additional information about what that number means. If I give you a `float` with value `9.8`, you have no idea if it is in miles, meters per second, hours, or even megabytes.

A powerful language feature for combating these dimensional analysis issues is *units of measure*. Units of measure allow you to pass along unit information with a floating-point value—`float`, `float32`, `decimal`—or signed integer types in order to prevent an entire class of software defects. Consider Example 7-1, which describes a temperature. Notice how the parameter `temp` is encoded to take only `fahrenheit` values. I will cover exactly what `float<_>` means later in this section.

Example 7-1. Converting Fahrenheit to Celsius with units of measure

```
[<Measure>]
type fahrenheit

let printTemperature (temp : float<fahrenheit>) =

    if   temp < 32.0<_>  then
        printfn "Below Freezing!"
    elif temp < 65.0<_>  then
        printfn "Cold"
    elif temp < 75.0<_>  then
        printfn "Just right!"
    elif temp < 100.0<_> then
        printfn "Hot!"
    else
        printfn "Scorching!"
```

Because the function accepts only `fahrenheit` values, it will fail to work with any floating-point values encoded with a different unit of measure. Calling the function with an invalid unit of measure will result in a compile-time error (and prevent potentially disastrous results at runtime):

```
> let seattle = 59.0<fahrenheit>;;

val seattle : float<fahrenheit> = 59.0

> printTemperature seattle;;
Cold
val it : unit = ()
> // ERROR: Different units
[<Measure>]
type celsius

let cambridge = 18.0<celsius>;;

[<Measure>]
type celsius
val cambridge : float<celsius> = 18.0

> printTemperature cambridge;;
```

```
    printTemperature cambridge;;
    -----------------^^^^^^^^^

stdin(18,18): error FS0001: Type mismatch. Expecting a
    float<fahrenheit>
but given a
    float<celsius>.
The unit of measure 'fahrenheit' does not match the unit of measure 'celsius'
```

Units of measure also can be compounded by multiplication or division. So if you divide a `meter` unit of measure by another such as `second`, the result will be encoded as `float<meter/second>`:

```
> // Define a measure for meters
[<Measure>]
type m;;

[<Measure>]
type m

> // Multiplication, goes to meters squared
1.0<m> * 1.0<m>;;

val it : float<m ^ 2> = 1.0
> // Division, drops unit entirely
1.0<m> / 1.0<m>;;

val it : float = 1.0
> // Repeated division, results in 1 / meters
1.0<m> / 1.0<m> / 1.0<m>;;

val it : float</m> = 1.0
```

Defining Units of Measure

To define a unit of measure, simply add the [<Measure>] attribute on top of a type declaration. A unit of measure type can only contain static methods and properties, and typically they are defined as *opaque types*, meaning they have no methods or properties at all.

Sometimes it can be quite useful to add functions for conversions between units of measures to their type itself. The following snippet defines units of measure for fahrenheit and celsius like before, except with the addition of static methods to do conversion between the two. Note the use of the **and** keyword so that the type far knows about type cel as part of its declaration:

```
> // Adding methods to units of measure
[<Measure>]
type far =
    static member ConvertToCel(x : float<far>) =
        (5.0<cel> / 9.0<far>) * (x - 32.0<far>)
```

```
    and [<Measure>] cel =
        static member ConvertToFar(x : float<cel>) =
            (9.0<far> / 5.0<cel> * x) + 32.0<far>;;

    [<Measure>]
    type far =
      class
        static member ConvertToCel : x:float<far> -> float<cel>
      end
    [<Measure>]
    and cel =
      class
        static member ConvertToFar : x:float<cel> -> float<far>
      end

    > far.ConvertToCel(100.0<far>);;
    val it : float<cel> = 37.77777778
```

Unit of measure types can also be abbreviated to be relative to other units of measure. In Example 7-2, a new unit of measure s, for seconds, is defined as well as a relative unit of measure Hz, for hertz, which stands for cycles per second. Because the units are relative to one another, two values with the same semantic meaning are considered equal.

Example 7-2. Defining new units of measure

```
> // Define seconds and hertz
[<Measure>]
type s

[<Measure>]
type Hz = s ^ -1;;

[<Measure>]
type s
[<Measure>]
type Hz =/s

> // If Hz was not convertible to s, this
// would result in a compile error.
3.0<s ^ -1> = 3.0<Hz>;;
val it : bool = true
```

Converting Between Units of Measure

Not every function takes a measured value as a parameter. To convert between a measured parameter and the base type, simply pass the value to the appropriate conversion function. Example 7-3 shows how to drop units of measure when calling the sin and cos trigonometric functions because they do not accept values marked them.

Example 7-3. Converting units of measure

```
> // Radians
[<Measure>]
type rads;;

[<Measure>]
type rads

> let halfPI = System.Math.PI * 0.5<rads>;;

val halfPI : float<rads>

> // ERROR: Pass a float<_> to a function accepting a float
sin halfPI;;

  sin halfPI;;
  ----^^^^^^^

stdin(7,5): error FS0001: The type 'float<rads>' does not match type 'float'.
> // Drop the units from value halfPi, to convert float<_> to float
sin (float halfPI);;
val it : float = 1.0
```

Generic Units of Measure

Relying on custom conversion can be a pain, especially if you want to create a generic function. Fortunately, you can allow the F# type system to infer complications to a unit of measure type. If you leave the unit of measure type off and use **float<_>** instead, the F# type inference system will define the value as a generic unit of measure:

```
> let squareMeter (x : float<m>) = x * x;;

val squareMeter : float<m> -> float<m ^ 2>

> let genericSquare (x : float<_>) = x * x;;

val genericSquare : float<'u> -> float<'u ^ 2>

> genericSquare 1.0<m/s>;;
val it : float<m ^ 2/s ^ 2> = 1.0
> genericSquare 9.0;;
val it : float = 81.0
```

If you want to create a type that is generic with regard to a unit of measure, add the [<Measure>] attribute to a generic type parameter. That generic type parameter will allow you to refer to the unit of measure, but it cannot be anything else. In fact, the compiled form of the type will not expose the generic type parameter at all.

Example 7-4 shows defining a point type that preserves a unit of measure.

Example 7-4. Creating a type that is generic with respect to a unit of measure

```
// Represents a point respecting the unit of measure
type Point< [<Measure>] 'u >(x : float<'u>, y : float<'u>) =

    member this.X = x
    member this.Y = y

    member this.UnitlessX = float x
    member this.UnitlessY = float y

    member this.Length =
        let sqr x = x * x
        sqrt <| sqr this.X + sqr this.Y

    override this.ToString() =
        sprintf
            "{%f, %f}"
            this.UnitlessX
            this.UnitlessY
```

When executed in an FSI session, Example 7-4 looks like the following. Notice how the unit of measure is persisted through the `Length` property—taking the square root of the sum of two squares:

```
> let p = new Point<m>(10.0<m>, 10.0<m>);;

val p : Point<m>

> p.Length;;
val it : float<m> = 14.14213562
```

 Units of measure are specific to the F# language and not to the Common Language Runtime. As a result, custom types you create in F# will not have their units of measure types exposed across assembly boundaries. So types that are `float<'a>` will only be exported as `float` when referenced from C#.

Units of measure are not only suited for "real-world" values, but they can also be helpful when dealing with abstract units, such as clicks, pixels, dollar amounts, and so on.

Active Patterns

Pattern matching adds power to your programming by giving you a way to be much more expressive in code branching than using `if` expressions alone. It allows you to match against constants, capture values, and match against the structure of data. However, pattern matching has a significant limitation. Namely, it only has the ability to match against literal values such as `string`, or a limited range of class types like arrays and lists.

Ideally, pattern matching could be used to match against higher-level concepts such as elements in a seq<_>. The following is an example of what you would like to write; however, it fails to compile:

```
// Does not compile
let containsVowel (word : string) =
    let letters = word.Chars
    match letters with
    | ContainsAny [ 'a'; 'e'; 'i'; 'o'; 'u' ]
        -> true
    | SometimesContains [ 'y' ]
        -> true
    | _ -> false
```

To check if elements exist in a seq<_>, you need to resort to using when guards, which are ugly at best. The following snippet creates a Set type filled with the letters of a string, and then searches for specific letters in a pattern-match rule's when guard:

```
let containsVowel (word : string) =
    let letters = word |> Set.ofSeq
    match letters with
    | _ when letters.Contains('a') || letters.Contains('e') ||
             letters.Contains('i') || letters.Contains('o') ||
             letters.Contains('u') || letters.Contains('y')
        -> true
    | _ -> false
```

Fortunately, in F#, there is a feature that captures all the succinct expressiveness you want with the elegance of pattern matching, called *active patterns*.

Active patterns are just special functions that can be used inside of pattern-match rules. Using them eliminates the need for when guards as well as adding clarity to the pattern match, which you can use to make the code look as though it maps more to the problem you are solving.

Active patterns take several forms; each takes an input and converts it into one or more new values:

- Single-case active patterns convert the input into a new value.
- Partial-case active patterns carve out an incomplete piece of the input space, such as only matching against strings which contain the letter 'e'.
- Multi-case active patterns partition the input space into one of several values, such as partitioning all possible integers into odds, evens, or zero.

Single-Case Active Patterns

The simplest type of active pattern is the single-case active pattern, which converts data from one type to another. This enables you to use the existing pattern-match syntax on classes and values that couldn't otherwise be expressed in a pattern-match rule. We will see an example of this shortly.

To define an active pattern, define the function enclosed with *banana clips* or (| |).

Example 7-5 defines an active pattern for converting a file path into its extension. This allows you to pattern match against the file extension, without having to resort to using a when guard.

To use the `FileExtension` active pattern, simply use it in place of a pattern-match rule. The result of the active pattern will come immediately after the active pattern's name, and will behave just like any other pattern-match rule. So in the example, the constant value `".jpg"` is matched against the result of the active pattern. In another pattern-match rule, a new value `ext` is bound to the result of the active pattern.

Example 7-5. Single-case active pattern

```
open System.IO

// Convert a file path into its extension
let (|FileExtension|) filePath = Path.GetExtension(filePath)

let determineFileType (filePath : string) =
    match filePath with

    // Without active patterns
    | filePath when Path.GetExtension(filePath) = ".txt"
        -> printfn "It is a text file."

    // Converting the data using an active pattern
    | FileExtension ".jpg"
    | FileExtension ".png"
    | FileExtension ".gif"
        -> printfn "It is an image file."

    // Binding a new value
    | FileExtension ext
        -> printfn "Unknown file extension [%s]" ext
```

Partial-Case Active Patterns

Using single-case active patterns is helpful for cleaning up pattern matches; however, there are many situations where the data doesn't convert. For example, what happens when you write an active pattern for converting strings to integers?

```
> // Active pattern for converting strings to ints
open System
let (|ToInt|) x = Int32.Parse(x);;

val ( |ToInt| ) : string -> int

> // Check if the input string parses as the number 4
let isFour str =
    match str with
    | ToInt 4 -> true
    | _ -> false;;
```

```
val isFour : string -> bool

> isFour " 4 ";;
val it : bool = true
> isFour "Not a valid Integer";;
System.FormatException: Input string was not in a correct format.
    at System.Number.StringToNumber(String str, NumberStyles options,
    NumberBuffer& number, NumberFormatInfo info, Boolean parseDecimal)
    at System.Number.ParseInt32(String s, NumberStyles style, NumberFormatInfo info)
    at FSI_0007.IsFour(String str)
    at <StartupCode$FSI_0009>.$FSI_0009._main()
stopped due to error
```

Partial-case active patterns allow you to define active patterns that don't always convert the input data. To do this, a partial active pattern returns an **option** type. (Which if you recall has only two values, Some('a) and None.) If the match succeeds, it returns Some; otherwise, it returns None. The option type is removed as part of the pattern match when the result is bound.

Example 7-6 shows how to define a partial active pattern that doesn't throw an exception for malformed input. To define a partial active pattern, simply enclose your active pattern with (|*ident*|_|) instead of the usual (|*ident*|). When used in the pattern match, the rule will only match if the partial active pattern returns Some.

Another way to think about partial active patterns is that they are optional single-case active patterns.

Example 7-6. Partial active patterns in action

```
open System
let (|ToBool|_|) x =
    let success, result = Boolean.TryParse(x)
    if success then Some(result)
    else         None

let (|ToInt|_|) x =
    let success, result = Int32.TryParse(x)
    if success then Some(result)
    else         None

let (|ToFloat|_|) x =
    let success, result = Double.TryParse(x)
    if success then Some(result)
    else         None

let describeString str =
    match str with
    | ToBool  b -> printfn "%s is a bool with value %b" str b
    | ToInt   i -> printfn "%s is an integer with value %d" str i
```

```
| ToFloat f -> printfn "%s is a float with value %f" str f
|  _            -> printfn "%s is not a bool, int, or float" str
```

An example of describeString is as follows:

```
> describeString " 3.141 ";;
 3.141  is a float with value 3.141000
val it : unit = ()
> describeString "Not a valid integer";;
Not a valid integer is not a bool, int, or float
val it : unit = ()
```

Parameterized Active Patterns

Active patterns can take parameters, too. Parameters for an active pattern are provided immediately after the active-pattern name, but before the result of the active pattern.

Example 7-7 shows creating parameterized active patterns to check if the given string matches a regular expression. Rather than having to keep track of the regular expression match and teasing out the individual groups, you can use active patterns to check whether the regular expression matches, as well as bind values to each group from within a pattern-match rule.

Example 7-7. Parameterized active patterns for regular expression matching

```
open System.Text.RegularExpressions

// Use a regular expression to capture three groups
let (|RegexMatch3|_|) (pattern : string) (input : string) =
    let result = Regex.Match(input, pattern)

    if result.Success then
        match (List.tail [ for g in result.Groups -> g.Value ]) with
        | fst :: snd :: trd :: []
            -> Some (fst, snd, trd)
        | [] -> failwith <| "Match succeeded, but no groups found.\n" +
                            "Use '(.*)' to capture groups"
        | _  -> failwith "Match succeeded, but did not find exactly three groups."
    else
        None

let parseTime input =
    match input with
    // Match input of the form "6/20/2008"
    | RegexMatch3 "(\d+)/(\d+)/(\d\d\d\d)" (month, day, year)
    // Match input of the form "2004-12-8"
    | RegexMatch3 "(\d\d\d\d)-(\d+)-(\d+)" (year, month, day)
        -> Some( new DateTime(int year, int month, int day) )
    | _ -> None
```

The result of this active pattern can be seen in the following FSI session:

```
> parseTime "1996-3-15";;
val it : DateTime option
= Some 3/15/1996 12:00:00 AM {Date = ...;
                              Day = 15;
                              DayOfWeek = Friday;
                              DayOfYear = 75;
                              Hour = 0;
                              Kind = Unspecified;
                              Millisecond = 0;
                              Minute = 0;
                              Month = 3;
                              Second = 0;
                              Ticks = 629624448000000000L;
                              TimeOfDay = 00:00:00;
                              Year = 1996;}
> parseTime "invalid";;
val it : DateTime option = None
```

 Active patterns can clean up match statements, but should be treated like .NET properties. They should not be computationally expensive to execute nor cause side effects. Otherwise, it can be difficult to isolate performance problems or anticipate where exceptions could be thrown.

Multi-Case Active Patterns

While single-case and partial active patterns are helpful for converting data, they have the drawback that they can only convert the input data into one other format. But sometimes you want to transform that data into multiple types, typically when you want to partition the input space into multiple categories.

Using a *multi-case active pattern*, you can partition the input space into a known set of possible values. To define a multi-case active pattern, simply use the banana clips again, but you may include multiple identifiers to identify the categories of output.

For example, consider doing a pattern match against a row in your Customers table in a database. You could write multiple partial active patterns to divide the customer into power user, non-user, valued customer, etc. Rather than defining a group of partial-case active patterns to determine which category the input falls into, a multi-case active pattern partitions the input space into exactly one of a group of possible results.

 Another way to think about multi-case active patterns is that they simply act as a way of converting the input data into a discriminated union type.

Example 7-8 takes a string and breaks it into `Paragraph`, `Sentence`, `Word`, and `Whitespace` categories. These categories, and associated data, can then be used as part of a pattern match.

Example 7-8. Multi-case active patterns

```
open System

// This active pattern divides all strings into their various meanings.
let (|Paragraph|Sentence|Word|WhiteSpace|) (input : string) =
        let input = input.Trim()

        if input = "" then
            WhiteSpace
        elif input.IndexOf(".") <> -1 then
            // Paragraph contains a tuple of sentence counts and sentences.
            let sentences = input.Split([|"."|], StringSplitOptions.None)
            Paragraph (sentences.Length, sentences)
        elif input.IndexOf(" ") <> -1 then
            // Sentence contains an array of string words
            Sentence (input.Split([|" "|], StringSplitOptions.None))
        else
            // Word contains a string
            Word (input)

// Count the number of letters of a string by breaking it down
let rec countLetters str =
    match str with
    | WhiteSpace -> 0
    | Word x      -> x.Length
    | Sentence words
        -> words
            |> Array.map countLetters
            |> Array.sum
    | Paragraph (_, sentences)
        -> sentences
            |> Array.map countLetters
            |> Array.sum
```

Using Active Patterns

Active patterns can do more than just spice up the standard sort of pattern matches we have seen so far. You can combine, nest, and use active patterns outside of `match` expressions just like pattern-match rules.

Active patterns can be used in place of any pattern-matching element, which if you recall means that they can be used as part of `let` bindings or as parameters in lambda expressions, too.

The following code snippet applies the active pattern `ToUpper` to the first parameter of function `f`:

```
> let (|ToUpper|) (input : string) = input.ToUpper();;

val ( |ToUpper| ) : string -> string


> let f ( ToUpper x ) = printfn "x = %s" x;;

val f : string -> unit

> f "this is lower case";;
x = THIS IS LOWER CASE
val it : unit = ()
```

Combining active patterns

Active patterns can also be combined much like regular pattern-match rules using Or and And. Example 7-9 shows how to combine multiple active patterns into the same pattern-match rule using Or, |.

Example 7-9. Combining active patterns with Or

```
// Classify movies
let (|Action|Drama|Comedy|Documentary|Horror|Romance|) movie =
    // ...

// Specific movie awards
let (|WonAward|_|) awardTitle movie =
    // ...

// Rate the movie as a date
let goodDateMovie movie =
    match movie with
    // Matching cases of the multi-case active pattern
    | Romance
    | Comedy

    // Using the parameterized active pattern
    | WonAward "Best Picture"
    | WonAward "Best Adaptation"
        -> true

    | _ -> false
```

And, &, allows you to test against multiple active patterns simultaneously. Example 7-10 combines active patterns to determine if an image file is too large to send in an email. The example combines a multi-case active pattern that converts a file path into one of several size-active pattern tags and a second, partial active pattern that will determine if a file path is an image file.

Example 7-10. Combining active patterns with And

```
open System.IO

let (|KBInSize|MBInSize|GBInSize|) filePath =
    let file = File.Open(filePath, FileMode.Open)
    if   file.Length < 1024L * 1024L then
        KBInSize
    elif file.Length < 1024L * 1024L * 1024L then
        MBInSize
    else
        GBInSize

let (|IsImageFile|_|) filePath =
    match filePath with
    | EndsWithExtension ".jpg"
    | EndsWithExtension ".bmp"
    | EndsWithExtension ".gif"
        -> Some()
    | _ -> None

let ImageTooBigForEmail filePath =
    match filePath with
    | IsImageFile & (MBInSize | GBInSize)
        -> true
    | _ -> false
```

Nesting active patterns

With all the power that active patterns have for converting data within pattern matching, a problem you'll quickly run into is transforming data multiple times. However, binding the result of an active pattern and immediate pattern matching against the value leads to tedious and error-prone code.

Fortunately, just as with pattern matching, you can nest active patterns. You can also use an active pattern in place of the result of an active pattern, which will then apply the result of the first active pattern to the second.

Example 7-11 defines a few simple active patterns for parsing XML elements. One is for converting an XML node into its child elements, another is for converting the value of an XML element's attributes, and so on. By nesting active patterns within a single match statement, you can match against the full structure of an XML document within a single rule of a pattern match. This shows the full extent to which active patterns add power to pattern matching.

Example 7-11. Nesting active patterns within a match expression

```
// This example requires a reference to System.Xml.dll
#r "System.Xml.dll"
open System.Xml

// Match an XML element
let (|Elem|_|) name (inp : XmlNode) =
```

```
        if inp.Name = name then Some(inp)
        else                    None


// Get the attributes of an element
let (|Attributes|) (inp : XmlNode) = inp.Attributes


// Match a specific attribute
let (|Attr|) attrName (inp : XmlAttributeCollection) =
    match inp.GetNamedItem(attrName) with
    | null -> failwithf "Attribute %s not found" attrName
    | attr -> attr.Value


// What we are actually parsing
type Part =
    | Widget   of float
    | Sprocket of string * int


let ParseXmlNode element =
    match element with
    // Parse a Widget without nesting active patterns
    | Elem "Widget" xmlElement
        -> match xmlElement with
            | Attributes xmlElementsAttributes
                -> match xmlElementsAttributes with
                    | Attr "Diameter" diameter
                        -> Widget(float diameter)

    // Parse a Sprocket using nested active patterns
    | Elem "Sprocket" (Attributes (Attr "Model" model & Attr "SerialNumber" sn))
        -> Sprocket(model, int sn)

    |_ -> failwith "Unknown element"
```

When executed through FSI, Example 7-11 has the following output:

```
> // Load the XML Document
let xmlDoc =
    let doc = new System.Xml.XmlDocument()
    let xmlText =
        "<?xml version=\"1.0\" encoding=\"utf-8\"?>
        <Parts>
            <Widget Diameter='5.0' />
            <Sprocket Model='A' SerialNumber='147' />
            <Sprocket Model='B' SerialNumber='302' />
        </Parts>
        "
    doc.LoadXml(xmlText)
    doc;;

val xmlDoc : XmlDocument

> // Parse each document node
xmlDoc.DocumentElement.ChildNodes
|> Seq.cast<XmlElement>
|> Seq.map ParseXmlNode;;
val it : seq<Part> = seq [Widget 5.0; Sprocket ("A",1024); Sprocket ("B",306)]
```

Using active patterns, you can easily add a great deal of flexibility to your pattern matching. The best time to use an active pattern is whenever you find yourself writing a lot of similar when guards or when you would like to be more expressive in pattern matches. For instance, XML doesn't lend itself naturally to pattern matching, but with a few simple active patterns, you can use it as part of any pattern match.

Using Modules

If you recall from Chapter 2, namespaces are a way to organize types. Modules behave much like namespaces, except that instead of being able to contain only types, modules can contain values as well.

While modules' ability to contain values makes it easy to write simple applications, they are not well suited for being shared with other programmers and .NET languages. A well-designed class can stand on its own, and is simple and intuitive to use because all of its complex inner workings are hidden. With a module, you are given a loose collection of values, functions, and types, and it can be unclear how they all relate.

Identifying when and how to convert a module into a namespace and class is important for mastering functional programming in F#.

Converting Modules to Classes

Simply put, code defined in modules doesn't scale as well as typical object-oriented hierarchies. Ten modules with dozens of values and types is manageable, but hundreds of modules with thousands of values and types is not. Eliminating the loose values and just relying on classes is one way to help combat complexity.

The code in Example 7-12 creates a simple screen scraper, or a program that downloads the images at a particular URL. You can see how code like this can easily grow out of a long FSI session: typing some code in the FSI window until it works and then copying it to the code editor later. While the code works in the context of a single code file and an FSI session, it cannot easily be integrated into an existing project.

Example 7-12. Web scraper in a module

```
open System.IO
open System.Net
open System.Text.RegularExpressions

let url = @"http://oreilly.com/"

// Download the webpage
let req = WebRequest.Create(url)
let resp = req.GetResponse()
let stream = resp.GetResponseStream()
let reader = new StreamReader(stream)
let html = reader.ReadToEnd()
```

```
// Extract all images
let results = Regex.Matches(html, "<img src=\"([^\"]*)\"")
let allMatches =
    [
        for r in results do
            for grpIdx = 1 to r.Groups.Count - 1 do
                yield r.Groups.[grpIdx].Value
    ]

let fullyQualified =
    allMatches
    |> List.filter (fun url -> url.StartsWith("http://"))

// Download the images
let downloadToDisk (url : string) (filePath : string) =
    use client = new System.Net.WebClient()
    client.DownloadFile (url, filePath)

fullyQualified
|> List.map(fun url -> let parts = url.Split( [| '/' |] )
                       url, parts.[parts.Length - 1])
|> List.iter(fun (url, filename) -> downloadToDisk url (@"D:\Images\" + filename))
```

The problem with Example 7-12 is that it is an unorganized series of values. While the code makes perfect sense when executing a series of steps from top to bottom, the next programmer just sees module properties like `results` and `allMatches`, which are meaningless out of context.

The first step to convert this code is to abstract elements into a series of functions, removing the need for any purely local values. By indenting everything four spaces and adding a function declaration up top, the module's contents could be placed inside of a function. Doing this allows us to break up the code into several pieces:

```
let downloadWebpage (url : string) =
    let req = WebRequest.Create(url)
    let resp = req.GetResponse()
    let stream = resp.GetResponseStream()
    let reader = new StreamReader(stream)
    reader.ReadToEnd()

let extractImageLinks html =
    let results = Regex.Matches(html, "<img src=\"([^\"]*)\"")
    [
        for r in results do
            for grpIdx = 1 to r.Groups.Count - 1 do
                yield r.Groups.[grpIdx].Value
    ] |> List.filter (fun url -> url.StartsWith("http://"))

let downloadToDisk (url : string) (filePath : string) =
    use client = new System.Net.WebClient()
    client.DownloadFile (url, filePath)
```

```
let scrapeWebsite destPath (imageUrls : string list) =
    imageUrls
    |> List.map(fun url ->
            let parts = url.Split( [| '/' |] )
            url, parts.[parts.Length - 1])
    |> List.iter(fun (url, filename) ->
            downloadToDisk url (Path.Combine(destPath, filename)))
```

This refactoring would enable you to use the web scraper in the following fashion:

```
downloadWebpage "http://oreilly.com/"
|> extractImageLinks
|> scrapeWebsite @"C:\Images\"
```

But loose functions aren't that useful for the same reasons that loose values aren't useful. Namely, they don't abstract or simplify anything. You still need to figure out how to get the functions to work together. So the next step would be to create classes that could then be used by other programmers. All you need to do then is replace the function value with a type declaration, and its parameters are simply parameters to the constructor.

In Example 7-13, all the loose functions are brought into the class, so that they are encapsulated. This leaves only a class with a constructor and a member SaveImagesTo Disk.

Example 7-13. Web scraper converted to a class

```
type WebScraper(url) =

    let downloadWebpage (url : string) =
        let req = WebRequest.Create(url)
        let resp = req.GetResponse()
        let stream = resp.GetResponseStream()
        let reader = new StreamReader(stream)
        reader.ReadToEnd()

    let extractImageLinks html =
        let results = Regex.Matches(html, "<img src=\"([^\"]*)\"")
        [
            for r in results do
                for grpIdx = 1 to r.Groups.Count - 1 do
                    yield r.Groups.[grpIdx].Value
        ] |> List.filter (fun url -> url.StartsWith("http://"))

    let downloadToDisk (url : string) (filePath : string) =
        use client = new System.Net.WebClient()
        client.DownloadFile (url, filePath)

    let scrapeWebsite destPath (imageUrls : string list) =
        imageUrls
        |> List.map(fun url ->
                let parts = url.Split( [| '/' |] )
                url, parts.[parts.Length - 1])
```

```
        |> List.iter(fun (url, filename) ->
                downloadToDisk url (Path.Combine(destPath, filename)))

    // Add class fields
    let m_html   = downloadWebpage url
    let m_images = extractImageLinks m_html

    // Add class members
    member this.SaveImagesToDisk(destPath) =
        scrapeWebsite destPath m_images
```

Modules serve a valuable purpose in F# code, especially in the development of simple programs. However, mastering the conversion of modules to classes is important for sharing and reusing your F# code with other .NET languages.

Intentional Shadowing

In F#, the notion of a value is simply a name bound to some data. By declaring a new value with the same name, you can shadow the previous value with that name:

```
let test() =
    let x = 'a'
    let x = "a string"
    let x = 3
    // The function returns 3
    x
```

In the same vein, opening a module dumps a series of new name/value pairs into the current environment, potentially shadowing existing identifiers. So if you have a value in scope named x, and you open a module that also contains a value named x, after the module is opened x will refer to the module's value. This will silently shadow the previous value x, leaving no way to access it.

While this has the potential for introducing subtle bugs, using modules to intentionally shadow values can be beneficial too. This is exactly the approach F# uses for checking for arithmetic overflow.

Consider the case of *checked arithmetic*, that is, arithmetic that throws an exception if there is an overflow. By default, F#'s mathematical operators do not support this, so when you overflow the bounds of an integer value, it just wraps around:

```
> let maxInt = System.Int32.MaxValue;;

val maxInt : int

> maxInt;;
val it : int = 2147483647
> maxInt + 1;;
val it : int = -2147483648
```

The `Microsoft.FSharp.Core.Operators.Checked` module defines common arithmetic operators such as +, -, and so on, that check for overflow conditions and throw the

OverflowException. By opening the Checked module, you shadow all of the existing arithmetic functions and essentially replace them with new ones. Opening that module effectively redefines all those operators for you:

```
> let maxInt = System.Int32.MaxValue;;

val maxInt : int

> open Checked;;
> maxInt + 1;;
System.OverflowException: Arithmetic operation resulted in an overflow.
    at <StartupCode$FSI_0009>.$FSI_0009._main()
stopped due to error
```

> The reason you only need to write open Checked instead of open Microsoft.FSharp.Core.Operators.Checked is because F# automatically opens the Microsoft.FSharp.Core.Operators namespace for you.

This ability to intentionally shadow values can be handy for customizing the behavior of code in a file, but you should be careful to make sure you have the right usage semantics for the modules you write.

Controlling Module Usage

What if a library writer wants to ensure that people are only accessing module values through the module's name? For example, opening the List module would bring a lot of simple functions like map and length into scope, but it would be easy to confuse those functions with other common functions like Seq.map or Array.length:

```
open List
open Seq

// Confusion: Is this List.length or Seq.length?
length [1 .. 10];;
```

To prevent a module from being opened in this way, you can simply add the [<RequireQualifiedAccess>] to the module, which bars them from being imported:

```
[<RequireQualifiedAccess>]
module Foo

let Value1 = 1

[<RequireQualifiedAccess>]
module Bar =
    let Value2 = 2
```

When you try to open a module with the [<RequireQualifiedAccess>] attribute you will get an error; e.g., in the F# library, the List module requires qualified access:

```
> open List;;

  open List;;
  ^^^^^^^^^

stdin(10,1): error FS0892: This declaration opens the module
'Microsoft.FSharp.Collections.List',which is marked as 'RequireQualifiedAccess'.
Adjust your code to use qualified references to the elements of the module instead,
e.g., 'List.map' instead of 'map'. This will ensure that your code is robust as new
constructs are added to libraries
```

However, some modules are especially useful and always having their values and types in scope would be good. In Chapter 6, you learned about extension methods, which allowed you to augment the members of a class. If you define a set of extension methods that are especially useful when used with a given namespace, you can mark the module to be automatically opened as soon as the parent namespace is opened with the [<AutoOpen>] attribute.

Example 7-14 defines a namespace that contains an auto-opened module. After opening the parent namespace with open Alpha.Bravo, you can access any values in the module Charlie without needing to fully qualify them because module Charlie was opened implicitly.

Example 7-14. The AutoOpen attribute

```
namespace Alpha.Bravo

[<AutoOpen>]
module Charlie =
    let X = 1
```

The first half of this chapter showed you how to take advantage of language elements in F# and syntax to enable you to write code in the functional style. The rest of the chapter will focus not on syntax, but theory. Specifically, how to take full advantage of the unique characteristics of functional programming.

Mastering Lists

Whereas arrays and the List<_> type make up the backbone data structure for imperative programming, lists are the cornerstone of functional programming. Lists offer a guarantee of immutability, which helps support function composition and recursion, as well as free you from needing to allocate all the memory up front (such as fixed size array).

Although lists are pervasive when programming in the functional style, I have not yet covered how to use them efficiently. Lists in F# have unique performance characteristics that you should be aware of or else you run the risk of unexpectedly poor performance.

F# lists are represented as a linked list, visualized in Figure 7-1. Every element of the list has a value as well as a reference to the next element in the list (except of course the last element of the list).

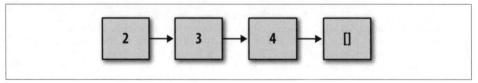

Figure 7-1. Structure of an FSharpList type

List Operations

Perhaps the greatest benefit of the `FSharpList` type is how simple it is to use. While the `List` module offers plenty of functionality for using existing lists, when you build up lists dynamically, there are only two operations to choose from, *cons* and *append*.

Cons

The cons operator, `::`, adds an element to the front of an existing list. When the cons operator is used, the result is a new list; the input list is unchanged because all the work is done by simply allocating a new list element and setting its next element to the start of the input list.

This can be seen visually in Figure 7-2. Notice that a new list is returned, and the input list is reused:

```
> let x = [2; 3; 4];;

val x : int list = [2; 3; 4]

> 1 :: x;;
val it : int list = [1; 2; 3; 4]

> x;;
val it : int list = [2; 3; 4]
```

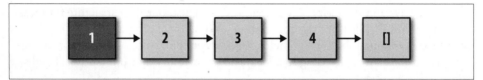

Figure 7-2. Cons operator on lists

Because only one list node is introduced, the cons operation for lists is very fast. Remember, if you were adding an element to a `List<_>`, and the internal array were already filled, a new array could need to be allocated, resulting in a very expensive operation. With lists, cons will always be fast.

Append

The append function, @, joins two lists together. Rather than the last element of the first list ending, it instead points to the beginning of the second list (forming a new, longer list). However, because the last element of the first list provided to append needs to be modified, an entire copy of that list is made.

You can see this in Figure 7-3:

```
> // Append
let x = [2; 3; 4]
let y = [5; 6; 7];;

val x : int list = [2; 3; 4]
val y : int list = [5; 6; 7]

> x @ y;;
val it : int list = [2; 3; 4; 5; 6; 7]
```

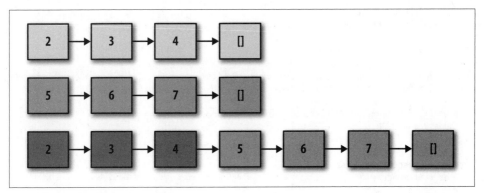

Figure 7-3. Append operator on lists

Looking at Figures 7-2 and 7-3, it is easy to see that cons is a very fast operation because all you do is create a new element and you are done. Append, on the other hand, is potentially more expensive because you need to clone the first list, meaning that for very long lists, append takes a proportionally long time. (Copying the list not only takes twice as much time but also twice as much memory!)

Using Lists

Once you know the performance characteristics of lists, you can then use them effectively. Cons should almost always be preferred over append, except in special circumstances.

Consider Example 7-15. Both functions defined remove consecutive duplicate elements in a list. The first implementation uses a fold, going from left to right. This makes producing the list costly, because append must be used in each iteration of the fold. (For those familiar with asymptotic time complexity, this is an $O(n^2)$ operation.)

Notice that the accumulator for `fold` is a tuple of the last letter and the new list with duplicate items removed.

The second implementation uses `foldBack`, which means this implementation can build up the list in order by using cons. This is precisely the reason for having two separate fold operations. For this particular problem, `foldBack` enables the use of cons, which is much more efficient than `fold`, which requires the use of append.

Example 7-15. Effective list manipulation

```
(*
Removes consecutive duplicate letters.
e.g., [1; 1; 2; 2; 3; 4] => [1; 2; 3; 4]
*)

// Slow implementation...
let removeConsecutiveDupes1 lst =

    let foldFunc acc item =
        let lastLetter, dupesRemoved = acc
        match lastLetter with
        | Some(c) when c = item
                    -> Some(c), dupesRemoved
        | Some(c) -> Some(item), dupesRemoved @ [item]
        | None    -> Some(item), [item]

    let (_, dupesRemoved) = List.fold foldFunc (None, []) lst
    dupesRemoved

// Fast implementation...
let removeConsecutiveDupes2 lst =
    let f item acc =
        match acc with
        | []
            -> [item]
        | hd :: tl when hd <> item
            -> item :: acc
        | _ -> acc

    List.foldBack f lst []
```

When using lists, think of append as a "code smell"—it is usually indicative of a sub-optimal solution.

Tail Recursion

You can now use lists to process large amounts of data efficiently, but there is trouble looming. Because lists are immutable, the primary way they are built is with recursion. Consider the following two ways to construct two lists of integers:

```
> // Creating a List<_> of 100,000 integers
open System.Collections.Generic
```

```
let createMutableList() =
    let l = new List<int>()
    for i = 0 to 100000 do
        l.Add(i)
    l;;

val createMutableList : unit -> List<int>

> // Creating a list of 100,000 integers
let createImmutableList() =
    let rec createList i max =
        if i = max then
            []
        else
            i :: createList (i + 1) max
    createList 0 100000;;

val createImmutableList : unit -> int list
```

Both solutions look identical, but the `createImmutableList` function won't work. (In fact, it will crash.) I'll explain the reason why the function is flawed as well as how to fix it by introducing tail recursion.

You may have heard of *tail recursion* before; in fact, you may have even written tail-recursive functions before without even knowing it. Tail recursion is a special form of recursion, where the compiler can optimize the recursive call to not consume any additional stack space. When a function makes a recursive call, the rest of the calling function may still need to execute some code, so the state of what's left to execute is stored on the stack.

However, as recursive functions call themselves deeper and deeper, the limited stack space can be exhausted, leading to an unrecoverable type of CLR error: the dreaded `StackOverflowException`. Because tail recursion doesn't use any additional stack space, it provides you a way to use recursion safely.

Understanding tail recursion is crucial for writing efficient and safe functional code. As you saw in the previous sections, many functional data structures require recursion to be built up. With this reliance on recursion, stack overflows can become a real threat and limit the size of data a recursive function can process. However, writing functions in a tail-recursive style can help avoid this.

Understanding the Stack

Before you can identify and write tail-recursive functions, you need to understand the stack and how it works with regard to recursive functions.

Whenever you call a function, the *instruction pointer*, the address in the program code that identifies the next operation to execute, is pushed onto the stack. Once the called function returns a value, the stack is cleared and the instruction pointer is restored, resuming the calling function in its previous state.

Consider this simple, recursive function for computing the factorial of a number:

```
let rec factorial x =
    if x <= 1
    then 1     // Base case
    else x * factorial (x - 1)
```

If you set a breakpoint on the base case and call `factorial` with a value of 10, and attach the Visual Studio debugger, you will see this call stack in Figure 7-4. Notice that each recursive call creates a new stack frame. Here you can clearly see the recursive function breaking the parameter x down into smaller and smaller values until x is less than or equal to 1 and the base case is executed.

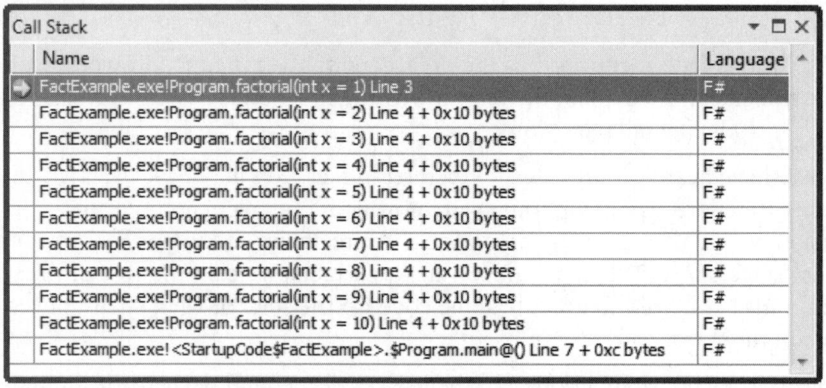

Figure 7-4. Call stack while executing the factorial function

Once the base case executes, it will return the value 1. The stack will be restored to when `factorial` was called with 2 as its parameter, which will return 2×1. Then the stack will be restored to when `factorial` was called with 3 as its parameter, returning 3×2, and so on.

But remember that the stack is in a fixed block of memory, and generally limited to 1MB. So the `factorial` function will exhaust the stack for sufficiently large values. An easier demonstration of this is this `infLoop` function in Example 7-16. Notice how `fsi.exe` is launched from the command line, and when the `StackOverflow` exception is thrown, the process terminates because you cannot catch the `StackOverflowException`.

Example 7-16. Overflowing the stack with recursion

```
C:\Program Files\Microsoft F#\v4.0>Fsi.exe

Microsoft F# Interactive, (c) Microsoft Corporation, All Rights Reserved
F# Version 1.9.8.0, compiling for .NET Framework Version v4.0.20620
```

```
Please send bug reports to fsbugs@microsoft.com
For help type #help;;

> let rec infLoop() = 1 + infLoop();;

val infLoop : unit -> int

> // Go hunting for the StackOverflowException
try
      printfn "%d" <| infLoop()
with
| _ -> printfn "Exception caught";;

Process is terminated due to StackOverflowException.

C:\Program Files\Microsoft F#\v4.0>
```

Figure 7-5 shows the same `infLoop` program but from within the Visual Studio debugger.

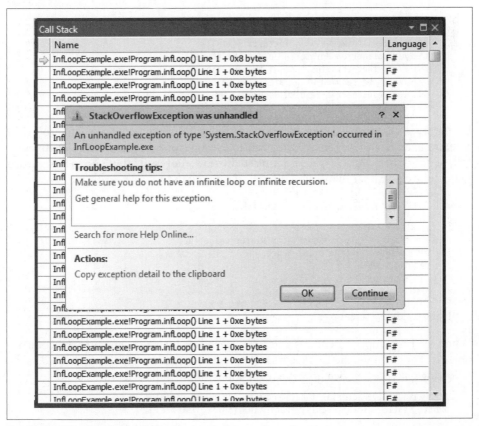

Figure 7-5. The dreaded StackOverflow exception

Introducing Tail Recursion

So how can you solve this problem of recursive calls consuming too much stack space? Tail recursion.

If there are no additional instructions to execute, there is no need to store the instruction pointer on the stack because the only thing left to do once the recursive call exits is restore the stack to the previous function. So rather than needlessly modifying the stack, *tail calls* (or recursive calls from a tail-recursive function) drop the current stack frame before making the recursive call. And once the recursion eventually succeeds, the function will return to the original instruction pointer location.

The previous implementation of `factorial` was not tail-recursive because after the recursive call to `factorial (x-1)` completed, the function needed to multiply that result by x, the original parameter. This is made clearer if you rewrite the function as follows:

```
let rec factorial x =
    if x <= 1
    then
        1
    else
        // Recurse
        let resultOfRecusion = factorial (x - 1)
        // Instruction Pointer needed to be stored
        // so that this instance of the function
        // can be resumed at a later time.
        let result = x * resultOfRecusion
        result
```

Example 7-17 is the tail-recursive version of `factorial`. By passing the data around as an extra parameter, you remove the need to execute code after the recursive function call, so no additional stack space is required. Instead, the result is built up to be returned in the base case rather than being unwound from all the recursive calls.

Example 7-17. Tail-recursive version of factorial

```
let factorial x =
    // Keep track of both x and an accumulator value (acc)
    let rec tailRecursiveFactorial x acc =
        if x <= 1 then
            acc
        else
            tailRecursiveFactorial (x - 1) (acc * x)
    tailRecursiveFactorial x 1
```

When the F# compiler identifies a function as tail-recursive, it generates the code differently. For example, the `tailRecursiveFactorial` function would be generated as the following C# code. Notice how the recursion is simply replaced with a `while` loop:

```
// tailRecursiveFactorial function as it would get compiled in C#.
public static int tailRecursiveFactorial (int x, int acc)
{
    while (true)
```

```
    {
        if (x <= 1)
        {
            return acc;
        }
        acc *= x;
        x--;
    }
}
```

If you fire up the Visual Studio debugger and set a breakpoint on the base case of the tailRecursiveFactorial function, you'll see that only one stack frame has been used, as shown in Figure 7-6.

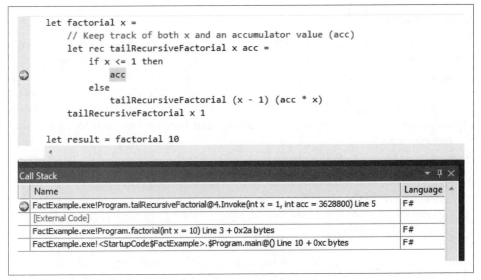

Figure 7-6. The call stack when the function is tail-recursive

To review the benefits of using tail recursion:

- The function executes slightly faster because fewer stack pushes and pops are required.
- The function can recurse indefinitely.
- No StackOverflowException is thrown.

And to review, a function is considered tail-recursive if and only if there is no work to be performed after a recursive call is executed. We will see more examples of this in the next section.

There is no indication from Visual Studio if a function will be compiled as tail-recursive. When you write recursive functions in the functional style, be careful to write them as tail-recursive.

Tail-Recursive Patterns

There are two main ways to ensure that a recursive function is tail-recursive. The simplest applies to when you are whittling down the input while at the same time building up the answer. The second, and much more mind-bending approach, is used when you need to have two recursive calls and branch code flow.

Accumulator pattern

The simplest way to master tail recursion is to have your code follow certain patterns of usage. The easiest thing to do is to add additional parameters, just as in the previous example of `tailRecursiveFactorial`. This is known as the *accumulator pattern*. Rather than waiting for a recursive call to return, instead you pass an accumulator parameter to the recursive call so that the base case will return the final state of the accumulator. (The location of the stack pointer can be forgotten because no execution is left after the recursive call.)

To illustrate the point, let's write a naive implementation of `List.map`, which transforms a list based on a provided function:

```
let rec map f list =
    match list with
    | []      -> []
    | hd :: tl -> (f hd) :: (map f tl)
```

However, that code is not tail-recursive because on the fourth line the recursive call to `map` completes and then the cons operation completes. To combat this, you can use the accumulator pattern to simply store the completed result. In Example 7-18, a nested recursive function is defined that takes the mapped list as a parameter and returns it in the base case.

Example 7-18. The accumulator pattern

```
let map f list =
    let rec mapTR f list acc =
        match list with
        | [] -> acc
        | hd :: tl -> mapTR f tl (f hd :: acc)
    mapTR f (List.rev list) []
```

For simple recursive functions the accumulator pattern is all you need. But what if there is some sort of branching? A function where in order for the function to return, you need to make two recursive calls? (So-called *binary recursion*.) One recursive call at the very least won't be in tail position. Consider Example 7-19, which is an implementation of a binary tree and an `iter` operation that applies a function to each node in the tree.

Example 7-19. Non-tail-recursive iter implementation

```
type BinTree<'a> =
    | Node of 'a * BinTree<'a> * BinTree<'a>
    | Empty

let rec iter f binTree =
    match binTree with
    | Empty -> ()
    | Node(x, l, r) ->
        f x
        iter f l  // NOT in tail position
        iter f r  // In tail position
```

Because there are two recursive calls to make, there simply is no way to use the accumulator pattern. Is all hope lost? Is the dream of entirely tail-recursive code a myth? Fortunately no. But it will take some functional programming magic to achieve.

Continuations

Imagine rather than passing the current state of the accumulator so far as a parameter to the next function call, you passed a function value representing the rest of the code to execute; i.e., rather than storing "what's left" on the stack, you store it in a function. This is known as the *continuation passing style* or simply using a *continuation*.

Continuations are when you return a function value that represents the rest of the code to execute when the current recursive call completes. This allows you to write tail-recursive functions even though there is more work to be done. Conceptually, you are trading stack space (the recursive calls) with heap space (the function values).

Consider Example 7-20, which prints a list of integers in reverse. The printing is done as part of the continuation, which grows larger with each recursive call. In the base case, the continuation is called. The function `printListRevTR` as well as the built continuation are both tail-recursive, so no matter how much input was processed or how large the resulting continuation becomes, it will not overflow the stack.

Example 7-20. Building up a function value

```
> // Print a list in revere using a continuation
let printListRev list =
    let rec printListRevTR list cont =
        match list with
        // For an empy list, execute the continuation
        | [] -> cont()
        // For other lists, add printing the current
        // node as part of the continuation.
        | hd :: tl ->
            printListRevTR tl (fun () -> printf "%d " hd
                                         cont() )
```

```
    printListRevTR list (fun () -> printfn "Done!");;

val printListRev : int list -> unit

> printListRev [1 .. 10];;
10 9 8 7 6 5 4 3 2 1 Done!
val it : unit = ()
```

Admittedly the act of building up a function value is a little mind-bending. But this technique allows you to write functions that otherwise would be impossible to implement in a tail-recursive fashion.

Let's revisit the binary tree `iter` operation. This operation needed to perform two recursive calls, and therefore the function cannot be tail-recursive using the accumulator pattern. However, in order to write code that can perform operations on large trees, you need to convert the function to be tail-recursive.

There are several ways to do this using continuations, but the simplest to understand is to use a *custom iterator type*. This is a pattern where rather than building up a single continuation to perform all the computation you need in tail-recursive fashion, you *linearize* what needs to happen through a custom data type.

Example 7-21 defines a custom iterator type `ContinuationStep`, which has two data tags `Finished` and `Step`, which is a tuple of a value and a function to produce the next `ContinuationStep`.

The function `linearize` uses a continuation to convert the binary tree into a `ContinuationStep` object. Each node is converted into a `Step` union tag in addition to breaking the recursive calls to the left and right subtrees in lambdas. Finally, the `processSteps` function breaks apart the `ContinuationStep` object to actually perform the `iter` operation on the binary tree.

Example 7-21. Building a custom iterator

```
type ContinuationStep<'a> =
    | Finished
    | Step of 'a * (unit -> ContinuationStep<'a>)

let iter f binTree =

    let rec linearize binTree cont =
        match binTree with
        | Empty -> cont()
        | Node(x, l, r) ->
            Step(x, (fun () -> linearize l (fun() -> linearize r cont)))

    let steps = linearize binTree (fun () -> Finished)

    let rec processSteps step =
        match step with
        | Finished -> ()
```

```
  | Step(x, getNext)
      -> f x
         processSteps (getNext())

  processSteps steps
```

While this example will take some time staring at to make sense, it is one way to break apart recursive functions and write tail-recursive code.

Admittedly, such a complicated solution is likely not the best one. Perhaps using a mutable data structure to store nodes to visit, in the order in which to visit them, would make more sense. (For example, keeping a mutable `Stack<_>` of nodes.) But when programming in F#, you have options to find the solution that works best for you.

Programming with Functions

Although tail recursion and modules allow us to get more out of the functional style of programming, there is still more we can learn about functions as values. Next, we will look at function currying and closures. While they may not be the most important aspect of functional programming, having a good understanding of their capabilities will make it easier for you to write code in the purely functional style.

Currying

Recall that function currying is the ability to specify a subset of a function's parameters and return new functions taking fewer parameters. On the surface, this seems like a strange feature to add. What does only providing a subset of a function's parameters actually buy you? The most visible benefit of function currying is the pipe-forward operator, which makes data transformation much more elegant:

```
getCustomers()
|> List.filter (fun cust -> datesEqual cust.Birthday DateTime.Today)
|> List.map (fun cust -> cust.EmailAddress)
|> List.filter Option.isSome
|> sendSpam "Happy Birthday... Now buy our product!"
```

Each line of the previous expression is a curried function whose last parameter is provided by the previous line of code. Writing code in this style enables you to write code exactly the way you conceptualize it in your head. But function currying has another way of cleaning up your code as well.

Passing functions as parameters

Using function currying can potentially eliminate the need for many lambda expressions. Consider the following code, which maps the function f to all the elements of a list:

```
List.map (fun x -> f x) lst
```

Note that the lambda's parameter x is passed as the last parameter to the function f. Whenever you see code like this, you can remove the lambda altogether because f can be passed as a parameter to the function List.map (which is the way you see most functions passed to List.map):

```
List.map f lst
```

In much the same vein, you can simplify functions even if they accept more than one parameter. In the following example, g takes four parameters a, b, c, and x. However, because the lambda takes only one parameter, x, you can just pass the partially applied function value as a parameter:

```
List.map (fun x -> g a b c x) lst
```

Again, the code can be simplified again by just currying the function:

```
List.map (g a b c) lst
```

 Although passing functions as parameters can be elegant, it can also obfuscate code. Remember that one day someone else will be debugging your programs, so always take care to ensure that they are readable.

Eliminating Redundant Code

A common need in refactoring is to eliminate redundancy through reuse, typically through inheritance in object-oriented code. However, you can also eliminate redundant code in the functional style using higher-order functions.

Consider these two functions to help you decide what to have for dinner. pickCheapest returns the cheapest entrée from the list, while pickHealthiest returns the item with the fewest calories. Remember that reduce behaves just like fold except that the initial value of the accumulator is the first element of the list:

```
[<Measure>]
type usd

type Entree = { Name : string; Price : float<usd>; Calories : int }

// Picks the cheapest item on the menu
let pickCheapest menuItems =
    List.reduce
        (fun acc item -> if item.Price < acc.Price
                         then item
                         else acc)
        menuItems

let pickHealthiest menuItems =
    List.reduce
        (fun acc item -> if item.Calories < acc.Calories
                         then item
                         else acc)
        menuItems
```

Both of these functions are nearly identical and differ only in how they compare the given element. Why not factor that out? If you define the compare function as a parameter, you can swap out implementations much more easily, potentially resulting in more readable code. Note that the functions `pickCheapest2` and `pickHealthiest2` rely on function currying from their partially applied call to `pickItem`:

```
let private pickItem cmp menuItems =
    let reduceFunc acc item =
        match cmp acc item with
        | true  -> acc
        | false -> item
    List.reduce reduceFunc menuItems

let pickCheapest2   = pickItem (fun acc item -> item.Price < acc.Price)
let pickHealthiest2 = pickItem (fun acc item -> item.Calories < acc.Calories)
```

Closures

Closures is the term used to describe an inner or nested function being able to access values not explicitly passed in as parameters to that function. Like currying, this too may seem like some strange concept that isn't particularly applicable, but you have actually been using closures constantly throughout the book without knowing it.

A simple example of a closure would be the following function `mult`, which multiplies every element in a list by a given number. Notice that `i` is a parameter to the first function, but not a parameter to the lambda expression. So you might be wondering, how can `i` be used inside that lambda if it isn't explicitly passed in as a parameter? That's the beauty of closures. Because value `i` is in scope, it is *captured* by the closure of the lambda, and therefore accessible. Behind the scenes the compiler actually links the value `i` to the lambda so that at runtime the value is accessible, but this is all done for you:

```
> let mult i lst = List.map (fun x -> x * i) lst;;

val mult : int -> int list -> int list

> mult 10 [1; 3; 5; 7];;
val it : int list = [10; 30; 50; 70]
```

In essence, with closures a function may capture some additional data with it, which enables the function to know about values in the scope where the function was declared. With this we can achieve some interesting results.

Imagine creating an abstract data type, like a class, without any explicit fields to store the type's state. It doesn't sound like it is possible—because in order for the type to have some meaning, it must store its internal data somewhere. But with closures that isn't the case.

Consider Example 7-22, which defines a record type `Set` where its two fields are functions, one to add items to the `Set`, and another to check if an item exists in the set. To create an instance of Set, simply access the static property Empty. Once you have an instance of Set, adding and removing items works entirely by capturing the data in closures. The function makeSet is passed in a list—which comprises the items contained in the set. When new items are added to the list, a recursive call to makeSet is returned, capturing the original set's item list and the new item to be added in the closure of the updated Add function.

Example 7-22. Data encapsulation via closures

```
// Data type for a set. Notice the implementation is
// stored in record fields...
type Set =
    {
        // Add an item to the set
        Add     : int -> Set
        // Checks if an element exists in the set
        Exists : int -> bool
    }

    // Returns an empty set
    static member Empty =
        let rec makeSet lst =
            {
                Add     = (fun item -> makeSet (item :: lst))
                Exists = (fun item -> List.exists ((=) item) lst)
            }
        makeSet []
```

You can see the Set type in action in the following FSI session:

```
> // Set in action
let s    = Set.Empty
let s'   = s.Add(1)
let s''  = s'.Add(2)
let s''' = s''.Add(3);;

val s : Set
val s' : Set
val s'' : Set
val s''' : Set

> s.Exists 2;;
val it : bool = false
> s'''.Exists 2;;
val it : bool = true
```

Just like writing super-complicated continuations, there are likely better ways to write types than by storing internal data entirely in closures. However, understanding that functions can contain more than just their parameters opens up new possibilities.

Functional Patterns

Now that we have covered some advanced concepts in the functional style of programming, let's examine some common design patterns they enable. Describing solutions to problems in terms of design patterns makes it easier to explain and reuse such solutions.

Memoization

When you write in the functional style, most of the functions you write will be pure, meaning that for the same input they will always produce the same output. However, if you call the same pure function many times, it can be a waste of resources to recompute known values. Instead, it would be more efficient to store those values in a `Dictionary<_,_>` type that maps input values to function results.

The process of storing known input/result pairs of a function is known as *memoization*, and can be done automatically by taking advantage of higher-order functions and closures in F#.

Example 7-23 defines a `memoize` function, which takes a function as a parameter and returns a memoized version of that function as its result. The memoized version stores a dictionary of previous results in its closure, and calls the provided function only when necessary.

Example 7-23. Memoizing pure functions

```
open System.Collections.Generic

let memoize (f : 'a -> 'b) =
    let dict = new Dictionary<'a, 'b>()

    let memoizedFunc (input : 'a) =
        match dict.TryGetValue(input) with
        | true,  x -> x
        | false, _ ->
            // Evaluate and add to lookup table
            let answer = f input
            dict.Add(input, answer)
            answer

    // Return our memoized version of f dict is captured in the closure
    memoizedFunc
```

The following FSI session shows the `memoize` function in action. The function `f` simply waits a given number of seconds, and calling the function twice with the same input will cause it to wait twice. Calling the memoized version will simply look up the cached value the second time, so the function doesn't need to actually be evaluated:

```
> // Some long running function...
let f x =
    // Sleep for x seconds
    System.Threading.Thread.Sleep(x * 1000)
    // Return x
    x;;

val f : int -> int

> // Benchmark
#time;;

--> Timing now on

> f 10;;
Real: 00:00:10.007, CPU: 00:00:00.000, GC gen0: 0, gen1: 0, gen2: 0
val it : int = 10
> f 10;;
Real: 00:00:10.008, CPU: 00:00:00.000, GC gen0: 0, gen1: 0, gen2: 0
val it : int = 10
> let memoizedF = memoize f;;
Real: 00:00:00.004, CPU: 00:00:00.000, GC gen0: 0, gen1: 0, gen2: 0

val memoizedF : (int -> int)

> memoizedF 10;;
Real: 00:00:10.009, CPU: 00:00:00.000, GC gen0: 0, gen1: 0, gen2: 0
val it : int = 10
> memoizedF 10;;
Real: 00:00:00.000, CPU: 00:00:00.000, GC gen0: 0, gen1: 0, gen2: 0
val it : int = 10
```

Memoizing recursive functions

Memoizing recursive functions can be a bit more tricky. In Example 7-23, the function memoize took a function f and returned a new function that checked whether the value of f had already been computed for a given input. However, what if in its evaluation f calls itself? Unfortunately, it will call the non-memoized version—which eliminates any benefits of memoization. Memoization will only occur for the first input value to the function; it will not check for memoized values for any recursive calls.

The correct thing to do is have any recursive calls to the function be through the memoized version. If you think about it, this shouldn't work, because the memoized function needs to be called before the memoized function is even finished being defined! Fortunately, the F# compiler does the extra work to make it happen, albeit with a warning.

Example 7-24 shows an FSI session illustrating both the correct and incorrect ways of memoizing the fib function. Notice how the function fib in the definition of memFib2 calls memFib2 (the memoized function) instead of recursively calling itself.

Example 7-24. Memoization of recursive functions

```
> // WRONG way to memoize the function - fib doesn't call the
// memoized version recursively.
let wrongMemFib =
    let rec fib x =
        match x with
        | 0 | 1 -> 1
        | 2 -> 2
        | n -> fib (n - 1) + fib (n - 2)

    memoize fib;;

val wrongMemFib : (int -> int)

> // CORRECT way to memoize the function - fib  does call
// the memoized version recursively.
let rec rightMemFib =
    let fib x =
        match x with
        | 0 | 1 -> 1
        | 2 -> 2
        | n -> rightMemFib (n - 1) + rightMemFib (n - 2)

    memoize fib;;

val rightMemFib : (int -> int)

> #time;;

--> Timing now on

> wrongMemFib 45;;
Real: 00:00:21.553, CPU: 00:00:21.528, GC gen0: 0, gen1: 0, gen2: 0
val it : int = 1836311903
> rightMemFib 45;;
Real: 00:00:00.001, CPU: 00:00:00.000, GC gen0: 0, gen1: 0, gen2: 0
val it : int = 1836311903
```

Mutable Function Values

Function values provide a simple way to pass around the implementation of a function. However, a function value can also be mutable, allowing you to easily swap out the *implementation* of a function. Much in the same way that a mutable integer allows you to update its value, a mutable function can be updated as well.

Example 7-25 shows how you can change out the implementation of the generate Widget function on the fly. This allows customization of implementation without resorting to heavyweight solutions like polymorphism and inheritance.

In the example, the generateWidget function is initialized to generate Sprockets. However, once the generateWidget function is updated, subsequent calls will generate Cogs.

Example 7-25. Using mutable function values

```
> // Code to produce Widgets, the backbone of all .NET applications
type Widget =
    | Sprocket of string * int
    | Cog of string * float

let mutable generateWidget =
    let count = ref 0
    (fun () -> incr count
                Sprocket("Model A1", !count));;

type Widget =
    | Sprocket of string * int
    | Cog of string * float
val mutable generateWidget : (unit -> Widget)

> // Produce a Widget
generateWidget();;
val it : Widget = Sprocket ("Model A1",1)
> // ... and another
generateWidget();;
val it : Widget = Sprocket ("Model A1",2)
> // Now update the function...
generateWidget <-
    let count = ref 0
    (fun () -> incr count
                Cog( (sprintf "Version 0x%x" !count), 0.0));;
val it : unit = ()
> // Produce another Widget - with the updated function
generateWidget();;
val it : Widget = Cog ("Version 0x1",0.0)
> generateWidget();;
val it : Widget = Cog ("Version 0x2",0.0)
```

To be clear, calling a function when you aren't 100% sure what it does can lead to heinous bugs. But being able to change the implementation of a function can be very helpful in certain situations.

Lazy Programming

I mentioned lazy programming briefly in Chapter 3, but it is a style in and of itself. In short, lazy programming means computing values only when needed—as opposed to *eagerly*, which is as soon as they are declared.

Lazy programming can have a few distinct advantages if used correctly.

Reducing memory usage

Earlier we looked at continuations as a way of making operations on a binary tree tail-recursive. But even if you didn't need to worry about overflowing the stack, for very large trees those operations can take a long time to compute. What if you wanted to map a function to every node in a tree with a million elements? Moreover, what if you only needed to access a small subset of the resulting nodes? If you lazily evaluated the map operation, you would only compute the values you need.

Example 7-26 defines a binary tree where the nodes are evaluated lazily. So in the implementation of map, the function f is applied to the child nodes only once their evaluation has been forced (by accessing the Value property).

Defining the map operation in this way, the input tree isn't duplicated. Instead, new nodes are only created as they are accessed. So for very large trees that are minimally inspected, using lazy programming can lead to a dramatic savings in memory usage.

Example 7-26. Lazy type

```
type LazyBinTree<'a> =
    | Node of 'a * LazyBinTree<'a> Lazy * LazyBinTree<'a> Lazy
    | Empty

let rec map f tree =
    match tree with
    | Empty -> Empty
    | Node(x, l, r) ->
        Node(
            f x,
            lazy (
                let lfNode = l.Value
                map f lfNode),
            lazy (
                let rtNode = r.Value
                map f rtNode)
        )
```

Abstracting data access

Another example of lazy programming is abstracting data access. Example 7-27 loads an entire directory full of comma-separated-value (CSV) files and returns the data as a single sequence of string arrays. However, the files aren't actually opened and accessed until necessary, so while on the surface the result of processFile looks to be a constant sequence of data, it is in fact opening and closing separate files behind the scenes. With Seq.map and Seq.concat, the file provided to processFile isn't opened until the actual sequence elements are required. Or put another way, the sequences are produced lazily.

Example 7-27. Lazy programming for processing CSV files

```
open System
open System.IO

let processFile (filePath : string) =
    seq {
        use fileReader = new StreamReader(filePath)
```

```
        // Skip header row
        fileReader.ReadLine() |> ignore

        while not fileReader.EndOfStream do
            let line = fileReader.ReadLine()
            yield line.Split( [| ',' |] )
    }

let rootPath = @"D:\DataFiles\"
let csvFiles = Directory.GetFiles(rootPath, "*.csv")

let allCsvData =
    csvFiles
    |> Seq.map processFile
    |> Seq.concat
```

CHAPTER 8

Applied Object-Oriented Programming

This chapter could also be called *Being Functional in an Object-Oriented World*. By now, you've mastered the F# syntax and style, but there is still plenty to be said about using F# in the object-oriented landscape of the .NET platform.

In this chapter, you will learn how to create F# types that integrate better with other object-oriented languages like C# when consumed: for example, adding operator over-loading to allow your types to be used with symbolic code as well as adding events to your code to allow consumers to receive notifications when certain actions occur. This not only enables you to be more expressive in your F# code, but it also reduces the friction with non-F# developers when sharing your code.

Operators

Using a symbolic notation for manipulating objects can simplify your code by elimi-nating the need to call methods like **Add** and **Remove**, instead using more intuitive coun-terparts like + and -. Also, if an object represents a collection of data, being able to index directly into it with the .[ ] or .[*expr .. expr*] notation can make it much easier to access the data an object holds.

Operator Overloading

Operator overloading is a term used for adding new meaning to an existing operator, like + or -. Instead of only working on primitive types, you can *overload* those operators to accept custom types you create. Operator overloading in F# can be done by simply adding a static method to a type. After that, you can use the operator as if it natively supported the type. The F# compiler will simply translate the code into a call to your static method.

 When overloading operators, be sure to use a semantic that makes sense based on the operator. For example, overloading + for a custom type shouldn't subtract values or remove items from a collection.

When you overload an operator, the operator's name must be in parentheses, for example (+) to overload the plus operator. To overload a unary operator, simply prefix the operator with a tilde ~.

Example 8-1 overloads the + and - operators to represent operators on a bottle. Note the ~- operator allows for unary negation.

Example 8-1. Operator overloading

```
[<Measure>]
type ml

type Bottle(capacity : float<ml>) =

    new() = new Bottle(0.0<ml>)

    member this.Volume = capacity

    static member (+) ((lhs : Bottle), rhs) =
        new Bottle(lhs.Volume + rhs)

    static member (-) ((lhs : Bottle), rhs) =
        new Bottle(lhs.Volume - rhs)

    static member (~-) (rhs : Bottle) =
        new Bottle(rhs.Volume * -1.0<1>)

    override this.ToString() =
        sprintf "Bottle(%.1fml)" (float capacity)
```

Once the proper operators have been added, then you can intuitively use the class using the standard symbolic operators you would expect. (Well, a bottle really can't have a negative volume, but you get the idea.)

```
> let half = new Bottle(500.0<ml>);;

val half : Bottle = Bottle(500.0ml)

> half + 500.0<ml>;;
val it : Bottle = Bottle(1000.0ml) {Volume = 1000.0;}
> half - 500.0<ml>;;
val it : Bottle = Bottle(0.0ml) {Volume = 0.0;}
> -half;;
val it : Bottle = Bottle(-500.0ml) {Volume = -500.0;}
```

You can also add overloaded operators to discriminated unions and record types in the same way as they are added to class types:

```
type Person =
    | Boy of string
    | Girl of string
    | Couple of Person * Person
    static member (+) (lhs, rhs) =
        match lhs, rhs with
        | Couple(_), _
```

```
    | _, Couple(_)
        -> failwith "Three's a crowd!"
    | _ -> Couple(lhs, rhs)
```

Using the + operator, we can now take two `Person` objects and convert them into a `Couple` union case:

```
Boy("Dick") + Girl("Jane");;
val it : Person = Couple (Boy "Dick",Girl "Jane")
```

 F# allows you to define arbitrary symbolic operators for types; however, only a subset of these can be used natively with C# and VB.NET. Only the following operators are recognized by those languages:

Binary operators:

```
+, -, *, /, %, &, |, <<, >>
+=, -=, *=, /=, %=
```

Unary operators:

```
~+, ~-, ~!, ~++, ~--
```

Otherwise the method will be exposed as a friendly name describing the symbols used. For example, overloading operator +-+ will be exposed as a static method named `op_PlusMinusPlus`.

Indexers

For types that are a collection of values, an indexer is a natural way to extend the metaphor by enabling developers to index directly into the object. For example, you can get an arbitrary element of an array by using the .[ ] operator.

In F#, you can add an indexer by simply adding a property named `Item`. This property will be evaluated whenever you call the .[ ] method on the class.

Example 8-2 creates a class `Year` and adds an indexer to allow you to look up the *n*th day of the year.

Example 8-2. Adding an indexer to a class

```
open System

type Year(year : int) =

    member this.Item (idx : int) =
        if idx < 1 || idx > 365 then
            failwith "Invalid day range"

        let dateStr = sprintf "1-1-%d" year
        DateTime.Parse(dateStr).AddDays(float (idx - 1))
```

The following FSI session shows using the indexer for type `Year`:

```
> // Using a custom indexer
let eightyTwo   = new Year(1982)
let specialDay = eightyTwo.[171];;

val eightyTwo : Year
val specialDay : DateTime = 6/20/1982 12:00:00 AM

> specialDay.Month, specialDay.Day, specialDay.DayOfWeek;;
val it : int * int * DayOfWeek = (6, 20, Sunday)
```

But what if you want to not only read values from an indexer, but write them back as well? Also, what if you wanted the indexer to accept a non-integer parameter? The F# language can accommodate both of those requests.

Example 8-3 defines an indexer for a type that accepts a non-integer parameter. In a different take on the `Year` class example, the indexer takes a month and date tuple.

Example 8-3. Non-integer indexer

```
type Year2(year : int) =

    member this.Item (month : string, day : int) =
        let monthIdx =
            match month.ToUpper() with
            | "JANUARY" -> 1  | "FEBRUARY" -> 2  | "MARCH"     -> 3
            | "APRIL"   -> 4  | "MAY"      -> 5  | "JUNE"      -> 6
            | "JULY"    -> 7  | "AUGUST"   -> 8  | "SEPTEMBER" -> 9
            | "OCTOBER" -> 10 | "NOVEMBER" -> 11 | "DECEMBER"  -> 12
            | _ -> failwithf "Invalid month [%s]" month

        let dateStr = sprintf "1-1-%d" year
        DateTime.Parse(dateStr).AddMonths(monthIdx - 1).AddDays(float (day - 1))
```

`Year2` uses a more intuitive indexer that makes the type easier to use:

```
> // Using a non-integer index
let O'seven = new Year2(2007)
let randomDay = O'seven.["April", 7];;

val O'seven : Year2
val randomDay : DateTime = 4/7/2007 12:00:00 AM

> randomDay.Month, randomDay.Day, randomDay.DayOfWeek;;
val it : int * int * DayOfWeek = (4, 7, Saturday)
```

The read-only indexers you've seen so far aren't ideal for every situation. What if you wanted to provide a read/write indexer to not only access elements but also update their values? To make a read/write indexer, simply add an explicit getter and setter to the `Item` property.

Example 8-4 defines a type `WordBuilder` that allows you to access and update letters of a word at a given index.

Example 8-4. Read/write indexer

```
open System.Collections.Generic

type WordBuilder(startingLetters : string) =
    let m_letters = new List<char>(startingLetters)

    member this.Item
        with get idx   = m_letters.[idx]
        and  set idx c = m_letters.[idx] <- c

    member this.Word = new string (m_letters.ToArray())
```

The syntax for writing a new value using the indexer is the same as updating a value in an array:

```
> let wb = new WordBuilder("Jurassic Park");;

val wb : WordBuilder

> wb.Word;;
val it : string = "Jurassic Park"
> wb.[10];;
val it : char = 'a'
> wb.[10] <- 'o';;
val it : unit = ()
> wb.Word;;
val it : string = "Jurassic Pork"
```

Adding Slices

Similar to indexers, slices allow you to index into a type that represents a collection of data. The main difference is that where an indexer returns a single element, a slice produces a new collection of data. Slices work by providing syntax support for providing an optional lower bound and an optional upper bound for an indexer.

To add a one-dimensional slice, add a method named `GetSlice` that takes two option types as parameters. Example 8-5 defines a slice for a type called `TextBlock` where the slice returns a range of words in the body of the text.

Example 8-5. Providing a slice to a class

```
type TextBlock(text : string) =
    let words = text.Split([| ' ' |])

    member this.AverageWordLength =
        words |> Array.map float |> Array.average

    member this.GetSlice(lowerBound : int option, upperBound : int option) =
        let words =
            match lowerBound, upperBound with
            // Specify both upper and lower bounds
            | Some(lb), Some(ub) -> words.[lb..ub]
            // Just one bound specified
```

```
        | Some(lb), None     -> words.[lb..]
        | None,    Some(ub) -> words.[..ub]
        // No lower or upper bounds
        | None,      None -> words.[*]
    words
```

Using our `TextBlock`, class we can see:

```
> // Using a custom slice operator
let text = "The quick brown fox jumped over the lazy dog"
let tb = new TextBlock(text);;

val text : string = "The quick brown fox jumped over the lazy dog"
val tb : TextBlock

> tb.[..5];;
val it : string [] = [|"The"; "quick"; "brown"; "fox"; "jumped"; "over"|]
> tb.[4..7];;
val it : string [] = [|"jumped"; "over"; "the"; "lazy"|]
```

If you need a more refined way to slice your data, you can provide a two-dimensional slicer. This allows you to specify two ranges of data. To define a two-dimensional slice, simply add a method called `GetSlice` again, except that the method should now take four option-type parameters. In order, they are first dimension lower bound, first dimension upper bound, second dimension lower bound, and second dimension upper bound.

Example 8-6 defines a class that encapsulates a sequence of data points. The type provides a 2D slice that returns only those points within the given range.

Example 8-6. Defining a two-dimensional slice

```
open System

type DataPoints(points : seq<float * float>) =
    member this.GetSlice(xlb, xub, ylb, yub) =

        let getValue optType defaultValue =
            match optType with
            | Some(x) -> x
            | None    -> defaultValue

        let minX = getValue xlb Double.MinValue
        let maxX = getValue xub Double.MaxValue

        let minY = getValue ylb Double.MinValue
        let maxY = getValue yub Double.MaxValue

        // Return if a given tuple representing a point is within range
        let inRange (x, y) =
            (minX < x && x < maxX &&
             minY < y && y < maxY)

        Seq.filter inRange points
```

The following FSI session shows the 2D slice in action. The slice allows you to get data points that fall only within a specific range, allowing you to isolate certain sections for further analysis:

```
> // Define 1,000 random points with value between 0.0 to 1.0
let points =
  seq {
      let rng = new Random()
      for i = 0 to 1000 do
          let x = rng.NextDouble()
          let y = rng.NextDouble()
          yield (x, y)
  };;

val points : seq<float * float>

> points;;
val it : seq<float * float> =
  seq
    [(0.6313018304, 0.8639167859); (0.3367836328, 0.8642307673);
     (0.7682324386, 0.1454097885); (0.6862907925, 0.8801649925); ...]

> let d = new DataPoints(points);;

val d : DataPoints

> // Get all values where the x and y values are greater than 0.5.
d.[0.5.., 0.5..];;

val it : seq<float * float> =
  seq
    [(0.7774719744, 0.8764193784); (0.927527673, 0.6275711235);
     (0.5618227448, 0.5956258004); (0.9415076491, 0.8703156262); ...]
> // Get all values where the x-value is between 0.90 and 0.99,
// with no restriction on the y-value.
d.[0.90 .. 0.99, *];;

val it : seq<float * float> =
  seq
    [(0.9286256581, 0.08974070246); (0.9780231351, 0.5617941956);
     (0.9649922103, 0.1342076446); (0.9498346559, 0.2927135142); ...]
```

Slices provide an expressive syntax for extracting data from types. However, you cannot add a slice notation for a type higher than two dimensions.

Generic Type Constraints

Adding generic type parameters to a class declaration enables the type to be used in conjunction with any other type. However, what if you want the class to actually *do* something with that generic type? Not just hold a reference to an instance 'a, but do something meaningful with 'a as well. Because 'a could be anything, you would appear to be out of luck.

Fortunately, you can add a *generic type constraint*, which will enable you still to have the class be generic but put a restriction on the types it accepts. For example, you can force the generic class to only accept types that implement a specific interface. This allows you to restrict which types can be used as generic type parameters so that you can do more with those generic types.

A generic type constraint is simply a form of type annotation. Whenever you would have written a generic type 'a, you can add type constraints using the when keyword.

Example 8-7 defines a generic class GreaterThanList where the type parameter must also implement the IComparable interface. This allows instances of the generic type to be cast to the IComparable interface, and ultimately enables items to be checked if they are greater than the first element in the list.

Example 8-7. Generic type constraints

```
open System
open System.Collections.Generic

exception NotGreaterThanHead

/// Keep a list of items where each item added to it is
/// greater than the first element of the list.
type GreaterThanList< 'a when 'a :> IComparable<'a> >(minValue : 'a) =

    let m_head = minValue

    let m_list = new List<'a>()
    do m_list.Add(minValue)


    member this.Add(newItem : 'a) =
        // Casting to IComparable wouldn't be possible
        // if 'a weren't constrainted
        let ic = newItem :> IComparable<'a>

        if ic.CompareTo(m_head) >= 0 then
            m_list.Add(newItem)
        else
            raise NotGreaterThanHead

    member this.Items = m_list :> seq<'a>
```

There are six ways to constrain types in F# and using multiple type constraints allows you to refine a type parameter. To combine multiple type constraints, simply use the and keyword:

```
open System

let compareWithNew (x : 'a when 'a : (new : unit -> 'a) and
                        'a :> IComparable<'a>) =
```

```
// Creating new instance of 'a because the type constraint enforces
// there be a valid constructor.
let clone = new 'a()

// Comparing x with a new instance, because we know 'a implements IComparable
let ic = x :> IComparable<'a>
ic.CompareTo(clone)
```

Subtype constraint

The subtype constraint enforces that the generic type parameter must match or be a subtype of a given type. (This also applies to implementing interfaces.) This allows you to cast 'a as a known type. The syntax for a subtype constraint is as follows:

```
'a :> type
```

Default constructor constraint

The default constructor constraint enforces that the type parameter must have a default (parameter-less) constructor. This allows you to instantiate new instances of the generic type. The syntax for a default constructor constraint is as follows:

```
'a : (new : unit -> 'a)
```

Delegate constraint

The delegate constraint requires that the type argument must be a delegate type, with the given signature and return type. (Delegates will be covered in the next section.) The syntax for defining a delegate constraint is as follows:

```
'a : delegate<tupled-args, return-type>
```

Struct constraint

The struct constraint enforces that the type argument must be a value type. The syntax for the struct constraint is as follows:

```
'a : struct
```

Reference constraint

The reference constraint enforces that the type argument must be a reference type. The syntax for the reference constraint is as follows:

```
'a : not struct
```

Enumeration constraint

With the enumeration constraint the type argument must be an enumeration type whose underlying type must be of the given base type (such as `int`). The syntax for the enumeration constraint is as follows:

```
'a : enum<basetype>
```

In addition, F# defines `comparison` and `equality` constraints. But in practice, they are seldom required or even needed.

Delegates and Events

So far the classes and types we have created have been useful, but they needed to be acted upon in order for something to happen. However, it would be beneficial if types could be *proactive* instead of *reactive*. That is, you want types that act upon others, and not the other way around.

Consider Example 8-8, which defines a type `CoffeeCup` that lets interested parties know when the cup is empty. This is helpful in case you want to automatically get a refill and avoid missing out on a tasty cup of joe. This is done by keeping track of a list of functions to call when the cup is eventually empty.

Example 8-8. Creating proactive types

```
open System.Collections.Generic

[<Measure>]
type ml

type CoffeeCup(amount : float<ml>) =
    let mutable m_amountLeft = amount
    let mutable m_interestedParties = List<(CoffeeCup -> unit)>()

    member this.Drink(amount) =
        printfn "Drinking %.1f..." (float amount)
        m_amountLeft <- min (m_amountLeft - amount) 0.0<ml>
        if m_amountLeft <= 0.0<ml> then
            this.LetPeopleKnowI'mEmpty()

    member this.Refil(amountAdded) =
        printfn "Coffee Cup refilled with %.1f" (float amountAdded)
        m_amountLeft <- m_amountLeft + amountAdded

    member this.WhenYou'reEmptyCall(func) =
        m_interestedParties.Add(func)

    member private this.LetPeopleKnowI'mEmpty() =
        printfn "Uh oh, I'm empty! Letting people know..."
        for interestedParty in m_interestedParties do
            interestedParty(this)
```

When used in an FSI session, the following transpires after a refreshing cup of coffee has been emptied:

```
> let cup = new CoffeeCup(100.0<ml>);;

val cup : CoffeeCup

> // Be notified when the cup is empty
cup.WhenYou'reEmptyCall(
    (fun cup ->
        printfn "Thanks for letting me know..."
        cup.Refil(50.0<ml>) ));;
```

```
val it : unit = ()

> cup.Drink(75.0<ml>);;

Drinking 75.0...
val it : unit = ()

> cup.Drink(75.0<ml>);;
Drinking 75.0...
Uh oh, I'm empty! Letting people know...
Thanks for letting me know...
Coffee Cup refilled with 50.0
val it : unit = ()
```

Abstractly, we can describe the CoffeeCup class as a pattern enabling *consumers*—people who have an instance of the class—to subscribe to an *event*—when the cup is empty. This turns out to be very useful, and makes up the foundation of most graphical programming environments (so-called event-driven programming). For example, windowing systems allow you to provide functions to be called when a button is clicked or when a check box is toggled. However, our custom implementation of keeping a list of function values is clunky at best.

Fortunately, the .NET framework has rich support for this pattern through the use of *delegates* and *event-driven programming*. A *delegate* is very similar to F#'s function values. An *event* is simply the mechanism for calling the functions provided by all interested parties.

When used together, delegates and events form a contract. The first class *publishes* an event, which enables other classes to *subscribe* to that event. When the class's event is fired, the delegates provided by all subscribers are executed.

Delegates can be thought of as an alternate form of function values. They represent a function pointer to a method and can be passed around as parameters or called directly, just like function values. Delegates, however, offer a couple of advantages over the F# functions you are used to, as we will see shortly.

Defining Delegates

To define a delegate, simply use the following syntax. The first type represents the parameters passed to the delegate, and the second type is the return type of the delegate when called:

```
type ident = delegate of type1 -> type2
```

Example 8-9 shows how to create a simple delegate and how similar it is to a regular function value. Notice how to instantiate a delegate type you use the new keyword and pass the body of the delegate in as a parameter, whereas to execute a delegate you must call its Invoke method.

Example 8-9. Defining and using delegates

```
let functionValue x y =
    printfn "x = %d, y = %d" x y
    x + y

// Defining a delegate
type DelegateType = delegate of int * int -> int

// Construct a delegate value
let delegateValue1 =
    new DelegateType(
        fun x y ->
            printfn "x = %d, y = %d" x y
            x + y
    )

// Calling function values and delegates
let functionResult = functionValue 1 2
let delegateResult = delegateValue1.Invoke(1, 2)
```

F# has a bit of magic that eliminates the need for instantiating some delegate types. If a class member takes a delegate as a parameter, rather than passing an instance of that delegate type you can pass in a lambda expression, provided it has the same signature as the delegate.

The following code snippet defines a delegate `IntDelegate` and a class method `Apply Delegate`. `ApplyDelegate` is called twice, the first time using an explicit instance of `IntDelegate`, and again using an implicit instance. The lambda expression provided would create a valid instance of `IntDelegate` and so the F# compiler creates one behind the scenes.

This dramatically cleans up F# code that interacts with .NET components that expect delegates, such as the Parallel Extensions to the .NET Framework, which we'll discuss in Chapter 11:

```
type IntDelegate = delegate of int -> unit

type ListHelper =
    /// Invokes a delegate for every element of a list
    static member ApplyDelegate (l : int list, d : IntDelegate) =
        l |> List.iter (fun x -> d.Invoke(x))

// Explicitly constructing the delegate
ListHelper.ApplyDelegate([1 .. 10], new IntDelegate(fun x -> printfn "%d" x))

// Implicitly constructing the delegate
ListHelper.ApplyDelegate([1 .. 10], (fun x -> printfn "%d" x))
```

Combining Delegates

While delegates are very similar to function values, there are two key differences. First, delegates can be combined. Combining multiple delegates together allows you to execute multiple functions with a single call to `Invoke`. Delegates are coalesced by calling the `Combine` and `Remove` static methods on the `System.Delegate` type, the base class for all delegates.

Example 8-10 shows combining delegates so that a single call to `Invoke` will execute multiple delegates at once.

Example 8-10. Combining delegates

```
open System.IO

type LogMessage = delegate of string -> unit

let printToConsole =
    LogMessage(fun msg -> printfn "Logging to console: %s..." msg)

let appendToLogFile =
    LogMessage(fun msg -> printfn "Logging to file: %s..." msg
                          use file = new StreamWriter("Log.txt", true)
                          file.WriteLine(msg))

let doBoth = LogMessage.Combine(printToConsole, appendToLogFile)
let typedDoBoth = doBoth :?> LogMessage
```

The following is the output from the FSI session. Invoking the `typedDoBoth` delegate executes both the `printToConsole` delegate and the `appendToLogFile` delegate. F# function values cannot be combined in this way.

```
> typedDoBoth.Invoke("[some important message]");;
Logging to console: [some important message]...
Logging to file: [some important message]...
val it : unit = ()
```

The second main difference between delegate types and function values is that you can invoke a delegate asynchronously, so the delegate's execution will happen on a separate thread and your program will continue as normal. To invoke a delegate asynchronously, call the `BeginInvoke` and `EndInvoke` methods.

Unfortunately, delegates created in F# do not have the `BeginInvoke` and `EndInvoke` methods, so to create delegates that can be invoked asynchronously, you must define them in VB.NET or C#. In Chapter 11, we will look at parallel and asynchronous programming in F# and simple ways to work around this.

Events

Now that you understand delegates, let's look at how to take advantage of them to create events. Events are just syntactic sugar for properties on classes that are delegates. So when an event is raised, it is really just invoking the combined delegates associated with the event.

Creating Events

Let's start with a simple example and work backward from that. Unlike C# or VB.NET, there is no event keyword in F#.

Example 8-11 creates a NoisySet type that fires events whenever items are added and removed from the set. Rather than keeping track of event subscribers manually, it uses the Event<'Del, 'Arg> type, which will be discussed shortly.

Example 8-11. Events and the Event<_,_> type

```
type SetAction = Added | Removed

type SetOperationEventArgs<'a>(value : 'a, action : SetAction) =
    inherit System.EventArgs()

    member this.Action = action
    member this.Value = value

type SetOperationDelegate<'a> = delegate of obj * SetOperationEventArgs<'a> -> unit

// Contains a set of items that fires events whenever
// items are added.
type NoisySet<'a when 'a : comparison>() =
    let mutable m_set = Set.empty : Set<'a>

    let m_itemAdded =
        new Event<SetOperationDelegate<'a>, SetOperationEventArgs<'a>>()

    let m_itemRemoved =
        new Event<SetOperationDelegate<'a>, SetOperationEventArgs<'a>>()

    member this.Add(x) =
        m_set <- m_set.Add(x)
        // Fire the 'Add' event
        m_itemAdded.Trigger(this, new SetOperationEventArgs<_>(x, Added))

    member this.Remove(x) =
        m_set <- m_set.Remove(x)
        // Fire the 'Remove' event
        m_itemRemoved.Trigger(this, new SetOperationEventArgs<_>(x, Removed))

    // Publish the events so others can subscribe to them
    member this.ItemAddedEvent   = m_itemAdded.Publish
    member this.ItemRemovedEvent = m_itemRemoved.Publish
```

Delegates for events

The first thing to point out in the example is the delegate used for the event. In .NET, the idiomatic way to declare events is to have the delegate return unit and take two parameters. The first parameter is the source, or object raising the event; the second parameter is the delegate's arguments passed in an object derived from System.EventArgs.

In the example, the SetOperationEventArgs type stores all relevant information for the event, such as the value of the item being added or removed. Many events, however, are raised without needing to send any additional information, in which case, the EventArgs class is not inherited from.

Creating and raising the event

Once the delegate has been defined for the event, the next step is to actually create the event. In F#, this is done by creating a new instance of the Event<_,_> type:

```
let m_itemAdded =
        new Event<SetOperationDelegate<'a>, SetOperationEventArgs<'a>>()
```

We will cover the Event<_,_> type shortly, but note that whenever you want to raise the event or add subscribers to it, you must use that type. Raising the event is done by calling the Trigger method, which takes the parameters to the delegates to be called:

```
// Fire the 'Add' event
m_itemAdded.Trigger(this, new SetOperationEventArgs<_>(x, Added))
```

Subscribing to events

Finally, to subscribe to a class's events, use the AddHandler method on the event property. From then on, whenever the event is raised, the delegate you passed to AddHandler will be called. If you no longer want your event handler to be called, call the RemoveHandler method.

> Be sure to remove an event handler when an object no longer needs to subscribe to an event. Or, the event raiser will still have a reference to the object and will prevent the subscriber from being garbage collected.

Example 8-12 shows the NoisySet<_> type in action.

Example 8-12. Adding and removing event handlers

```
> // Using events
let s = new NoisySet<int>()

let setOperationHandler =
    new SetOperationDelegate<int>(
        fun sender args ->
            printfn "%d was %A" args.Value args.Action
    )
```

```
s.ItemAddedEvent.AddHandler(setOperationHandler)
s.ItemRemovedEvent.AddHandler(setOperationHandler);;

val s : NoisySet<int>
val setOperationHandler : SetOperationDelegate<int>

> s.Add(9);;
9 was Added
val it : unit = ()
> s.Remove(9);;
9 was Removed
val it : unit = ()
```

As you can see from Example 8-12, all the work of combining delegates and eventually raising the event was handled by the Event<'Del, 'Arg> class. But what is it exactly? And why does it need two generic parameters?

The Event<_,_> Class

The Event<'Del, 'Arg> type keeps track of the delegates associated with the event, and makes it easier to fire and publish an event. The type takes two generic parameters. The first is the type of delegate associated with the event, which in the previous example was SetOperationDelegate. The second generic parameter is the type of the delegate's argument, which was SetOperationEventArgs. (Note that this ignores the delegate's actual first parameter, the sender object.)

If your events don't follow this pattern where the first parameter is the sender object, then you should use the DelegateEvent<'del> type instead. It is used the same way, except that its arguments are passed in as an obj array.

Example 8-13 defines a clock type with a single event that gets fired every second, notifying subscribers of the current hour, minute, and second. Note that in order to trigger an event with type DelegateEvent<_>, you must pass in an obj array for all of its parameters. As a reminder, the box function converts its parameter to type obj.

Example 8-13. The DelegateEvent type

```
open System

type ClockUpdateDelegate = delegate of int * int * int -> unit

type Clock() =

    let m_event = new DelegateEvent<ClockUpdateDelegate>()

    member this.Start() =
        printfn "Started..."
        while true do
            // Sleep one second...
            Threading.Thread.Sleep(1000)
```

```
let hour   = DateTime.Now.Hour
let minute = DateTime.Now.Minute
let second = DateTime.Now.Second

m_event.Trigger( [| box hour; box minute; box second |] )

member this.ClockUpdate = m_event.Publish
```

When finally run, Example 8-13 produces the following output:

```
> // Non-standard event types
let c = new Clock();;

val c : Clock

> // Adding an event handler
c.ClockUpdate.AddHandler(
    new ClockUpdateDelegate(
        fun h m s -> printfn "[%d:%d:%d]" h m s
    )
);;
val it : unit = ()

> c.Start();;
Started...
[14:48:27]
[14:48:28]
[14:48:29]
```

The Observable Module

Using events as a way to make class types proactive and notify others when particular events occur is helpful. However, events in F# don't have to be associated with a particular class, much as functions in F# don't have to be members of a particular class, either.

The `Observable` module defines a series of functions for creating instances of the `I Observable<_>` interface, which allows you to treat events as first-class citizens, much like objects and functions. So you can use functional programming techniques like composition and data transformation on events.

Example 8-14 defines a `JukeBox` type that raises an event whenever a new song is played. (The specifics of the mysterious `CLIEvent` attribute will be covered later.)

Example 8-14. Compositional events

```
[<Measure>]
type minute

[<Measure>]
type bpm = 1/minute

type MusicGenre = Classical | Pop | HipHop | Rock | Latin | Country
```

```
type Song = { Title : string; Genre : MusicGenre; BPM : int<bpm> }

type SongChangeArgs(title : string, genre : MusicGenre, bpm : int<bpm>) =
    inherit System.EventArgs()

    member this.Title = title
    member this.Genre = genre
    member this.BeatsPerMinute = bpm

type SongChangeDelegate = delegate of obj * SongChangeArgs -> unit

type JukeBox() =
    let m_songStartedEvent = new Event<SongChangeDelegate, SongChangeArgs>()

    member this.PlaySong(song) =
        m_songStartedEvent.Trigger(
            this,
            new SongChangeArgs(song.Title, song.Genre, song.BPM)
        )

    [<CLIEvent>]
    member this.SongStartedEvent = m_songStartedEvent.Publish
```

Rather than just adding event handlers directly to the JukeBox type, we can use the Observable module to create new, more specific event handlers. In Example 8-15, the Observable.filter and Observable.partition methods are used to create two new events, slowSongEvent and fastSongEvent, which will be raised whenever the JukeBox plays songs that meet a certain criterion.

The advantage is that you can take an existing event and transform it into new events, which can be passed around as values.

Example 8-15. Using the Event module

```
> // Use the Observable module to only subscribe to specific events
let jb = new JukeBox()

let fastSongEvent, slowSongEvent =
    jb.SongStartedEvent
    // Filter event to just dance music
    |> Observable.filter(fun songArgs ->
            match songArgs.Genre with
            | Pop | HipHop | Latin | Country -> true
            | _ -> false)
    // Split the event into 'fast song' and 'slow song'
    |> Observable.partition(fun songChangeArgs ->
            songChangeArgs.BeatsPerMinute >= 120<bpm>);;

val jb : JukeBox
val slowSongEvent : IObservable<SongChangeArgs>
val fastSongEvent : IObservable<SongChangeArgs>
```

```
> // Add event handlers to the IObservable event
slowSongEvent.Add(fun args -> printfn
                               "You hear '%s' and start to dance slowly..."
                               args.Title)

fastSongEvent.Add(fun args -> printfn
                               "You hear '%s' and start to dance fast!"
                               args.Title);;
> jb.PlaySong( { Title = "Burnin Love"; Genre = Pop; BPM = 120<bpm> } );;
You hear 'Burnin Love' and start to dance fast!
val it : unit = ()
```

However, `Observable.filter` and `Observable.partition` are not the only useful methods in the module.

Observable.add

`Observable.add` simply subscribes to the event. Typically, this method is used at the end of a series of forward-pipe operations and is a cleaner way to subscribe to events than calling `AddHandler` on the event object.

`Observable.add` has the following signature:

```
val add : ('a -> unit) -> IObservable<'a> -> unit
```

Example 8-16 pops up a message box whenever the mouse moves into the bottom half of a form.

Example 8-16. Subscribing to events with Observable.add

```
open System.Windows.Forms

let form = new Form(Text="Keep out of the bottom!", TopMost=true)

form.MouseMove
|> Observable.filter (fun moveArgs -> moveArgs.Y > form.Height / 2)
|> Observable.add    (fun moveArgs -> MessageBox.Show("Moved into bottom half!")
                                      |> ignore)

form.ShowDialog()
```

Observable.merge

`Observable.merge` takes two input events and produces a single output event, which will be fired whenever either of its input events is raised.

`Observable.merge` has the following signature:

```
val merge: IObservable<'a> -> IObservable<'a> -> IObservable<'a>
```

This is useful when trying to combine and simplify events. For example, in the previous example, if a consumer didn't care about specifically dancing to slow or fast songs, both the song events could be combined into a single justDance event:

```
> // Combine two song events
let justDanceEvent = Observable.merge slowSongEvent fastSongEvent
justDanceEvent.Add(fun args -> printfn "You start dancing, regardless of tempo!");;

val justDanceEvent : System.IObservable<SongChangeArgs>

> // Queue up another song
jb.PlaySong(
    { Title = "Escape (The Pina Colada Song)"; Genre = Pop; BPM = 70<bpm> } );;
You hear 'Escape (The Pina Colada Song)' and start to dance slowly...
You start dancing, regardless of tempo!
val it : unit = ()
```

Observable.map

Sometimes when working with an event value, you want to transform it into some sort of function that is easier to work with. Observable.map allows you to convert an event with a given argument type into another. It has the following signature:

```
val map: ('a -> 'b) -> IObservable<'a> -> IObservable<'b>
```

When using Windows Forms, all mouse-click events are given in pixels relative to the top left of the form. So for a given form f the top left corner is at position (0, 0) and the bottom right corner is at position (f.Width, f.Height). Example 8-17 uses Event.map to create a new Click event that remaps the positions to points relative to the center of the form.

Example 8-17. Transforming event arguments with Event.map

```
> // Create the form
open System.Windows.Forms

let form = new Form(Text="Relative Clicking", TopMost=true)

form.MouseClick.AddHandler(
    new MouseEventHandler(
        fun sender clickArgs ->
            printfn "MouseClickEvent    @ [%d, %d]" clickArgs.X clickArgs.Y
    )
);;

val form : System.Windows.Forms.Form =
  System.Windows.Forms.Form, Text: Relative Clicking

> // Create a new click event relative to the center of the form
let centeredClickEvent =
    form.MouseClick
    |> Observable.map (fun clickArgs -> clickArgs.X - (form.Width  / 2),
                                        clickArgs.Y - (form.Height / 2))
```

```
// Subscribe
centeredClickEvent
|> Observable.add (fun (x, y) -> printfn "CenteredClickEvent @ [%d, %d]" x y);;

val centeredClickEvent : System.IObservable<int * int>

> // The output is from clicking the dialog twice, first in the
// top left corner and then in the center.
form.ShowDialog();;
MouseClickEvent      @ [4, 8]
CenteredClickEvent @ [-146, -142]
MouseClickEvent      @ [150, 123]
CenteredClickEvent @ [0, -27]
val it : DialogResult = Cancel
```

Using the `Observable` module enables you to think about events in much the same way as function values. This adds a great deal of expressiveness and enables you to do more with events in F# than you can in other .NET events.

Creating .NET Events

There is just one extra step for creating events in F#. To create an event in F# code, you simply need to create a property that returns an instance of the `IEvent<_, _>` interface. However, to create an event that can be used by other .NET languages, you must also add the `[<CLIEvent>]` attribute. This is just a hint to the F# compiler specifying how to generate the code for the class. To F# consumers of your code, the class will behave identically; however, to other .NET languages, rather than being a property of type `IEvent<_,_>`, there will be a proper .NET event in its place.

Example 8-18 revisits our coffee cup example, but rather than keeping an explicit list of functions to notify when the coffee cup is empty, a proper .NET event is used instead.

Example 8-18. Creating .NET-compatible events

```
open System

[<Measure>]
type ml

type EmptyCoffeeCupDelegate = delegate of obj * EventArgs ->  unit

type EventfulCoffeeCup(amount : float<ml>) =
    let mutable m_amountLeft = amount
    let m_emptyCupEvent = new Event<EmptyCoffeeCupDelegate, EventArgs>()

    member this.Drink(amount) =
        printfn "Drinking %.1f..." (float amount)
        m_amountLeft <- min (m_amountLeft - amount) 0.0<ml>
        if m_amountLeft <= 0.0<ml> then
            m_emptyCupEvent.Trigger(this, new EventArgs())
```

```
member this.Refil(amountAdded) =
    printfn "Coffee Cup refilled with %.1f" (float amountAdded)
    m_amountLeft <- m_amountLeft + amountAdded

[<CLIEvent>]
member this.EmptyCup = m_emptyCupEvent.Publish
```

PART II

Programming F#

CHAPTER 9

Scripting

In previous chapters, you saw how F# can be effective across programming paradigms. But F# is not only well suited for different *styles* of programming, it can also be effective for writing different *types* of programs as well. F# is not only useful for client applications but it can also be effective as a scripting language too.

Scripting is the general term used to describe programs that don't have a UI and are focused on solving a particular task. In most scripting languages, the script consists entirely of code—as opposed to an executable program—that is then interpreted by a runtime engine.

Programming in this mode typically sacrifices execution speed for the convenience of being able to easily modify and deploy the program. Rather than creating a complex solution designed to work everywhere, you can simply move a script from machine to machine and modify it as necessary.

While F# may be best suited for client application programming, using it in a scripting context has one major advantage: you already know it. Rather than learning a separate language for your scripts, employing F# for your scripting needs lets you reuse your existing code and knowledge about F# programming. Also, F# code is never interpreted; it is always compiled first. So F# can be comparatively faster than pure scripting languages.

If you have a simple problem and don't need a complicated interface, consider scripting the solution. In this chapter, you will learn about some constructs available to script files as well as see some recipes for creating useful F# scripts that you can put to good use right away.

F# Script Files

When F# is installed on a system, it registers *.fsx* files as *F# script* files. These are F# source files specifically designed to be easy to execute. Double-clicking on an F# script file will bring up Visual Studio to edit the script. Right-clicking on the file in Windows Explorer enables you to execute it directly by selecting the "Run with F# Interactive" context menu item, seen in Figure 9-1.

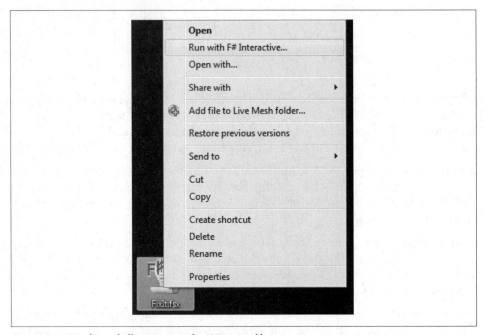

Figure 9-1. Windows shell integration for F# script files

Executing an F# script file simply sends the contents of the file to the console version of F# Interactive, `fsi.exe`.

F# script files behave just as if you had opened the code file within Visual Studio and sent it all directly to FSI. (In fact, that is exactly what happens.) The code will then be compiled and executed, performing whatever actions are in the script. In F# script files, you have full usage of the F# language and a few additional features to help make writing scripts easier.

Directives

The most noticeable difference between normal F# source files and F# script files is the usage of compiler directives. These are special hints and commands to the F# compiler.

General Directives

The following directives are available in any F# source program but are mostly applicable to F# scripts.

__SOURCE_DIRECTORY__

The Source Directory directive, available with __SOURCE_DIRECTORY__, returns the current directory of the executing code. This is especially helpful in scripts for determining where the script file is located. Any instance of __SOURCE_DIRECTORY__ will be replaced with a constant string as soon as the file is compiled:

```
C:\Program Files\Microsoft F#\v4.0>fsi.exe

Microsoft F# Interactive, (c) Microsoft Corporation, All Rights Reserved
F# Version 1.9.8.0, compiling for .NET Framework Version v4.0.20620

Please send bug reports to fsbugs@microsoft.com
For help type #help;;

> __SOURCE_DIRECTORY__;;
val it : string = "C:\Program Files\Microsoft F#\v4.0"
> #q;;

C:\Program Files\Microsoft F#\v4.0>
```

__SOURCE_FILE__

The __SOURCE_FILE__ directive returns the current filename. When you combine this directive with __SOURCE_DIRECTORY__, you can determine the actual script being executed.

Example 9-1 runs a script that prints the __SOURCE_FILE__ to the console. Like __SOURCE_DIRECTORY__, __SOURCE_FILE__ will be replaced with a string as soon as the file is compiled.

Example 9-1. Using __SOURCE_FILE__ and __SOURCE_DIRECTORY__

```
C:\Program Files\Microsoft F#\v4.0>type AweomestScriptEver.fsx
printfn "__SOURCE_DIRECTORY__ = %s" __SOURCE_DIRECTORY__
printfn "__SOURCE_FILE__      = %s" __SOURCE_FILE__

C:\Program Files\Microsoft F#\v4.0>fsi AweomestScriptEver.fsx
__SOURCE_DIRECTORY__ = C:\Program Files\Microsoft F#\v4.0
__SOURCE_FILE__      = AweomestScriptEver.fsx
```

F# Script-Specific Directives

The following directives are not available in regular F# source files. Rather, they are specifically designed to be used in F# script files to provide an experience as though they were single-file projects within Visual Studio. These directives are also available from within an FSI session in Visual Studio.

#r

The #r directive references an assembly. This allows your F# script file to reference types defined in a separate .NET assembly, perhaps written in another language, such as C#. The string passed to the #r directive can be as simple as the assembly's shortened file name or the full assembly name containing the name, version, culture, and so on.

Example 9-2 shows how to load the Windows Forms libraries to display a list of files located in the *Pictures* folder on a data grid.

Example 9-2. Loading assembly references in scripts

```
#r "System.Windows.Forms.dll"
#r "System.Drawing.dll"

open System
open System.IO
open System.Collections.Generic
open System.Drawing
open System.Windows.Forms

// val images : seq<string * System.Drawing.Image>
let images =
    let myPictures =
        Environment.GetFolderPath(Environment.SpecialFolder.MyPictures)

    Directory.GetFiles(myPictures, "*.JPG")
    |> Seq.map (fun filePath ->
            Path.GetFileName(filePath),
            Bitmap.FromFile(filePath))

// Create the data grid and put on a form
let dg = new DataGridView(Dock = DockStyle.Fill)
dg.DataSource <- new List<_>(images)

let f = new Form()
f.Controls.Add(dg)

f.ShowDialog()
```

 The order for reference resolution is:

1. The Include Path (discussed next)
2. The same directory as the script
3. The .NET Global Assembly Cache

#I

The #I directive adds a new directory to the search path for references. If you want to keep your scripts and the assemblies they depend on in separate folders, you can use the #I directive to add a new folder to the search path so that those assemblies can be found when using #r.

The following example adds several directories to F#'s search path so that when it comes time to actually load a reference with #r, the desired assembly can be found:

```
// Reference whatever version of Managed DirectX is installed...
#I @"C:\WINDOWS\Microsoft.NET\DirectX for Managed Code\1.0.2904.0"
#I @"C:\WINDOWS\Microsoft.NET\DirectX for Managed Code\1.0.2905.0"
#I @"C:\WINDOWS\Microsoft.NET\DirectX for Managed Code\1.0.2906.0"
#I @"C:\WINDOWS\Microsoft.NET\DirectX for Managed Code\1.0.2907.0"

#r "Microsoft.DirectX.dll"
#r "Microsoft.DirectX.Direct3D.dll"
#r "Microsoft.DirectX.Direct3Dx.dll"

// ...
```

#load

The #load directive opens up another F# file with a relative path and executes it. This is for when you want scripts to be broken up across multiple files, or if you want to reuse some existing F# code. Loading a code file will work as if you had opened the file and sent its entire contents directly into the FSI session. Example 9-3 shows loading a code file for displaying charts and plots while the actual script file does the computation.

Example 9-3. Loading a code file into an F# script

```
#load "Plotting.fs"

open System

let data =
    seq {
        let rng = new Random()
        for i in 1 .. 10000 do
            yield (rng.NextDouble(), rng.NextDouble())
    }

// Function plot is defined in 'Plotting.fs'
plot "Random plot" data
```

 Use #load sparingly in F# scripts. They make scripts more difficult to maintain and deploy. If your script needs multiple code files to work, consider creating an actual project.

F# Script Recipes

This section will highlight some simple utilities that can help make your F# scripts more effective—such as taking advantage of console coloring or automating data input to Microsoft Excel.

Colorful Output

Scripts don't primarily invest in a UI, rather they are designed not to need any user input. However, taking advantage of a color console can dramatically improve the readability of your script's output. Example 9-4 defines a `cprintfn` function that behaves just like `printfn`, taking a string filled with format specifiers and additional arguments, except that it also takes a color parameter.

Example 9-4. Producing colorful output

```
/// Colorful printing for helpful diagnostics
let cprintfn c fmt =
    Printf.kprintf
        (fun s ->
            let orig = System.Console.ForegroundColor
            System.Console.ForegroundColor <- c;
            System.Console.WriteLine(s)
            System.Console.ForegroundColor <- orig)
        fmt
```

The `cprintfn` function takes advantage of the `Printf.kprintf` function in the F# library, which does all the conversion of the format string, such as `"%d %f %s"`, and the additional arguments, and calls the provided function once they have been combined into the final result. The `cprintfn` function then simply updates the console color before doing the actual printing.

The following code prints text to the console in various colors. The last section of the code uses a little functional programming magic to print a string where each letter is in a different color—see if you can figure out how it works (hint: a `string` type can be treated as if it were a `seq<char>`):

```
open System

cprintfn ConsoleColor.Blue  "Hello, World! in blue!"
cprintfn ConsoleColor.Red   "... and in red!"
cprintfn ConsoleColor.Green "... and in green!"

let rotatingColors =
    seq {
        let i = ref 0
        let possibleColors = Enum.GetValues(typeof<ConsoleColor>)
        while true do
            yield (enum (!i) : ConsoleColor)
            i := (!i + 1) % possibleColors.Length
    }
```

```
"Experience the rainbow of possibility!"
|> Seq.zip rotatingColors
|> Seq.iter (fun (color, letter) -> cprintfn color "%c" letter)
```

Producing Sound

Similar to using the console's ability to color output as a way of improving your scripts, you can also take advantage of the console's ability to beep. To have your script make sounds, you can use the `System.Console.Beep` method, which takes a frequency and duration as parameters. While potentially very annoying, having an audible cue for when a script is complete or when a special event has occurred can be helpful.

The following code defines two functions, `victory` and `defeat`, which play sounds to indicate success or failure. `victory` beeps ascending tones to convey the sheer joy of success, while `defeat` beeps a series of increasingly depressing low tones:

```
open System

/// Victory!
let victory() =
    for frequency in [100 .. 50 .. 2000] do
        Console.Beep(frequency, 25)

/// Defeat :(
let defeat() =
    for frequency in [2000 .. -50 .. 37] do
        Console.Beep(frequency, 25)
```

Walking a Directory Structure

You'll often want a script to process all the files under a certain directory. An easy and effective way to process every file is to use the sequence expression defined in Example 9-5. Remember that in a sequence expression, `yield!` merges a sequence of elements into the master sequence, similar to the `Seq.concat` function.

Example 9-5. Getting all sub files under a directory

```
open System.IO

let rec filesUnder basePath =
    seq {
        yield! Directory.GetFiles(basePath)
        for subDir in Directory.GetDirectories(basePath) do
            yield! filesUnder subDir
    }
```

This following script can be applied to walk a directory tree and identify specific files, which can then be processed by your script. Notice that using the __SOURCE_DIREC TORY__ directive allows you to scan each file under the directory where the script resides.

The following code uses the `filesUnder` function to copy all JPEG files under the script's directory into a new folder:

```
open System.IO

let rec filesUnder basePath =
    seq {
        yield! Directory.GetFiles(basePath)
        for subDir in Directory.GetDirectories(basePath) do
            yield! filesUnder subDir
    }

let NewImageFolder = @"D:\NewImagesFolder\"

__SOURCE_DIRECTORY__
|> filesUnder
|> Seq.filter(fun filePath -> filePath.ToUpper().EndsWith("JPG"))
|> Seq.iter(fun filePath -> let fileName = Path.GetFileName(filePath)
                            let destPath = Path.Combine(NewImageFolder, fileName)
                            File.Copy(filePath, destPath))
```

Starting Processes Easily

Another common task for scripts is to launch a separate tool. The functionality for spawning new processes is built into the .NET base class libraries. The simplest way to do this is to use the `Process.Start` method, and simply wait for it to complete:

```
open System.Diagnostics
Process.Start("notepad.exe", "file.txt").WaitForExit()
```

For more sophisticated scripts, you will probably need to check the result of the process, either the process exit code or its console output.

Example 9-6 defines a function called `shellExecute` that launches a program with the given arguments and returns its exit code and output as a tuple.

Example 9-6. Launching a new process

```
open System.Text
open System.Diagnostics

/// Spawns a new process. Returns (exit code, stdout)
let shellExecute program arguments =

    let startInfo = new ProcessStartInfo()
    startInfo.FileName <- program
    startInfo.Arguments <- arguments

    startInfo.UseShellExecute        <- false
    startInfo.RedirectStandardOutput <- true

    let proc = new Process()
    proc.EnableRaisingEvents <- true
```

```
// Add a handler to the 'OutputDataRecieved' event, so we can store
// the STDOUT stream of the process.
let driverOutput = new StringBuilder()
proc.OutputDataReceived.AddHandler(
    DataReceivedEventHandler(
        (fun sender args -> driverOutput.AppendLine(args.Data) |> ignore)
    )
)

proc.StartInfo <- startInfo
proc.Start() |> ignore
proc.BeginOutputReadLine()

proc.WaitForExit()
(proc.ExitCode, driverOutput.ToString())
```

Automating Microsoft Office

Yet another possible application for F# scripts is automation, or programmatically performing otherwise mundane tasks. The following scripts show you how to automate simple tasks for Microsoft Office.

Example 9-7 automates Microsoft Word. It prints out all documents in the same folder as the script modifying the print options so that pages are printed with four pages per sheet.

The APIs for manipulating Microsoft Word are fairly straightforward; the only bit of trickiness in Example 9-7 is that the Word COM APIs expect to take **byref<obj>** objects as parameters, so the **comarg** function is introduced to convert a value into a mutable **obj**. (The byref<_> type is discussed in more detail in Appendix B.)

Example 9-7. Printing all documents in a folder

```
#r "stdole.dll"
#r "Microsoft.Office.Interop.Word"

open Microsoft.Office.Interop.Word

let private m_word : ApplicationClass option ref = ref None

let openWord()        = m_word := Some(new ApplicationClass())
let getWordInstance() = Option.get !m_word
let closeWord()       = (getWordInstance()).Quit()

// COM objects expect byref<obj>, ref cells will be
// converted to byref<obj> by the compiler.
let comarg x = ref (box x)

let openDocument filePath =
    printfn "Opening %s..." filePath
    getWordInstance().Documents.Open(comarg filePath)

let printDocument (doc : Document) =
```

```
        printfn "Printing %s..." doc.Name

        doc.PrintOut(
            Background  = comarg true,
            Range       = comarg WdPrintOutRange.wdPrintAllDocument,
            Copies      = comarg 1,
            PageType    = comarg WdPrintOutPages.wdPrintAllPages,
            PrintToFile = comarg false,
            Collate     = comarg true,
            ManualDuplexPrint = comarg false,
            PrintZoomColumn = comarg 2,  // Pages 'across'
            PrintZoomRow    = comarg 2)  // Pages 'up down'

let closeDocument (doc : Document) =
    printfn "Closing %s..." doc.Name
    doc.Close(SaveChanges = comarg false)

// ----------------------------------------------------------------

open System
open System.IO

try
    openWord()

    printfn "Printing all files in [%s]..." __SOURCE_DIRECTORY__

    Directory.GetFiles(__SOURCE_DIRECTORY__, "*.docx")
    |> Array.iter
        (fun filePath ->
            let doc = openDocument filePath
            printDocument doc
            closeDocument doc)
finally
    closeWord()

printfn "Press any key..."
Console.ReadKey(true) |> ignore
```

Example 9-8 creates a new Microsoft Excel workbook and dumps the contents of the *Pictures* folder to a spreadsheet. You could just as easily store the results of some computations.

The script starts up by loading up the Excel application, creating a new workbook, and allowing spreadsheet cells to be set using the **setCellText** function. The script then walks through each file in the *My Pictures* folder and prints the filename, size, etc.

Example 9-8. Creating Excel worksheets

```
#r "Microsoft.Office.Interop.Excel"

open System
open System.IO
open System.Reflection
open Microsoft.Office.Interop.Excel
```

```fsharp
let app = ApplicationClass(Visible = true)

let sheet = app.Workbooks
               .Add()
               .Worksheets.[1] :?> _Worksheet

let setCellText (x : int) (y : int) (text : string) =
    let range = sprintf "%c%d" (char (x + int 'A')) (y+1)
    sheet.Range(range).Value(Missing.Value) <- text


let printCsvToExcel rowIdx (csvText : string) =
    csvText.Split([| ',' |])
    |> Array.iteri (fun partIdx partText -> setCellText partIdx rowIdx partText)


let rec filesUnderFolder basePath =
    seq {
        yield! Directory.GetFiles(basePath)
        for subFolder in Directory.GetDirectories(basePath) do
            yield! filesUnderFolder subFolder
    }

// Print header
printCsvToExcel 0 "Directory, Filename, Size, Creation Time"

// Print rows
filesUnderFolder (Environment.GetFolderPath(Environment.SpecialFolder.MyPictures))
|> Seq.map (fun filename -> new FileInfo(filename))
|> Seq.map (fun fileInfo -> sprintf "%s, %s, %d, %s"
                                fileInfo.DirectoryName
                                fileInfo.Name
                                fileInfo.Length
                                (fileInfo.CreationTime.ToShortDateString()))
|> Seq.iteri (fun idx str -> printCsvToExcel (idx + 1) str)
```

F# scripts allow you to use F# code outside of the normal "projects and solution" format of Visual Studio. F# scripts enable many new scenarios that would otherwise be prohibitively annoying to automate in a language like C#, or easy in a language like Python but would require additional software to be installed and configured.

Using F# scripts, you can automate tasks such as uploading files to a web server, analyzing and extracting data from log files, and so on. Using F# in a scripting context is just one more way you can apply the language to help you be more productive.

CHAPTER 10

Computation Expressions

In Chapters 2, 3, and 4, we covered list, sequence, and array comprehensions, which are ways to write integrated F# code that ultimately produce a collection of ordered elements in list, sequence, or array form. These comprehensions are not just syntactic sugar built into the language, but rather an advanced feature at work called *computation expressions* (less formally referred to as *workflows*).

In fact, this same technique that simplifies declaring sequences can also be applied to asynchronous programming or creating domain-specific languages.

In short, computation expressions allow you to take F# code and determine *how* it gets executed. Having the workflow do all the heavy lifting behind the scenes can dramatically reduce redundant code and in some ways extend the F# language itself.

Toward Computation Expressions

Let's briefly review what's possible with sequence expressions—they allow you to define a sequence by embedding some F# code into a **seq** computation expression. Example 10-1 shows a sequence expression for generating the days of the year.

Notice that you can write pretty much any F# code inside the **seq** { } block, and elements are produced from the sequence as items are returned with the **yield** keyword.

Example 10-1. Sequence expression for enumerating days of the year

```
> // Sequence for producing month, day tuples
let daysOfTheYear =
    seq {
        let months =
            [
                "Jan"; "Feb"; "Mar"; "Apr"; "May"; "Jun";
                "Jul"; "Aug"; "Sep"; "Oct"; "Nov"; "Dec"
            ]
```

```
    let daysInMonth month =
        match month with
        | "Feb"
            -> 28
        | "Apr" | "Jun" | "Sep" | "Nov"
            -> 30
        | _ -> 31

    for month in months do
        for day = 1 to daysInMonth month do
            yield (month, day)
};;

val daysOfTheYear : seq<string * int>

> daysOfTheYear;;
val it : seq<string * int> =
  seq [("Jan", 1); ("Jan", 2); ("Jan", 3); ("Jan", 4); ...]
> Seq.length daysOfTheYear;;
val it : int = 365
```

It is clear that the code you can put inside of a sequence expression—and by extension computation expression—is sufficient for performing powerful computations. In fact, the only limitations to the F# code you can put inside of a computation expression are:

- No new types may be declared within a computation expression.
- Mutable values cannot be used inside computation expressions; you must use `ref` cells instead.

I've claimed that computation expressions can dramatically simplify code. To demonstrate this, let me provide an example. Example 10-2 tries to do some basic math, except rather than leaving division up to chance—and potentially throwing a `DivideByZeroEx ception`—each division is wrapped into a custom type that will indicate success or failure.

The computation preformed is a simple electrical calculation: the total resistance of three resistors in parallel, which requires four division operations. Because we want to check the result of division against `Success` or `DivByZero`, the code ends up looking excessively complex because after each division, we much check whether we want to continue the computation or stop with a `DivByZero`.

Example 10-2. Setting the state for custom workflows

```
type Result = Success of float | DivByZero

let divide x y =
    match y with
    | 0.0 -> DivByZero
    | _   -> Success(x / y)
```

```
// Total resistance of three resistors in parallel is given
// by: 1/R_e = 1/R_1 + 1/R_2 + 1/R_3
let totalResistance r1 r2 r3 =
    let r1Result = divide 1.0 r1
    match r1Result with
    | DivByZero
        -> DivByZero
    | Success(x)
        -> let r2Result = divide 1.0 r2
           match r2Result with
           | DivByZero
               -> DivByZero
           | Success(y)
               -> let r3Result = divide 1.0 r3
                  match r3Result with
                  | DivByZero
                      -> DivByZero
                  | Success(z)
                      -> let finalResult = divide 1.0 (x + y + z)
                         finalResult
```

While this code works as expected, it is clear that programming in this style is tedious and error-prone. Ideally, you could define a new function called let_with_check to do the result checking for you. This function could check the result of a call to divide, and if it was Success, then the next line of code would execute; otherwise, the function would return DivByZero:

```
let totalResistance r1 r2 r3 =
    let_with_check x = divide 1.0 r1
    let_with_check y = divide 1.0 r2
    let_with_check z = divide 1.0 r3
    return_with_check 1.0 (x + y + z)
```

However, the special function let_with_check cannot be added to the F# language because it would have to abnormally break control flow. That is, in F# there is no way to exit a function prematurely, other than throwing an exception or using cascading if/match expressions.

If only there were a way to chop up this function into different parts, and have the let_with_check take two parameters, the first being the result of divide, and the second being a function that represents the rest of the computation to be performed. (If you recall from Chapter 7, this is known as a *continuation*.)

Example 10-3 defines a function let_with_check that does just that. It takes two parameters: the result of a division operation and a function representing the rest of the computation. And if the result returned DivByZero, then the rest of the computation is not executed.

Example 10-3. Defining let_with_check

```
let let_with_check result restOfComputation =
    match result with
    | DivByZero  -> DivByZero
    | Success(x) -> restOfComputation x

let totalResistance r1 r2 r3 =
    let_with_check
        (divide 1.0 r1)
        (fun x ->
            let_with_check
                (divide 1.0 r2)
                (fun y ->
                    let_with_check
                        (divide 1.0 r3)
                        (fun z -> divide 1.0 (x + y + z))
                )
        )
```

With the code indented and the additional lambda expressions, the code looks worse than it did originally. However, let's try to rewrite our `totalResistance` function again, but this time putting the lambdas on the same line.

If we write it the following way, the code almost looks like we originally wanted, giving the appearance that the function will abruptly stop as soon as the first `DivByZero` is encountered:

```
let totalResistance r1 r2 r3 =
    let_with_check (divide 1.0 r1) (fun x ->
    let_with_check (divide 1.0 r2) (fun y ->
    let_with_check (divide 1.0 r3) (fun z ->
    divide 1.0 (x + y + z) ) ) )
```

Computation Expression Builders

Computation expressions in a nutshell are syntactic transforms for F# code, just like `let_with_check` in the previous example. Let's look at how you can leverage F#'s support for computation expressions to simplify your code.

Example 10-4 shows how to create a custom workflow. We'll go over what's going on behind the scenes in a moment. For now, just look at the implementation of the `Bind` method, the `defined { }` block, and the use of the `let!` keyword.

Example 10-4. The success/failure computation expression

```
type Result = Success of float | DivByZero

let divide x y =
    match y with
    | 0.0 -> DivByZero
    | _   -> Success(x / y)
```

```
type DefinedBuilder() =

    member this.Bind ((x : Result), (rest : float -> Result)) =
        // If the result is Success(_) then execute the
        // rest of the function. Otherwise terminate it
        // prematurely.
        match x with
        | Success(x) -> rest x
        | DivByZero  -> DivByZero

    member this.Return (x : 'a) = x

// Create an instance of our computation expression builder
let defined = DefinedBuilder()

let totalResistance r1 r2 r3 =
    defined {
        let! x = divide 1.0 r1
        let! y = divide 1.0 r2
        let! z = divide 1.0 r3
        return divide 1.0 (x + y + z)
    }
```

You can test this in FSI and verify that the computation expression version gets the same results, and in one-third the lines of code!

```
> totalResistance 0.01 0.75 0.33;;
val it : Result = Success 0.009581881533
> totalResistance 0.00 0.55 0.75;;
val it : Result = DivByZero
```

All computation expressions do is break the expression into multiple function calls to the *computation expression builder*. In the previous example, it was of type Defined Builder. To use the computation expression builder, all you need to do is put an instance of it out in front of two curly braces { } surrounding the code you want to execute. In this example, it was an instance of DefinedBuilder via value defined.

Every let! is replaced with a call to the builder's Bind method, where the evaluation of the righthand side of the equals sign is the first parameter, and the second parameter is the function representing the rest of the computation to be performed. This is how the computation stops after the first DivByZero is reached. In the computation expression builder's implementation of Bind, the rest of the computation isn't executed if the result is DivByZero. If the result is Success, then the rest of the computation is performed.

Example 10-5 shows the expansion of this in a desugared form of the defined workflow, which is strikingly similar to the code you saw in Example 10-3.

Example 10-5. Desugared form of a computation expression

```
// De-sugared form
let totalResistance r1 r2 r3 =
    defined.Bind(
        (divide 1.0 r1),
```

```
(fun x ->
    defined.Bind(
        (divide 1.0 r2),
        (fun y ->
            defined.Bind(
                (divide 1.0 r3),
                (fun z ->
                    defined.Return(
                        divide 1.0 (x + y + z)
                    )
                )
            )
        )
    )
)
```

Inside of a custom workflow builder, you can write normal F# code, but in addition you have access to new keywords and abilities such as let!, return, and yield. By using these new primitives in the body of the computation expression, you can extend how F# processes the code. (For example, adding custom semantics for when the yield keyword is encountered.)

By providing a Bind function, you provided a way to determine how let! was computed. Similarly, providing a Return function will enable you to determine how the return keyword works. But a workflow builder can provide more methods for determining how F# code gets executed. A full list is shown in Table 10-1.

 Another way to think about computation expressions is that they enable you to insert code in between the various steps of the computation, doing any necessary background processing without requiring you to explicitly write the code.

Table 10-1. Computation expression methods

Method signature	Description
member For: seq<'a> * ('a -> Result<unit>) -> Result<unit>	Enables execution of for loops. The parameters are the values which the loop executes on and the body of the for loop.
member Zero: unit -> Result<unit>	Enables execution of unit expressions, such as the result of an if expression without a matching else if the predicate evaluates to false.
member Combine: Result<unit> * Result<'a> -> Result<'a>	Used to link together computation expression parts, for example, two for loops in sequence.
member While: (unit -> bool) * Result<unit> -> Result<unit>	Enables execution of while loops. The parameters are the function which determines whether or not the while loop should continue and the body of the loop.
member Return: 'a -> Result<'a>	Enables execution of the return keyword.

Method signature	Description
member ReturnFrom: 'a -> Result<'a>	Enables execution of the return! keyword.
member Yield: 'a -> Result<'a>	Enables execution of the yield keyword.
member YieldFrom: seq<'a> -> Result<'a>	Enables execution of the yield! keyword.
member Delay: (unit -> Result<'a>) -> Result<'a>	This operation is typically used in conjunction with Combine, to make sure that operations get executed in the correct order (in case they have side effects).
member Run: Result<'a> -> Result<'a>	If provided, the method will be called at the very start of the computation expression.
member Using: 'a * ('a -> Result<'b>) -> Result<'b> when 'a :> System.IDisposable	Enables execution of use and use! keywords. The implementation of Using is responsible for calling IDisposable.Dispose.
member Bind: Result<'a> * ('a -> Result<'b>) -> Result<'b>	Enables execution of the let! and do! keywords. (do! is a specialized form of let!, when binding against Result<unit>.)
member TryFinally: Result<'a> * (unit -> unit) -> Result<'a>	Enables execution of try/finally expressions. The parameters are the result of the try block and the function representing the finally block.
member TryWith: Result<'a> * (exn -> Result<'a>) -> Result<'a>	Enables execution of try/with expressions. The parameters are the result of the try block and the function representing the with block.

If your computation expression builder contains an implementation for the given function, then you can use the associated construct inside the computation expression. In the previous example, if you didn't include the Return method, you would get an error because you used the return keyword on the last line.

```
        return divide 1.0 (x + y + z)
--------^^^^^^^^^^^^^^^^^^^^^^^^^^^^^^^
```

```
  stdin(259,9): error FS0039: The field, constructor or member 'Return' is not defined.
```

The pattern of looking for a computation expression method by its name alone has a couple of interesting ramifications. First, computation expression builder methods can be added via extension methods—enabling unexpected types to be the root of computation expressions. Second, due to method overloading, you can have multiple implementations of computation expression methods like Bind.

Custom Computation Expression Builders

Now you have the capability to customize how various language constructs get executed by defining extra work to be carried out. But when would this be useful? It is clear that F# workflows were helpful when trying to determine the success or failure of a computation, but you might be skeptical that the same technique can make asynchronous programming easier.

Asynchronous Workflows

Think about the most tedious aspects of parallel and asynchronous programming—dealing with threads. If you want your program to have two things going on at once, you need to spawn new threads, give them appropriate work, and then marshal their results back. It is just as painful to exploit IO-level parallelism. The .NET Framework provides asynchronous IO operations via `FileStream.BeginRead` and `FileStream.Begin Write`. However, using these constructs requires a messy combination of `IAsyncRe sult` interfaces, `AsyncCallback` delegates, and a lot of tedious code.

Even if you didn't mind handling all the thread hopping and the managing of incomplete tasks yourself, it is still a pain to deal with exceptions. In addition, there is no good way to cancel the operation once it starts.

If only there were a way to abstract the code and wire in the thread hopping.... Fortunately, this library does exist and it is built into F#. *F# asynchronous workflows* are a type of computation expression builder specifically designed for asynchronous tasks.

Example 10-6 shows how to use an asynchronous workflow for reading and writing file data asynchronously. Note the use of `let!` to perform asynchronous operations; all the thread hopping will be performed in the implementation of the `async` builder's `Bind` method. The details for how the `async` computation expression builder and `Async.Start` work will be covered in more detail in Chapter 11, which is devoted entirely to the subject of parallel and asynchronous programming.

Example 10-6. F# asynchronous workflows

```
open System.IO

let asyncProcessFile (filePath : string) (processBytes : byte[] -> byte[]) =
    async {

        printfn "Processing file [%s]" (Path.GetFileName(filePath))

        let fileStream = new FileStream(filePath, FileMode.Open)
        let bytesToRead = int fileStream.Length

        let! data = fileStream.AsyncRead(bytesToRead)

        printfn
            "Opened [%s], read [%d] bytes"
            (Path.GetFileName(filePath))
            data.Length

        let data' = processBytes data

        let resultFile = new FileStream(filePath + ".results", FileMode.Create)
        do! resultFile.AsyncWrite(data', 0, data'.Length)
```

```
    printfn "Finished processing file [%s]" <| Path.GetFileName(filePath)
} |> Async.Start
```

Computation expressions weren't added to the F# language with ultra-useful asynchronous workflows in mind, rather they just enable certain patterns of code that have the potential to be quite useful.

> If you want to get fancy, you could call computation expressions a form of *monoids in the category of endo-functors*, but I don't recommend it.

The Rounding Workflow

When doing some types of mathematical calculation it can be desirable to enforce a specific degree of precision, for example, to make sure calculations to compute real world lengths are feasible. (Unless, of course, they start selling rulers that go down to the picometer.)

Example 10-7 defines the Rounding workflow. Notice that the `Bind` method changes the value of what is passed to it. In addition, because `Bind` constrains its input to type `float`, you will get a compiler error if you use `let!` with any other type.

Example 10-7. Implementation of a rounding workflow

```
open System

// Computation expression builder which rounds bound computations
// to a fix number of significant digits.
type RoundingWorkflow(sigDigs : int) =

    let round (x : float) = Math.Round(float x, sigDigs)

    // Due to result being constrained to type float, you can only use
    // let! against float values. (Otherwise will get a compiler error.)
    member this.Bind(result : float, rest : float -> float) =
        let result' = round result
        rest result'

    member this.Return (x : float) = round x

let withPrecision sigDigs = new RoundingWorkflow(sigDigs)
```

The following shows the rounding workflow in action:

```
> // Test the rounding workflow
let test =
    withPrecision 3 {
        let! x = 2.0 / 12.0
        let! y = 3.5
        return x / y
```

```
    };;
val test : float = 0.048
```

The State Workflow

To see a more real-world example of a useful computation expression, consider a workflow to keep track of state. Imagine creating a library for web scripting. Each action such as clicking a link or button, changes the current state—current URL, HTML, session cookies, etc.—which needs to be passed to the next step of the computation.

Example 10-8 shows some hypothetical code to script a web session, which quickly becomes tedious, as the state information needs to be piped through to every single stage of the computation. (It may seem tempting to simply use the pipe-forward operator |>. The problem with using the pipe-forward operator in a situation like this is that it would require that every method in the sequence return the same state object, which wouldn't make sense for some functions.)

Example 10-8. Code passing around a state object

```
let reviewBook() =
    let state1 = openPage "www.fsharp.net"
    let state2 = clickLink "F# Books" state1
    let (table, state3) = getHtmlTableFromHeader "Programming F#" (state2)
    let state4 = clickButton table "Five Star Rating" state3
    ...
```

By using a computation expression, you can eliminate the need for passing a state object throughout the computation. The intuition here is that computation expressions are used to do "extra work" behind the scenes of normal F# code, so perhaps we can have that extra work persist state information:

```
let reviewBook() =
    state {
        do! OpenPage "www.fsharp.net"
        do! ClickLink "F# Books"
        let! table = GetHtmlTableWithHeader "Programming F#"
        do! ClickButton table "Five Star Rating"
    }
```

Building up the computation

We can achieve this illusion of persisting state information by using a single-case discriminated union type called StatefulFunc, which represents a function that takes an initial state and returns a tuple of the result and updated state:

```
type StatefulFunc<'state, 'result> = StatefulFunc of ('state -> 'result * 'state)
```

Each call to `Bind` will take an existing `StatefulFunc` object and produce a new, larger `StatefulFunc` object by executing the function attached to the existing `StatefulFunc` object and then executing the rest of the computation (the continuation that is passed to `Bind`).

So, for example, we want to write a workflow to power the following code:

```
state {
    do! OpenWebpage "www.bing.com"    // Sets the state
    do! EnterText "Jellyfish"         // Uses the state
    do! ClickButton "Search"          // Uses and Sets the state
}
```

When encoded into the `StatefulFunc` type, the steps would look something like the following:

```
// do! OpenWebpage "www.Bing.com"
let step1 =
    StatefulFunc(fun initialState ->
        let result, updatedState = OpenWebpage "www.bing.com" initialState
        result, updatedState)

// do! EnterText
let step2 =
    StatefulFunc(fun initialState ->
        let result, updatedState = EnterText "Jellyfish" initialState
        result, updatedState)

// do! ClickButton "Search"
let step3 =
    StatefulFunc(fun initialState ->
        let result, updatedState = ClickButton "Search" initialState
        result, initialState)
```

The result of a `state` workflow then is a single `StatefulFunc` object that has associated with it a function that will perform the full computation, passing along a state object, built out of the calls to `Bind` within the workflow.

Once the `StatefulFunc` has been built up, the full computation would end up looking similar to the following:

```
StatefulFunc(fun initialState ->

    let result1, updatedState1 = OpenWebPage "www.bing.com" initialState

    updatedState1 |> (fun initialState ->
        let result2, updatedState2 = EnterText "Jellyfish" initialState

        updatedState3 |> (fun initialState ->
            let result3, updatedState3 = ClickButton "Search" initialState

            result3, updatedState3
        )
    )
```

Implementation

Example 10-9 shows the implementation of the full `state` workflow. With additional methods like `Combine` and `TryFinally`, the full range of possible F# code is available within the workflow.

 Explicit type annotations have been provided to each method signature to make it clear what the signatures are, but in practice they can usually be omitted.

Example 10-9. Implementation of a state workflow in F#

```
open System

// Type to represent a stateful function. A function which takes an input state and
// returns a result combined with an updated state.
type StatefulFunc<'state, 'result> = StatefulFunc of ('state -> 'result * 'state)

// Run our stateful function
let Run (StatefulFunc f) initialState = f initialState

type StateBuilder() =

    member this.Bind(
                    result : StatefulFunc<'state, 'a>,
                    restOfComputation : 'a -> StatefulFunc<'state, 'b>
                 ) =

        StatefulFunc(fun initialState ->
            let result, updatedState = Run result initialState
            Run (restOfComputation result) updatedState
        )

    member this.Combine(
                    partOne : StatefulFunc<'state, unit>,
                    partTwo : StatefulFunc<'state, 'a>
                 ) =

        StatefulFunc(fun initialState ->
            let (), updatedState = Run partOne initialState
            Run partTwo updatedState
        )

    member this.Delay(
                    restOfComputation : unit -> StatefulFunc<'state, 'a>
                 ) =

        StatefulFunc (fun initialState ->
            Run ( restOfComputation() ) initialState
        )
```

```
member this.For(
                elements : seq<'a>,
                forBody : ('a -> StatefulFunc<'state, unit>)
                ) =

    StatefulFunc(fun initialState ->
        let state = ref initialState

        for e in elements do
            let (), updatedState = Run (forBody e) (!state)
            state := updatedState

        // Return unit * finalState
        (), !state
    )

member this.Return(x : 'a) =
    StatefulFunc(fun initialState -> x, initialState)

member this.Using<'a, 'state,
                'b when 'a :> IDisposable>(
                  x : 'a,
                  restOfComputation : 'a -> StatefulFunc<'state, 'b>
                ) =

    StatefulFunc(fun initialState ->
        try
            Run (restOfComputation x) initialState
        finally
            x.Dispose()
    )

member this.TryFinally(
                tryBlock : StatefulFunc<'state, 'a>,
                finallyBlock : unit -> unit
                ) =

    StatefulFunc(fun initialState ->
        try
            Run tryBlock initialState
        finally
            finallyBlock()
    )


member this.TryWith(
                tryBlock : StatefulFunc<'state, 'a>,
                exnHandler : exn -> StatefulFunc<'state, 'a>
                ) =

    StatefulFunc(fun initialState ->
        try
            Run tryBlock initialState
        with
```

```
            | e ->
                Run (exnHandler e) initialState
    )

    member this.While(
                        predicate : unit -> bool,
                        body : StatefulFunc<'state, unit>
                    ) =

        StatefulFunc(fun initialState ->

            let state = ref initialState
            while predicate() = true do
                let (), updatedState = Run body (!state)
                state := updatedState

            // Return unit * finalState
            (), !state
        )

    member this.Zero() =
        StatefulFunc(fun initialState -> (), initialState)

// Declare the state workflow builder
let state = StateBuilder()

// Primitive functions for getting and setting state
let GetState          = StatefulFunc (fun state -> state, state)
let SetState newState = StatefulFunc (fun prevState -> (), newState)
```

With the full workflow defined, Example 10-10 uses the `state` workflow to script a four-function calculator. (You can use the same `state` workflow for creating a web crawler, but the code to do that properly would easily dwarf the text in this chapter.)

The state is represented by the current total and the calculator's operational history. The functions `Add`, `Subtract`, `Multiply`, and `Divide` will take an input state, modify it, and return a new `StatefulFunc` object.

Example 10-10. Using the state workflow to create a calculator

```
let Add x =
    state {
        let! currentTotal, history = GetState
        do! SetState (currentTotal + x, (sprintf "Added %d" x) :: history)
    }

let Subtract x =
    state {
        let! currentTotal, history = GetState
        do! SetState (currentTotal - x, (sprintf "Subtracted %d" x) :: history)
    }


let Multiply x =
    state {
```

```
        let! currentTotal, history = GetState
        do! SetState (currentTotal * x, (sprintf "Multiplied by %d" x) :: history)
    }

let Divide x =
    state {
        let! currentTotal, history = GetState
        do! SetState (currentTotal / x, (sprintf "Divided by %d" x) :: history)
    }
```

Using functions like Add and Subtract within the state workflow will give the illusion that you are not passing the state around, while in actuality a large StatefulFunc object is built, which can be executed by passing it to the Run function:

```
> // Define the StatefulFunc we will use, no need to thread
// the state parameter through each function.
let calculatorActions =
    state {
        do! Add 2
        do! Multiply 10
        do! Divide 5
        do! Subtract 8

        return "Finished"
    }

// Now run our SatefulFunc passing in an intial state
let sfResult, finalState = Run calculatorActions (0, []);;

val calculatorActions : StatefulFunc<(int * string list),string> =
  StatefulFunc <fun:Delay@324>
val sfResult : string = "Finished"
val finalState : int * string list =
  (-4, ["Subtracted 8"; "Divided by 5"; "Multiplied by 10"; "Added 2"])
```

F# workflows are a very advanced concept that even expert developers can have a hard time grasping. But they can be used to simplify code by giving you the ability to execute code in between computation steps. If you find yourself writing a lot of redundant, boilerplate code, consider looking into whether you can wrap that functionality inside of a computation expression.

CHAPTER 11

Asynchronous and Parallel Programming

The reason for mastering asynchronous and parallel programming is that without it, you simply cannot take advantage of your hardware's potential. This is especially true in intensive CPU-bound domains, like technical computing. Previously there was a good reason for not writing programs in an asynchronous or parallel fashion: added complexity and the risk of introducing bugs. However, with the great libraries available in Visual Studio 2010, combined with a side effect–free style of functional programming, this concern has been elegantly mitigated.

This chapter will focus on how to speed up computation in F# using asynchronous and parallel programming. By the end of this chapter, you will be able to execute code in different contexts (threads), use the F# asynchronous workflows library for mastering asynchronous programming, and also take advantage of the Parallel Extensions to .NET.

Before we begin, let's first examine what exactly asynchronous and parallel programming mean and why they matter.

Asynchronous programming
   Asynchronous programming describes programs and operations that once started are executed in the background and terminate at some "later time." For example, in most email clients, new emails are retrieved asynchronously in the background so the user doesn't have to force checking for new mail.

Parallel programming
   Parallel programming is dividing up work among processing resources in order to speed up execution. For example, converting a song into an MP3 can be parallelized—dividing the song into pieces and converting each segment in parallel.

Asynchronous and parallel programming adds a great deal of complexity to applications; however, using these techniques provides some clear benefits:

Take advantage of multiple processors and cores
> Modern computers come with multiple processors, each equipped with multiple cores. These logical units allow multiple different computations to happen at the same time, so rather than executing your program sequentially, you can take advantage of these extra processors and cores by splitting up your programs. For example, a computer with two quad-core processors can execute eight operations at once.

Asynchronous IO
> Historically IO operations such as reading and writing to disk have been the bottleneck in high-performance applications. Modern hardware has the ability to do asynchronous IO, and can greatly improve overall performance.

Application responsiveness
> Perhaps the most compelling reason to introduce asynchronous programming into your applications is to increase application responsiveness. For any long-running computation, if you run it asynchronously, your application is still free to process user input, which enables users to continue working or perhaps even cancel operations in progress.

Working with Threads

Asynchronous and parallel programming is done using *threads*, which are different computational units. Once started, the operating system will give each thread on the system a certain amount of time to execute before passing control to another thread.

What separates threads from *processes* is that processes are kept isolated from each other. Threads belong to the process that spawned them and can access the same memory heap as any other thread spawned by that process, so communication between threads is as simple as writing data to shared memory. Processes, on the other hand, cannot easily access each other's memory, and so communication is more difficult.

At any given moment, the operating system determines which threads are executing. The ones that aren't executing are suspended, and simply waiting for their next slice of processor time.

Spawning multiple threads on a single-processor system won't hurt anything—but the processor can only execute one of those threads at a time, so there will be switching between the different threads. The same program on a multi-processor or multi-core machine, on the other hand, would be able to execute several threads concurrently, so it would often go much faster.

The drawback is that with multiple things going on at once it can be difficult to keep track of data being read or written. Is the data that thread *alpha* read out of date because thread *beta* just updated the value? What if thread *alpha* needs to access a file that thread *beta* has locked for writing? When you're dealing with multiple threads, several classes of synchronization issues can occur, which we will cover later.

Spawning Threads

To spin up a new thread and have it execute in the background, simply create a new instance of `System.Threading.Thread` and pass in a `ThreadStart` delegate to its constructor. Then, call the `Thread` object's `Start` method.

Example 11-1 spawns a couple of threads that each count to five.

 Remember that in F# if a function takes a delegate as a parameter, you can pass in a lambda expression or function value and the compiler will treat it as though you had created an instance of the delegate type. So, in the example, `threadBody` was passed into the constructor of `Thread`, when in actuality it was a new instance of `ThreadStart`.

Example 11-1. Creating threads

```
// Creating new threads
open System
open System.Threading

// What will execute on each thread
let threadBody() =
    for i in 1 .. 5 do
        // Wait 1/10 of a second
        Thread.Sleep(100)
        printfn "[Thread %d] %d..."
            Thread.CurrentThread.ManagedThreadId
            i

let spawnThread() =
    let thread = new Thread(threadBody)
    thread.Start()

// Spawn a couple of threads at once
spawnThread()
spawnThread()
```

When executed, Example 11-1 will output the following (or something like it; there is no way to tell how the OS will schedule threads and/or assign thread IDs):

```
[Thread 5] 1...
[Thread 6] 1...
[Thread 5] 2...
[Thread 6] 2...
[Thread 5] 3...
[Thread 6] 3...
[Thread 5] 4...
```

```
[Thread 6] 4...
[Thread 5] 5...
[Thread 6] 5...
```

Spawning multiple threads that count to five is a good start, but imagine that the threadBody function now calculated insurance premiums or did gene sequence alignment. Getting multiple threads executing code concurrently is actually just as simple as spinning up a new thread and calling Start.

Other than Start, there are two methods on a Thread object that you should be aware of: Sleep and Abort.

Thread.Sleep

Thread.Sleep is a static method that puts the currently executing thread to sleep for a given number of milliseconds. In Example 11-1, both threads had a 100 millisecond sleep—or one-tenth of a second—in between when they printed to the console.

Typically Thread.Sleep is used to put in a static delay or simply yield execution of the current thread so the OS can devote processor time to a different thread.

Thread.Abort

The Thread.Abort method kills the thread, attempting to stop its execution by raising a ThreadAbortException execution somewhere in the executing thread. (With a few exceptions, wherever the thread's instruction pointer happens to be at the time the thread is aborted.) With the .NET memory model, the abrupt termination of the thread likely won't leak any memory, but you should always avoid using Thread.Abort.

Later in this chapter, we will look at more advanced libraries built on top of System.Thread to enable friendly notions such as task cancellation to avoid the need for Thread.Abort.

The .NET Thread Pool

Spawning new threads can be costly. For example, each thread has its own stack to keep track of its execution, which can be several megabytes in size. For short-lived actions, rather than continually allocating memory for new threads, it is recommended that you use the *.NET thread pool*, which is a collection of threads just waiting around to do your bidding.

You can spawn a task on the .NET thread pool using the ThreadPool.QueueUserWorkI tem function, which takes a delegate of type WaitCallback. The following example does the same printing numbers to the console, except that it doesn't need to manually allocate and start the threads.

WaitCallback takes a parameter of type obj, because in one overload of the QueueUser WorkItem method you can pass in an obj parameter, which will be passed to the callback.

If no parameter is specified when calling `QueueUserWorkItem`, the callback's parameter will be `null`:

```
open System.Threading

ThreadPool.QueueUserWorkItem(fun _ -> for i = 1 to 5 do printfn "%d" i)

// Our thread pool task, note that the delegate's
// parameter is of type obj
let printNumbers (max : obj) =
    for i = 1 to (max :?> int) do
        printfn "%d" i

ThreadPool.QueueUserWorkItem(new WaitCallback(printNumbers), box 5)
```

Sharing Data

With multiple threads executing, you will want to share data between them for coordination and storing intermediate results. This, however, leads to a couple of problems: race conditions and deadlocks.

Race conditions

A *race condition* is when you have two threads trying to read or write the same value at the same time. If two threads are writing a value, the last one wins, and the first write operation is lost forever. Similarly, if one thread reads a value and the other immediately overwrites that value, the first thread's data is out of date and potentially invalid.

Example 11-2 simply loops through an array and adds up its elements on two threads. Both threads are constantly updating the `total` reference cell, which leads to a data race.

Example 11-2. Race conditions

```
open System.Threading

let sumArray (arr : int[]) =
    let total = ref 0

    // Add the first half
    let thread1Finished = ref false

    ThreadPool.QueueUserWorkItem(
        fun _ -> for i = 0 to arr.Length / 2 - 1 do
                    total := arr.[i] + !total
                 thread1Finished := true
    ) |> ignore

    // Add the second half
    let thread2Finished = ref false
```

```
ThreadPool.QueueUserWorkItem(
    fun _ -> for i = arr.Length / 2 to arr.Length - 1 do
                total := arr.[i] + !total
             thread2Finished := true
) |> ignore

// Wait while the two threads finish their work
while !thread1Finished = false ||
      !thread2Finished = false do

    Thread.Sleep(0)

!total
```

The results of the sumArray function in an FSI session are quite troubling. Not only does this function fail to work, it returns a different value each time! An array with a million elements with value 1 should sum to exactly one million; instead, sumArray is returning about half that:

```
> // Array of 1,000,000 ones
let millionOnes = Array.create 1000000 1;;

val millionOnes : int array =
  [|1; 1; 1; 1; 1; 1; 1; 1; 1; 1; 1; 1; 1; 1; 1; 1; 1; 1; 1; 1; 1; 1; 1; 1; 1;
    1; 1; 1; 1; 1; 1; 1; 1; 1; 1; 1; 1; 1; 1; 1; 1; 1; 1; 1; 1; 1; 1; 1; 1; 1;
    1; 1; 1; 1; 1; 1; 1; 1; 1; 1; 1; 1; 1; 1; 1; 1; 1; 1; 1; 1; 1; 1; 1; 1; 1;
    1; 1; 1; 1; 1; 1; 1; 1; 1; 1; 1; 1; 1; 1; 1; 1; 1; 1; 1; 1; 1; 1; 1; 1; 1;
    ...|]

> sumArray millionOnes;;
val it : int = 547392
> sumArray millionOnes;;
val it : int = 579574
> sumArray millionOnes;;
val it : int = 574109
> sumArray millionOnes;;
val it : int = 573321
> sumArray millionOnes;;
val it : int = 550012
```

The problem arises from the fact that updating total consists of three separate operations: reading the value, incrementing it, and then writing it back. Ideally updating total would occur as a single, atomic operation.

A solution for data races is to *lock* the shared data, that is, to prevent other threads from accessing it while you update its value. For example, there would be no problem with the implementation of sumArray if only one thread could read and update the value of total at a time.

In F#, you can lock a value by using the lock function, which has the following signature. It takes a reference value, which is the value being locked on, and will lock that value until the provided function is finished executing.

```
val lock : ('a -> (unit -> 'b) -> 'b) when 'a : not struct
```

Example 11-3 is the same as Example 11-2 except that this time all access to the total value is done inside of lock, meaning that all other threads must wait to access it until the provided predicate has finished executing.

Example 11-3. Array summing using lock

```
let lockedSumArray (arr : int[]) =
    let total = ref 0

    // Add the first half
    let thread1Finished = ref false
    ThreadPool.QueueUserWorkItem(
        fun _ -> for i = 0 to arr.Length / 2 - 1 do
                    lock (total) (fun () -> total := arr.[i] + !total)
                 thread1Finished := true
    ) |> ignore

    // Add the second half
    let thread2Finished = ref false
    ThreadPool.QueueUserWorkItem(
        fun _ -> for i = arr.Length / 2 to arr.Length - 1 do
                    lock (total) (fun () -> total := arr.[i] + !total)
                 thread2Finished := true
    ) |> ignore

    // Wait while the two threads finish their work
    while !thread1Finished = false ||
          !thread2Finished = false do

        Thread.Sleep(0)

    !total
```

Now the function works exactly as we want; the sum of an array with a million ones is exactly one million. However, with the locking there is no longer any performance gain from summing the array elements in parallel because the counting is actually done one element at a time as the lock is released and immediately acquired, over and over again.

Later in this chapter, you will learn how to use concurrent data structures, which are built for high performance, while still using locking internally to maintain data integrity:

```
> lockedSumArray millionOnes;;
val it : int = 1000000
> lockedSumArray millionOnes;;
val it : int = 1000000
> lockedSumArray millionOnes;;
val it : int = 1000000
> lockedSumArray millionOnes;;
val it : int = 1000000
```

Deadlocks

Locking solves the data race problem; however, it unfortunately introduces more problems down the road. What if you ever need to acquire a lock while you are locking something else? This has the potential to lead to a *deadlock*.

Deadlocks are when you want to access a resource that is locked by another thread, but that other thread won't let up until you release a resource that you have locked. So both you and the other thread are left waiting indefinitely for the other to release its lock.

Whenever you have a lock on an object, you run the risk of a potential deadlock if another thread needs to access that value.

Example 11-4 shows a simple implementation of a bank account and a function to transfer funds between two bank accounts using locking.

Example 11-4. Deadlocks in F#

```
type BankAccount = { AccountID : int; OwnerName : string; mutable Balance : int }

/// Transfer money between bank accounts
let transferFunds amount fromAcct toAcct =

    printfn "Locking %s's account to deposit funds..." toAcct.OwnerName
    lock fromAcct
        (fun () ->
            printfn "Locking %s's account to withdrawl funds..." fromAcct.OwnerName
            lock toAcct
                (fun () ->
                    fromAcct.Balance <- fromAcct.Balance - amount
                    toAcct.Balance   <- toAcct.Balance + amount
                )
        )
```

The previous code snippet looks simple enough, but if there is ever a fund transfer between the same two accounts at the same time, the code will deadlock.

In the following example the first call to `transferFunds` will lock John Smith's account, while on a separate thread, the second call to `transferFunds` will lock Jane Doe's account. Then, when the `transferFunds` routine goes to lock the other account, both threads will stall indefinitely:

```
let john = { AccountID = 1; OwnerName = "John Smith"; Balance = 1000 }
let jane = { AccountID = 2; OwnerName = "Jane Doe";   Balance = 2000 }

ThreadPool.QueueUserWorkItem(fun _ -> transferFunds 100 john jane)
ThreadPool.QueueUserWorkItem(fun _ -> transferFunds 100 jane john)
```

Deadlocking doesn't mean that sharing data between threads is a no-win situation. You just need to be judicious in your use of locking and be aware of what dependencies threads have. There are many ways to write code with locks that don't have deadlocks. For example, in the previous example, if the function `transferFunds` always locked the account with the lower `AccountID` first, then there would be no deadlock.

Asynchronous Programming

Armed with a firm understanding of threads, you can now look at how you can begin writing asynchronous programs for .NET.

Asynchronous programming is when you begin an operation on a background thread to execute concurrently, and have it terminate at some later time, either ignoring the new task to complete in the background or polling it at a later time to check on its return value.

Modern hardware has facilities for parallel reading and writing, so performing asynchronous IO may improve your application's performance. This is especially true if you are writing data to disk that you will not need later—there is no need to "block" the program, waiting for the operation to complete, when you can begin the write asynchronously and continue execution of your program.

The way asynchronous programs have historically been written on .NET has been using the *asynchronous programming model*, or APM.

The APM is a pattern for dividing asynchronous operations into two methods called `BeginOperation` and `EndOperation`. When `BeginOperation` is called, the operation will begin asynchronously, and when complete will execute a provided delegate callback. The code within that callback must call `EndOperation`, which will retrieve the result of the asynchronous computation. Coordination, such as polling for when the operation has completed, happens through the use of the `IAsyncResult` interface.

Example 11-5 uses the APM to asynchronously open a file, perform some operation on the file's data, and then asynchronously write the updated data to disk. Doing this asynchronously effectively queues up all the IO operations so that the disk controller can work as fast as possible. More importantly, the thread isn't blocked while the operation completes.

Don't worry if all the `AsyncCallback` delegates and `IAsyncResult` interfaces seem complicated. The APM truly is a pain to work with, and in the next section, you will see a way to avoid using this model explicitly.

Example 11-5. Asynchronous IO using the AMP

```
open System
open System.IO

let processFileAsync (filePath : string) (processBytes : byte[] -> byte[]) =

    // This is the callback from when the AsyncWrite completes
    let asyncWriteCallback =
        new AsyncCallback(fun (iar : IAsyncResult) ->
            // Get state from the async result
            let writeStream = iar.AsyncState :?> FileStream

            // End the async write operation by calling EndWrite
```

```fsharp
        let bytesWritten = writeStream.EndWrite(iar)
        writeStream.Close()

        printfn
            "Finished processing file [%s]"
            (Path.GetFileName(writeStream.Name))
    )

// This is the callback from when the AsyncRead completes
let asyncReadCallback =
    new AsyncCallback(fun (iar : IAsyncResult) ->
        // Get state from the async result
        let readStream, data = iar.AsyncState :?> (FileStream * byte[])

        // End the async read by calling EndRead
        let bytesRead = readStream.EndRead(iar)
        readStream.Close()

        // Process the result
        printfn
            "Processing file [%s], read [%d] bytes"
            (Path.GetFileName(readStream.Name))
            bytesRead

        let updatedBytes = processBytes data

        let resultFile = new FileStream(readStream.Name + ".result",
                                        FileMode.Create)

        let _ =
            resultFile.BeginWrite(
                updatedBytes,
                0, updatedBytes.Length,
                asyncWriteCallback,
                resultFile)

        ()
    )

// Begin the async read, whose callback will begin the async write
let fileStream = new FileStream(filePath, FileMode.Open, FileAccess.Read,
                               FileShare.Read, 2048,
                               FileOptions.Asynchronous)

let fileLength = int fileStream.Length
let buffer = Array.zeroCreate fileLength

// State passed into the async read
let state = (fileStream, buffer)

printfn "Processing file [%s]" (Path.GetFileName(filePath))
let _ = fileStream.BeginRead(buffer, 0, buffer.Length,
                             asyncReadCallback, state)
()
```

To the mortal programmer, the code in Example 11-5 demonstrates just how painful and error-prone the APM is. Several problems with this pattern stand out:

- If several asynchronous computations happen back to back, you can no longer follow the flow of the program as it is spread across multiple callbacks.

- Forgetting to call `EndOperation` can lead to adverse effects, anything from memory leaks to exceptions to program hangs.

- Casting any state information from the `IAsyncResult.AsyncState` property can lead to type cast exceptions at runtime.

- Once you start looping with asynchronous calls, you encounter a nightmare of spaghetti callbacks.

These aren't the only pitfalls when using the APM. What if you wanted to do proper exception handling across the series of asynchronous operations? You can't wrap all of your callbacks inside of a single `try-with` expression; rather, you need to have an exception handler inside each callback.

The point of introducing the APM wasn't to scare you away from asynchronous programming, but rather to set the stage for how F# can improve upon this.

Ideally, there would be a way to eliminate the need for explicitly dividing up your code into what happens *before* the asynchronous operation (the code that calls `BeginOpera tion`) and what happens *after* the asynchronous operation (the callback, which calls `EndOperation`).

It would be useful if you could write your code in a synchronous fashion, and have some helper library do the "thread hopping" and "chopping up of your computation and passing it to a callback" for you. Ideally, you could write:

```
printfn "Opening file..."
let_wait_until_async_is_done data = openFileAsync filePath

let result = processFile data filePath

printfn "Writing result to disk..."
do_wait_until_async_is_done writeFileAsync (filePath + ".result") result

printfn "Finished!"
```

Didn't we run into a similar problem back in Chapter 10? We identified classes of problems where we wanted some background operation to occur behind the scenes but still to be allowed to write normal F# code. Perhaps that technique could be useful here as well....

That's right, F# computation expressions to the rescue!

Asynchronous Workflows

F# asynchronous workflows allow you to perform asynchronous operations without the need for explicit callbacks. So you can write the code as if it were using synchronous execution, but in actuality, the code will execute asynchronously, suspending and resuming the computation as asynchronous operations complete.

 F# asynchronous workflows don't introduce any new primitives to the .NET platform; rather, F#'s computation expression syntax makes the existing threading libraries much more palatable.

Example 11-6 repeats the same task of asynchronously reading and writing a file, except rather than using the APM, all of the asynchronous operations are handled by the F# asynchronous workflows library. The result is that the code is dramatically simpler to write and understand.

The magic of how async workflows works will be discussed shortly. But for now, just notice that the code is wrapped up in the `async` computation expression builder and the asynchronous operations begin with `let!` and `do!`. Also, note that the result of the `async` builder is passed to the mysterious `Async.Start` method.

Example 11-6. Asynchronous file IO using F# async workflows

```
open System.IO

let asyncProcessFile (filePath : string) (processBytes : byte[] -> byte[]) =
    async {

        printfn "Processing file [%s]" (Path.GetFileName(filePath))

        use fileStream = new FileStream(filePath, FileMode.Open)
        let bytesToRead = int fileStream.Length

        let! data = fileStream.AsyncRead(bytesToRead)

        printfn
            "Opened [%s], read [%d] bytes"
            (Path.GetFileName(filePath))
            data.Length

        let data' = processBytes data

        use resultFile = new FileStream(filePath + ".results", FileMode.Create)
        do! resultFile.AsyncWrite(data', 0, data'.Length)

        printfn "Finished processing file [%s]" <| Path.GetFileName(filePath)
    } |> Async.Start
```

The Async Library

The secret behind asynchronous workflows is that the code is wrapped in an `async` block and doesn't immediately execute. Rather, the computation that the code performs is returned in the form of an `Async<'T>` object, which you can think of as an asynchronous operation that will *eventually* return an instance of `'T`. Exactly how the `'T` will be extracted from the `Async<'T>` is the business of the `Async` module and the `async` computation expression builder.

Whenever a `let!`, `do!`, or similar action is performed, the `async` computation builder will begin the task asynchronously and then execute the rest of the computation once that task completes.

In the previous example, the function `AsyncRead` returns an `Async<byte[]>`. So if the code were written

```
let data = fileStream.AsyncRead(bytesToRead)
```

the type of `data` would be `Async<byte[]>`.

However, `let!` (pronounced let-bang) was used instead. This starts the `async` builder's machinery to begin the computation asynchronously, and return the result that was a byte array once that operation completes:

```
let! data : byte[] = fileStream.AsyncRead(bytesToRead)
```

 Please refer back to Chapter 10 for more information about how `let!` and `do!` translate to function calls on a computation expression builder.

Starting async tasks

There are several methods available to start asynchronous workflows. The simplest of these is the `Async.Start` method. `Async.Start` takes an `Async<unit>` as a parameter, and simply begins executing it asynchronously. If you want the async task to return a value, you need to wait for operation to complete by calling `Async.RunSynchronously`.

Example 11-7 defines a function `getHtml` that takes a URL as a parameter and returns the web page's content. The function returns an instance of type `Async<string>`.

Notice that a value is returned from the async workflow by using the `return!` keyword. `return` is also a valid way to return a value from an async workflow, and will have the workflow return an `Async<'T>` instead of a `'T`.

 Example 11-7 uses the `AsyncReadToEnd` extension method defined in `FSharp.PowerPack.dll`. For more information on how to obtain the F# PowerPack, refer to Appendix A.

Example 11-7. Retrieving values from async workflows

```
#r "FSharp.PowerPack.dll"

open System.IO
open System.Net
open System.Microsoft.FSharp.Control.WebExtensions

let getHtml (url : string) =
    async {

        let req = WebRequest.Create(url)
        let! rsp = req.AsyncGetResponse()

        use stream = rsp.GetResponseStream()
        use reader = new StreamReader(stream)

        return! reader.AsyncReadToEnd()
    }

let html =
    getHtml "http://en.wikipedia.org/wiki/F_Sharp_programming_language"
    |> Async.RunSynchronously
```

`Async.RunSynchronously` isn't especially useful on its own, because it blocks the starting thread waiting for the operation to complete—which is exactly the opposite of asynchronous execution. Usually this method is called immediately after the `Async.Paral lel` method, which takes a `seq< Async<'T> >`, and starts all of the sequence's computations in parallel. The results are combined into an instance of `Async<'T[]>`.

The following code snippet builds off the `getHtml` method, and retrieves a series of web pages in parallel:s

```
let webPages : string[] =
    [ "http://www.google.com"; "http://www.bing.com"; "http://www.yahoo.com" ]
    |> List.map getHtml
    |> Async.Parallel
    |> Async.RunSynchronously
```

In addition to simplifying asynchronous code, using F# asynchronous workflows has the added benefit of making it easier to handle exceptions and support cancellation, something that is prohibitively difficult when using the APM.

Exceptions

Earlier, when we were chopping up asynchronous tasks with `BeginOperation` and `EndOperation`, what if you wanted to properly handle an exception? Rather than having multiple exception handlers—each within an APM callback—when using asynchronous workflows, you can put the exception handler directly in the `async` block.

Even if the body of the `try` has several asynchronous operations (`let!`s and `do!`s) inside of it, the exception will be caught exactly the way you expect.

```
let asncOperation =
    async {
        try
            // ...
        with
        | :? IOException as ioe ->
            printfn "IOException: %s" ioe.Message
        | :? ArgumentException as ae ->
            printfn "ArgumentException: %s" ae.Message
    }
```

But what happens if an exception from an async workflow isn't caught? Does the exception bubble up and eventually bring down the whole process? Unfortunately, yes.

In asynchronous workflows, unhandled exceptions bring down the whole process because by default they are not caught. To catch unhandled exceptions from async workflows, you can use the `Async.StartWithContinuations` method, discussed later, or use the `Async.Catch` combinator.

The `Async.Catch` method takes an async workflow and wraps it into a success or exception result. It has the following signature:

```
val Catch : Async<'T> -> Async< Choice<'T,exn> >
```

The `Choice` type means that its value has one of several values; this is what multi-case active patterns compile to behind the scenes.

The following example uses the `Async.Catch` combinator to enable catching exceptions and then runs the async workflow. If the task completes successfully the result is printed to the screen; otherwise, the exception's message is printed:

```
asyncTaskX
|> Async.Catch
|> Async.RunSynchronously
|> function
    | Choice1Of2 result    -> printfn "Async operation completed: %A" result
    | Choice2Of2 (ex : exn) -> printfn "Exception thrown: %s" ex.Message
```

Cancellation

When you execute code asynchronously, it is important to have a cancellation mechanism just in case the user notices things going awry or gets impatient. Earlier, when we were working with raw threads, the only way to cancel an operation was to literally kill the thread using `Thread.Abort`, and in doing so introduce numerous problems.

Asynchronous workflows can be cancelled, but unlike `Thread.Abort`, cancelling an async workflow is simply a request. The task does not immediately terminate, but rather the next time a `let!`, `do!`, etc. is executed, the rest of the computation will not be run and a cancellation handler will be executed instead.

The simplest way to hook up cancellation is to use the `Async.TryCancelled` method. Similar to `Async.Catch`, it takes an `Async<'T>` and returns an updated `Async<'T>` that will call a provided function in the event that the workflow is cancelled.

Example 11-8 defines a simple task that counts to 10 and cancels it later. Notice how the cancellation is done by calling the `Async.CancelDefaultToken` method.

Example 11-8. Cancelling asynchronous operations

```
open System
open System.Threading

let cancelableTask =
    async {
        printfn "Waiting 10 seconds..."
        for i = 1 to 10 do
            printfn "%d..." i
            do! Async.Sleep(1000)
        printfn "Finished!"
    }

// Callback used when the operation is canceled
let cancelHandler (ex : OperationCanceledException) =
    printfn "The task has been canceled."

Async.TryCancelled(cancelableTask, cancelHandler)
|> Async.Start

// ...

Async.CancelDefaultToken()
```

Cancellation in F# asynchronous workflows is handled using the same mechanism of the Parallel Extensions to .NET, via the `CancellationToken` type. A `CancellationToken` simply keeps track of whether or not the operation has been cancelled. (Or more specifically, had cancellation requested.) So whenever a `let!` or `do!` is encountered, the `async` builder checks the workflow's `CancellationToken` to see if the operation should continue or terminate early.

The `Async.CancelDefaultToken` method cancels the last asynchronous workflow started. This is ideal most of the time but can cause issues if your application starts multiple asynchronous workflows.

If you want to be able to cancel an arbitrary asynchronous workflow, then you'll want to create and keep track of a `CancellationTokenSource` object. A `CancellationToken Source` is what signals the cancellation, which in turn updates all of its associated `CancellationTokens`.

The following snippet shows how to start an asynchronous workflow whose cancellation is tracked by a `CancellationTokenSource` object:

```
open System.Threading

let computation = Async.TryCancelled(cancelableTask, cancelHandler)
let cancellationSource = new CancellationTokenSource()

Async.Start(computation, cancellationSource.Token)

// ...

cancellationSource.Cancel()
```

The `Async` module may seem a bit complicated with so many ways to start and customize async workflow tasks. Most likely you will only use one method for hooking into unhandled exceptions and cancellations, and that is the `Async.StartWithContinuations` method. Essentially, it is `Async.Catch`, `Async.TryCancelled`, and `Async.Start` all rolled into one. It takes four parameters:

- The async workflow to execute
- A function to execute when the operation completes
- A function to call in case an exception is thrown
- A function to call in case the operation gets cancelled

The following snippet shows the `Async.StartWithContinuations` method in action:

```
Async.StartWithContinuations(
    superAwesomeAsyncTask,
    (fun result -> printfn "Task completed with result %A" result),
    (fun exn    -> printfn "Task threw an exception with Message: %s" exn.Message),
    (fun oce    -> printfn "Task was cancelled. Message: %s" oce.Message)
)
```

Async Operations

F# asynchronous workflows show the ease with which you can write asynchronous code, but how do you get an instance of `Async<'T>`? You can build your own async objects, as you will see shortly, but most likely you will be using the extension methods defined in the F# library.

The `System.IO.Stream` type is extended with several methods for reading and writing data synchronously. You've already seen examples of `AsyncRead` and `AsyncWrite`.

The `System.Net.WebRequest` class is extended with `AsyncGetResponse` for retrieving web pages asynchronously. However, to use this extension method, you must first open the `Microsoft.FSharp.Control.WebExtensions` namespace:

```
open System.IO
open System.Net

open Microsoft.FSharp.Control.WebExtensions

let getHtml (url : string) =
```

```
async {

    let req = WebRequest.Create(url)
    let! rsp = req.AsyncGetResponse()

    use stream = rsp.GetResponseStream()
    use reader = new StreamReader(stream)

    return reader.ReadToEnd()
}
```

The `Async.Sleep` method does a sleep just like `Thread.Sleep` except that it does not block the async workflow thread. Instead, the thread that begins the sleep will be reused by some other task, and when the sleep completes, another thread will be woken up and finish the execution.

The following code snippet suspends and resumes an async workflow each second to update a progress bar attached to a WinForm:

```
#r "System.Windows.Forms.dll"
#r "System.Drawing.dll"

open System.Threading
open System.Windows.Forms

let form = new Form(TopMost = true)

let pb   = new ProgressBar(Minimum = 0, Maximum = 15, Dock = DockStyle.Fill)
form.Controls.Add(pb)

form.Show()

async {
    for i = 0 to 15 do
        do! Async.Sleep(1000)
        pb.Value <- i
} |> Async.Start
```

Custom Async Primitives

You can build your own async workflow primitives by using the `Async.FromBeginEnd` function. As parameters, it takes the `BeginOperation` and `EndOperation` methods from the APM, but wraps them so that they can be used with an async workflow. (The `Async.FromBeginEnd` function is overloaded to accept various types of APM operations.)

Example 11-9 defines two extension methods for getting the files in a directory and copying a file asynchronously. Both async primitives work by using the `Func<_,_>` type, which is a way to create function values, except that it works using delegates. Remember that any delegate type defined in C# or VB.NET comes with a `BeginInvoke` and `EndInvoke` method that can serve as the basis for the APM.

Once the two new async primitives `AsyncGetFiles` and `AsyncCopy` have been created, they are used to copy all the files from one folder to another.

 Be careful when creating your own async primitives. Unless there is a specific reason for executing an operation asynchronously, such as an OS hook to improve IO throughput, you won't see any improvement, as the operation will complete synchronously and then switch to a different thread when the async workflow resumes.

Example 11-9. Creating custom async primitives

```
open System
open System.IO

type System.IO.Directory with
    /// Retrieve all files under a path asynchronously
    static member AsyncGetFiles(path : string, searchPattern : string) =
        let dele = new Func<string * string, string[]>(Directory.GetFiles)
        Async.FromBeginEnd(
            (path, searchPattern),
            dele.BeginInvoke,
            dele.EndInvoke)

type System.IO.File with
    /// Copy a file asynchronously
    static member AsyncCopy(source : string, dest : string) =
        let dele = new Func<string * string, unit>(File.Copy)
        Async.FromBeginEnd((source, dest), dele.BeginInvoke, dele.EndInvoke)


let asyncBackup path searchPattern destPath =
    async {
        let! files = Directory.AsyncGetFiles(path, searchPattern)

        for file in files do
            let filename = Path.GetFileName(file)
            do! File.AsyncCopy(file, Path.Combine(destPath, filename))
    }
```

Limitations

F# asynchronous workflows are great for enabling IO parallelism; however, because the library simply is a lightweight wrapper on top of the thread pool, using it won't guarantee that you will maximize performance. When executing code in parallel, there are numerous factors to take into account, for example:

- The number of processor cores
- Processor cache coherency
- The existing CPU workload

While F# asynchronous workflows make it easy to perform multiple computations at once, there is no throttling of executing threads to ensure an optimal usage. For example, if eight threads are vying for CPU time, but the machine is already under a heavy workload, then a lot of time is wasted context switching among those threads. Ideally, a governor would give some threads more processor time to reduce this context switching.

You should use F# asynchronous workflows for asynchronous programming, but for CPU-level parallelism, consider using the .NET Parallel Extensions, discussed later in this chapter.

Parallel Programming

Parallel programming is about dividing up a computation into *n* parts to obtain—hopefully—an *n*-times speedup (though in practice this is rarely achievable).

The simplest way to do parallel programming on .NET is through the Parallel Extensions to the .NET Framework (PFX); which is Microsoft-speak for new primitives to make it easier to write parallel programs. By using, the PFX you should have no need to manually control threads or the thread pool.

 The Parallel Framework only exists on CLR 4.0. If you create an F# application that targets the .NET 2.0, 3.0, or 3.5 runtime, you will not be able to take advantage of the PFX libraries. Also, to take advantage of the PFX libraries within an FSI session you must add a reference to System.Core.dll via:

```
#r "System.Core.dll"
```

F# asynchronous workflows, however, are available on down-level platforms.

Parallel.For

The first thing you can do to parallelize your applications is to just swap out your `for` loops with the `Parallel.For` and `Parallel.ForEach` methods in the `System.Threading` namespace. As their names imply, these functions can replace `for` loops and execute loop iterations in parallel.

Example 11-10 uses `Parallel.For` to multiply two matrices. The code to produce each row of the resulting matrix is in the **rowTask** function, so rows of the resulting matrix will be computed in parallel.

Example 11-10. Using Parallel.For

```
open System
open System.Threading.Tasks
```

```
/// Multiply two matricies using the PFX
let matrixMultiply (a : float[,]) (b : float[,]) =

    let aRow, aCol = Array2D.length1 a, Array2D.length2 a
    let bRow, bCol = Array2D.length1 b, Array2D.length2 b
    if aCol <> bRow then failwith "Array dimension mismatch."

    // Allocate space for the resulting matrix, c
    let c = Array2D.create aCol bRow 0.0
    let cRow, cCol = aCol, bRow

    // Compute each row of the resulting matrix
    let rowTask rowIdx =
        for colIdx = 0 to cCol - 1 do
            for x = 0 to aRow - 1 do
                c.[colIdx, rowIdx] <-
                    c.[colIdx, rowIdx] + a.[x, colIdx] * b.[rowIdx, x]
        ()

    let _ = Parallel.For(0, cRow, new Action<int>(rowTask))

    // Return the computed matrix
    c
```

Blindly swapping out for loops with Parallel.For will introduce bugs if the code executing inside the for loop depends on the previous iteration; for instance, if you are using a for loop to perform a fold-type operation. In the previous example, the order in which rows were computed didn't matter, so the code could safely be parallelized.

You can start to see the benefits of containing mutation and not sharing global state. In F#, you have to "'opt in" for mutating data, so your code by default is thread-safe.

The Array.Parallel Module

Built on top of the PFX, for F# developers, is the Array.Parallel module that contains some of the methods found in the Array module, such as map, mapi, and partition. The only difference is that these methods complete the operation in parallel.

Example 11-11 shows using the Array.Parallel module to open and search through files in parallel. Just like using Parallel.For, if the operation on each element of the array is independent, you can safely replace the parallel operations with the synchronous ones.

The code retrieves a list of classified files, decrypts them in parallel, then searches for keywords in parallel, and finally encrypts them again...in parallel.

Example 11-11. Using the Array.Parallel library

```
open System.IO

let getSecretData keyword =
```

```
let secretFiles = Directory.GetFiles(@"D:\TopSecret\", "*.classified")
```

```
Array.Parallel.iter File.Decrypt secretFiles
```

```
let secretData =
    Directory.GetFiles(@"D:\TopSecret\", "*.classified")
    |> Array.Parallel.map (fun filePath -> File.ReadAllText(filePath))
    |> Array.Parallel.choose (fun contents ->
            if contents.Contains(keyword)
            then Some(contents)
            else None)
```

```
Array.Parallel.iter File.Encrypt secretFiles
```

```
secretData
```

Parallel Extensions for .NET

In the previous section, we looked at how to execute operations in arrays and **for** loops in parallel; however, not every problem can decompose so nicely. Most likely you will see a way to cleanly break up a problem, but the divisions may not be equal. Or perhaps one part of the problem may need to be subdivided again and again in a "divide and conquer" approach.

Fortunately, the PFX allows you divide your operations however you see fit and the library will take care of scheduling and executing those pieces in parallel.

The core structure of PFX parallelism is the **Task** object. Similar to the **Async<'T>** type, a **Task** represents a body of work to be completed later. To see what the **Task** object offers, let's quickly review how to write parallel programs in F#.

Suppose you have two independent, long-running tasks. The naive implementation simply runs them in serial:

```
let result1 = longTask1()
let result2 = longTask2()
```

You can improve upon this by using the thread pool as you saw earlier; however, this makes a mess of the code and prevents you from cancelling the operation or handling exceptions properly:

```
let mutable completed = false
let mutable result1 = null

ThreadPool.QueueUserWorkItem(fun _ ->
    result1   <- longTask1()
    completed <- true
) |> ignore

let result2 = longTask2()

// Wait until task1 complete
```

```
    while not completed do
        Thread.Sleep(0)
```

Here is how you can solve this problem using the PFX:

```
open System.Threading.Tasks

let taskBody = new Func<string>(longTask1)
let task = Task.Factory.StartNew<string>(taskBody)

let result2 = longTask2()
let result1 = task.Result
```

Primitives

New tasks can be created using one of the overloads of the `Task.Factory.StartNew` method. Once created, the task will be scheduled to execute in parallel. However, the machinery of the PFX library will determine just how many tasks to spawn at a time, dependent upon factors such as current available CPU resources, number of processors, and so on.

The point is that you don't need to manage this explicitly; the PFX will do it for you. So whereas spawning numerous operations using F# asynchronous workflows would overwhelm the thread pool and CPU, the PFX properly modulates how many tasks are executing at once to get the best performance possible.

To retrieve a task's return value, all you need to do is access its `Result` property.

```
let x = task.Result
```

Accessing `Result` will do one of three things:

- Return the task's stored result if the task has already completed.
- Wait for the task to complete if it has already started.
- Start executing the task on the current thread if it hasn't begun executing.

You don't have to track individual tasks either. You can combine multiple tasks with synchronization primitives `Task.WaitAll` and `Task.WaitAny`. These functions take an array of tasks and wait until all the tasks have finished or any of the tasks has finished before continuing on.

Example 11-12 shows spawning several tasks to resize images in a directory, and using the `WaitAll` method to wait for all of the parallel operations to complete.

Example 11-12. Using Task.WaitAll to wait for tasks to complete

```
open System
open System.IO
open System.Drawing
open System.Drawing.Imaging
open System.Drawing.Drawing2D
open System.Threading.Tasks
```

```fsharp
/// Resize images to a new width, height
let resizeImage (newWidth : int, newHeight : int) (filePath : string) =
    let originalImage = Bitmap.FromFile(filePath)

    let resizedImage = new Bitmap(newWidth, newHeight)
    use g = Graphics.FromImage(resizedImage)
    g.InterpolationMode <- InterpolationMode.HighQualityBicubic
    g.DrawImage(originalImage, 0, 0, newWidth, newHeight)

    let fileName = Path.GetFileNameWithoutExtension(filePath)
    let fileFolder = Path.GetDirectoryName(filePath)
    resizedImage.Save(
        Path.Combine(fileFolder, fileName + ".Resized.jpg"),
        ImageFormat.Jpeg)

// Spawns a new PFX task to resize an image
let spawnTask filePath =
    let taskBody = new Action(fun () -> resizeImage (640, 480) filePath)
    Task.Factory.StartNew(taskBody)

let imageFiles = Directory.GetFiles(@"C:\2009-03-16 iPhone\", "*.jpg")

// Spawning resize tasks
let resizeTasks = imageFiles |> Array.map spawnTask

// Wait for them all to complete
Task.WaitAll(resizeTasks)
```

The `WaitAny` primitive may seem strange—why spawn several tasks and wait for only one to complete? There are two good reasons to use this primitive.

First, if you have a family of algorithms you can use to solve a problem, each with varying degrees of efficiency based on input, then it can make sense to start them all in parallel and just get the first one that completes. (You might want to cancel all the other tasks once you know their results won't be needed, though.)

Second, it can be helpful for creating more responsive applications. For example, if there were a UI attached to Example 11-13, the user might want to see the results of the resized images as they came in—not just after all of the operations have completed.

Cancellation

Another benefit of using the `Task` class, unlike manually controlling threads you spawn, is to take advantage of cancellation. Just like F# asynchronous workflows, cancellation is a request and doesn't immediately terminate the task. So if you want tasks to behave well when cancelled, you must explicitly check for it.

As mentioned earlier, the Parallel Extensions to .NET use the same cancellation mechanism as F# asynchronous workflows. Specifically, each task can be associated with a `CancellationToken` object, which keeps track of its cancellation status. A

CancellationToken is produced by a CancellationTokenSource object that actually signals cancellation.

Example 11-13 shows starting up a task that will execute for 10 seconds, unless it is
otherwise cancelled. The task is started with a CancellationToken associated with the
longTaskCTS CancellationTokenSource. Once signaled to be cancelled, a task must either
shut down as best it can or simply throw an OperationCancelledException.

Example 11-13. Cancelling tasks

```
open System
open System.Threading
open System.Threading.Tasks

let longTaskCTS = new CancellationTokenSource()

let longRunningTask() =
    let mutable i = 1
    let mutable loop = true

    while i <= 10 && loop do
        printfn "%d..." i
        i <- i + 1
        Thread.Sleep(1000)

        // Check if the task was cancelled
        if longTaskCTS.IsCancellationRequested then
            printfn "Cancelled; stopping early."
            loop <- false

    printfn "Complete!"

let startLongRunningTask() =
    Task.Factory.StartNew(longRunningTask, longTaskCTS.Token)

let t = startLongRunningTask()

// ...

longTaskCTS.Cancel()
```

Exceptions

Handling exceptions in conjunction with the PFX is a bit more involved. If a task throws
an exception, it returns an exception of type System.AggregateException. It may seem
strange that tasks don't surface the exception you originally threw, but remember that
tasks are executing in an entirely different context from where the exception will be
caught. What if the task had spawned child tasks—and they too threw exceptions?

The AggregateException type combines all exceptions originating from the target task,
which you can access later via the InnerExceptions collection.

Example 11-14 shows using the PFX for searching through a graph structure, which in the example is a magical cave filled with yeti and treasure. Whenever a fork is encountered, new tasks are spawned to visit the left and right branches.

Example 11-14. Using the PFX to search through a graph

```
open System
open System.Threading.Tasks

type CaveNode =
    | ManEatingYeti of string
    | BottomlessPit
    | Treasure
    | DeadEnd
    | Fork of CaveNode * CaveNode

let rec findAllTreasure node =
    match node with

    // Finding treasure in magical caves ain't easy...
    | ManEatingYeti(n) -> failwithf "Eaten by a yeti named %s" n
    | BottomlessPit    -> failwith "Fell into a bottomless pit"

    // Leaf nodes
    | DeadEnd  -> 0
    | Treasure -> 1

    // Branches. Send half of your expedition left, the other half goes right...
    // ... hopefully not to only be eaten by a Yeti
    | Fork(left, right) ->
        let goLeft  = Task.Factory.StartNew<int>(fun () -> findAllTreasure left)
        let goRight = Task.Factory.StartNew<int>(fun () -> findAllTreasure right)
        goLeft.Result + goRight.Result
```

The following code snippet calls the `findAllTreasure` function and catches the `Aggre gateException`. Notice how the `decomposeAggregEx` function is used to extract all the non-`AggregateExceptions`:

```
let colossalCave =
    Fork(
        Fork(
            DeadEnd,
            Fork(Treasure, BottomlessPit)
        ),
        Fork(
            ManEatingYeti("Umaro"),
            Fork(
                ManEatingYeti("Choko"),
                Treasure
            )
        )
    )

try
    let treasureFindingTask =
```

```
            Task.Factory.StartNew<int>(fun () -> findAllTreasure colossalCave)

        printfn "Found %d treasure!" treasureFindingTask.Result

    with
    | :? AggregateException as ae ->

        // Get all inner exceptions from the aggregate exception.
        let rec decomposeAggregEx (ae : AggregateException) =
            seq {
                for innerEx in ae.InnerExceptions do
                    match innerEx with
                    | :? AggregateException as ae -> yield! decomposeAggregEx ae
                    | _ -> yield innerEx
            }

        printfn "AggregateException:"

        // Alternately, you can use ae.Flatten() to put all nested
        // exceptions into a single AggregateException collection.
        decomposeAggregEx ae
        |> Seq.iter (fun ex -> printfn "\tMessage: %s" ex.Message)
```

Concurrent Data Structures

Mastering the `Task` type is crucial for exploiting the PFX and writing parallel programs without a lot of extra fuss. However, the `Task.Result` property alone is insufficient to store the results for many parallel applications. Ideally, you will have tasks working in concert to fill out a shared data structure.

However, sharing data structures between tasks can be problematic due to the data races you saw early in the chapter. You could lock the data type every single time you access the value, but acquiring an exclusive lock is an expensive operation, and can dramatically hamper performance if it is never used. (That is, you acquire a lock during a time nobody else accesses the data.) Also, should you acquire a lock for a read operation?

The PFX introduces several new collection types to solve this problem. The `System.Col` `lections.Concurrent` namespace contains the standard sort of collection types you would expect, except that they can all be shared freely between threads. Each collection uses locking to ensure data is consistent, but does so in a way so as to maximize performance. (Or if possible, simply use a lock-free algorithm.)

Concurrent queue

A common pattern in parallel programming is having a list of work to be done and dividing it among various threads. However, there is an inherent contention for the list of things to do. Fortunately, the `ConcurrentQueue` data type solves this problem.

The type is a first-in, first-out queue that can safely be used across threads. The main methods on the type are `TryDequeue` and `Enqueue`. The `Try` prefix indicates that the function will return `true` if the operation completed successfully and `false` if it didn't. (In the context of concurrent data structures, this is typically due to a data race.)

Similar to `Dictionary.TryGetValue`, the result of `TryDequeue` will be returned as a tuple, with the first element indicating success or failure of the operation:

```
open System.Collections.Concurrent

let cq = new ConcurrentQueue<int>()
[1 .. 10] |> List.iter cq.Enqueue

let success, firstItem = cq.TryDequeue()
if success then
    printfn "%d was successfully dequeued" firstItem
else
    printfn "Data race, try again later"
```

Concurrent dictionary

The `ConcurrentDictionary` type behaves like a normal dictionary. Example 11-15 uses a `ConcurrentDictionary` to associate words with the number of times they are encountered in a set of files.

In the example, the `AddOrUpdate` method is used. The `ConcurrentDictionary` has different methods for adding new items to the dictionary, and `AddOrUpdate` takes a key, a value to add if the key doesn't exist, and a function to update the value if the key is already present in the dictionary. Using this method makes it easier to insert items into the dictionary rather than checking the result of `TryAdd`.

Example 11-15. Using the ConcurrentDictionary

```
open System
open System.IO
open System.Collections.Concurrent

// Queue of files to process
let filesToProcess =
    Directory.GetFiles(@"D:\Book\", "*.txt")
    |> (fun files -> new ConcurrentQueue<_>(files))

// Dictionary to store the occurances of particular words
let wordUsage = new ConcurrentDictionary<string, int>()

let processFile filePath =
    let text = File.ReadAllText(filePath)
    let words =
        text.Split([| ' '; '\r'; '\n' |], StringSplitOptions.RemoveEmptyEntries)
        |> Array.map (fun word -> word.Trim())

    // Add the word to our lookup table. Inserts value '1', or if the key
    // is already present updates it to be 'count + 1'.
```

```
    Array.Parallel.iter(fun word ->
        wordUsage.AddOrUpdate(
            word,
            1,
            new Func<string,int,int>(fun _ count -> count + 1)
        ) |> ignore
    )

// Begins updating the wordUsage dictionary
let fillDictionary() =
    let mutable continueWorking = true

    while continueWorking do

        let dequeueSuccessful, filePath = filesToProcess.TryDequeue()

        if not dequeueSuccessful then
            // If the queue is empty, then we are done working
            if filesToProcess.IsEmpty then
                continueWorking <- false
            // ... otherwise, two tasks tried to dequeue
            // at the same time. Try again.
            else
                continueWorking <- true

        // Process the file
        processFile filePath

// Start three tasks to count word usage
fillDictionary()
fillDictionary()
fillDictionary()
```

Concurrent bag

The ConcurrentBag class behaves much like the HashSet<_> type we covered in Chapter 4, except that it allows duplicate items to be added. This isn't a world-shattering loss because once the bag has been filled you can filter out duplicates on your own.

A ConcurrentBag is ideal for aggregating results from several tasks you have spawned.

Example 11-16 spawns several tasks to compute a list of prime numbers up to a maximum value in parallel using a ConcurrentBag. If a HashSet<_> type were used instead, some of the values added to the collection would be "dropped" because of the race conditions when trying to update the HashSet's internal data structures. (Or even worse, the data itself could get corrupted.)

The function computePrimes returns the ConcurrentBag cast as a seq<int> and then passed to a HashSet<_>. (ConcurrentBag, like most collection types, implements the IEnumerable<_> interface and therefore can be cast as a seq<_>.)

Example 11-16. Using the ConcurrentBag class to store parallel results

```fsharp
open System
open System.Threading.Tasks
open System.Collections.Concurrent
open System.Collections.Generic

/// Check if a number is prime
let isPrime x =
    let rec primeCheck count =
        // If the counter has reaced x, then we know x is prime
        if count = x       then true
        // If x is divisible by the counter, we know x isn't prime
        elif x % count = 0 then false
        else primeCheck (count + 1)
    // Special case 1 as prime
    if x = 1
    then true
    else primeCheck 2

let computePrimes tasksToSpawn maxValue =
    let range = maxValue / tasksToSpawn
    let primes = new ConcurrentBag<int>()

    // Spawn several tasks at once, adding any primes they find
    // to the ConcurrentBag
    let tasks =
        [|
        for i in 0 .. tasksToSpawn - 1 do
            yield Task.Factory.StartNew(
                Action(fun () ->
                    for x = i * range to (i + 1) * range - 1 do
                        if isPrime x then primes.Add(x)
                )
            )
        |]
    Task.WaitAll(tasks)

    new HashSet<_>(primes :> seq<int>)
```

Now you can write asynchronous and parallel programs in F# by taking advantage of the great libraries available. You can also see why an emphasis on functional programming is beneficial when doing parallel programming. Composing pure, immutable functions makes it easy to decompose tasks to execute independently, without worrying about introducing bugs.

 Remember that adding parallelism to an application doesn't always make it perform better. Whenever doing any architectural changes for performance, be sure to benchmark your application early and often.

CHAPTER 12

Reflection

We have covered almost all of the raw syntax of F#, and the programming paradigms it enables. In this chapter, you won't learn any new capabilities of the F# language per se; instead you will learn how to harness the *.NET Reflection APIs*.

Reflection allows you to access the runtime metadata information about executing code. Metadata can be raw type information, such as the methods a class has, or it can come in the form of *attributes*, which are programmer-supplied code annotations.

.NET reflection is most commonly used for *metaprogramming*, which is writing programs that reason about themselves, or modify themselves, such as those that can load plug-ins to add new functionality at runtime; in other words, they allow other developers to extend your application without their needing to have access to the source code.

But before you can do full-on metaprogramming, you must first understand how to annotate code to provide metadata.

Attributes

Attributes are a form of metadata you can attach to assemblies, methods, parameters, and so on. These annotations can then be inspected at runtime using reflection, which we will get to later in this chapter. The F# compiler will recognize attributes as well; in fact, you have been using attributes for a while now to provide hints for how to compile your code.

Recall from Chapter 5 that in order to mark a class as abstract, you need to provide the [<Abstract>] attribute to the type declaration. When the F# compiler sees that attribute, it will generate the code differently than if the attribute had not been present. The same is true for the [<Struct>], [<ReferenceEquality>], and other attributes:

```
[<AbstractClass>]
type Animal =
    abstract Speak : unit -> unit
    abstract NumberOfLegs : int with get
```

In .NET programming, there are many common attributes that the F# compiler will recognize as well. For example, the System.ObsoleteAttribute is used to mark deprecated methods and classes. When using code entities marked with [<Obsolete>], the F# compiler will generate an error or warning based on usage.

Example 12-1 shows some F# code that has been refactored since originally written. An [<Obsolete>] attribute has been added to help guide consumers of the class to update their code.

As you saw earlier, to place an attribute, simply insert the attribute's name surrounded by [< >] above the class or method you want the attribute to apply to. When applying an attribute, if the attribute's name is suffixed with *Attribute*, you can omit the word *Attribute*. For example, to apply an instance of System.ObsoleteAttribute, you just need to write [<Obsolete>] if the System namespace has been opened.

Example 12-1. The Obsolete attribute

```
open System

type SafetyLevel =
    | RecreationalUse  = 1
    | HaveMcCoyOnDuty  = 3
    | SetPhasersToKill = 4

type HoloDeck(safetyLevel : SafetyLevel) =

    let mutable m_safetyLevel = safetyLevel

    member this.SafetyLevel with get () = m_safetyLevel

    [<Obsolete("Deprecated. Cannot update protocols once initialized.", true)>]
    member this.SafetyLevel with set x = m_safetyLevel <- x
```

Figure 12-1 shows the Visual Studio 2010 editor when trying to call a method or property marked with [<Obsolete>].

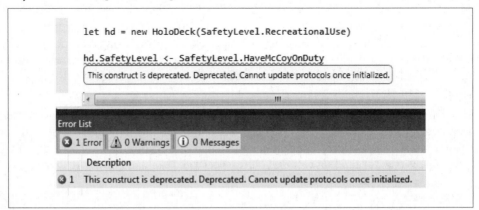

Figure 12-1. Warnings and errors in the Visual Studio Editor

Applying Attributes

Later in this chapter, we will look at how to analyze type information to examine any attributes provided. But first, we need to have metadata to analyze, so let's take a deeper look at adding attributes to your code.

Attribute targets

Most of the time putting the attribute directly above the type or method you want to annotate will be sufficient. However, there will be times when the attribute's target can be ambiguous. To have the attribute apply to a specific construct, you can use an *attribute target*, which is a keyword indicating what the attribute applies to.

For example, assembly-level attributes are global in the sense that they do not belong to a particular class or method, but rather apply to the whole assembly. So an attribute target is required to make clear that the assembly-level attribute doesn't apply to the next type or value declared.

The most common assembly-level attributes are those for setting the assembly's version and copyright information. Note in the example that character trigraphs \169 and \174 are used to encode the © and " characters, respectively:

```
open System.Reflection

[<assembly:AssemblyDescription("RemoteCombobulator.exe")>]
[<assembly:AssemblyCompany("Initech Corporation")>]
[<assembly:AssemblyCopyright("\169 Initech Corporation.  All rights reserved.")>]
[<assembly:AssemblyProduct("Initech \174 RemoteCombobulator")>]
do()
```

 In F#, assembly-level attributes must be placed inside of a module on a do binding.

The list of common attribute targets are described in Table 12-1.

Table 12-1. Attribute targets

Target Name	Description
assembly	Applies to the assembly
field	Applies to a class field
parameter	Applies to a parameter of a method
return	Applies to the return value of a method or property

Applying multiple attributes

When you apply multiple attributes, you have the choice to either place each attribute individually or group all the attributes together in a semicolon-delimited list.

Example 12-2 shows the same assembly-level attributes from the previous code snippet, but in a slightly cleaned-up form.

Example 12-2. Applying multiple attributes

```
open System.Reflection

[<
    assembly:AssemblyDescription("RemoteCombobulator.exe");
    assembly:AssemblyCompany("Initech Corporation");
    assembly:AssemblyCopyright("\169 Initech Corporation.  All rights reserved.");
    assembly:AssemblyProduct("Initech \174 RemoteCombobulator")
>]
do()
```

Defining New Attributes

To define new attributes of your own, simply create a class that inherits from `System.Attribute`. Defining your own custom attributes is instrumental for creating custom type annotations.

Example 12-3 defines a couple of custom attributes for adding descriptions for classes and methods. XML-Doc comments are unavailable at runtime, whereas the custom `ClassDescription` and `MethodDescription` attributes will be.

Note that the custom attributes have the optional `AttributeUsage` attribute applied to them. This attribute for custom attributes determines where the attribute can be applied. (Meta-meta-programming indeed!) In Example 12-3, the `AttributeUsage` attribute indicates that the `MethodDescriptionAttribute` can only be applied to methods, otherwise, an error will be issued by the F# compiler. Similarly, the `ClassDescriptionAttribute` can only be applied to classes.

Example 12-3. Defining custom attributes

```
open System

/// Provide a description for a given class
[<AttributeUsage(AttributeTargets.Class)>]
type ClassDescriptionAttribute(desc) =
    inherit Attribute()
    member this.Description = desc

/// Provide a description for a given method
[<AttributeUsage(AttributeTargets.Method)>]
type MethodDescriptionAttribute(desc) =
    inherit Attribute()
    member this.Description = desc

type Widget =
    | RedWidget
    | GreenWidget
    | BlueWidget
```

```
/// XML Doc comments like this one are great for describing a class,
/// but are only available at compile-time. Metadata encoded into
/// attributes is available at run-time.
[<ClassDescription("Represents a stack of Widgets.")>]
type WidgetStack() =

    let mutable m_widgets : Widget list = []

    [<MethodDescription("Pushes a new Widget onto the stack.")>]
    member this.Push(x) = m_widgets <- x :: m_widgets

    [<MethodDescription("Access the top of the Widget stack.")>]
    member this.Peek()  = List.head m_widgets

    [<MethodDescription("Pops the top Widget off the stack.")>]
    member this.Pop()   = let top = List.head m_widgets
                          m_widgets <- List.tail m_widgets
                          top
```

Type Reflection

So you have learned how to attribute code, but what if you wanted to inspect those attributes? You can access attributes on code through *type reflection*.

Recall that everything in .NET inherits from `System.Object`, and therefore every value in .NET has a `GetType` method, which returns an instance of `System.Type`. The `Type` class describes everything there is to know about a type—including its attributes.

Accessing Types

The following FSI session defines a custom type named `Sprocket` and then uses two different methods to access its type information. The first method used in the sample is the generic `typeof<_>` type function, which returns the type of the supplied type parameter. The second method used is to call the `GetType` method found on an instance of `Sprocket` because it inherits from `obj`:

```
> // Simple sprocket type
type Sprocket() =
    member this.Gears = 16
    member this.SerialNumber = "WJM-0520";;

type Sprocket =
  class
    new : unit -> Sprocket
    member Gears : int
    member SerialNumber : string
  end

> // Get type information via typeof<_>
let type1 = typeof<Sprocket>;;
```

```
val type1 : System.Type = FSI_0002+Sprocket

> // Get type information via GetType
let aSprocket = new Sprocket()
let type2 = aSprocket.GetType();;

val aSprocket : Sprocket
val type2 : System.Type = FSI_0002+Sprocket

> type1 = type2;;
val it : bool = true
> type1.Name;;
val it : string = "Sprocket"
```

Accessing generic types

While typeof<_> is helpful for getting type information, when used on generic types it must fix any unknown generic type parameter to obj. If you want the returned type to be fully generic, use the typedefof<_> type function.

The following snippet shows getting type information from a sequence. Notice that the returned type information from using typedefof<_> is fully generic, whereas typeof<_> indicates that the sequence is of type obj, which is potentially incorrect:

```
> let fixedSeq = typeof< seq<float> >;;

val fixedSeq : Type = System.Collections.Generic.IEnumerable`1[System.Double]

> let genSeq = typeof< seq<'a> >;;

val genSeq : Type = System.Collections.Generic.IEnumerable`1[System.Object]

> let fullyGenSeq = typedefof< seq<'a> >;;

val fullyGenSeq : Type = System.Collections.Generic.IEnumerable`1[T]
```

Inspecting methods

Once you have an instance of Type, you can inspect the type's methods and properties by calling GetMethods and GetProperties, and so on.

Example 12-4 defines a function called describeType, which will print all methods, properties, and fields for a type to the console.

The BindingFlags enum is passed in to filter the results. For example, Binding Flags.DeclaredOnly is used so that the call to GetMethods doesn't return inherited methods, such as GetHashCode and ToString.

Example 12-4. Inspecting and analyzing types

```
open System
open System.Reflection
```

```
/// Prints the methods, properties, and fields of a type to the console
let describeType (ty : Type) =

    let bindingFlags =
        BindingFlags.Public    ||| BindingFlags.NonPublic |||
        BindingFlags.Instance  ||| BindingFlags.Static    |||
        BindingFlags.DeclaredOnly

    let methods =
        ty.GetMethods(bindingFlags)
        |> Array.fold (fun desc meth -> desc + sprintf " %s" meth.Name) ""

    let props =
        ty.GetProperties(bindingFlags)
        |> Array.fold (fun desc prop -> desc + sprintf " %s" prop.Name) ""

    let fields =
        ty.GetFields(bindingFlags)
        |> Array.fold (fun desc field -> desc + sprintf " %s" field.Name) ""

    printfn "Name: %s" ty.Name
    printfn "Methods:    \n\t%s\n" methods
    printfn "Properties: \n\t%s\n" props
    printfn "Fields:     \n\t%s" fields
```

The following FSI session shows using describeType on string:

```
Name: String
Methods:
    Join get_FirstChar Join nativeCompareOrdinal nativeCompareOrdinalEx
nativeCompareOrdinalWC SmallCharToUpper EqualsHelper CompareOrdinalHelper
Equals Equals Equals Equals Equals op_Equality op_Inequality get_Chars CopyTo
To CharArray ToCharArray IsNullOrEmpty GetHashCode get_Length get_ArrayLength
get_Capacity Split Split Split Split Split Split InternalSplitKeepEmptyEntries
InternalSplitOmitEmptyEntries MakeSeparatorList MakeSeparatorList Substring
Substring InternalSubStringWithChecks InternalSubString Trim TrimStart
TrimEnd CreateString

    ...snip...

Properties:
    FirstChar Chars Length ArrayLength Capacity

Fields:
    m_arrayLength m_stringLength m_firstChar Empty WhitespaceChars TrimHead
                                       TrimTail TrimBoth
charPtrAlignConst alignConst
```

Now let's use describeType on a custom class. First, define a type called Cog. Note the private accessibility modifiers on the class's field and property:

```
/// Unit of measure for milliliter
[<Measure>]
type ml
```

```
type Cog =

    val mutable private m_oilLevel : float<ml>

    new() = { m_oilLevel = 100.0<ml> }

    member private this.Gears = 16
    member this.SerialNumber = "1138-THX"

    member this.Rotate() =
        // Rotating loses a bit of oil on each turn...
        this.m_oilLevel <- this.m_oilLevel - 0.01<ml>
```

Now, in an FSI session, call describeType on the type of Cog. Notice how all type information is printed out, including members marked with the **private** accessibility modifiers.

 Code accessibility is a language-level restriction to help programmers; however, declaring something private or internal offers no security at runtime. When using .NET reflection, you can access any fields and members of objects. You should keep this in mind when persisting sensitive information in memory.

```
> describeType (typeof<Cog>);;
Name: Cog
Methods:
    get_Gears get_SerialNumber Rotate

Properties:
    SerialNumber Gears

Fields:
    m_oilLevel
val it : unit = ()
```

Inspecting attributes

Inspecting a type's attributes is done in much the same way as inspecting its methods and properties. The only difference, however, is that attributes can be put in many more places.

Example 12-5 shows inspecting a type for the ClassDescription and MethodDescription attributes from earlier in this chapter. Note how the full list of custom attributes on a type needs to be pared down to just the ClassDescription or MethodDescription attributes.

Example 12-5. Inspecting type attributes

```
open System

/// Displays data attributed with the MethodDesc or ClassDesc attributes
let printDocumentation(ty : Type) =
```

```
// Return if a object has a given type
let objHasType ty obj = (obj.GetType() = ty)

let classDescription : string option =
    ty.GetCustomAttributes(false)
    |> Seq.tryFind(objHasType typeof<ClassDescriptionAttribute>)
    |> Option.map(fun attr -> (attr :?> ClassDescriptionAttribute))
    |> Option.map(fun cda -> cda.Description)

let methodDescriptions : seq<string * string option> =
    ty.GetMethods()
    |> Seq.map(fun mi -> mi, mi.GetCustomAttributes(false))
    |> Seq.map(fun (methodInfo, methodAttributes) ->
        let attributeDescription =
            methodAttributes
            |> Seq.tryFind(objHasType typeof<MethodDescriptionAttribute>)
            |> Option.map(fun atr -> (atr :?> MethodDescriptionAttribute))
            |> Option.map(fun mda -> mda.Description)
        methodInfo.Name, attributeDescription)

let getDescription = function
                    | Some(desc) -> desc
                    | None       -> "(no description provided)"

printfn "Info for class: %s" ty.Name
printfn "Class Description:\n\t%s" (getDescription classDescription)
printfn "Method Descriptions:"

methodDescriptions
|> Seq.iter(fun (methName, desc) -> printfn
                                "\t%15s - %s"
                                methName
                                (getDescription desc))
```

When run on the `WidgetStack` type from Example 12-3, the `printDocumentation` function has the following output:

```
> printDocumentation (typeof<WidgetStack>);;
Info for class: WidgetStack
Class Description:
    Represents a stack of Widgets.
Method Descriptions:
            Push - Pushes a new Widget onto the stack.
            Peek - Access the top of the Widget stack.
             Pop - Pops the top Widget off the stack.
        ToString - (no description provided)
          Equals - (no description provided)
     GetHashCode - (no description provided)
         GetType - (no description provided)
val it : unit = ()
```

Reflecting on F# Types

While the .NET reflection APIs are easy to use, they were written long before F# existed and as such don't have any concept of special F# types. As a result, when inspecting things like records or discriminated unions, you might get unexpected results.

Consider the following discriminated union to describe playing cards. Conceptually the PlayingCard type is a very simple data structure:

```
type Suit =
    | Club
    | Diamond
    | Heart
    | Spade

type PlayingCard =
    | Ace    of Suit
    | King   of Suit
    | Queen of Suit
    | Jack   of Suit
    | ValueCard of int * Suit
    | Joker
```

However, when it is analyzed using reflection by our inspectType function, you can see all the work the F# compiler does behind the scenes to map the discriminated union onto the object-oriented .NET runtime:

```
> describeType (typeof<PlayingCard>);;
Name: PlayingCard
Methods:
    get_Joker get_IsJoker NewValueCard get_IsValueCard NewJack get_IsJack NewQueen
    get_IsQueen NewKing get_IsKing NewAce get_IsAce get_Tag __DebugDisplay CompareTo
    CompareTo CompareTo GetHashCode GetHashCode Equals Equals Equals

Properties:
    Tag Joker IsJoker IsValueCard IsJack IsQueen IsKing IsAce

Fields:
    _tag _unique_Joker
```

Fortunately, the F# library contains a few additional APIs for reflecting over functional types in the Microsoft.FSharp.Reflection namespace.

Tuples

The underlying type used for tuples is System.Tuple<_>. To decompose a particular instance of a tuple and get the type of its elements, you can use the FSharpType.GetTupleElements method, which will return the types of the tuple's elements in order as an array:

```
> let xenon = ("Xe", 54);;

val xenon : string * int = ("Xe", 54)
```

```
> // Get the tuple's element's types
open Microsoft.FSharp.Reflection
let tupleElementTypes = FSharpType.GetTupleElements (xenon.GetType());;

val tupleElementTypes : Type [] = [|System.String; System.Int32|]
```

Discriminated unions

You can reflect over discriminated union data tags by using the FSharpType.GetUnion
Cases method. This will return an array of the UnionCaseInfo type, which will describe
each data tag.

The following snippet reflects over the PlayingCard type and prints each data tag name
to the console:

```
> // Reflect the PlayingCard discriminated union type
FSharpType.GetUnionCases typeof<PlayingCard>
|> Array.iter (fun unionCase -> printfn "%s" unionCase.Name);;
Ace
King
Queen
Jack
ValueCard
Joker
val it : unit = ()
```

Records

You can use the FSharpType.GetRecordFields method to get all of the properties on a
record type:

```
> // Type definitions
[<Measure>]
type far // Degrees fahrenheit

type Outlook = Sunny | Cloudy | Rainy

type Weather = { Outlook : Outlook; High : float<far>; Low : float<far> };;

...snip...

> // Reflect over the Weather record type
FSharpType.GetRecordFields typeof<Weather>
|> Array.iter (fun propInfo -> printfn
                              "Name [%s], Type [%s]"
                              propInfo.Name propInfo.PropertyType.Name);;

Name [Outlook], Type [Outlook]
Name [High], Type [Double]
Name [Low], Type [Double]
val it : unit = ()
```

Dynamic Instantiation

In the previous section, you saw ways to examine types and reflect on their metadata. However, the real power of reflection lies in *dynamic instantiation*, which is a fancy way of saying "creating values at runtime whose type you didn't know about at compile time." In other words, given an instance of System.Type, create a new instance of the type it describes.

Instantiating Types

Dynamically instantiating types can be done using the Activator class. Example 12-6 defines a type PoliteWriter, and creates a new instance dynamically using Activator.CreateInstance.

The parameters to PoliteWriter's constructor are passed in as an obj array. The result of CreateInstance is an obj, which will need to be cast as the type you want.

Example 12-6. Dynamic instantiation

```
> // Definte a polite text writer
open System.IO

type PoliteWriter(stream : TextWriter) =

    member this.WriteLine(msg : string) =
        sprintf "%s... please" msg
        |> stream.WriteLine;;

type PoliteWriter =
  class
    new : stream:IO.TextWriter -> PoliteWriter
    member WriteLine : msg:string -> unit
  end

> // Dynamically create an instance of that class
let politeConsole =
    Activator.CreateInstance(typeof<PoliteWriter>, [| box Console.Out |]);;

val politeConsole : obj

> (politeConsole :?> PoliteWriter).WriteLine("Hello, World!");;
Hello, World!... please
val it : unit = ()
```

Now you have the ability to not only load types but also to create new instances of them at runtime. This opens up powerful new capabilities for F# applications such as loading plug-ins.

Instantiating F# Types

Just like the custom F# reflection APIs for doing type inspection of functional code, there are special methods for doing dynamic instantiation as well. Table 12-2 shows some common methods in the `FSharpValue` module for dynamically instantiating functional types like tuples and discriminated unions.

Table 12-2. Common methods in the FSharpValue module

Signature	Description
MakeTuple: obj[] * Type -> obj	Creates a new tuple value.
MakeRecord: Type * obj[] -> obj	Creates a new record value.
MakeUnion: UnionCaseInfo * obj[] -> obj	Creates a new instance of a discriminated union. You can get an instance of UnionCaseInfo by calling FSharpType.GetUnionCases.

Dynamic Invocation

If you can go about dynamically loading and instantiating types, why stop there? In .NET you can do *dynamic invocation*, which is a fancy term for *late binding*, which is in turn a fancy way of saying "calling methods at runtime which you didn't know about at compile time." Using reflection you can get an instance of a method or property and call it.

Example 12-7 defines a class `Book` and dynamically gets an instance of the type's `CurrentPage` property. That property can then be updated dynamically without manipulating an instance of `Book` directly, but rather calling `SetValue` on the returned `PropertyInfo` object.

Example 12-7. Dynamic invocation

```
> // Type for representing a book
type Book(title, author) =
    // Current page, if the book is opened
    let mutable m_currentPage : int option = None

    member this.Title  = title
    member this.Author = author
    member this.CurrentPage with get () = m_currentPage
                            and  set x  = m_currentPage <- x

    override this.ToString() =
        match m_currentPage with
        | Some(pg) -> sprintf "%s by %s, opened to page %d" title author pg
        | None     -> sprintf "%s by %s, not currently opened" title author;;
```

```
...snip...

> let afternoonReading = new Book("The Mythical Man Month", "Brooks");;

val afternoonReading : Book =
  The Mythical Man Month by Brooks, not currently opened

> let currentPagePropertyInfo = typeof<Book>.GetProperty("CurrentPage");;

val currentPagePropertyInfo : PropertyInfo =
  Microsoft.FSharp.Core.FSharpOption`1[System.Int32] CurrentPage

> currentPagePropertyInfo.SetValue(afternoonReading, Some(214), [| |]);;
val it : unit = ()
> afternoonReading.ToString();;
val it : string = "The Mythical Man Month by Brooks, opened to page 214"
```

Using late binding isn't that common because normally if you are given an `obj`, you know what types to expect, so you can use a dynamic cast (`:?>`) and then call the expected method. Late binding is typically used in dynamic languages, in which methods and properties can be added to objects at runtime. So you need to look up whether the given method or property even exists before calling it!

The Question Mark Operators

As you saw in the previous example, dynamically getting a property and calling it can feel clunky in F#. For that reason, the question mark `?` and question mark setter `?<-` operators were introduced. Functions defined with that name are treated specially by the F# compiler, and make late binding much easier to perform.

If a symbolic operator named `?` is defined, then when it is called the first parameter will be the expression on the lefthand side and the text on the righthand side will be passed in as a `string` parameter.

The following example defines a question mark operator that checks whether a property exists on a type, printing the result to the screen. When using the `.` operator to access class members, whether the member exists is checked at compile time. You get the text of the member name and can do the check at runtime:

```
> // Use the Question Mark operator to check if a type
// contains a given property.
let (?) (thingey : obj) (propName : string) =
    let ty = thingey.GetType()

    match ty.GetProperty(propName) with
    | null -> false
    | _    -> true;;

val ( ? ) : obj -> string -> bool

> // All strings have a Length property
"a string"?Length;;
```

```
val it : bool = true
> // Integers don't have an IsPrime property
42?IsPrime;;
val it : bool = false
> // Cast a string as an obj, works because check is dynamic
("a string" :> obj) ? Length;;
val it : bool = true
```

Using the question mark operator, we can clean up our code in Example 12-7. The following snippet defines both a question mark and question mark setter for dynamically accessing a class and updating a class property:

```
> // Get a property value. Notice that the return type is generic.
let (?) (thingey : obj) (propName: string) : 'a =
    let propInfo = thingey.GetType().GetProperty(propName)
    propInfo.GetValue(thingey, null) :?> 'a

// Set a property value.
let (?<-) (thingey : obj) (propName : string) (newValue : 'a) =
    let propInfo = thingey.GetType().GetProperty(propName)
    propInfo.SetValue(thingey, newValue, null);;

val ( ? ) : obj -> string -> 'a
val ( ?<- ) : obj -> string -> 'a -> unit

> let book = new Book("Foundation", "Asimov");;

val book : Book = Foundation by Asimov, not currently opened

> book?CurrentPage <- Some(14);;
val it : unit = ()
> let currentPage : int option = book?CurrentPage;;

val currentPage : int option = Some 14
```

In most applications, you will rarely encounter a type for which you know its available properties but not its actual type. So the question mark operators are of somewhat limited use. But consider situations where the property being checked contains additional information; for example, book?CurrentPageTextInSpanish. The question mark operators add extra flexibility when pushing the limits of what F# code can do.

Using Reflection

So now that you know all about reflection, what *do* you do with it? In other words, what is metaprogramming?

Next, we will look at two specific applications of .NET reflection: declarative programming and writing plug-in systems.

Declarative Programming

Perhaps the simplest thing to do when using reflection is to create more declarative code. Rather than hardcoding data into properties and methods, you can encode data by using attributes instead. This leads to potentially cleaner and more readable code.

Consider Example 12-8, which defines a function determineBoxToUse to calculate the proper container to ship an item in. Each item that can be shipped inherits from the ShippingItem class and overrides the Weight and Dimension properties, which are used to determine the correct box size.

No reflection or declarative programming is used just yet; we'll see how we can improve upon this code next.

Example 12-8. Simple shipping software

```
/// Pounds
[<Measure>]
type lb

[<Measure>]
type inches

type Container =
    | Envelope
    | Box
    | Crate

type Dimensions =
    { Length : float<inches>; Width : float<inches>; Height : float<inches> }

[<AbstractClass>]
type ShippingItem() =
    abstract Weight : float<lb>
    abstract Dimension : Dimensions

// Piece of paper describing what is in the box
type ShippingManifest() =
    inherit ShippingItem()

    override this.Weight = 0.01<lb>
    override this.Dimension =
                {
                    Length = 11.0<inches>
                    Width  = 8.5<inches>
                    Height = 0.01<inches>
                }

// Will it blend?
type Blender() =
    inherit ShippingItem()

    override this.Weight = 14.00<lb>
    override this.Dimension =
```

```
                    {
                        Length =  6.0<inches>;
                        Width  =  5.0<inches>
                        Height = 12.0<inches>
                    }

/// Partial active pattern which matches only if the input is
/// greater than its parameter.
let (|GreaterThan|_|) (param : float<'a>) input =
    if param > input
    then Some()
    else None


let determineBoxToUse(item : ShippingItem) =

    match item.Weight, item.Dimension with
    // Heavy orders must always go into a crate
    | GreaterThan 10.0<lb>, _
        -> Crate

    // Large orders must always go into a crate
    | _, { Length = GreaterThan 24.0<inches>; Width = _; Height = _}
    | _, { Length = _; Width = GreaterThan 24.0<inches>; Height = _}
    | _, { Length = _; Width = _; Height = GreaterThan 24.0<inches>}
        -> Crate

    // Beefy orders must go into a box
    | GreaterThan 2.0<lb> _, _
        -> Box

    // Min dimensions for a box
    | _, { Length = GreaterThan 10.0<inches>; Width = _; Height = _}
    | _, { Length = _; Width = GreaterThan 10.0<inches>; Height = _}
    | _, { Length = _; Width = _; Height = GreaterThan 10.0<inches>}
        -> Box

    // Looks like an envelope will do
    | _ -> Envelope
```

Example 12-8 seems simple enough, but the code doesn't scale very well. Imagine you need to extend it so that you can add special handling instructions. For example, suppose you need to account for the fact that some shipping items are fragile or flammable.

Using the full object-oriented approach, one approach would be to extend the ShippingItem base class and add new properties:

```
[<AbstractClass>]
type ShippingItem() =
    abstract Weight : float<lb>
    abstract Dimension : Dimensions
    abstract Fragile  : bool
    abstract Flammable : bool
```

But because you are adding a new property to the base class, you either need to give the `Fragile` property a default implementation, or you need to provide an implementation for every single class that inherits from `ShippingItem`. You then suffer this same problem every time you want to extend `ShippingItem` in some way—edit every single class or provide a default implementation.

Providing a default implementation may seem simple, but remember that it adds complexity to the type. If you are inheriting from `ShippingItem` and see 15+ abstract methods or properties, it may take some time to determine which ones are important and which ones are not.

For many items, it would be far easier to have them declare any special handling needs themselves, rather than adding dozens of "one-off" properties to the `ShippingItem` base class. You can use attributes to annotate these types with their special needs.

Example 12-9 defines several attributes for annotating types to be shipped, so that later special shipping requirements can be determined. This frees the base type from needing to modify any special flags, and allows new shipping items to be written in a more declarative way. (In fact, the `Weight` and `Dimension` properties could also be replaced with attributes.)

Example 12-9. Using attributes for declarative programming

```
open System

type FragileAttribute() =
    inherit System.Attribute()

type FlammableAttribute() =
    inherit System.Attribute()

type LiveAnimalAttribute() =
    inherit System.Attribute()


/// A real, live wombat delivered right to your door!
[<LiveAnimal>]
type Wombat() =
    inherit ShippingItem()

    override this.Weight = 60.0<lb>
    override this.Dimension =
            {
                Length = 39.0<inches>
                Width  = 10.0<inches>
                Height = 13.0<inches>
            }

[<Fragile; Flamable>]
type Fireworks() =
    inherit ShippingItem()
```

```
override this.Weight = 5.0<lb>
override this.Dimension =
        {
            Length = 10.0<inches>
            Width  = 8.0<inches>
            Height = 5.0<inches>
        }
```

The following snippet defines a getShippingRequirements function that uses an inner function named containsAttribute to check whether a given object is marked with a specific attribute. This is then used to check the items to be shipped and determine additional requirements:

```
open System.Collections.Generic

type ShippingRequirements =
    | NeedInsurance  of ShippingItem
    | NeedSignature  of ShippingItem
    | NeedBubbleWrap of ShippingItem

/// Get any additional requirements for shipping the package
let getShippingRequirements (contents : ShippingItem list) =

    let containsAttribute (targetAttrib : Type) x =
        x.GetType().GetCustomAttributes(false)
        |> Array.tryFind(fun attr -> attr.GetType() = targetAttrib)
        |> Option.isSome

    let itemsWithAttribute attr =
        contents |> List.filter (containsAttribute attr)

    let requirements = new HashSet<ShippingRequirements>()

    // Include fragile items
    itemsWithAttribute typeof<FragileAttribute>
    |> List.iter (fun item -> requirements.Add(NeedBubbleWrap(item)) |> ignore)

    // Include flammable items
    itemsWithAttribute typeof<FlammableAttribute>
    |> List.iter (fun item -> requirements.Add(NeedInsurance(item)) |> ignore)

    // Include live animals
    itemsWithAttribute typeof<LiveAnimalAttribute>
    |> List.iter (fun item -> requirements.Add(NeedSignature(item)) |> ignore)

    // Return the list of special shipping requirements
    Seq.toList requirements
```

Plug-in Architecture

Another use of reflection is to allow for a plug-in architecture, where other developers can extend your application by creating new .NET assemblies that conform to a specific contract. You can then use reflection to dynamically load those assemblies and call into the other programmer's code.

Typically this is done through a two-step process. First, you create an assembly to define the core infrastructure pieces, such as an interface and/or custom attributes to define new plug-ins. Then, you have your application search other assemblies for types that look like plug-ins and instantiate them.

The following examples will continue our delivery system implementation by allowing other developers to create new methods for delivering packages.

Plug-in interfaces

Example 12-10 defines the code for `DeliverySystem.Core.dll`, which is a library that future plug-ins will have to reference. It defines an interface `IDeliveryMethod`, which future plug-ins must implement.

Example 12-10. DeliverySystem.Core.dll

```
// DeliverySystem.Core.dll

namespace DeliverySystem.Core

/// Represents a package to be delivered
type Package =
    class
    (* ... *)
    end

/// Package destination
type Destination =
    {
        Address : string
        City    : string
        State   : string
        Zip     : int
        Country : string
    }

/// Interface for new delivery systems to be added
type IDeliveryMethod =
    interface
        abstract MethodName : string
        abstract DeliverPackage : Package * Destination -> unit
    end
```

Next, let's author a simple plug-in. Example 12-11 defines a new assembly, which references `DeliverySystem.Core.dll`, and implements a new high-speed delivery system called `CarrierPigeon`.

Example 12-11. CarrierPigeonPlugin.dll

```
// CarrierPigeonPlugin.dll

// References DeliverySystem.Core.dll

open DeliverySystem.Core

type CarrierPigeon() =
    interface IDeliveryMethod with

        member this.MethodName = "Carrier Pigeon"

        member this.DeliverPackage (pkg, dest) =
            (* A lot of code using the System.Animals.Pigeon APIs *)
            ()
```

Loading assemblies

The final piece to our plug-in system is loading other assemblies and any desired types into the executing process.

You can dynamically load assemblies by using the `Assembly.Load` method, which will return an instance of `System.Assembly`. Once you have an `Assembly` object, you can then examine its types and reflect over them—inspecting and/or instantiating the types.

Example 12-12 defines a method `loadAsm` that opens an assembly by name and later prints out the number of types in a set of common assemblies.

The 1,317 types defined in `FSharp.Core` certainly may seem like a lot, but remember you don't need to know them all.

Example 12-12. Loading assemblies

```
> // Load the assembly
open System.Reflection
let loadAsm (name : string) = Assembly.Load(name)

// Prints assembly info to the console
let printAssemblyInfo name =
    let asm = loadAsm name
    printfn "Assembly %s has %d types" name (asm.GetTypes().Length);;

val loadAsm : string -> Assembly
val printAssemblyInfo : string -> unit

> // Some common assemblies
[ "System"; "System.Core"; "FSharp.Core"; "System.Windows.Forms" ]
|> List.iter printAssemblyInfo;;
Assembly System has 2034 types
Assembly System.Core has 927 types
```

```
Assembly FSharp.Core has 1317 types
Assembly System.Windows.Forms has 2265 types
val it : unit = ()
```

Loading plug-ins

Now that we can load assemblies, let's finish our plug-in demo. Example 12-13 defines a method loadPlugins, which searches the current directory for *.dll* files, loads the assemblies, gets their types, and then filters them for those that implement IDeliveryMethod.

Finally, it uses the Activator class to instantiate external plug-ins.

Example 12-13. Loading plug-ins

```
// DeliverySystem.Application.dll

open System
open System.IO
open System.Reflection

open DeliverySystem.Core

let loadPlugins() =

    // Returns whether or not a type implements the given interface
    let typeImplementsInterface (interfaceTy : Type) (ty : Type) =
        printfn "Checking %s" ty.Name
        match ty.GetInterface(interfaceTy.Name) with
        | null -> false
        | _    -> true

    Directory.GetFiles(Environment.CurrentDirectory, "*.dll")
    // Load all of the assembly's types
    |> Array.map (fun file -> Assembly.LoadFile(file))
    |> Array.map(fun asm -> asm.GetTypes())
    |> Array.concat
    // Just get types that implement IDeliveryMethod
    |> Array.filter (typeImplementsInterface typeof<IDeliveryMethod>)
    // Instantiate each plugin
    |> Array.map (fun plugin -> Activator.CreateInstance(plugin))
    // Cast the obj to IDeliveryMethod
    |> Array.map (fun plugin -> plugin :?> IDeliveryMethod)

[<EntryPoint>]
let main(_) =

    let plugins = loadPlugins()

    plugins |> Array.iter (fun pi -> printfn "Loaded Plugin - %s" pi.MethodName)

    (* Ship some packages! *)

    0
```

It may seem like a lot of extra work to go loading external assemblies and instantiating their types, but remember that the final application has *no knowledge* of the types it will load ahead of time. So by using reflection, you can extend and modify the behavior of an application without actually modifying its source.

CHAPTER 13
Quotations

In the previous chapter, we looked at .NET reflection as a way to do metaprogramming: analyzing static type information to reason about program code. While metaprogramming using reflection can do things like load program plug-ins, if you want to reason about how that code *operates*, you are out of luck. The .NET reflection APIs allow you to get at the raw MSIL op codes, but you have to reverse engineer what that code does—a daunting task at best.

However, there are many applications where knowing not only the structure of program code but also how it operates can be beneficial: for example, taking a function written in F# and converting it into a form that can execute on a graphics card's GPU. (Presumably to be executed much, much faster.)

F# provides a mechanism called `quotation expressions` by which you can access not only the static type information for a block of code, but also see how the code is structured—that is, the F# compiler's internal representation (sometimes referred to as an `abstract syntax tree`, or AST).

Using F# quotations, you can:

- Perform code analysis and inspection
- Defer computation to other platforms (SQL, GPU, and so on)
- Generate new code

We will look at these capabilities shortly, but first let's look at how we can get started with this language feature. Quotations are deep wizardry though, and not for the faint of heart. This chapter only provides a crash course on the subject. To truly master quotations, refer to online resources at the F# developer center at *http://fsharp.net*.

Quotation Basics

Simply put, a quotation is an object representing the structure of some F# code. You can get hold of a quotation by placing quotation markers `<@ @>` or `<@@ @@>` around an expression:

```
> // Simple addition
<@ 1 + 1 @>;;

val it : Quotations.FSharpExpr<int> =
  Call (None, Int32 op_Addition[Int32,Int32,Int32](Int32, Int32),
     [Value (1), Value (1)])
  {CustomAttributes = [NewTuple (Value ("DebugRange"),
        NewTuple (Value ("stdin"), Value (7), Value (3), Value (7), Value (8)))];
     Raw = ...;
     Type = System.Int32;}

> // Lambda expression
<@@ fun x -> "Hello, " + x @@>;;

val it : Quotations.FSharpExpr =
  Lambda (x,
      Call (None,
            System.String op_Addition[String,String,String]
            (System.String, System.String),
            [Value ("Hello, "), x]))
    {CustomAttributes = [NewTuple (Value ("DebugRange"),
        NewTuple (Value ("stdin"), Value (10), Value (4), Value (10),
               Value (26)))];
     Type = Microsoft.FSharp.Core.FSharpFunc`2[System.String,System.String];}
```

F# exposes quotations using the `Expr<_>` type defined in the `Microsoft.FSharp.Quota` `tions` namespace. The generic type parameter of `Expr<_>` is the result of the expression; for example, `<@ 1 + 1 @>` evaluates to `Expr<int>` because the expression `1 + 1` evaluates to an integer.

Using `<@@ @@>` will produce an untyped quotation, of type `Expr`, which doesn't contain the expression's return type. In most situations it won't matter which way you quote code. Note that an `Expr<_>` can always be converted into an `Expr` by accessing its `Raw` property.

You can quote any arbitrary F# expression, with the only restrictions being that you cannot quote the use of an object expression. (Which if you recall is how F# introduces anonymous classes.)

Decomposing Quotations

Once you have a quotation, deconstructing the AST is done using active patterns defined in the F# library. So while an `Expr<_>` represents a complicated tree-like data structure, you can use pattern matching to match against what the code represents with the additional benefit of being able to bind new values from the results of the pattern match.

Example 13-1 defines a function describeCode, which takes a quotation expression and prints a description of the code to the console. Notice that the pattern match does not use a dynamic type test to get the type of the expression, but rather is matching against what the computation represents. So you can not only check if the quoted code is a function call, but even bind that call's parameters.

Example 13-1. Basic quotations

```
open Microsoft.FSharp.Quotations
open Microsoft.FSharp.Quotations.Patterns
open Microsoft.FSharp.Quotations.DerivedPatterns

let rec describeCode (expr : Expr) =
    match expr with

    // Literal value
    | Int32(i)  -> printfn "Integer with value %d" i
    | Double(f) -> printfn "Floating-point with value %f" f
    | String(s) -> printfn "String with value %s" s

    // Calling a method
    | Call(calledOnObject, methInfo, args)
        -> let calledOn = match calledOnObject with
                          | Some(x) -> sprintf "%A" x
                          | None    -> "(Called a static method)"

            printfn "Calling method '%s': \n\
                     On value:  %s \n\
                     With args: %A" methInfo.Name calledOn args

    // Lambda expressions
    | Lambda(var, lambdaBody) ->
        printfn
            "Lambda Expression - Introduced value %s with type %s"
            var.Name var.Type.Name
        printfn "Processing body of Lambda Expression..."
        describeCode lambdaBody

    | _ -> printfn "Unknown expression form:\n%A" expr
```

Using this, we can call our describeCode method in an FSI session, which will produce the following output:

```
> describeCode <@ 27 @>;;
Integer literal with value 27
val it : unit = ()

> describeCode <@ 1.0 + 2.0 @>;;
Calling method 'op_Addition':
On value:  (Called a static method)
With args : [Value (1.0); Value (2.0)]
```

```
val it : unit = ()
> let localVal = "a string";;

val localVal : string = "a string"

> describeCode <@ localVal.ToUpper() @>;;
Calling method 'ToUpper':
On value:  PropertyGet (None, System.String localVal, [])
With args : []
val it : unit = ()

> describeCode <@ fun x y -> (x, y) @>;;
Lambda Expression-Introduced on value 'x' with type 'Object'
Processing body of Lambda Expression...
Lambda Expression-Introduced on value 'y' with type 'Object'
Processing body of Lambda Expression...
Unknown expression form:
NewTuple (x, y)
val it : unit = ()
```

The F# library provides a full range of active patterns for discerning any form of quotation expression. All available active patterns can be found in the `Microsoft.FSharp.Quotations.Patterns` namespace.

Before continuing, let's take a closer look at the active patterns used in Example 13-1.

Literal values

There are active patterns available for every type of primitive value type in F#, from `int` to `float` to `string` and so on. Matching against these constant literals gives you an opportunity to bind their value:

```
// Literal value
| Int32(i)  -> printfn "Integer with value %d" i
| Double(f) -> printfn "Floating-point with value %f" f
| String(s) -> printfn "String with value %s" s
```

Function calls

Function calls can be matched against the `Call` active pattern. If it matches, the pattern introduces three values: the instance of the object on which the method is called (or `None` if the method is static), the `MethodInfo` containing reflection information for the method, and the list of arguments passed to the method.

```
// Calling a method
| Call(calledOnObject, methInfo, args)
   -> let calledOn = match calledOnObject with
                     | Some(x) -> sprintf "%A" x
                     | None    -> "(Called a static method)"

      printfn "Calling method '%s': \n\
               On value:  %s \n\
               With args: %A" methInfo.Name calledOn args
```

The `Call` active pattern can be cumbersome to use if you are looking for a specific function call, however. For this reason, the `SpecificCall` active pattern was created. Using it within a pattern match allows you to identify when a certain function is used and allows you to bind the function call's parameters. (It also binds the types of any generic function parameters required, but usually those can be safely ignored.) So rather than matching any function call, `SpecificCall` matches only the function you want.

Example 13-2 shows using the `SpecificCall` active pattern for describing an arithmetic operation. In the example, only the function's parameters are bound and the generic types instantiated are ignored.

Example 13-2. The SpecificCall active pattern

```
let describeArithmatic operation =
    match operation with
    | SpecificCall <@ (+) @> (_, _, [lhs; rhs]) ->
        printfn "Addition."

    | SpecificCall <@ (-) @> (_, _, [lhs; rhs]) ->
        printfn "Subtraction."

    | SpecificCall <@ (*) @> (_, _, [Int32(0); _])
    | SpecificCall <@ (*) @> (_, _, [_; Int32(0)]) ->
        printfn "Multiplication by zero."

    | SpecificCall <@ (*) @> (_, _, [lhs; rhs]) ->
        printfn "Multiplication."

    | SpecificCall <@ (/) @> (_, _, [lhs; Int32(0)]) ->
        printfn "Division by zero."

    | SpecificCall <@ (/) @> (_, _, [lhs; rhs]) ->
        printfn "Division."

    | _ -> failwith "Unknown quotation form."
```

Function values

Function values are matched using the `Lambda` active pattern. The two values bound in the active pattern are of type `Var` and `Expr`:

```
// Lambda expressions
| Lambda(var, lambdaBody) ->
    printfn
        "Lambda Expression - Introduced Value %s of type %s"
        var.Name var.Type.Name
    printfn "Processing body of Lambda Expression..."
    describeCode lambdaBody
```

The `Expr` is simply the body of the lambda expression. The `Var` represents the new value introduced by the lambda expression (its parameter).

When quoting code, anytime you decompose an expression that introduces a new value, such as a `let` binding, the newly introduced value is represented as a `Var`.

Quoting Method Bodies

While enclosing an expression in `<@ @>` marks returns the F# compiler's representation of that code, it is usually insufficient because that code calls into functions, which then call into other functions and so on. To get the full abstract syntax tree of the expression, you need to drill into method bodies as well. By default, the F# compiler cannot return the quoted form of functions and class member bodies in a quotation.

To allow function bodies to be included inside of a quotation, you can provide the `[<ReflectedDefinition>]` attribute. Methods marked with this attribute can be further expanded upon when processing the quotation by using the `(|MethodWithReflectedDefinition|_|)` active pattern.

Example 13-3 is the same `describeCode` function with a slight modification to add support for processing methods attributed with the `[<ReflectedDefinition>]` attribute. The function checks the `MethodInfo` object returned by the `(|Call|_|)` active pattern and checks if the body of the method is known. If so, then the body of the method being called is processed as well.

Example 13-3. Using the ReflectedDefinition attribute

```
open Microsoft.FSharp.Quotations
open Microsoft.FSharp.Quotations.Patterns
open Microsoft.FSharp.Quotations.DerivedPatterns

let rec describeCode2 (expr : Expr) =
    match expr with

    // Literal value
    | Int32(i)  -> printfn "Integer literal with value %d" i
    | Double(f) -> printfn "Floating point literal with value %f" f
    | String(s) -> printfn "String literal with value %s" s

    // Calling a method
    | Call(calledOnObject, methInfo, args)
        -> let calledOn = match calledOnObject with
                          | Some(x) -> sprintf "%A" x
                          | None    -> "(static method)"

           printfn "Calling method '%s': \n\
                   On intance:  %s \n\
                   With args : %A" methInfo.Name calledOn args

           match methInfo with
           | MethodWithReflectedDefinition(methBody) ->
               printfn
                   "Expanding method body of '%s'..." methInfo.Name
               describeCode2 methBody
```

```
            | _ ->
                printfn
                    "Unable to expand body of '%s'. Quotation stops here."
                    methInfo.Name

    // Lambda expressions
    | Lambda(var, lambdaBody) ->
        printfn
            "Lambda Expression on value '%s' with type '%s'"
            var.Name var.Type.Name

        printfn "Processing body of Lambda Expression..."
        describeCode2 lambdaBody

    | _ -> printfn "Unknown expression form:\n%A" expr
```

The following FSI session shows the processing of two quotation expressions. describeCode2 can process the body of the invertNumberReflected function because it has been decorated with the [<ReflectedDefinition>] attribute:

```
> // Define functions with and without ReflectedDefinition
let invertNumber x = -1 * x

[<ReflectedDefinition>]
let invertNumberReflected x = -1 * x;;

val invertNumber : int -> int
val invertNumberReflected : int -> int

> // Describe code without ReflectedDefinition
describeCode2 <@ invertNumber 10 @>
;;
Calling method 'invertNumber':
On intance:  (static method)
With args : [Value (10)]
Unable to expand body of 'invertNumber'. Quotation stops here.
val it : unit = ()

> // Describe code with ReflectedDefinition
describeCode2 <@ invertNumberReflected 10 @>
;;
Calling method 'invertNumberReflected':
On intance:  (static method)
With args : [Value (10)]
Expanding method body of 'invertNumberReflected'...
Lambda Expression on value 'x' with type 'Int32'
Processing body of Lambda Expression...
Calling method 'op_Multiply':
On intance:  (static method)
With args : [Value (-1); x]
Unable to expand body of 'op_Multiply'. Quotation stops here.
val it : unit = ()
```

Decomposing Arbitrary Code

Armed with just a few active patterns we were able to decompose many code types in the describeCode method. However, whenever code wasn't matched it fell through the pattern match and threw an exception.

Most applications of active patterns decompose an arbitrary AST, intercepting only the nodes that the code cares about and ignoring the rest. However, it is important to traverse the entire AST. Abruptly stopping the traversal at a given node isn't a valid option because it ignores a large amount of the tree and potentially some code constructs you care about.

However, it also doesn't make sense to match against every possible active pattern available, from ForIntegerRangeLoop (for loops) to IfThenElse (if expressions) to LetRecursive (recursive let bindings) and so on.

Fortunately there is a "catchall" active pattern that matches the most general forms of F# expressions. The catchall active pattern is in the ExprShape module and converts any F# quotation expression into a ShapeVar, ShapeLambda, or ShapeCombination.

Example 13-4 introduces a new function, generalizedDescribeCode, for decomposing any quotation. The quotation matches against a ShapeVar if the expression is looking up a value and ShapeLambda is matched whenever a new function value is introduced. The majority of F# quotations fall into the third active pattern case, ShapeCombination. ShapeCombination is intentionally nondescript, only giving you an opaque handle to what was used to generate it and the subexpressions from the code construct. (Meaning that you cannot determine what the code represents—you are just given a list of its subexpressions.)

Example 13-4. Generalized quotation traversal

```
open Microsoft.FSharp.Quotations
open Microsoft.FSharp.Quotations.ExprShape

let rec generalizedDescribeCode indentation expr =

    let indentedMore = indentation + "    "

    match expr with
    // A variable being used
    | ShapeVar(var) ->
        printfn "%s Looking up value '%s'" indentation var.Name

    // A new lambda expression
    | ShapeLambda(var, lambdaBody) ->
        printfn
            "%s Lambda expression, introducing var '%s'"
            indentation var.Name
        generalizedDescribeCode indentedMore lambdaBody

    // Other
```

```
| ShapeCombination(_, exprs) ->
    printfn "%s ShapeCombination:" indentation
    exprs |> List.iter (generalizedDecribeCode indentedMore)
```

The following FSI session shows the generalizedDescribeCode method in action:

```
> generalizedDescribeCode "" <@ (fun x y z -> x + y + z) @>;;
  Lambda expression, introducing var 'x'
      Lambda expression, introducing var 'y'
          Lambda expression, introducing var 'z'
              ShapeCombination:
                  ShapeCombination:
                      Looking up value 'x'
                      Looking up value 'y'
                  Looking up value 'z'
val it : unit = () >
```

You are then free to add new pattern-match rules earlier in the match expression to "intercept" the things you care about, as in earlier versions of the describeCode method.

Application: Deferring Computation to Other Platforms

You have seen ways to decompose F# quotation expressions to analyze the compiler-generated form of the code, but what do you *do* with it? Perhaps the best usage of F# quotations is deferring computation to other platforms. By processing the F# quotation expressions, you can take F# code and transport it to another platform, such as a GPU or on an SQL database. By walking the AST, you can transform the F# code into a format that is amenable to another computing environment. This technique allows you to avoid the use of a second language and use the existing F# toolset (IntelliSense, type checking, and so on).

For example, rather than writing assembly code for your graphics card encoded as a string, you can write F# code, and then convert that quotation of that code to the appropriate assembly language.

To provide a simple example of this, let's use quotations to convert F# mathematical expressions into *reverse polish notation*, or RPN.

RPN is a form of expressing mathematical equations without the need for parentheses. It works by using a hypothetical stack of numbers, where algebraic functions such as addition, pop the top two items from the stack and push the result back on.

For example, the expression 2 * 3 + 4 would be represented by the operations listed in Table 13-1.

*Table 13-1. Evaluation of 2 * 3 + 4 in RPN*

Operation	Stack
Push 2	2
Push 3	3, 2

Operation	Stack
Call (*)	6
Push 4	4, 6
Call (+)	10

Encoding functions in RPN can be difficult and error-prone. Instead, you can use quotations to write F# code—letting compiler build up the expression tree preserving the order of operations—and then transform the quotation of that code into RPN.

Example 13-5 defines a function called fsharpToRPN, which takes a quotation expression and decomposes the expression building up a list of operations to express the equation in RPN.

The example works by intercepting arithmetic operations and recursively generating the list of RPN operations to compute the left- and righthand sides of the operator. Then, it simply adds those operators to the list of RPN operations in the correct order.

Example 13-5. Converting F# code to RPN

```
open Microsoft.FSharp.Quotations
open Microsoft.FSharp.Quotations.Patterns
open Microsoft.FSharp.Quotations.DerivedPatterns

let rec fsharpToRPN code stackOperations =
    match code with

    | Int32(n)  -> (sprintf "Push %d" n) :: stackOperations
    | Double(f) -> (sprintf "Push %f" f) :: stackOperations

    | SpecificCall <@ (+) @> (_, _, [lhs; rhs]) ->
        let lhs = fsharpToRPN lhs stackOperations
        let rhs = fsharpToRPN rhs stackOperations
        lhs @ rhs @ ["Call (+)"]

    | SpecificCall <@ (-) @> (_, _, [lhs; rhs]) ->
        let lhs = fsharpToRPN lhs stackOperations
        let rhs = fsharpToRPN rhs stackOperations
        lhs @ rhs @ ["Call (-)"]

    | SpecificCall <@ (*) @> (_, _, [lhs; rhs]) ->
        let lhs = fsharpToRPN lhs stackOperations
        let rhs = fsharpToRPN rhs stackOperations
        lhs @ rhs @ ["Call (*)"]

    | SpecificCall <@ (/) @> (_, _, [lhs; rhs]) ->
        let lhs = fsharpToRPN lhs stackOperations
        let rhs = fsharpToRPN rhs stackOperations
        lhs @ rhs @ ["Call (/)"]

    | expr -> failwithf "Unknown Expr:\n%A" expr
```

The following snippet shows the `fsharpToRPN` function in action:

```
> fsharpToRPN <@ 1 + 2 @> [];;
val it : string list = ["Push 1"; "Push 2"; "Call (+)"]
> fsharpToRPN <@ 2 * 3 + 4 @> [];;
val it : string list = ["Push 2"; "Push 3"; "Call (*)"; "Push 4"; "Call (+)"]
> // A little more complex
fsharpToRPN <@ (2 + 10) / (3 * (2 - 6 / 7 - 2)) @> []
|> List.iter (printfn "%s");;
Push 2
Push 10
Call (+)
Push 3
Push 2
Push 6
Push 7
Call (/)
Call (-)
Push 2
Call (-)
Call (*)
Call (/)
```

Generating Quotation Expressions

Decomposing quotation expressions gives you a way to inspect and transform ASTs, but you can build up quotation expressions dynamically at runtime as well.

Generating quotation expressions is especially useful when creating mini-programming languages. Rather than writing F# code and processing the AST, you can parse another, perhaps simpler, language to generate the expression tree and then process that.

Any active pattern you see for decomposing quotation expressions has a complementary static method on the `Expr` class for producing an equivalent `Expr<_>` value.

The following snippet shows taking the quotation of a simple expression and the equivalent way to build up that same expression value:

```
let organicQuotation =
    <@
        let x = (1, 2, 3)
        (x, x)
    @>

let syntheticQuotation =
    Expr.Let(
        new Var("x", typeof<int * int * int>),
        Expr.NewTuple( [ Expr.Value(1); Expr.Value(2); Expr.Value(3) ] ),
        Expr.NewTuple( [ Expr.GlobalVar("x").Raw; Expr.GlobalVar("x").Raw ] )
    )
```

Expression Holes

Using methods on the `Expr` type isn't the only way to generate quotation expressions. Quotations may contain *expression holes*, which are locations for new instances of `Expr<_>` to be placed, allowing you to build up expression trees by simply patching holes in an existing expression.

To declare an expression hole, simply use a percent sign `%` in front of any expression within the quotation, and the result of that expression will be bound to the generated quotation expression tree. (Similar to `<@@ @@>`, using `%%` will leave a hole for an `Expr` type instead of `Expr<_>`.)

Example 13-6 defines a function called `addTwoQuotations` that takes two quoted values and builds a new expression, adding the two `Expr<_>`s together. So calling `addTwoQuo tations` with the quoted form of two integer literals `<@ 1 @>` and `<@ 2 @>` is the same as quoting `<@ 1 + 2 @>`. Moreover, the generated quotation is identical to the static version of the quotation.

Example 13-6. Quotation holes

```
> let addTwoQuotations x y = <@ %x + %y @>;;

val addTwoQuotations : Expr<int> -> Expr<int> -> Expr<int>

> // Generate the quotation and describe it
addTwoQuotations <@ 1 @> <@ 2 @>
|> describeCode;;
Calling method 'op_Addition':
On value:  (Called a static method)
With args: [Value (1); Value (2)]
val it : unit = ()

> // Generate and describe a more complex quotation
addTwoQuotations <@ "a string".Length @> <@ (2 * 2) @>
|> describeCode;;
Calling method 'op_Addition':
On value:  (Called a static method)
With args: [PropGet (Some (Value ("a string")), Int32 Length, []);
 Call (None, Int32 op_Multiply[Int32,Int32,Int32](Int32, Int32),
     [Value (2), Value (2)])]
val it : unit = ()
```

Evaluating Quotations

You can not only analyze quotations—but *execute* them, too. The F# PowerPack contains an experimental library for converting F# quotation expressions to LINQ expression trees. LINQ expression trees are very similar to F# quotation expressions: both are ways to represent compiler ASTs. While F# quotation expressions can express more forms of code than expression trees alone, the main advantage is expression trees can be compiled and executed.

The F# PowerPack does not come with Visual Studio 2010 and is a separate download from the F# PowerPack's home page on CodePlex, *www.codeplex.com*. For more information on the F# PowerPack, refer to Appendix A.

To evaluate or compile F# quotations, you will need to download and add a reference to `FSharp.PowerPack.dll` and `FSharp.PowerPack.Linq.dll` and open up the `Micro soft.FSharp.Linq.QuoationEvaluation` namespace. That will add extension methods to `Expr` and `Expr<_>` allowing you to evaluate and compile quotations via the `Eval` and `Compile` methods.

The following example shows simple evaluation and compilation of F# quotation expressions:

```
> // Reference required libraries
#r "System.Core.dll"
#r "FSharp.PowerPack.dll"
#r "FSharp.PowerPack.Linq.dll"

// Adds extension methods to Expr<_>
open Microsoft.FSharp.Linq.QuotationEvaluation;;

--> Referenced 'C:\Program Files\Reference
Assemblies\Microsoft\Framework\v3.5\System.Core.dll'


--> Referenced 'C:\Program Files\MicrosoftF#\PowerPack\FSharp.PowerPack.dll'


--> Referenced 'C:\Program Files\MicrosoftF#\PowerPack\FSharp.PowerPack.Linq.dll'

> // Evaluate a simple expression
let x = <@ 1 + 2 * 3 @>

val x : Expr<int> =
  Call (None, Int32 op_Addition[Int32,Int32,Int32](Int32, Int32),
     [Value (1),
      Call (None, Int32 op_Multiply[Int32,Int32,Int32](Int32, Int32),
          [Value (2), Value (3)])])

> x.Eval();;
val it : int = 7
> // Compile a function value expression
let toUpperQuotation = <@ (fun (x : string) -> x.ToUpper()) @>
let toUpperFunc = toUpperQuotation.Compile() ();;

val toUpperQuotation : Expr<(string -> string)> =
  Lambda (x, Call (Some (x), System.String ToUpper(), []))
val toUpperFunc : (string -> string)

> toUpperFunc "don't panic";;
val it : string = "DON'T PANIC"
```

Application: Generating Derivatives

The ability to evaluate or compile F# quotation expressions adds a bold new capability to your F# applications—namely, the ability to generate new code. Example 13-7 analyzes the raw quotation and then generates a new Expr<_> representing the function's derivative.

The derivative of a function f(x) is the rate at which function f changes at point x. If f is increasing in value from f(x) to f(x+0.0001) then the derivative will be positive. Likewise, if f(x) is decreasing at point x, the derivative will be negative. Derivatives may seem like complicated business, but computing them is simple with a few easy rules.

Example 13-7 defines a function generateDerivative, which just like previous examples, matches basic arithmetic functions. When each arithmetic operation is encountered, the corresponding derivative rule is applied so that the resulting Expr represents the derivative of the operation. From there, you can use the F# PowerPack to compile and execute the generated function.

Example 13-7. Using quotations to create a derivative

```
#r "FSharp.PowerPack.dll"
#r "FSharp.PowerPack.Linq.dll"

// Adds extension methods to Expr<_>
open Microsoft.FSharp.Linq.QuotationEvaluation

open Microsoft.FSharp.Quotations
open Microsoft.FSharp.Quotations.Patterns
open Microsoft.FSharp.Quotations.DerivedPatterns

// Get the 'MethodInfo' object corresponding to basic arithmatic functions.
// These will be used to generate new Expr<_>.
type Operations =
    static member Add (x, y) : float = x + y
    static member Sub (x, y) : float = x - y
    static member Mul (x, y) : float = x * y
    static member Div (x, y) : float = x / y

let addMi = (typeof<Operations>).GetMethod("Add")
let subMi = (typeof<Operations>).GetMethod("Sub")
let mulMi = (typeof<Operations>).GetMethod("Mul")
let divMi = (typeof<Operations>).GetMethod("Div")

let rec generateDerivative (equation : Expr) =

    match equation with

    // Lamda - Begining of a function
    | Lambda(arg, body) ->
        Expr.Lambda(arg, generateDerivative body)

    // Method Call - Begining of a function
```

```
| Call(None, MethodWithReflectedDefinition(methBody), [ arg ]) ->
    generateDerivative methBody

// Property Getter - For module-bound properties
| PropertyGet(None, PropertyGetterWithReflectedDefinition(body), []) ->
    generateDerivative body

// Addition
// [d/dx] f(x) + g(x) = f'(x) + g'(x)
| SpecificCall <@ (+) @> (_, _, [f; g]) ->
    let f' = generateDerivative f
    let g' = generateDerivative g
    Expr.Call(addMi, [f'; g'])

// Subtraction
// [d/dx] f(x) - g(x) = f'(x) - g'(x)
| SpecificCall <@ (-) @> (_, _, [f; g]) ->
    let f' = generateDerivative f
    let g' = generateDerivative g
    Expr.Call(subMi, [f'; g'])

// Product Rule
// [d/dx] f(x) * g(x) = (f'(x) * g(x)) + (f(x) * g'(x))
| SpecificCall <@ (*) @> (_, _, [f; g]) ->
    let f' = generateDerivative f
    let g' = generateDerivative g
    Expr.Call(addMi,
        [ Expr.Call(mulMi, [f'; g]);
          Expr.Call(mulMi, [f; g']) ]
    )

// Quotient Rule
// [d/dx] f(x) / g(x) = ((f '(x) * g(x)) - (f(x) * g'(x))) / (g^2(x))
| SpecificCall <@ (/) @> (_, _, [f; g]) ->
    let f' = generateDerivative f
    let g' = generateDerivative g

    let numerator =
        Expr.Call(subMi,
            [ Expr.Call(mulMi, [f'; g])
              Expr.Call(mulMi, [f; g'])]
        )
    let denominator = Expr.Call(mulMi, [g; g])

    Expr.Call(divMi, [numerator; denominator])

// Value
// [d/dx] x = 1
| Var(x) ->
    Expr.Value(1.0, typeof<double>)

// Constant
// [d/dx] C = 0.0
| Double(_) ->
    Expr.Value(0.0, typeof<double>)
```

```
    | _ -> failwithf "Unrecognized Expr form: %A" equation

let f = (fun x -> 1.5*x*x*x + 3.0*x*x + -80.0*x + 5.0)

let f'  =
    let quote : Expr =
        generateDerivative <@ (fun x -> 1.5*x*x*x + 3.0*x*x + -80.0*x + 5.0) @>

    let typedQuote : Expr<float -> float> = Expr.Cast quote

    // Compile the Expr<_> into an actual method
    let compiledDerivative = typedQuote.Compile()
    compiledDerivative()
```

With function f and its derivative f', we can quickly plot their values on a graph, resulting in Figure 13-1:

```
open System.IO

let generatePlot() =
    use csvFile = new StreamWriter("Plot.csv")
    csvFile.WriteLine("x, f(x), f'(x)")

    [-10.0 .. 0.1 .. 10.0]
    |> List.iter (fun x -> csvFile.WriteLine(sprintf "%f, %f, %f" x (f x) (f' x)))

    csvFile.Close()
```

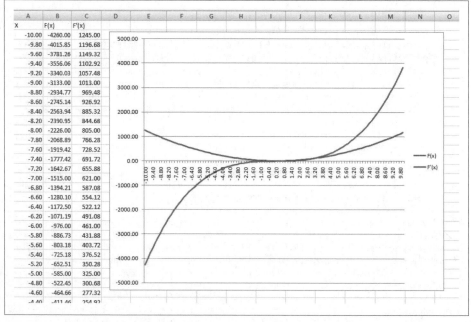

Figure 13-1. Graph of a computed derivative

Quotations allow you to write applications that would otherwise require you to write your own parser, compiler, or both. Using the F# compiler's representation of code allows you to focus on transforming the AST instead of parsing another language and building up an internal representation yourself.

> For more information about F# quotation expressions, refer to the F# developer center at *http://fsharp.net*.

Overview of .NET Libraries

The .NET ecosystem has incredible breadth—by enabling you to run .NET code on various platforms, like on the Internet via Silverlight, or on mobile devices with the Compact Framework. It also has incredible depth—by having a wealth of powerful libraries, from visualization, to communications, to databases, and so on.

This appendix will provide a quick overview of some existing .NET libraries so you can transition from the sample applications in this book to real-world problem solving. The APIs covered will be divided into three main areas: visualization, data processing, and storing data. We'll end with a quick look at the F# library, including the F# PowerPack.

Visualization

F# is a great tool for processing raw data, but visualizing that data doesn't need to be constrained to just the command line.

There are two main visualization APIs available for .NET: Windows Forms (Win-Forms) and Windows Presentation Foundation (WPF). WinForms is the older of the two and is an object-oriented wrapper on top of core Windows APIs. With WinForms it is easy to create a functional UI with buttons and common controls, but it can be difficult to create a rich and dynamic interface. WPF on the other hand is a much more design-centric library that allows for sophisticated interfaces at the cost of added complexity and a steeper learning curve.

 F# doesn't support code generation, so you cannot use the WYSIWYG editors of Visual Studio. The examples you see in this chapter will build UIs programmatically; however, it is recommended that you write your presentation layer code in C# or VB.NET to take advantage of the rich tool support available.

Windows Forms

WinForms is conceptually very simple. Each window on the screen is an instance of a `Form`, which contains a collection of UI elements of type `Control`. As users interact with the Form's controls, they will raise events, which the programmer can listen to. For example, a `Button` control has a `Click` event, which will be fired whenever the button is clicked:

```
#r "System.Windows.Forms.dll"
#r "System.Drawing.dll"

open System.Windows.Forms

// Create a form
let form = new Form()

// Create a button
let btn = new Button(Text = "Click Me")
btn.Click.AddHandler(fun _ _ ->
    MessageBox.Show("Hello, World")
    |> ignore)

// Add the button to the form
form.Controls.Add(btn)

// Display the form
form.ShowDialog()
```

Example A-1 creates a form that displays a progress bar while counting the number of words in the complete works of Shakespeare. The form contains two controls, a `ProgressBar` and a `Label` (a control that displays text). As files are processed asynchronously, the two form controls will be updated to indicate progress.

Note the assembly references to `System.Windows.Forms.dll` and `System.Drawing.dll`; these are required for WinForms development.

Example A-1. Using Windows Forms

```
#r "System.Windows.Forms.dll"
#r "System.Drawing.dll"

open System.IO
open System.Windows.Forms

// Count the number of words in a given text file.
let countWords filePath =
    System.Threading.Thread.Sleep(2000)
    let lines = File.ReadAllText(filePath)
    let words = lines.Split([| ' ' |])
    words.Length

// The complete works of Shakespeare
let filesToProcess = Directory.GetFiles(@"D:\CompleteWorksOfShakespeare\")
```

```
// Setup the WinForm
let form = new Form(Text = "The Words of Shakespeare", TopMost=true, Height=130)

let wordCountText = new Label(Dock = DockStyle.Bottom)
let progress = new ProgressBar(Minimum = 0,
                               Maximum = filesToProcess.Length - 1,
                               Dock = DockStyle.Fill)

form.Controls.Add(progress)
form.Controls.Add(wordCountText)
form.Show()

// Begin processing files asynchronously. Once each file has been
// processed the status of the progress bar and label will be updated.
async {

    let totalWords = ref 0

    for i in 0 .. filesToProcess.Length - 1 do
        totalWords := !totalWords + (countWords filesToProcess.[i])

        // Update progress bar value and text
        progress.Value <- i
        wordCountText.Text <- sprintf "%d words counted so far..." (!totalWords)

} |> Async.Start
```

When the code from Example A-1 is executed, a form similar to Figure A-1 will be displayed.

Figure A-1. Windows forms

Windows Presentation Foundation

WinForms provides a simple API for putting together a functional user interface, but to build more advanced UIs with "sizzle," you will need to take a different approach. Windows Presentation Foundation was added as part of .NET 3.0 with the aim of changing how people write and develop UIs.

WPF was designed around a couple of key tenets:

Enable rich media

Make it easy to embed rich media like video and animation into an application. Whereas WinForms applications typically rely on bland operating system controls, the hallmarks of a WPF application are smooth corners, translucency, and clear text. In addition, WPF applications will benefit from hardware acceleration where possible.

Declarative programming model

Another problem with WinForms applications is that the design of the UI and the code that powers it are inextricably linked. It is nearly impossible to change the interface of a WinForms application without needing to rewrite most of the program code. In WPF, the UI layout is separate from the code, and therefore much easier to refactor.

Getting a simple WPF app up and running doesn't take much more work than Win-Forms. Example A-2 does the prototypical "Hello, World"–style application using WPF.

Example A-2. Hello, World in WPF

```
#r "WindowsBase.dll"
#r "PresentationCore.dll"
#r "PresentationFramework.dll"

open System
open System.Windows
open System.Windows.Controls


let win = new Window(Height = 128.0, Width = 360.0)


let label = new Label()
label.FontSize <- 62.0
label.Content <- "Hello, World"

win.Content <- label

let app = new Application()
app.Run(win)
```

Figure A-2 shows our "Hello, World" application in action. Notice how smooth the text looks. This is because WPF is vector-based, meaning that displays created with WPF can be zoomed without pixelation, making the overall experience much cleaner and more visually appealing.

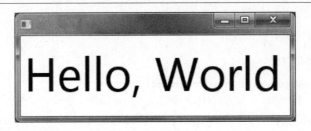

Figure A-2. Hello, World in WPF

XAML, the eXtensible Application Markup Language

While you can create WPF user interfaces entirely in code, a key component of WPF development is *XAML* (pronounced "zam-el") or the eXtensible Application Markup Language. XAML is an XML-dialect that enables you to express application UI elements declaratively. This enables black-turtleneck-wearing designers to create application interfaces without impacting the coding done by caffeine-guzzling programmers. In addition to enabling designers to add "sizzle" to applications, XAML solves the problems we experienced with WinForms programming where the code and UI were too tightly coupled.

Example A-3 defines a simple WPF application that accepts user input, and when a button is pressed, displays **"Hello, *Name*"**. The application interface is described in XAML, which is then parsed at runtime using the `XamlReader` class. (The specifics of the XAML itself won't be covered here.)

Example A-3. The SayHello application

```
#r "WindowsBase.dll"
#r "PresentationCore.dll"
#r "PresentationFramework.dll"
#r "System.Xaml.dll" // Only on CLR 4.0


open System
open System.Windows
open System.Windows.Controls
open System.Windows.Markup

/// Declare the UI in XAML
let windowXaml = "
<Window
    xmlns='http://schemas.microsoft.com/winfx/2006/xaml/presentation'
    xmlns:sys='clr-namespace:System;assembly=mscorlib'
    xmlns:x='http://schemas.microsoft.com/winfx2006/xaml' >

    <StackPanel>
        <TextBlock>Who do you want to say hello to?</TextBlock>
        <TextBox Name='NameTextBox'> [name goes here] </TextBox>
        <Button  Name='SayHelloButton'>Say Hello!</Button>
    </StackPanel>
```

```
    </Window>
" // End string-based XAML

// Load our XAML markup
let getWindow() =
    let xamlObj = XamlReader.Parse(windowXaml)
    xamlObj :?> Window

let win = getWindow()

// Get instance of the XAML-based UI controls, and wire up event handlers
let textBox = win.FindName("NameTextBox")    :?> TextBox
let button  = win.FindName("SayHelloButton") :?> Button

button.Click.AddHandler(fun _ _ -> let msg = sprintf "Hello, %s" textBox.Text
                                   MessageBox.Show(msg) |> ignore)

let app = new Application()
app.Run(win)
```

The example enabled us to express the UI layout in XAML, but the program code and interface are still too tightly coupled. Because the program code gets a reference to the TextBox and Button controls by their Name property, the layout *has* to have a button and text box with specific names or else the application will stop working. Ideally, there would be a way to write code so that it didn't depend on the specific type of interface elements.

Binding

The designers of WPF wanted to make progress and enable a true separation of the UI and the code powering it. To achieve this, XAML supports *binding*, or linking live program objects with UI elements.

Let's rewrite our "Say Hello" application by first focusing on what we want the code to model, and grafting an interface on top of it later.

To power our "Say Hello" application, we want a class that has an introductory message, a Name property the user can set, and a command to greet the user. Example A-4 defines this simple Greeter class as well as a GreetUserCommand, which displays a message box. This is all the code required to power our WPF application. Note the lack of any reference to UI elements.

Example A-4. Greeter for the SayHello application

```
// Greeter.fs

namespace GreetersNamespace

open System
open System.Windows
open System.Windows.Input
```

```
/// Greet command - when executed displays a message box
type GreetUserCommand() =

    let m_canExecuteChangedEvent = new Event<System.EventHandler, EventArgs>()

    interface ICommand with
        member this.CanExecute(param : obj) = true

        member this.Execute(param : obj) =
            MessageBox.Show(sprintf "Hello, %s" (string param))
            |> ignore

        [<CLIEvent>]
        member this.CanExecuteChanged with get() = m_canExecuteChangedEvent.Publish


/// Greeter class - Used to model greeting an end user
type Greeter() =

    let m_greetCommand = new GreetUserCommand()
    let mutable m_name = " [name goes here] "

    /// Introductory text
    member this.Introduction = "Hello, what is your name?"

    member this.Name with get () = m_name
                     and  set x  = m_name <- x

    member this.GreetCommand = m_greetCommand
```

Now that we have a model for how the code should execute, we want to define some XAML to use that model.

First, we need to let our XAML know about the namespace where our code lives. The following snippet defines a new XML namespace, g, to be the GreetersNamespace in the current assembly (named WPFinFSharp):

```
<Window
    xmlns='http://schemas.microsoft.com/winfx/2006/xaml/presentation'
    xmlns:x='http://schemas.microsoft.com/winfx/2006/xaml'
    xmlns:g='clr-namespace:GreetersNamespace;assembly=WPFinFSharp'
    Title='Greeter' Height='220' Width='450'>
```

Then, we add a resource to the window of type Greeter called TheGreeter. With this resource in the XAML code, an instance of Greeter will be created behind the scenes and stored in a resource dictionary. This will enable future UI elements to bind to it:

```
<!-- Add an instance of 'Greeter' to the Window's resources -->
<Window.Resources>
    <g:Greeter x:Key='TheGreeter' />
</Window.Resources>
```

Now, we can refer to that live object using WPF binding. The following XAML associates the live `Greeter` object with the `StackPanel`. It then adds a `TextBlock`, which will display the `Introduction` property of resource `TheGreeter`:

```
<StackPanel DataContext='{Binding Source={StaticResource TheGreeter}}'>

    <TextBlock Margin='7.5' FontSize='36.0'
        Text='{Binding Introduction}' />
```

Likewise, we can bind the `TextBox`'s value to `TheGreeter`'s `Name` property. So whenever the textbox is updated, the `Name` property is updated accordingly:

```
<TextBox Margin='7.5' FontSize='36.0'
    Text='{Binding Name}' />
```

Finally, we bind clicking the button to our `GreetCommand` property, which is an instance of `GreetUserCommand`. When activated, this will carry out greeting the user by calling the `Execute` method of the command:

```
<Button
    Margin='7.5' FontSize='36.0'
    Content='Say Hello' Command='{Binding GreetCommand}'
    CommandParameter='{Binding Name}' />
```

This introduction of another abstraction layer—the window resource—seems like additional complexity, but the code is no longer explicitly tied to the layout of the UI.

Example A-5 shows the updated XAML, which uses proper WPF binding, and the rest of the refactored "Say Hello" application. The XAML also adds a `LinearGradient Brush` element to add a vibrant splash of color to the UI.

 Note that the code references the `Greeters` namespace from the currently executing assembly, `WPFinFSharp`. You'll need to update that with the name of the application you build, which may be different, for example, *Application1*.

Example A-5. XAML for the SayHello application

```
// Program.fs

open System
open System.Windows
open System.Windows.Input
open System.Windows.Markup

module XamlCode =
    let xamlUI = "
        <Window
            xmlns='http://schemas.microsoft.com/winfx/2006/xaml/presentation'
            xmlns:x='http://schemas.microsoft.com/winfx/2006/xaml'
            xmlns:g='clr-namespace:GreetersNamespace;assembly=WPFinFSharp'
            Title='Greeter' Height='240' Width='450'>

            <!-- Add an instance of 'Greeter' to the Window's resources -->
```

```
        <Window.Resources>
            <g:Greeter x:Key='TheGreeter' />
        </Window.Resources>

        <StackPanel DataContext='{Binding Source={StaticResource TheGreeter}}'>

            <!-- Add a gratutious use of gradient brushes -->
            <StackPanel.Background>
                <LinearGradientBrush>
                    <GradientStop Color='Red'    Offset='0.00' />
                    <GradientStop Color='Orange' Offset='0.16' />
                    <GradientStop Color='Yellow' Offset='0.33' />
                    <GradientStop Color='Green'  Offset='0.50' />
                    <GradientStop Color='Blue'   Offset='0.66' />
                    <GradientStop Color='Indigo' Offset='0.83' />
                    <GradientStop Color='Violet' Offset='1.00' />
                </LinearGradientBrush>
            </StackPanel.Background>

            <!-- Set the TextBlock's Text property equal to the Greeter's
                 Introduction property -->
            <TextBlock Margin='7.5' FontSize='36.0'
                Text='{Binding Introduction}' />

            <!-- Bind the TextBox's data to the Greeter's Name property -->
            <TextBox Margin='7.5' FontSize='36.0'
                Text='{Binding Name}' />

            <!-- When you click the button, execute the Greeter's GreetCommand,
                 passing in the Name property as its parameter -->
            <Button
                Margin='7.5' FontSize='36.0'
                Content='Say Hello' Command='{Binding GreetCommand}'
                CommandParameter='{Binding Name}' />
        </StackPanel>
    </Window>
    "

[<EntryPoint; STAThread>]
let main(args) =

    let getWindow() =
        let o = XamlReader.Parse(XamlCode.xamlUI)
        o :?> Window

    let win = getWindow()

    let app2 = new Application()
    let result = app2.Run(win)

    result
```

When the "Say Hello" application is compiled and executed, the result looks like Figure A-3.

Figure A-3. Data-bound XAML

It is impossible to show the full extent of WPF data binding in a single example. But you now have a glimpse of how WPF's support for data binding allows you to cleanly separate presentation layer from code and write rich media applications.

 There is far more to learn about WPF. If you are interested in doing serious WPF development, I recommend *WPF Unleashed* by Adam Nathan (Sams).

Data Processing

Once you have a fancy user interface set up for your application, the next step is *doing* something. There are plenty of great data-processing libraries in .NET for whatever your application needs.

Regular Expressions

Manipulating text is one of the most common tasks you will encounter. Because strings in .NET are immutable, it can be difficult to search and modify them. Fortunately .NET has the full support for regular expressions.

Regular expressions are a formal language for searching text for particular words or sequences of characters. You can use regular expressions in .NET to simplify processing textual data to do things like:

- Validate input against a particular form
- Identify substrings that match a particular structure
- Create new strings that are modified versions of the input

To start with, consider the following code snippet. It defines a symbolic function =~= that takes a string and a regular expression—the format for which we will cover shortly—and returns if the string matches the given regular expression. The regular expression provided, "\d+", checks if the string contains a number:

```
> // Simple regular expressions
open System.Text.RegularExpressions

let (=~=) str regex = Regex.IsMatch(str, regex);;

val ( =~= ) : string -> string -> bool

> "Does this contain a number?" =~= "\d+";;
val it : bool = false
> "Does this (42) contain a number?" =~= "\d+";;
val it : bool = true
```

Metacharacters

Regular expressions are built on their own language of metacharacters. The metacharacters and syntax for .NET regular expressions are defined in Table A-1.

Table A-1. Regular expression metacharacters

Character	Description
Most characters	Characters other than `. $ { [(	)] } * + ?` are matched verbatim.
`.`	Matches any character except for `\n`.
`[aeiou0-9]`	Matches any of a series of characters, including those in a range.
`[^aeiou0-9]`	Matches any character except those specified.
`\w`	Matches any word character `[a-zA-Z_0-9]`.
`\W`	Matches any non-word character `[^a-zA-Z_0-9]`.
`\d`	Matches any decimal digit `[0-9]`.
`\D`	Matches any non-decimal digit `[^0-9]`.
`\s`	Matches any whitespace character.
`\S`	Matches any non-whitespace character.
`\`	Used to escape metacharacters, such as matching `. $ { [(	)] } * + ?`.
`+`	Match the previous character one or more times.
`*`	Match the previous character zero or more times.
`?`	Match the previous character zero or one times.

In the previous code, snippet the regular expression \d was used to match any digit character, and with the + suffix the regular expression matched any digit one or more times. So "1", "42", and "888" would match the regular expression, but not "foo" or "bar".

A great application for regular expressions is to validate input. Consider the following regular expression for validating if the input is a phone number:

```
"(\(\d\d\d\))?\s*\d\d\d\s*-\s*\d\d\d\d"
```

Even for regular expression pros, the syntax can seem cryptic. Let's look at this regex piece by piece.

First, a phone number can start with an optional three-digit area code. This is done by writing a regular expression to look for parentheses around three digits. Note that the parentheses need to be escaped:

```
\(\d\d\d\)
```

To indicate that the optional area code can only be matched zero or one times, it is enclosed in parentheses and suffixed with a question mark. The parentheses around \(\d\d\d\) treat the sequence of five characters as a single entity, for which the question mark will apply:

```
(\(\d\d\d\))?
```

Next, there can be zero or more whitespace characters \s* followed by three digits \d\d\d, then optional whitespace on either side of a dash separating the first three digits of a phone number from the rest \s*-\s*, and finally four sequential digits \d\d\d\d.

Example A-6 defines a function isValidPhoneNumber for validating input. The regular expression itself is processed using the static Regex.IsMatch method.

Example A-6. Validating input with regular expressions

```
> // Matching a phone number
open System.Text.RegularExpressions

let phoneNumberRegEx = "(\(\d\d\d\))?\s*\d\d\d\s*-\s*\d\d\d\d"
let isValidPhoneNumber text = Regex.IsMatch(text, phoneNumberRegEx);;

val phoneNumberRegEx : string = "(\(\d\d\d\))?\s*\d\d\d\s*-\s*\d\d\d\d"
val isValidPhoneNumber : string -> bool

> isValidPhoneNumber "(707) 827-7000";;
val it : bool = true
> isValidPhoneNumber "123-4567";;
val it : bool = true
> isValidPhoneNumber "123      -      4567";;
val it : bool = true
> isValidPhoneNumber "(this is not a phone number)";;
val it : bool = false
> isValidPhoneNumber "(123) 456-????";;
val it : bool = false
```

String manipulation

The `Regex` class offers methods to help build new strings based on existing ones. `Split` can be used to break a string into parts separated by a regex; `Replace` replaces all instances of a regex with a static string.

Using these two methods we can go a long way toward parsing semi-structured textual data.

The most widely used file-format for storing Chess games is in *Portable Game Notation*, or PGN. The format starts with data/value pairs enclosed in brackets, can have comments enclosed in curly braces, and each move is prefixed with a number and one or three dots.

The following snippet shows an example PGN file describing a match between Bobby Fischer and Boris Spassky:

```
[Event "F/S Return Match"]
[Site "Belgrade, Serbia Yugoslavia|JUG"]
[Date "1992.11.04"]
[Round "29"]
[White "Fischer, Robert J."]
[Black "Spassky, Boris V."]
[Result "1/2-1/2"]

1. e4 e5 2. Nf3 Nc6 3. Bb5 {This opening is called the Ruy Lopez.} 3... a6
4. Ba4 Nf6 5. 0-0 Be7 6. Re1 b5 7. Bb3 d6 8. c3 0-0 9. h3 Nb8  10. d4 Nbd7
11. c4 c6 12. cxb5 axb5 13. Nc3 Bb7 14. Bg5 b4 15. Nb1 h6 16. Bh4 c5 17. dxe5
Nxe4 18. Bxe7 Qxe7 19. exd6 Qf6 20. Nbd2 Nxd6 21. Nc4 Nxc4 22. Bxc4 Nb6
23. Ne5 Rae8 24. Bxf7+ Rxf7 25. Nxf7 Rxe1+ 26. Qxe1 Kxf7 27. Qe3 Qg5 28. Qxg5
hxg5 29. b3 Ke6 30. a3 Kd6 31. axb4 cxb4 32. Ra5 Nd5 33. f3 Bc8 34. Kf2 Bf5
35. Ra7 g6 36. Ra6+ Kc5 37. Ke1 Nf4 38. g3 Nxh3 39. Kd2 Kb5 40. Rd6 Kc5 41. Ra6
Nf2 42. g4 Bd3 43. Re6 1/2-1/2
```

In order to access the game move data, first all comments and metadata must be removed. Using `Regex.Replace` this task is very straightforward. In the game format all comments and metadata are enclosed between [ ] or { }. So with two regular expressions, any text that matches any sequence of characters between [ ] or { } can be replaced with the empty string, effectively stripping out all comments and metadata:

```
// Remove comments and markup from the PGN file
let removeMarkup text =
    let tagPairs = new Regex(@"\[(^\])+\]")
    let noTagPairs = tagPairs.Replace(text, "")

    let comments = new Regex(@"\{(^\})+\}")
    let noComments = comments.Replace(noTagPairs, "")

    // Trim any leading whitespace and convert to a single-line
    noComments.Trim().Replace("\r", "").Replace("\n", " ")
```

Within the raw move-data blob, the next step is to separate the list of chess moves from the move markers. This can be done using `Regex.Split` on any sequences of digits followed by periods:

```
// Get the list of moves, each prefixed with a number and one or three dots
let getMoves text =
    let movePrefix = new Regex(@"\d+\.+")
    movePrefix.Split(text)
```

Using the `removeMarkup` and `getMoves` methods in conjunction will get you access to the meat of the PGN file. While there certainly is need for more format-specific code to be written, Example A-7 shows how using regular expressions can quickly transform a chunk of textual data into a form that can be more easily processed.

Example A-7. PGN file parser

```
> // Starting to parse a PGN file
open System.Text.RegularExpressions

let pgnGameText = "
[Event \"F/S Return Match\"]
[Site \"Belgrade, Serbia Yugoslavia|JUG\"]
[Date \"1992.11.04\"]
[Round \"29\"]
[White \"Fischer, Robert J.\"]
[Black \"Spassky, Boris V.\"]
[Result \"1/2-1/2\"]

1. e4 e5 2. Nf3 Nc6 3. Bb5 {This opening is called the Ruy Lopez.} 3... a6
4. Ba4 Nf6 5. O-O Be7 6. Re1 b5 7. Bb3 d6 8. c3 O-O 9. h3 Nb8  10. d4 Nbd7
11. c4 c6 12. cxb5 axb5 13. Nc3 Bb7 14. Bg5 b4 15. Nb1 h6 16. Bh4 c5 17. dxe5
Nxe4 18. Bxe7 Qxe7 19. exd6 Qf6 20. Nbd2 Nxd6 21. Nc4 Nxc4 22. Bxc4 Nb6
23. Ne5 Rae8 24. Bxf7+ Rxf7 25. Nxf7 Rxe1+ 26. Qxe1 Kxf7 27. Qe3 Qg5 28. Qxg5
hxg5 29. b3 Ke6 30. a3 Kd6 31. axb4 cxb4 32. Ra5 Nd5 33. f3 Bc8 34. Kf2 Bf5
35. Ra7 g6 36. Ra6+ Kc5 37. Ke1 Nf4 38. g3 Nxh3 39. Kd2 Kb5 40. Rd6 Kc5 41. Ra6
Nf2 42. g4 Bd3 43. Re6 1/2-1/2
"

// Remove comments and markup from the PGN file
let removeMarkup text =
    let tagPairs = new Regex(@"\[.*\]")
    let noTagPairs = tagPairs.Replace(text, "")

    let comments = new Regex(@"\{.*\}")
    let noComments = comments.Replace(noTagPairs, "")

    // Trim any leading whitespace and convert to a single-line
    noComments.Trim().Replace("\r", "").Replace("\n", " ")

// Get the list of moves, each prefixed with a number and one or three dots
let getMoves text =
    let factRegex = new Regex(@"\d+\.+", RegexOptions.Multiline)
    factRegex.Split(text)

let normalizedText = removeMarkup pgnGameText
```

```
let listMoves() =
    getMoves normalizedText
    |> Array.map (fun move -> move.Trim())
    |> Array.iter (printfn "%s");;

val pgnGameText : string =
  "
[Event "F/S Return Match"]
[Site "Belgrade, Serbia Yugoslavi"+[684 chars]
val removeMarkup : string -> string
val getMoves : string -> string []
val normalizedText : string =
  "1. e4 e5 2. Nf3 Nc6 3. Bb5   3... a6 4. Ba4 Nf6 5. 0-0 Be7 6. "+[464 chars]
val printGameMoves : unit -> unit

> printGameMoves();;

e4 e5
Nf3 Nc6
Bb5
a6
Ba4 Nf6
0-0 Be7
Re1 b5
Bb3 d6
c3 0-0
h3 Nb8
d4 Nbd7
c4 c6
...
```

Capture groups

Regular expressions can be used for more than just validating input and manipulating text. You can also use regular expressions to extract textual data that matches a given format.

If you want to use a metacharacter like ?, +, or * to apply to a sequence of characters, you can group them in parentheses. For example, "(foo)+" matches the phrase "foo" one or more times. Without the parentheses, "foo+" the regular expression would match the letters f, o, and then another o one or more times.

Grouping can be more useful than adding expressiveness to regular expression syntax. If you use the Regex.Match method, a Match object will be returned that you can use to refer back to the string captured in each captured group.

Example A-8 defines a regular expression to parse out word analogies found on standardized tests. Each part of the regular expression associated with a word is enclosed in parentheses, and therefore is its own group.

The example takes the returned `Match` object and prints each captured group to the console. Notice that the full regular expression is considered the "first" group, which in the example is the full word analogy.

Example A-8. Capturing regular expression groups

```
> // Capturing regex groups
open System
open System.Text.RegularExpressions

let analogyRegex = "(\w+):(\w+)::(\w+):(\w+)"
let m = Regex.Match("dog:bark::cat:meow", analogyRegex);;

val analogyRegex : string = "(\w+):(\w+)::(\w+):(\w+)"
val m : Match = dog:bark::cat:meow

> // Print captures
printfn "Group captures..."
for i = 0 to  m.Groups.Count - 1 do
    printfn "[%d] %s" i (m.Groups.[i].Value);;
Group captures...
[0] dog:bark::cat:meow
[1] dog
[2] bark
[3] cat
[4] meow
```

We've already seen a great example of when to use regular expression group captures, and that is in conjunction with active patterns.

Example A-9 is from Chapter 7. Notice how the partial active pattern returns a tuple of three strings, which are the result of three captures in the given regular expression. `List.tl` is used to skip the first group's value—the fully matched string—and instead returns each individual group capture.

The example uses the (|Match3|_|) partial active pattern to match different ways to specify a date, binding the year, month, and day to values in the pattern match rule.

Example A-9. Regular expression captures via active patterns

```
let (|RegexMatch3|_|) (pattern : string) (input : string) =
    let result = Regex.Match(input, pattern)

    if result.Success then
        match (List.tl [ for g in result.Groups -> g.Value ]) with
        | fst :: snd :: trd :: []
            -> Some (fst, snd, trd)
        | [] -> failwith "Match succeeded, but no groups found.\n \
                          Use '(.*)' to capture groups"
        | _  -> failwith "Match succeeded, but did not find exactly three groups."
    else
        None

let parseTime input =
```

```
match input with
// Match input of the form "6/20/2008"
| RegexMatch3 "(\d+)/(\d+)/(\d+)" (month, day, year)
// Match input of the form "2000-3-6"
| RegexMatch3 "(\d+)-(\d+)-(\d+)" (year, month, day)
    -> Some( new DateTime(int year, int month, int day) )
| _ -> None
```

 If you are interested in learning more about regular expressions, consider reading *Mastering Regular Expressions* by Jeffrey E. F. Friedl
(O'Reilly).

Working with XML

Working with XML allows you to easily create and store structured data without the
fuss of writing your own parser. It means that you can leverage .NET APIs for manipulating XML documents as well.

There are two separate XML libraries for .NET, an early version in the
System.Xml.dll assembly, which is somewhat painful to use, and a newer, friendlier
library in System.Linq.XML.dll which will be covered here.

Writing XML

Writing XML documents is as simple as constructing a hierarchy of XElement objects.
Example A-10 defines a Book type that knows how to convert itself into an XML document, via the ToXml method.

 In order to work with XML, you must first add a reference to both
System.Xml.dll and System.Xml.Linq.dll.

Example A-10. Writing XML documents

```
#r "System.Xml.dll"
#r "System.Xml.Linq.dll"

open System.Xml.Linq

// Convert a string into an XName object
let xname thing = XName.Get(thing.ToString())

type Book =
    | ComicBook of string * int
    | Novel of string * string
    | TechBook of string * string
    member this.ToXml() =
        match this with
        | ComicBook(series, issue) ->
```

```
                    new XElement(xname "ComicBook",
                        new XElement(xname "Series", series),
                        new XElement(xname "Issue",  issue))

            | Novel(author, title) ->
                new XElement(xname "Novel",
                    new XElement(xname "Author", author),
                    new XElement(xname "Title",  title))

            | TechBook(author, title) ->
                new XElement(xname "TechBook",
                    new XElement(xname "Author", author),
                    new XElement(xname "Title",  title))

/// Generates an XML document from a list of books
let bookshelfToXml (bookshelf : Book list) =
    let books = bookshelf
                |> List.map (fun book -> book.ToXml())
                |> Array.ofList
    new XElement(xname "Bookshelf", books)
```

When used in an FSI session, you can see how easy it is to construct XML documents. Saving XML documents is as simple as calling the **Save** method on an **XElement** object:

```
> // Convert a list of Book union cases to an XML document
[
    ComicBook("IronMan", 1)
    ComicBook("IronMan", 2)
    TechBook("Machine Learning", "Mitchell")
    TechBook("Effective C++", "Meyers")
    Novel("World War Z", "Max Brooks")
    ComicBook("IronMan", 3)
]
|> bookshelfToXml
|> (printfn "%A");;

<Bookshelf>
  <ComicBook>
    <Series>IronMan</Series>
    <Issue>1</Issue>
  </ComicBook>
  <ComicBook>
    <Series>IronMan</Series>
    <Issue>2</Issue>
  </ComicBook>
  <TechBook>
    <Author>Machine Learning</Author>
    <Title>Mitchell</Title>
  </TechBook>
  <TechBook>
    <Author>Effective C++</Author>
    <Title>Meyers</Title>
  </TechBook>
  <Novel>
    <Author>World War Z</Author>
```

```
      <Title>Max Brooks</Title>
    </Novel>
    <ComicBook>
      <Series>IronMan</Series>
      <Issue>3</Issue>
    </ComicBook>
  </Bookshelf>
val it : unit = ()
```

Reading XML

To open XML documents, use the static methods XElement.Parse and XElement.Load. Parse takes a string containing structured XML data and returns an instance of XElement; Load will take a file path to a valid XML file:

```
> // Load an existing XML document from disk
do
    let shelf = XElement.Load("LordOfTheRings.xml")
    printfn "Loaded Document:\n%A" shelf;;

Loaded Document:
<Bookshelf>
  <Novel>
    <Author>The Two Towers</Author>
    <Title>Tolkien</Title>
  </Novel>
  <Novel>
    <Author>Fellowship of the Ring</Author>
    <Title>Tolkien</Title>
  </Novel>
  <Novel>
    <Author>The Return of the King</Author>
    <Title>Tolkien</Title>
  </Novel>
</Bookshelf>
val it : unit = ()

> // Parse an XML document from a string
do
    let shelf = XElement.Parse("<Bookshelf>
                                  <TechBook>
                                    <Author>Steve McConnell</Author>
                                    <Title>CodeComplete</Title>
                                  </TechBook><TechBook>
                                    <Author>Charles Petzold</Author>
                                    <Title>Code</Title>
                                  </TechBook>
                                </Bookshelf>")
    printfn "Parsed Document:\n%A" shelf;;

Parsed Document:
<Bookshelf>
  <TechBook>
    <Author>Steve McConnell</Author>
    <Title>CodeComplete</Title>
```

```
    </TechBook>
    <TechBook>
      <Author>Charles Petzold</Author>
      <Title>Code</Title>
    </TechBook>
  </Bookshelf>
  val it : unit = ()
```

Storing Data

Once you've computed the values you need, you will probably want to save that data to disk or in a database. There are numerous ways to store data in .NET, each with varying degrees of performance and ease of use.

File IO

Most .NET IO facilities are based around the abstract `System.IO.Stream` class, which defines a primitive interface between the stream and the backing store. (Backing store is just a fancy term for "where the data comes from.") Classes inherit from `Stream` and add specialized ways to read or write from a particular backing store. For example, `MemoryStream` is used to read or write data from memory, `NetworkStream` is used to read or write data from a network connection, `FileStream` is used to read or write data from a file, and so on.

The simplest way to read or write data from disk is to use the `File.ReadAllLines` and `File.WriteAllLines` methods. `WriteAllLines` takes a file path and a string array of textual data to be written to the file, while `ReadAllLines` takes a file path and returns the string array of the file's lines:

```
> // Solving the fizz buzz problem
open System.IO

let computeFileContents() =
    [| 1 .. 100 |]
    |> Array.map(function
                  | x when x % 3 = 0 && x % 5 = 0 -> "FizzBuzz"
                  | x when x % 3 = 0 -> "Fizz"
                  | x when x % 5 = 0 -> "Buzz"
                  | _ -> ".");;

val computeFileContents : unit -> string array

> File.WriteAllLines("FizzBuzzSln.txt", computeFileContents());;
val it : unit = ()

> let fileContents = File.ReadAllLines("FizzBuzzSln.txt");;

val fileContents : string [] =
  [|"."; "."; "Fizz"; "."; "Buzz"; "Fizz"; "."; "."; "Fizz"; "Buzz"; ".";
    "Fizz"; "."; "."; "FizzBuzz"; "."; "."; "Fizz"; "."; "Buzz"; "Fizz"; ".";
```

```
"."; "Fizz"; "Buzz"; "."; "Fizz"; "."; "."; "FizzBuzz"; "."; "."; "Fizz";
"."; "Buzz"; "Fizz"; "."; "."; "Fizz"; "Buzz"; "."; "Fizz"; "."; ".";
"FizzBuzz"; "."; "."; "Fizz"; "."; "Buzz"; "Fizz"; "."; "."; "Fizz";
"Buzz"; "."; "Fizz"; "."; "."; "FizzBuzz"; "."; "."; "Fizz"; "."; "Buzz";
"Fizz"; "."; "."; "Fizz"; "Buzz"; "."; "Fizz"; "."; "."; "FizzBuzz"; ".";
"."; "Fizz"; "."; "Buzz"; "Fizz"; "."; "."; "Fizz"; "Buzz"; "."; "Fizz";
"."; "."; "FizzBuzz"; "."; "."; "Fizz"; "."; "Buzz"; "Fizz"; "."; ".";
"Fizz"; "Buzz"|]
```

Data Serialization

While the ability to read and write data to files is quite useful, you're still out of luck
if you have no way to convert your classes to a form that can be easily written to disk.
For that, you will need to use *serialization*. Serialization is the process of converting an
object into a binary format, which can then be persisted on disk or transferred across
a network.

You can write your own mechanisms for serialization, but built into the .NET framework is support to do this for you. To opt into the default serialization provided
by .NET simply add the [<Serializable>] attribute to the type.

Just because a type has the [<Serializeable>] attribute doesn't mean
that a type can be serialized in arbitrary ways, however. Different forms
of serialization apply special constraints.

For example, the .NET XML serializer, which serializes objects into
XML, requires that types have a parameterless constructor. This restriction disallows you from using F# types such as records and
discriminated unions with XML serialization.

Consider the following types defining a baseball team from a discriminated union,
record, and class; each is marked with the [<Serializable>] attribute:

```
open System
open System.Collections.Generic

// Discrimianted Union
[<Serializable>]
type Position =
    // Battery
    | Pitcher      | Catcher
    // Infield
    | ShortStop    | FirstBase     | SecondBase    | ThirdBase
    // Outfield
    | LeftField    | CenterField   | RightField

// Record
[<Serializable>]
type BaseballPlayer =
    {
        Name : string
```

```
            Position : Position
            BattingAvg : float
    }

// Class
[<Serializable>]
type BaseballTeam(name : string ) =

    let m_roster = new List<BaseballPlayer>()

    member this.TeamName = name

    member this.DraftPlayer(player) = m_roster.Add(player)
    member this.BenchPlayer(player) = m_roster.Remove(player)

    member this.Roster = m_roster |> Seq.toArray
```

Serializing an object to a byte[] is as simple as passing a stream to an instance of
BinaryFormatter. Example A-11 shows an FSI session where the method serializeTh
ing serializes an arbitrary obj into a byte[] and a method saveTeam, which saves a
BaseballTeam object to disk.

The serializeThing method works by creating a MemoryStream, which allows the binary
BinaryFormatter to write the serialized version of the obj into memory. Then, the function returns the MemoryStream's data in the form of a byte[].

Example A-11. Serialization

```
> // Serializing an object
open System.IO
open System.Runtime.Serialization.Formatters.Binary

/// Serialize an object
let serializeThing(thing) =
    let bf = new BinaryFormatter()
    use mstream = new MemoryStream()
    bf.Serialize(mstream, thing)

    mstream.ToArray()

/// Saves a baseball team to disk
let saveTeam(team : BaseballTeam, filePath : string) =

    let byteArr = serializeThing team

    use fileStream = new FileStream(filePath, FileMode.CreateNew)
    fileStream.Write(byteArr, 0, byteArr.Length)
    fileStream.Close()

    ()
;;

val serializeThing : 'a -> byte []
val saveTeam : BaseballTeam * string -> unit
```

```
> // Creating a baseball team
let M's = new BaseballTeam("Mariners")
let ichiro =
    {
        Name = "Ichiro Suzuki"
        Position = RightField
        BattingAvg = 0.330
    }
let griffeyJr =
    { Name = "Ken Griffey, Jr."; Position = LeftField; BattingAvg = 0.287 }
M's.DraftPlayer(ichiro)
M's.DraftPlayer(griffeyJr);;

val M's : BaseballTeam
val ichiro : BaseballPlayer = {Name = "Ichiro Suzuki";
                                Position = RightField;
                                BattingAvg = 0.33;}
val griffeyJr : BaseballPlayer = {Name = "Ken Griffey, Jr.";
                                Position = LeftField;
                                BattingAvg = 0.287;}

> // Serialize poor Ichiro into a byte[]
serializeThing ichiro;;
val it : byte [] =
  [|0uy; 1uy; 0uy; 0uy; 0uy; 255uy; 255uy; 255uy; 255uy; 1uy; 0uy; 0uy; 0uy;
    0uy; 0uy; 0uy; 0uy; 12uy; 2uy; 0uy; 0uy; 0uy; 67uy; 70uy; 83uy; 73uy; 45uy;
    65uy; 83uy; 83uy; 69uy; 77uy; 66uy; 76uy; 89uy; 44uy; 32uy; 86uy; 101uy;
    114uy; 115uy; 105uy; 111uy; 110uy; 61uy; 48uy; 46uy; 48uy; 46uy; 48uy;
    46uy; 48uy; 44uy; 32uy; 67uy; 117uy; 108uy; 116uy; 117uy; 114uy; 101uy;
    61uy; 110uy; 101uy; 117uy; 116uy; 114uy; 97uy; 108uy; 44uy; 32uy; 80uy;
    117uy; 98uy; 108uy; 105uy; 99uy; 75uy; 101uy; 121uy; 84uy; 111uy; 107uy;
    101uy; 110uy; 61uy; 110uy; 117uy; 108uy; 108uy; 5uy; 1uy; 0uy; 0uy; 0uy;
    23uy; 70uy; 83uy; 73uy; 95uy; ...|]
> saveTeam(M's, @"D:\MarinersTeam.bbt");;
val it : unit = ()
```

Deserialization

Deserializing data is done in much the same way it is serialized, but the `Deserialize` method is called on the `BinaryFormatter`. `Deserialize` returns an `obj`, which will need to be cast as another type.

Example A-12 provides the complement of `saveTeam`, called `loadTeam`. The method opens up a `FileStream` object, which the `BinaryFormatter` will read from and deserialize a `BaseballTeam` type.

Example A-12. Deserialization

```
> // Deserialization
let loadTeam(filePath) =

    use fileStream = new FileStream(filePath, FileMode.Open)

    let bf = new BinaryFormatter()
```

```
    let result = bf.Deserialize(fileStream)

    (result :?> BaseballTeam);;

val loadTeam : string -> BaseballTeam

> let loadedM's = loadTeam @"D:\MarinersTeam.bbt";;

val loadedM's : BaseballTeam

> // Print the loaded data
loadedM's.Roster
|> Array.iter (fun player -> printfn "%s - Batting %.3f"
                                     player.Name
                                     player.BattingAvg);;
Ichiro Suzuki - Batting 0.330
Ken Griffey, Jr. - Batting 0.287
val it : unit = ()
```

The F# Libraries

Like most modern languages, F# comes with its own standard library. The F# library, however, comes in two parts:

FSharp.Core.dll

    FSharp.Core.dll is implicitly referenced by every single F# application and is *the* F# library. It contains the definitions for common types such as list, Async, option, and so on.

The F# PowerPack

    The F# PowerPack is a set of experimental extensions and additional functionality meant to augment the F# library: for example, modules enabling F# applications to be source-level-compatible with the OCaml programming language.

FSharp.Core.dll

Learning more about FSharp.Core.dll will enable you to get the most out of your F# projects. We've covered a lot of functionality in the F# library throughout the book so far, but there are several gems tucked away under the Microsoft.FSharp namespace, the most useful of which are a couple of purely functional (immutable) data structures.

Chapter 4 introduced mutable collection types as an easier-to-use alternative to list and seq. However, if you want to strive for pure functional programming, you can use functional collection types instead.

The Set<_> and Map<_,_> types behave much like the HashSet<_> and Dictionary<_,_> types from Chapter 4, except that you cannot modify any instance. So when you add a new element to the collection by using the Add method, rather than returning unit and updating the internal data structure, a new instance of the `Set<_>` or `Map<_,_>` is returned instead.

Example A-13 uses the `Set<_>` type to get the list of unique words from a given web page, which in the example is the text of the book *Frankenstein* by Mary Shelley.

Notice how the `Set<_>` type is built up using the **Array.fold** method. In order to fill a functional collection type, you must use some form of recursion. Also, just as the `List` and `Seq` modules provide a series of functions for working with types of the same name, there is a `Set` module containing methods like `Set.add` and `Set.count`.

Example A-13. Using the Set type

```
> // The functional Set type
open System
open System.IO
open System.Net

let getHtml (url : string) =
    let req = WebRequest.Create(url)
    let rsp = req.GetResponse()

    use stream = rsp.GetResponseStream()
    use reader = new StreamReader(stream)

    reader.ReadToEnd()

let uniqueWords (text : string) =
    let words = text.Split([| ' ' |], StringSplitOptions.RemoveEmptyEntries)

    let uniqueWords =
        Array.fold
            (fun (acc : Set<string>) (word : string) -> Set.add word acc)
            Set.empty
            words

    uniqueWords;;

val getHtml : string -> string
val uniqueWords : string -> Set<string>

> let urlToShelley'sFrankenstein = "http://www.gutenberg.org/files/84/84.txt";;

val urlToShelley'sFrankenstein : string =
  "http://www.gutenberg.org/files/84/84.txt"

> // Produce the Set of unique words
let wordsInBook =
    urlToShelley'sFrankenstein
    |> getHtml |> uniqueWords;;

val wordsInBook : Set<string>
```

```
> Set.count wordsInBook;;
val it : int = 16406
```

Example A-14 uses the Map<_,_> type to associate each word with the number of times it is used in the book. Then, the Map<_,_> is converted to a sequence of key-value tuples, sorted, and the top 20 most frequently occurring words are printed to the screen.

Just as the Set<_> was built up in the previous example, the Map<_,_> is also produced during a fold operation.

Example A-14. Using the Map type

```
> // The functional Map type
let wordUsage (text : string) =
    let words = text.Split([| ' ' |], StringSplitOptions.RemoveEmptyEntries)

    let wordFrequency =
        Array.fold
            (fun (acc : Map<string, int>) (word : string) ->
                if Map.contains word acc then
                    let timesUsed = acc.[word]
                    Map.add word (timesUsed + 1) acc
                else
                    Map.add word 1 acc)
            Map.empty
            words

    wordFrequency

let printMostFrequentWords (wordFrequency : Map<string, int>) =
    let top20Words =
        wordFrequency
        |> Map.toSeq
        |> Seq.sortBy (fun (word, timesUsed) -> -timesUsed)
        |> Seq.take 20

    printfn "Top Word Usage:"
    top20Words
    |> Seq.iteri(fun idx (word, timesUsed) ->
        printfn "%d\t '%s' was used %d times" idx word timesUsed);;

val wordUsage : string -> Map<string,int>
val printMostFrequentWords : Map<string,int> -> unit

> // Print the most frequent words
urlToShelley'sFrankenstein
|> getHtml |> wordUsage |> printMostFrequentWords
;;
Top Word Usage:
0        'the' was used 3408 times
1        'and' was used 2569 times
2        'of' was used 2405 times
3        'I' was used 2333 times
4        'to' was used 1900 times
5        'my' was used 1389 times
```

```
6       'a' was used 1212 times
7       'in' was used 980 times
8       'that' was used 876 times
9       'was' was used 874 times
10      'with' was used 573 times
11      'had' was used 571 times
12      'but' was used 480 times
13      'me' was used 478 times
14      'which' was used 465 times
15      'as' was used 437 times
16      'not' was used 432 times
17      'his' was used 413 times
18      'by' was used 411 times
19      'you' was used 404 times
val it : unit = ()
```

The F# PowerPack

When F# was still a research project by Microsoft Research, the original F# library was quite large. Not only did it contain all the functionality found in `FSharp.Core.dll`, but it also contained many experimental library extensions. When Microsoft made the decision to integrate F# into Visual Studio 2010, it meant putting just the core set of functionality into `FSharp.Core.dll` and leaving the rest for the F# PowerPack (to either be used just by language power users or stabilized and eventually put into the proper F# library).

Inside the F# PowerPack, you'll find tools and utilities such as:

- Functions and modules found in the OCaml library
- Plotting and graphing libraries
- Tools for generating parsers
- Libraries for enabling LINQ-like support in F#
- An F# CodeDOM, or library for generating F# source code

The F# PowerPack does not ship with Visual Studio 2010; instead you must download it from CodePlex (*http://www.codeplex.com*).

While most F# PowerPack functionality is specialized and targeted for only select developers, there are two features you might be interested in using.

SI units of measure

In Chapter 7, you learned how to eliminate dimensional analysis bugs by adding units of measure. However, rather than define standard units such as seconds and meters for every F# application you write, the F# PowerPack contains built-in units of measure from the French *Système International d'Unités* (known to folks in the United States as the metric system).

A subset of SI units of measure found in the F# library is listed in Table A-2. To access the built-in units of measure, open the `Microsoft.FSharp.Core.SI` module. (Or just `SI`, because `Microsoft.FSharp.Core` is in scope by default.)

```
> // Use the SI units of measure defined in the F# PowerPack
#r "FSharp.PowerPack.dll"
open SI
let g = -9.8<m/s>;;

val g : float<m/s>
```

Table A-2. Common units of measure in the F# PowerPack

Measure	Name	Description
m	Meter	SI unit of length
kg	Kilogram	SI unit of mass
s	Second	SI unit of time
K	Kelvin	SI unit of thermodynamic temperature
Hz	Hertz	SI unit of frequency
N	Newton	SI unit of force

FSLex and FSYacc

A common task required for creating domain-specific languages is to create a parser, or a library that accepts a body of text (program code) and translates it into a tree structure (abstract syntax tree or AST). There are many ways to write parsers, the simplest of which is to avoid writing it all together and to generate the parser directly from a formal grammar.

Included in the F# PowerPack are tools `FSLex.exe` and `FSYacc.exe`, which are used for generating parsers. In fact, the F# compiler's parser is written using `FSLex.exe` and `FSYacc.exe`. `FSLex.exe` is used to create a lexer, which takes source code and produces a token stream. Then, `FSYacc.exe` produces the parser that converts the token stream into an actual AST.

Using `FSLex.exe` and `FSYacc.exe`, you can quickly develop and debug parsers so that you spend your time on implementing your language, rather than manipulating parse trees.

The syntax for these tools could easily fill a chapter—or even an entire book—on their own. For more information and tutorials on these tools, refer to the F# PowerPack's home page on CodePlex.

F# Interop

This book presents F# as a great language for helping you to be more productive and one that can also seamlessly integrate with the existing .NET stack. While it is true that F# is a great language, the word *seamlessly* may need to be qualified.

The dominant languages used in .NET today are C# and Visual Basic .NET, and while in F# you can write and call into object-oriented assemblies to interact with C# and VB.NET code, some concepts may get lost in translation.

This appendix is focused on how to ease interop with F#. By the end of this appendix, you'll be able to identify problem areas when doing multilanguage programming. In addition, you'll be able to make your F# interoperate with unmanaged (native) code using Platform Invoke and COM.

 Although F# allows you to work with both C# and Visual Basic .NET, in this appendix, I'm just going to refer to C#, for convenience. Whenever you see the term C#, you can replace it with the phrase *C# or Visual Basic .NET*, depending on your preference.

.NET Interop

The key to interoperation between .NET languages is to make sure that the types and methods in the public surface area of a class library are available to all languages consuming the code. Intuitively, if a library exposes constructs that are not native to the consuming language, things can look a little strange.

C# Interoperating with F#

When writing F# code you should refrain from exposing functional types such as discriminated unions, records, and function values directly. (Instead use them only for internal types and values, and expose regular class types for public-facing methods.)

Discriminated unions

Discriminated unions are types that define a series of possible data tags, and an instance of the discriminated union may only hold the value of one data tag at a time. To enforce this property, the F# compiler relies on inheritance and polymorphism behind the scenes.

Example B-1 shows a simple discriminated union in F# for describing the employees of a company.

Example B-1. Discriminated union exposed from F#

```
// HumanResources.fs - F# code declaring a discrimianted union

namespace Initech.HumanResources

type PersonalInfo = { Name : string; EmployeeID : int }

type Employee =
    | Manager of PersonalInfo * Employee list
    | Worker  of PersonalInfo
    | Intern
```

Discriminated unions seem simple in F# when you have pattern matching and syntax support; however, when consumed from C# they are quite a pain to use.

Example B-2 shows the same F# code for the `Initech.HumanResources.Employee` discriminated union as it would look in C# (and therefore the API a C# developer would have to program against). In the example, interfaces and compiler-generated methods have been omitted.

You can see how treacherous navigating the type is in C#, but it should also give you an appreciation for how much legwork the F# compiler is doing to make pattern matching so elegant.

Example B-2. F# discriminated unions when viewed from C#

```
using System;
using Microsoft.FSharp.Collections;

namespace Initech.HumanResources
{
    [Serializable, CompilationMapping(SourceConstructFlags.SumType)]
    public abstract class Employee
    {
        // Fields
        internal static readonly Employee _unique_Intern = new _Intern();

        // Methods
        internal Employee()
        {
        }

        [CompilationMapping(SourceConstructFlags.UnionCase, 0)]
```

```
public static Employee NewManager(PersonalInfo item1,
FSharpList<Employee> item2)
{
    return new Manager(item1, item2);
}

[CompilationMapping(SourceConstructFlags.UnionCase, 1)]
public static Employee NewWorker(PersonalInfo item)
{
    return new Worker(item);
}

// Properties
public static Employee Intern
{
    [CompilationMapping(SourceConstructFlags.UnionCase, 2)]
    get
    {
        return _unique_Intern;
    }
}

public bool IsIntern
{
    [CompilerGenerated, DebuggerNonUserCode]
    get
    {
        return (this is _Intern);
    }
}

public bool IsManager
{
    [CompilerGenerated, DebuggerNonUserCode]
    get
    {
        return (this is Manager);
    }
}

public bool IsWorker
{
    [CompilerGenerated, DebuggerNonUserCode]
    get
    {
        return (this is Worker);
    }
}

public int Tag
{
        get
        {
                Employee employee = this;
                return (!(employee is _Intern) ? (!(employee is Worker)
```

```
                        ? 0 : 1) : 2);
        }
}

// Nested Types
[Serializable]
internal class _Intern : Employee
{
    // Methods
    internal _Intern()
    {
    }
}

[Serializable]
public class Manager : Employee
{
    // Fields
    internal readonly PersonalInfo item1;
    internal readonly FSharpList<Employee> item2;

    // Methods
    internal Manager(PersonalInfo item1, FSharpList<Employee> item2)
    {
        this.item1 = item1;
        this.item2 = item2;
    }

    // Properties
    [CompilationMapping(SourceConstructFlags.Field, 0, 0)]
    public PersonalInfo Item1
    {
        get
        {
            return this.item1;
        }
    }

    [CompilationMapping(SourceConstructFlags.Field, 0, 1)]
    public FSharpList<Employee> Item2
    {
        get
        {
            return this.item2;
        }
    }
}

public static class Tags
{
    // Fields
    public const int Intern = 2;
    public const int Manager = 0;
    public const int Worker = 1;
}
```

```
[Serializable]
public class Worker : Employee
{
    // Fields
    internal readonly PersonalInfo item;

    // Methods
    internal Worker(PersonalInfo item)
    {
        this.item = item;
    }

    // Properties
    [CompilationMapping(SourceConstructFlags.Field, 1, 0)]
    public PersonalInfo Item
    {
        get
        {
            return this.item;
        }
    }
}
```

Function values

Function values represent a similar problem when consuming F# code from C#. While
C# supports lambda expressions just like F#, the way the C# compiler handles them
is very different.

In C# the method for representing function values is to use delegates, and in C# 3.0
two generic delegate types were introduced to help aid C# developers when doing
functional programming: System.Action<_> and System.Func<_,_>.

The Action<_> type represents a function that does not return a value. The Func<_,_>
type, on the other hand, does return a value. In both cases, the generic type parameters
are the types of the function's parameters.

The following snippet shows F# code for creating Action<_> and Func<_,_> function
values:

```
> // Using the System.Action type
#r "System.Core.dll"

open System

let fsAction = new Action<string>(fun arg -> printfn "Hello, %s" arg);;

--> Referenced 'C:\Windows\Microsoft.NET\Framework\v4.0.20620\System.Core.dll'


val fsAction : Action<string>
```

```
> fsAction.Invoke("World");;
Hello, World
val it : unit = ()
> // Using the System.Func type
let fsFunc = new Func<string, int>(fun s -> Int32.Parse(s) * Int32.Parse(s));;

val fsFunc : Func<string,int>

> fsFunc.Invoke("4");;

val it : int = 16
```

Function values created in F# are not of type Action<_> or Func<_,_>, but instead of type FSharpFunc<_,_>. In F#, function values may be curried, so passing in the first parameter of a function returns a new function with one less parameter.

Example B-3 shows the type MathUtilities, which has a method named GetAdder that returns an F# function value taking three string parameters.

Example B-3. Function values in F#

```
namespace Initech.Math

open System

type MathUtilities =
    static member GetAdder() =
        (fun x y z -> Int32.Parse(x) + Int32.Parse(y) + Int32.Parse(z))
```

The type returned by GetAdder is an FSharpFunc<_,_> object, which in F# can be expressed by:

```
string -> string -> string -> int
```

However, to declare that same function type in C#, you must write:

```
FSharpFunc <string, FSharpFunc <string, FSharpFunc <string, int>>>
```

Just imagine what the function signature would look like if it took more parameters! Curried function values are an elegant way to simplify code in functional languages, but be wary of exposing them to languages that don't support currying natively.

F# Interoperating with C#

Consuming C# code from F# is typically no problem because F# contains most all of the language features found in C# and VB.NET. However, there are a few things you can do in C# that you cannot do easily in F#; so if you have control over the C# libraries, you will consume from F#, keep the following points in mind.

Byref and out parameters

In C#, you can declare out and ref parameters, which enables a function to return more than one value by modifying its parameters. ref indicates that a parameter's value may be changed during the execution of a function call, and out indicates that the parameter's value will be set as a result of the function call.

F# supports both ref and out parameters natively and it can make use of C# code that exposes them.

Consider the following C# code, which defines two functions taking both out and ref parameters:

```
public class CSharpFeatures
{
    public static bool ByrefParams(ref int x, ref int y)
    {
        x = x * x;
        y = y * y;
        return true;
    }

    public static bool OutParams(out int x, out int y)
    {
        x = 10;
        y = 32;
        return true;
    }
}
```

In F#, to pass a parameter to a function accepting ref arguments, you have two options: you can either pass in a ref<'a> value or use the F# address-of operator & on a mutable value.

The following FSI session shows calling into the CSharpFeatures.ByrefParams method using both a ref value and the address-of operator. Notice that after the function executes, both parameters have been modified:

```
> // Declare ref / out parameter values
let x = ref 3
let mutable y = 4;;

val x : int ref = {contents = 3;}
val mutable y : int = 4

> CSharpFeatures.ByrefParams(x, &y);;
val it : bool = true
> x;;
val it : int ref = {contents = 9;}
> y;;
val it : int = 16
```

In F#, out parameters have the special property that they are not required to be passed to the function, and if they are omitted, the out parameters are returned with the function's result as a tuple. To pass in an `out` parameter in F#, the same rules for `ref` arguments apply. It must be of type `ref<'a>` or mutable value called with the address-of operator.

The following FSI session shows calling into the `CSharpFeatures.OutParams` method three times. Notice how the return type of the function changes based on whether or not the `out` parameters were passed in:

```
> // Declare ref / out parameter values
let x = ref 0
let mutable y = 0;;

val x : int ref = {contents = 0;}
val mutable y : int = 0

> // Pass in both out parameters, return value is bool
CSharpFeatures.OutParams(x, &y);;
val it : bool = true
> // Pass in just one out parameter, return value is bool * int
CSharpFeatures.OutParams(x);;
val it : bool * int = (true, 32)
> // Pass in no out parameters, return value is bool * int * int
CSharpFeatures.OutParams();;
val it : bool * int * int = (true, 10, 32)
```

To expose a method parameter from F# as a `ref` parameter, simply give the parameter type `byref<'a>`. You can then treat that parameter as a local, mutable variable. To expose an `out` parameter, give the parameter type `byref<'a>` as well but also attribute it with `System.Runtime.InteropServices.OutAttribute`. The following snippet defines an F# function that takes a `ref` and an `out` parameter, respectively:

```
open System.Runtime.InteropServices

let fsharpFunc (x : byref<int>, [<Out>] y : byref<int>) =
    x <- x + 1
    y <- y + 1
```

Dealing with null

Another F#-C# interop area is dealing with `null`. Types created in F# cannot be `null`, but any reference type in C# can have `null` as a proper value. This can lead to sticky situations when round-tripping types defined in F# through C# libraries (because the C# library could return `null` when the F# library doesn't expect it).

To enable types defined in an F# assembly to permit `null` as a possible value, you can add the `AllowNullLiteral` attribute. This attribute is only available on class and interface types; so records, structs, and discriminated unions still may not be `null`.

The following FSI session shows the `AllowNullLiteral` attribute in action. Notice that when trying to create an instance of `Widget` with value of `null`, a compiler error is given. However, you can have a value of type `Sprocket` equal to `null` because it was decorated with the `AllowNullLiteral` attribute:

```
> // Define two classes, one with [<AllowNullLiteral>] and one without
type Widget() =
    override this.ToString() = "A Widget"

[<AllowNullLiteral>]
type Sprocket() =
    override this.ToString() = "A Sprocket";;

type Widget =
  class
    new : unit -> Widget
    override ToString : unit -> string
  end
type Sprocket =
  class
    new : unit -> Sprocket
    override ToString : unit -> string
  end

> // ERROR: Widget cannot be null
let x : Widget = null;;

  let x : Widget = null;;
  -----------------^^^^

stdin(12,18): error FS0043: The type 'Widget' does not have 'null' as a proper value
> // Works
let x : Sprocket = null;;

val x : Sprocket = null
```

Unmanaged Interop

While the .NET platform offers a wealth of functionality and is a great platform for writing new applications, there are many times when you will want to interoperate with legacy code: for example, calling into frameworks written in C or C++.

F# supports all the same mechanisms as C# for interoperating with unmanaged code.

Platform Invoke

Platform invoke, also referred to as P/Invoke, is how managed applications can call into unmanaged libraries, such as Win32 API functions. When you have a non-.NET library you wish to call into, P/Invoke is how you do it.

 P/Invoke isn't limited to just Windows. Any CLI implementation, such as Mono, may use P/Invoke in order to access libraries outside of the CLI runtime environment.

In F#, to make a P/Invoke call, you must first declare the function signature. This means defining the function signature so that the .NET framework knows how to call into it correctly (the library where the function exists, the number and types of parameters, and so on).

Example B-4 shows calling into the Win32 function `CopyFile`, defined in the library `kernel32.dll`. The `DllImport` attribute shows which library and the name of the method the F# function is bound to. After that the function is declared using the **extern** keyword followed by the function signature as it would be declared in a C-like language. (Types coming before parameter names.)

Once the P/Invoke signature is declared, the actual function can be called like any normal F# function value. The F# compiler will take care of passing data to the unmanaged library. The process of transferring data between managed and unmanaged code is known as *marshalling*.

Example B-4. Using platform invoke in F#

```
open System.Runtime.InteropServices

/// PInvoke signature for CopyFile
[<DllImport("kernel32.dll", EntryPoint="CopyFile")>]
extern bool copyfile(char[] lpExistingFile, char[] lpNewFile, bool bFailIfExists);

let file1 = @"D:\File.dat"
let file2 = @"D:\Backups\File.dat"

// Calls the CopyFile method defined in kernel32.dll
copyfile(file1.ToCharArray(), file2.ToCharArray(), false)
```

For more advanced interop scenarios, you can customize how data gets marshalled by providing hints to the F# compiler.

Example B-5 declares two structs, `SequentialPoint` and `ExplicitRect`, for use with the Win32 API function `PtInRect`. The function `PtInRect` returns whether or not a given point exists inside of a rectangle. However, because the Win32 function has no knowledge of the .NET type system, it simply expects structs with a specific layout to be passed on the stack.

The `StructLayout` attribute determines how the struct's data gets laid out in memory, to ensure that it lines up with the way data is expected to be received on the unmanaged half of the P/Invoke call.

For example, the `PtInRect` function expects the rectangle to be made up of four 4-byte integers in left, top, right, bottom order. In the example, the `ExplicitRect` doesn't declare its fields in that order. Instead, it uses the `FieldOffset` attributes so that when the F# compiler generates code for the `ExplicitRect` type, its fields are laid out in the expected order.

Example B-5. Customizing marshalling

```
open System.Runtime.InteropServices

/// Define a Point using the sequential layout
[<Struct; StructLayout(LayoutKind.Sequential)>]
type SequentialPoint =

    new (x, y) = { X = x; Y = y }

    val X : int
    val Y : int

/// Define a rectangle struct explicitly
[<Struct; StructLayout(LayoutKind.Explicit)>]
type ExplicitRect =

    new (l, r, t, b) = { left = l; top = t; right = r; bottom = b }

    [<FieldOffset(12)>]
    val mutable bottom : int
    [<FieldOffset(0)>]
    val mutable left : int
    [<FieldOffset(8)>]
    val mutable right : int
    [<FieldOffset(4)>]
    val mutable top : int

/// P/Invoke signature for PtInRect
[<DllImport("User32.dll", EntryPoint="PtInRect")>]
extern bool PointInRect(ExplicitRect &rect, SequentialPoint pt);
```

 There are many other ways to customize the marshaling of data between managed and unmanaged code. For more information, refer to MSDN documentation of the System.Runtime.InteropServices namespace.

COM Interop

The .NET world where multiple languages use the same runtime to interoperate seamlessly isn't a terribly new idea; in fact, many of .NET's core architectural principles are rooted in another technology called *Component Object Model* or COM. COM is a 1990s-era technology to support binary interoperability between different programs, so a C++ application written by one developer could interact with a Visual Basic application written by another.

Most large, unmanaged applications expose COM interfaces as their way of loading add-ins, enabling programmatic access, and so on. For example, rather than writing your own web browser you could just host the Internet Explorer COM control inside your application.

While COM components don't execute on top of the .NET runtime, just as with P/Invoke, you can call into COM objects from .NET applications.

The easiest and most common way to call into COM objects is through a *runtime callable wrapper* (RCW). An RCW is a .NET assembly that provides wrapper classes on top of COM interfaces. So to the developer it looks like you are programming against any other .NET assembly, when in fact every function call and class instantiated is actually using the COM-interop machinery of the .NET runtime.

To generate an RCW, use the `tlbimp.exe` tool, which comes with Visual Studio as part of the .NET framework SDK. The following snippet shows using `tlbimp.exe` to create an RCW for the Apple iTunes COM interfaces (declared in `iTunes.exe`). The iTunes COM interfaces allow programmatic control of the iTunes software, such as playing music or manipulating the music library:

```
C:\Program Files\iTunes>tlbimp iTunes.exe /out:NETiTunesLibrary.dll
Microsoft (R) .NET Framework Type Library to Assembly Converter 3.5.21022.8
Copyright (C) Microsoft Corporation.  All rights reserved.

Type library imported to C:\Program Files\iTunes\NETiTunesLibrary.dll
```

With the RCW in place, you can reference the library like any other .NET library and write applications that interact with iTunes. Example B-6 shows an FSI session where the RCW for calling into the iTunes APIs is used to print out a list of top-rated albums for the current music library.

This is done by creating an instance of the `iTunesAppClass`, and accessing the `Library Source` property. These all correspond to COM interfaces defined in the iTunes API, but with the generated RCW it looks just like any other .NET assembly. Moreover, if you add a reference to an RCW within Visual Studio, you will get full IntelliSense support.

Example B-6. COM interop

```
> // Reference required libraries
#r "System.Core.dll"
#r @"C:\Program Files\iTunes\NETiTunesLibrary.dll";;

--> Referenced 'C:\Program Files\Reference
Assemblies\Microsoft\Framework\v3.5\System.Core.dll'


--> Referenced 'C:\Program Files\iTunes\NETiTunesLibrary.dll'

> // Bind to the iTunes app
open System.Linq
open NetiTunesLibrary

// Load up the main iTunes library
let iTunes = new iTunesAppClass()
let iTunesLibrary = iTunes.LibrarySource.Playlists.[1];;
Binding session to 'C:\Program Files\iTunes\NetiTunesLibrary.dll'...
```

```
val iTunes : NetiTunesLibrary.iTunesAppClass
val iTunesLibrary : NetiTunesLibrary.IITPlaylist

> // Search my iTunes music library to sort albums by average song rating
// Return type is seq< albumName * avgRating * tracksInAlbum>
let albumsByAverageRating : seq<string * float * seq<IITTrack>> =
    iTunesLibrary.Tracks.OfType<IITTrack>()
    |> Seq.groupBy(fun track -> track.Album)
    |> Seq.map(fun (albumName, tracks) ->
        // Get average track rating
        let trackRatings = tracks |> Seq.map (fun track -> float track.Rating)
        albumName, (Seq.average trackRatings), tracks);;

val albumsByAverageRating : seq<string * float * seq<IITTrack>>

> // Return whether or not the majority of tracks in the album have been rated
let mostTracksRated tracks =
    let rated, notRated =
        Seq.fold
            (fun (rated, notRated) (track : IITTrack) ->
                if track.Rating <> 0 then
                    (rated + 1, notRated)
                else
                    (rated, notRated + 1))
            (0, 0)
            tracks
    if rated > notRated then
        true
    else
        false

// Print top albums, filtering out those with few ratings
let printTopAlbums() =
    albumsByAverageRating
    |> Seq.filter(fun (_,_,tracks) -> mostTracksRated tracks)
    |> Seq.sortBy(fun (_, avgRating, _) -> -avgRating)
    |> Seq.iter(fun (albumName, avgRating, _) ->
        printfn
            "Album [%-18s] given an average rating of %.2f"
            albumName avgRating);;

val mostTracksRated : seq<IITTrack> -> bool
val printTopAlbums : unit -> unit


> printTopAlbums();;
Album [Aloha From Hawaii ] given an average rating of 100.00
Album [Sample This - EP   ] given an average rating of 95.00
Album [Dark Passion Play  ] given an average rating of 83.08
Album [When I Pretend to Fall] given an average rating of 80.00
Album [Weezer (Red Album)] given an average rating of 78.30
Album [The Best Of The Alan Parsons Project] given an average rating of 76.36
Album [Karmacode          ] given an average rating of 64.00
val it : unit = ()
```

.NET and COM interop is a very complex subject, and attention must be paid to details like security models, threading, and garbage collection. Fortunately, F# doesn't have any special requirements over C# when it comes to COM interop.

 If you are interested in doing in-depth COM interop, I recommend *.NET and COM: The Complete Interoperability Guide* by Adam Nathan (Sams).

Index

A

& (ampersand)
  & (pattern matching 'and'), 67, 175
  && (Boolean 'and'), 20
  &&& (bitwise 'and'), 18
' (apostrophe), generic parameters, 25, 125
* (asterisk), 95
  multiplication operator, 15
  regular expressions, 339, 343
  tuple type separator, 30
@ (at sign), verbatim string, 20
brackets/parens, 244, 341
  ( ) pass to higher order functions, 56, 61
  ( )overloading an operator, 206
  (:) type annotation, 24
  ()unit, representation of void, 29
  (* *) multiline comments, 8
  (| |) active pattern, 170
  (| |_|) partial active pattern, 171
  .[ ] indexer, 19, 93, 205, 207
  <@ @> or <@@ @@> expression
      quotation markers, 312, 316
  [ ] list comprehension, 33
  [ ] lists, 32
  [< >] attribute, 288
  [| |] array values, 93
  { } define expression/record, 76, 81, 152
character escape sequences
  \" (double quote), 19
  \' (single quote), 19
  \b (backspace), 19
  \n (newline), 19
  \r (carriage return), 19
  \t (horizontal tab), 19

\\ (backslash), 19
.. (double dot/period), list range, 32
F# Interactive window output
  --^^, error, 23
  -> (right arrow) value reporting, 22
  > command line prompt, 10
(number sign) F# script-specific directives,
    232
operators, arithmetic
  % modulus, 15
  * multiplication, 15
  ** power, 15
  + plus, 15
  - subtraction, 15
  / division, 15
operators, comparison and equality
  < less than, 21
  <= less than or equal to, 21
  <> not equal to, 21
  = equal to operator, 21
  > greater than, 21
  >= greater than or equal to, 21
operators, other
  ! get ref cell value, 91
  -> right arrow, 34, 50, 63
  . dot, 300
  :: cons list, 32, 68, 184
  := set ref cell value, 91
  :> static cast, 141
  :? pattern type test, 143
  :?> dynamic cast, 142, 300
  <- left arrow, 90, 128
  << backward composition, 62
  <<< bitwise 'left shift', 18
  <| pipe-backward, 61

We'd like to hear your suggestions for improving our indexes. Send email to *index@oreilly.com*.

Bind computation expression method, 244, 248, 249
binding in XAML, 334
bitwise operations, 18
bool type, 20
Boolean values, 20
box function, 220
Byref parameters, 363
byref<obj> objects, 237
byte numerical primitive, 14–17, 350

C

C#, how F# differs from, 9
(see also troubleshooting: warnings/notes regarding)
behavior of equality on arrays, 97
cannot partially implement interface, 149
default constructors, 123
delegates do not have BeginInvoke, EndInvoke methods, 217
does not have break and continue keywords, 107
does not have event keyword, 218
does not have protected visibility, 135
does not have try-catch-finally expression, 111
extension methods cannot be consumed, 155
failure indicated by None, not -1, 99
for loop more powerful than foreach loop, 107
indexers require dot notation, 94
must explicitly implement base interface, 150
no native out or ref parameters, 363
types cannot be null, 364
use of arbitrary symbolic operators, 207
!x does not mean "not", 91
C#, how F# differs from.
does not have Main method, 42
does not have return keyword, 22
FSI improved code testing, 9
switch statement and pattern matching, 62
void compared to unit, 28
C#, interoperability with, 357
calculator example, 254
call stacks, 188
calls, tail, 190
cancellation, 280

CancellationToken type, 272
capture groups, 343
case sensitivity, 6
casting, 141
ceil function, 16
character trigraphs, 289
characters, 19
checked arithmetic, 16, 181
class hierarchy, 137
classes
abstract, 139, 140
adding indexers to, 207
adding slices to, 209
converting modules to, 178
derived, 153
generic, 125
methods and properties, 127–133
overview, 122
preferred way to create, 125
versus records, 76
sealed, 140
CLI (Common Language Infrastructure), xv, 145
CLIEvent attribute, 225
closures, 53, 90, 197
CLR (Common Language Runtime) restrictions, 90, 97, 187
code passing, 250
code, eliminating redundant, 196
color console output, 234
COM (Component Object Model), 367
Combine method, 217
combining active patterns, 175
Command Pattern, 116
comments, coding, 8
Common Language Infrastructure (CLI), xv, 145
compare function, 21
comparison operators, 21
compile order, 11
compiler directives, 230
SOURCE DIRECTORY, 231, 235
SOURCE FILE, 231
Component Object Model (COM), 367
comprehensions
array, 93
list, 33
computation expressions, 244
overview, 241

computed derivative, 326
concurrent data structures, 283
concurrent queue, 283
cons operator, 32, 68, 184, 185
console
    .Beep, 235
    color output, 234
    printf, printfn, sprintf, 41
    .Writeline, 133
constructors, 122, 129
continuation passing styles, 193
continuations, 243
control flow, 27
conversions, 17, 157, 166
core types, 29
cores, multiple, 258
cos function, 16
cprintfn function, 234
creating events, 218
CSV files, processing, 203
currying, 51, 59, 130, 195
custom attributes, 290
custom logic, 66
custom types, 112, 194, 291
custom workflows, 242, 244

D

data
    associating with union case, 71
    pattern matching, 68
    serialization, 349
    storing, 348
    using ref cells to mutate, 91
data encapsulation, 197
data processing libraries, 338–344
data races, 261, 283
deadlocks, 264
decimal numerical primitives, 14–17
decomposing quotations, 312, 318
decr function, 91
dedents, significance of, 7
default constructor, 160, 213
default values, 87
defined block, 244
delegate constraint, 213
DelegateEvent<_;gt type, 220
delegates, 214–217, 219, 259, 361
derivatives, 324
derived classes, 137, 153

describeType function, 292
deserialization, 351
design patterns, 116, 199
Dictionary type, 102, 199
dictionary, concurrent, 284
directives, compiler, 230
    SOURCE DIRECTORY, 235
    SOURCE FILE, 231
directives, F# script-specific, 231
directories
    adding new, 233
    walking, 235
discriminated unions
    adding overloaded operators to, 206
    defined, 70
    versus enum, 158
    equality of, 121
    generic, 126
    and interoperability, 358
    methods and properties of, 75
    and multi-case active patterns, 173
    pattern matching against, 73
    reflecting, 297
    for tree structures, 72
division operator, 15
do bindings, 124, 289
do! keyword, 268
download and install, xvi
downto keyword, 106
dynamic cast, 142, 143
dynamic instantiation, 298
dynamic invocation, 299
dynamic typing, 23
dynamically built lists, 184

E

eager evaluation, 79
elif (within if then expression), 28
else (within if then expression), 27
empty list, 32
encapsulation, 197
encryption, 93
end keyword, 150, 159
EndInvoke method, 217
EndOperation, 265, 274
EntryPoint attribute, 45
enumerable for loops, 107
enumeration constraint, 213
enumerations, 156–158

recursive, 53
returning functions, 52
treated as data, 50
types, 29, 52

G

garbage collection, 146
general directives, 231
generated equality, 120
generic classes, 125
generic functions, 24, 25
generic types, 211, 292
get keyword, 128
GetHashCode function, 292
GetMethods function, 292
GetProperties function, 292
GetSlice method, 209
GetType method, 291

H

handlers, event, 219
handling exceptions, 109
hash codes, 117
HashSet<_> type, 104, 285
heap, 86, 91
Hello, World examples, 3, 5, 332, 333
hexadecimal numerical primitive, 15
higher order functions, 50

I

#I directive, 233
IAsyncResult interface, 265
IComparer interface, 152
IConsumable interface, 148
IDisposable interface, 147
IEEE32, IEEE64 standards, 15
IEnumerable<'a>, 80
IEvent<_> interface, 225
if then expressions, 27, 63
ignore function, 29
immutability, 6, 49
imperative programming, xv, 49, 85
implementations, 201
implicit class construction, 124, 137
impure functional programming languages, 50
incr function, 91
indents, significance of, 6, 43
infinite loop example, 188

infix notation, 56
inheritance, 136
initializing enum array, 156
initializing of values, 87
installation, xvi
instantiation, 298
instruction pointer, 187
int core type, 29
int, int16, int32, int64 numerical primitives,
    14–17
Int32.TryParse function, 39
integers, 14
intentional shadowing, 181
interface keyword, 148, 150
interfaces, 148–153
interfaces, plug-in, 306
intermediate results, 30
internal accessibility modifier, 134
interoperability, 357
Invoke method, 215
IO operations, asynchronous, 248
IO.Stream type, 273, 348
IObservable<_> interface, 221
it (unnamed expression), 9
Item property, 207
iter implementation, 193
iTunes RCW example, 368

J

jagged arrays, 99
JIT (just-in-time), 145
just-in-time (JIT), 145

K

keyboard shortcuts, 10, 11

L

lambda expressions, 50, 259
lambda syntax for pattern matching, 70
late binding, 299
launching a new process, 236
lazy evaluation, 79–81, 202
let bindings, 14, 31, 69, 124, 174
let keyword, 6, 14
let! keyword, 244, 248, 268
libraries
    F# PowerPack, 352, 355
    FSharp.Core.dll, 352

extending, 155
intentional shadowing using, 181
vs. namespaces, 43, 178
scope of, 25, 182
when not recommended, 45
modulus operator, 15
Mono platform, xvi, 3
monoids, 249
mouse events, 223, 224
MSIL (Microsoft Intermediate Language), 145
multi-case active patterns, 173
multidimensional arrays, 99
multiple attributes, 289
multiple processors/cores, 258
multiple source files, managing, 11, 43
multiplication operator, 15
mutability
    collection types, 101
    record field, 92
    variable, 49, 90
mutable function values, 201
mutable keyword, 90, 92
mutual recursion, 55

N

named patterns, 68
namespaces, 43
naming
    .NET interfaces, 150
    self-identifiers, 127
Nathan, Adam, 338, 370
nesting
    of active patterns, 176
    of functions, 25, 197
    of modules, 43
.NET
    classes versus F# records, 76
    Common Language Infrastructure (CLI),
        145, 365
    equality in, 22
    events, 225
    interoperability, 8, 146, 357, 367
    IO facilities, 348
    memory in, 86, 146
    platform, 145–147
    Reflection APIs, 287, 296
    regular expressions, 338–344
    thread pool, 260

Windows Forms (WinForms), 224, 329,
    330
Windows Presentation Foundation (WPF),
    329, 331
XML libraries, 345
.NET and COM (Nathan), 370
new keyword, 215
newlines, 6
non integer index, 208
None value, 39
null, 40, 88, 364
numeric primitive conversion routines, 17
numeric primitives, 14
numeric values, comparing, 21

O

obj, 116, 141, 291
object expressions, 151
object-oriented programming
    advantages of, 115
    defined, xv
    disadvantages of, 116
    overview, 115
Observable module, 221
Obsolete attribute, 288
octal numerical primitive, 15
one-dimensional slice, 209
opaque types, 165
operator overloading, 205
operator precedence, 61
option type, 29, 39, 68, 99, 171
optional single-case active patterns, 171
order of
    compilation, 11
    operators, 61
    type inference, 58
Out parameters, 363
outscoping, 65
overflow in arithmetic operators, 16
overloading, 24, 133, 205, 279
override keyword, 138
overview, 108

P

P/Invoke, 365
Parallel Extensions to the .NET Framework
    (PFX), 276, 281
parallel for loops, 276

generic, 126
mutable, 92
pattern matching on, 77
reflecting, 297
versus structs, 161
types, 206
rectangular arrays, 99
recursion
in class methods, 130
in discriminated unions, 71
in discriminated unions, 74
mutual, 55
in sequences, 81
tail, 186
recursive functions, 53, 200
redundancy, avoiding, 196, 241
ref function, 91
ref type (ref cell), 91, 242
reference constraint, 213
reference types, 87, 89, 119
ReferenceEquality attribute, 122
referential equality, 22, 119
ReflectedDefinition attribute, 316
reflection
declarative programming, 302
dynamic instantiation, 298
overview, 287
plug-in architecture, 305
type, 291
regular expressions (Regex), 338–344
Remove method, 217
RemoveHandler method, 219
reordering files in FSI, 11
REPL (Read, Evaluate, Print, Loop), 9
RequireQualifiedAccess attribute, 182
reraise function, 111
Result property, 279
Return computation expression method, 246
return escape character (\r), 19
reverse polish notation (RPN), 319
rich media, 332
ROT13, 93
rounding workflows, 249
RPN (reverse polish notation), 319
runtime, 145, 146
runtime callable wrapper (RCW), 368

S

sbyte numerical primitive, 14–17

scope, 25, 52, 65, 182
screen, writing to, 41
scripting
advantages of F#, 229
defined, 229
editing, 230
recipes, 234
Sealed attribute, 140, 161
sealed class, 140
security issues
CLR restrictions, 90
at runtime, 294
spoofing, 141
self identifier, 123
self-identifier, 127
Seq class, 203, 235
Seq module, 82
seq type, 79, 169
sequence expressions, 81, 241
sequences versus lists, 80
Serializable attribute, 349
set keyword, 128
Set type, 352
shadowing, 26, 181
short circuit evaluation, 21
SI units of measure, 355
side effects, 39, 49, 85
sign function, 16
signature files, 135
sin function, 16
single-case active patterns, 169
slashes (/), 8
slices, 95, 100, 209
snd function, 30
Some('a) value, 39
sound, producing, 235
SOURCE DIRECTORY directive, 231, 235
spaces, 6
spawning new processes, 236
spawning threads, 259
speeding up computation, 257
spoofing, preventing, 141
sprintf function, 42
sqrt function, 16
stack, 86, 187
Stacktrace property, 108
state workflows, 250–255
static keyword/methods, 131
static typing, 23

static upcast, 141
statically typed, xv
string manipulation, 341
Struct attribute, 159
struct constraint, 213
struct keyword, 159
structs, 159–162
sub sequences, 81
subscribing to events, 219
subtraction operator, 15
subtype constraint, 213
suffixes for numeric primitives, 14, 19
sumArray function, 261
symbolic operators, 55
synchronization primitives, 279
syntactic transforms, 244
System.Collections.Generic lists, 101–104
System.Object, 116–118, 143

T

tab character, 7, 19, 20
tail calls, 190
tail recursion
    accumulator pattern, 192
    continuations, 193
    overview, 186, 190
tan function, 16
targets, attribute, 289
Task object, 278
then keyword, 123
Thread, 271
Thread methods, 259
threads, 258–264
    .NET thread pool, 260
    overview, 258
    spawning, 259
    thread hopping, 248
ToString method, 292
tree structures, 72
trigraphs, character, 289
troubleshooting: warnings and errors, 64
    (see also exceptions)
    FS0001, 23, 28, 31, 41, 165, 167
    FS0025, 64, 74
    FS0026, 65
    FS0039, 25, 55, 149, 155, 247
    FS0043, 89, 365
    FS0058, 7
    FS0072, 59

FS0191, 90, 161, 183
FS0366, 151
FS0809, 131
FS0945, 141
troubleshooting: warnings/notes regarding, 51, 127
    (see also C#, how F# differs from)
    .NET reflection, 294
    active patterns and match statements, 173
    arbitrary symbolic operators in C# and
        VB.NET, 207
    assembly-level attributes, 289
    constraints on serialization, 349
    creating async primitives, 275
    curried functions, 52
    exceptions and performance, 109
    explicit type annotations for method
        signature, 252
    F# PowerPack not in Visual Studio 2010,
        323
    hash codes and equality, 118
    large lambdas, 51
    modules in large scale projects, 45
    no CLR support for units of measure, 168
    overuse of #load, 233
    passing functions and code readability, 196
    persisting sensitive information in memory,
        294
    pipe-forward operator, 59
    presentation layer code, 329
    proper semantics when overloading
        operators, 205
    timely removal of event handlers, 219
    Visual Studio, 323, 329
    while loop with initial false predicate will
        not execute, 106
    wildcard matching against discriminated
        union, 75
    !x does not mean "not", 91
truth table example, 20
try-catch expressions, 109
try-finally expressions, 110
Tuple class, 30
tuple type, 29, 30, 68, 120, 296
two-dimensional slice, 210
type annotation, 24
type function, 87
type inference, 23, 41
    coding order of, 58

and pipe-forward, 59
for records, 77
and recursion, 55
and units of measure, 167
type instantiation, 299
type keyword, 70
type reflection, 291
typedefof function, 292
typeof function, 291, 292
types
Async<string>, 269
Boolean, 20
CancellationToken, 272
concurrent, 283, 284
core, 29
custom iterator, 194
defined, 13
FSharpList, 184
Func<_,_>, 274
generic, 211, 292
Lazy, 79
numeric, 14–18
opaque, 165
option, 39
in pattern matching, 63
primitive, 13, 314
proactive, 214, 221
record, 75
ref, 91
reference, 87
string, 19, 234
unit, 28
value, 87

U

Unicode, 19
uninitialized state, 87
union cases, 70
unit core type, 29
unit, uint16, uint32, uint64 numerical
    primitive, 14–17
units of measure, 163–168
unmanaged code, 145, 146, 365
URLs
CodePlex (www.codeplex.com), 323, 355
F# development center (http://fsharp.net),
    327
F# PowerPack (www.codeplex.com/
    FSharpPowerPack), 355

usage
memory, 97, 202
module, 182
use keyword, 147

V

val (FSI output), 9
val bindings, 124, 160
val keyword, 123
value captures, 65
value equality, 22
value types, 87, 119
values
accessibility modifiers on module, 135
case sensitivity in, 6
changing, 89
default, 87
in scope, 52
initializing of, 87
mutable, 89
naming syntax, 6
using fields to name, 75
versus variables, 49
variables, 49, 60, 86
VB.NET, how F# differs from, 9
(see also troubleshooting: warnings/notes
    regarding)
delegates do not have BeginInvoke,
        EndInvoke methods, 217
does not have event keyword, 218
FSI improved code testing, 9
indexers require dot notation, 94
use of arbitrary symbolic operators, 207
Visual Studio
and F# PowerPack, 323, 355
debugger, 188, 189, 191
download and install, xvi
features, 4, 257
online documentation, 3
RCW in, 368
script editing in, 230, 239
sending code to FSI, 10
warnings and errors in, 288
visualization APIs, 329
void, representation of, 29

W

walking a directory structure, 235

X

Y

Z

About the Author

Chris Smith works at Microsoft on the F# team. His role as a software design engineer in the testing group gives him a unique mastery of the F# language. Chris has a Master's degree in computer science from the University of Washington, and a burning passion for any tasty drink that comes with an umbrella. You can find him online at Chris Smith's Completely Unique View at *http://blogs.msdn.com/chrsmith/*.

Colophon

The image on the cover of *Programming F#* is a bullfinch (*Pyrrhula pyrrhula*). Members of the *Fringillidae* family, bullfinches are small passerine birds that can be found throughout central and northern Europe, from the Atlantic coast of western Europe and Morocco to the Pacific coasts of Russia and Japan. They primarily inhabit woodland areas, orchards, and farmlands, and are somewhat notorious for the damage they do by eating the buds of fruit trees and flowering shrubs in spring. Bullfinches are skittish, wary birds and are rarely seen on the ground.

The common bullfinch grows to about six inches long. It has a thick neck and a short, stubby bill. Both sexes are primarily black and white, though males have rose-colored undersides while females have duller, brownish breasts. The females make nests from small twigs, moss, and roots, and lay four or five eggs twice a year. Both parents share feeding responsibilities once the young have hatched.

Between 1968 and 1991, there was a significant decline in the bullfinch population. While the specific cause is not known, one theory is that the trend of deforestation and overtrimming hedges on agricultural land compromised many nesting sites and removed the birds' primary food sources. Increased use of herbicides is also a probable culprit, as well as the fact that trapping and killing bullfinches was not regulated until relatively recently. However, bullfinch numbers are now abundant over most of their range and, with the exception of some local populations and subspecies, the birds are not considered threatened.

The cover image is from *Cassell's Natural History*. The cover font is Adobe ITC Garamond. The text font is Linotype Birka; the heading font is Adobe Myriad Condensed; and the code font is LucasFont's TheSansMonoCondensed.

Buy this book and get access to the online edition for 45 days—for free!